Microcomputers

with tutorials for popular software packages

Larry Long
Nancy Long

PRENTICE HALL, Englewood Cliffs, N.J. 07632

Library of Congress Cataloging-in-Publication Data

LONG, LARRY
  Microcomputers: "with tutorials for popular software packages"
by Larry Long, Nancy Long.
    p. cm.

  Includes index.
  ISBN 0–13–580101–X.
  1. Microcomputers.   2. Computer programs.   I. Long, Nancy.
II. Title
QA76.5.L656   1988   87–32665
005.265 dc19   CIP

© 1988 by Prentice Hall
A Division of Simon & Schuster
Englewood Cliffs, New Jersey 07632

Editorial/production supervision: Colleen Brosnan
Interior design: Janet Schmid
Cover design: Janet Schmid
Page layout: Maureen Eide
Manufacturing buyer: Barbara Kittle

Printed in the United States of America

10 9 8 7 6 5 4 3 2

ISBN 0-13-580101-X

Prentice-Hall International (UK) Limited, *London*

Prentice-Hall of Australia Pty. Limited, *Sydney*

Prentice-Hall Canada Inc., *Toronto*

Prentice-Hall Hispanoamericana, S.A., *Mexico*

Prentice-Hall of India Private Limited, *New Delhi*

Prentice-Hall of Japan, Inc., *Tokyo*

Simon & Schuster Asia Pte. Ltd., *Singapore*

Editora Prentice-Hall do Brasil, Ltda., *Rio de Janeiro*

TRADEMARK AND COPYRIGHT INFORMATION

To Troy, our son

OVERVIEW

CONTENTS

PREFACE TO THE STUDENT

In microcomputers, technology has taken another giant step. Any company, government agency, or educational institution that has not already made micros an integral part of everyday operations is making plans to do so. This integration of microcomputers into the mainstream of society means that what you learn about micros and micro software from this book and this course will surely help you in your academic pursuits, your work, and, eventually, your career.

The first three chapters of this text offer an overview of microcomputer technology, operation, and applications. The remainder of the book is devoted to the presentation of concepts and skills that will enable you to learn the use and operation of DOS (the disk operating system) and a variety of popular software packages, including word processing, electronic spreadsheet, and database.

Getting the Most from This Text

The layout and organization of the text and its contents are designed to be interesting, to present concepts in a logical and informative manner, to provide a reference for the reinforcement of classroom lectures, and to provide you with an opportunity to get plenty of hands-on experience. To avoid inordinately long chapters, the Hands-On Tutorials in support of Chapter 5, "Word Processing Concepts," Chapter 7, "Electronic Spreadsheet Concepts: Spreadsheet Capabilities," and Chapter 10, "Database Concepts," are placed in separate chapters (Chapters 6, 8, and 11, respectively). Other Hands-On Tutorials follow the conceptual material in the same chapter (Chapters 9, 12, and 13).

Reading a Chapter.   A good way to approach each chapter is to:

1. Look over the Student Learning Objectives.
2. Read the Summary and Important Terms.
3. Read over the major headings and subheadings and think how they are related.
4. Read the chapter and note the important terms that are in **boldface** type and in *italic* type.

5. Relate photos and photo captions to the textual material (a picture is worth a thousand words).

6. Go over the Summary Outline and Important Terms again, paying particular attention to the boldface terms.

7. Take the Self-Test. Reread those sections that you do not fully understand.

8. Answer the questions in the Review Exercises.

9. Complete the Hands-On Tutorials at the end of the chapter (or in the following chapter) as directed by your instructor.

10. Complete the Hands-On Exercises as directed by your instructor.

The Learning Assistance Package.   The text is supported by a comprehensive learning assistance package. The purchase price of the text includes a *license* to use educational versions of WordPerfect, the TWiN (emulates Lotus 1–2–3), dBASE III PLUS, The OUTLINER, and Crosstalk XVI (interactive simulation) software, as well as SuperSoftware (an educational software supplement). An optional *Lab Manual* includes vocabulary exercises, hands-on exercises, quick reference guides (command summaries) for a variety of software packages, follow-up keystroke tutorials for the software packages presented in the text, and SuperSoftware activities. Ask your instructor about the availability of these learning supplements.

You, Computers, and the Future

Learning about micros and micro software is more than just education— it's an adventure! However, the microcomputer field is so dynamic that you have to run pretty fast just to stand still. When you complete this course, you will have acquired a base of knowledge that will enable you to race ahead of the pack.

Keep your course notes and this book because they will provide valuable reference material in other courses and in your career. The material addresses a broad range of microcomputer concepts and skills that pop up frequently in other classes, at work, and even at home.

PREFACE TO THE INSTRUCTOR

During the last decade, the presence of computers, especially micro-computers, has had an increasingly significant effect on all phases of life, including higher education and continuing education. Each year, people entering the work force need to know more and more about computers.

A decade ago, we challenged our noncomputer students and professionals to acquire a *passive* computer literacy; that is, we taught them enough about computers to enable them to articulate their automation and information processing requirements to computer specialists. Today, passive computer literacy is inadequate. Graduates in computer and noncomputer fields are encouraged to exploit the potential of microcomputers; therefore, both must pursue an *active* computer literacy. The material in this book is designed to provide its readers with an active computer literacy.

Objectives

The objectives of this text and its accompanying teaching/learning system are threefold:

1. To present microcomputers and micro software (oriented to the IBM PC and its compatibles) in a logical, informative, and interesting manner.
2. To instill in students, via hands-on experience, a confidence that they can use and apply microcomputers and popular microcomputer software to their own business, domestic, and academic needs.
3. To give you, the instructor, everything you need to accomplish the first two.

Organization

Microcomputers is organized in three parts.

- *Part I: The World of Computers*, Chapters 1 and 2, introduces students to micros and personal computing and presents those hardware, software, and data management concepts that they will need to know to make the most effective use of microcomputer productivity software.

■ *Part II: Interacting with a Microcomputer* consists of Chapters 3 and 4. Chapter 3 focuses on concepts that relate to interacting with a micro, configuring and caring for a micro, and buying micros and micro-related products. Chapter 4 is devoted to DOS concepts and commands, and it includes the Hands-On Tutorials for MS DOS and PC DOS.

■ *Part III: Microcomputer Productivity Software*, Chapters 5 through 13, comprises the bulk of this text. This part provides generic, yet detailed, conceptual coverage of word processing, integrated electronic spreadsheet (spreadsheet, database, and graphics capabilities), database, idea processor, and communications software. Each of the conceptual discussions of the various productivity tools is followed by keystroke tutorials for leading commercial software packages. Keystroke tutorials for the following software packages illustrate how these software packages would be used to develop the examples discussed in the conceptual presentation.

Word Processing
WordPerfect*   Webster's NewWorld Writer   WordStar Professional
MultiMate Advantage II   PFS:Professional Write

Electronic Spreadsheet
(spreadsheet, database, and graphics)
The TWiN (emulates Lotus 1–2–3)*   Lotus 1–2–3   SuperCalc4

Database
dBASE III PLUS*   Reflex: The Database Manager
PFS:Professional File

Idea Processor
The OUTLINER   ThinkTank

Communications
Crosstalk XVI*   PC-Talk4

Some topics are broader in scope than others, so naturally more attention was devoted to electronic spreadsheets (Chapters 7 through 9) than idea processors (Chapter 12). To avoid inordinately long chapters, the Hands-On Tutorials in support of Chapter 5, "Word Processing Concepts," Chapter 7, "Electronic Spreadsheet Concepts: Spreadsheet Capabilities," and Chapter 10, "Database Concepts," are placed in separate chapters (i.e., Chapters 6, 8, and 11, respectively). Other Hands-On Tutorials follow the conceptual material in the same chapter (i.e., Chapters 9, 12, and 13).

---

*An educational version of this package is part of the teaching/learning system. Those colleges or businesses adopting *Microcomputers* are awarded a site license to use this popular software package in support of the courses that require this book.

In Part III we have attempted to present hands-on skills in a pedagogical framework that will enable students to translate their understanding of the use and operation of microcomputers and software packages to a variety of computing environments. Once the student has read and understood the principles of these software tools, the student can easily relate what has been learned to the specifics of any hardware or software environment.

The Teaching/Learning System

Microcomputers is the cornerstone of a comprehensive teaching/learning system. Other components of the system are described in the paragraphs that follow.

Instructor's Resource Manual with Test Item File and Transparency Masters.   The *Instructor's Resource Manual* contains Teaching Hints (including the use of support software) and Lecture Notes (in outline format) to accompany the material presented in the text. Boldface terms, in-class discussion questions, and references to appropriate transparencies are embedded in the Lecture Notes.

The *Instructor's Resource Manual* also includes answers to exercises and solutions to appropriate hands-on assignments in the text and *Lab Manual*. The black-line *Transparency Masters* are provided to facilitate in-class explanation.

Computer-Based Test Generation.   The hard copy of the *Test Item File* is included in the *Instructor's Resource Manual*. A computerized version of the *Test Item File* and Prentice Hall's Text Generator software are available on diskettes for popular microcomputers. Three types of questions (true/false, multiple choice, and essay) are provided for each conceptual chapter (all but Chapters 6, 8, and 11, which contain only Hands-On Tutorials).

Lab Manual.   The *Lab Manual* includes hands-on exercises and follow-up keystroke tutorials for all of the software packages presented in the text. These tutorials illustrate both domestic and business applications for the various software tools, and they introduce students to the more advanced features of the packages.

The SuperSoftware Activities section of the *Lab Manual* contains lab activities and questions to be used with SuperSoftware, one of the software supplements.

Software Supplements.   Several *Software Supplements* accompany the text.

For IBM PC and Compatibles

- WordPerfect (word processing—educational version)
- The TWiN (emulates Lotus 1–2–3) (spreadsheet, graphics, and database—educational version)

- dBASE III PLUS (database—educational version)
- The OUTLINER (idea processor—fully functional)
- Crosstalk XVI (communications—interactive simulation)
- SuperSoftware (interactive educational software)
- Test Generator (exam preparation software distributed with test item file)
- Solutions Disk (files resulting from all hands-on tutorials in the text and *Lab Manual*)

For the Apple IIe and IIc

- SuperSoftware (interactive educational software)
- Test Generator (exam preparation software distributed with test item file)

Commercial Software Packages Available to Adopters. Arrangements have been made with WordPerfect Corporation (WordPerfect), Mosaic Software (The TWiN), Ashton-Tate (dBASE III PLUS), Long and Associates (The OUTLINER), and DCA/Crosstalk Communications (Crosstalk XVI) to offer educational versions of their software to adopters of *Microcomputers*. Comprehensive keystroke tutorials of these packages are included in the text and in the *Lab Manual*.

SuperSoftware. SuperSoftware, which contains 50-plus hours of hands-on lab activity for the IBM PC version (25-plus hours for the Apple version), is designed to instruct, intrigue, and motivate. With SuperSoftware, students can begin using and enjoying micros during the first class. The *Lab Manual* contains specific hands-on activities and exercises.

Scores of interesting and graphic programs, such as "Introduction to the PC," encourage students to become familiar with the computer. SuperSoftware interactively demonstrates micro software concepts (electronic spreadsheet, word processing, and so on) concepts through imaginative generic simulations.

Author "Hotline." Professors and administrators of colleges adopting *Microcomputers* are encouraged to call Larry or Nancy Long (the "hotline" number is in the preface of the *Instructor's Resource Manual*) to discuss specific questions relating to the use of the text and its support package or to discuss more general questions relating to course organization or curricula planning.

Introductory Computer Texts That Complement *Microcomputers*. *Introduction to Computers and Information Processing*, second edition (Prentice Hall, 1988) and *Computers in Business* (Prentice Hall, 1987), both by Larry Long, provide a general overview of computer and information processing concepts, the latter having a business orientation. *Microcomputers* and either of these introductory texts are designed such that they complement one another in a two-course sequence.

Pedagogical Philosophy

The Three Step Process.   Learning effectiveness was a key consideration in the design of this book. Consistent with this consideration, the premise of this text is that *students learn by doing*. We designed this text to get the student on the microcomputer and to enable the student to realize results as soon as possible. We do this in a three-step process.

1. *Students are introduced to the conceptual basis for each of the software productivity tools.* In the succinct and pedagogically sound conceptual presentation, students learn the purpose, function, concepts, and applications for a category (such as word processing) of software. The entire presentation is within the context of a typical application of the software. This type of presentation permits students to grasp the concepts quickly and move on to hands-on applications of these tools.

    In the interest of pedagogical effectiveness, concepts common to micros and micro software are discussed only once. For example, "universal" concepts such as scrolling, pull-down menus, cursor control, booting DOS, special-purpose keys, and so on are discussed in Chapters 1 through 4.

2. *Students work through keystroke tutorials to familiarize themselves with the fundamentals of the operation and use of a particular software package, such as WordPerfect or dBASE III PLUS.* The tutorials:

- Acquaint students with the functionality and the applications potential of a particular micro software package.
- Instill in students a confidence that they can make effective use of these packages.
- Expose students to the menu/command structure of the software packages.
- Demonstrate common operations, such as block moves in word processing, entering formulas in an electronic spreadsheet, and setting conditions for record selection from a data base.

3. *Students complete Hands-On Exercises that provide them with an opportunity to apply their micro skills to a variety of domestic and business applications.* After the successful completion of one or more Hands-On Exercises, students should be able to apply their skills and imagination to their own applications at work and at home.

Teaching/Learning Flexibility.   Teaching/learning flexibility remains a priority in our pedagogical strategy. The *Microcomputers* package is designed to give you the flexibility to create and teach a microcomputer course that is most appropriate for your environment. The text contains functional summaries and keystroke tutorials for DOS and a wide variety of commercial software. This variety permits colleges and businesses with established computing environments to continue using existing resources to meet local educational needs. This variety also permits the use of existing resources to be supplemented or replaced with software that is distributed to adopters of the text.

In Summary.   The examples in the conceptual presentation were carefully prepared to demonstrate the fundamental principles associated with the use and operation for a category of software packages. We are confident that the student who understands the conceptual material, completes the associated Hands-On Tutorials, and accomplishes one or more of the Hands-On Exercises will have acquired the skills needed to be an effective user of micro productivity software.

Acknowledgments

During the conceptualization and eventually the preparation of the *Microcomputers* manuscript, we talked personally with literally hundreds of professors about the evolution of microcomputer education and what they wanted for a text and as support material. Their collective comments have been the beacon that has guided our thinking with regard to content, organization, depth of coverage, and orientation. We would like to extend our deepest gratitude to these dedicated professionals. In addition, we wish to thank the many students who class tested the keystroke tutorials.

Microcomputers was signed, designed, and produced by our friends and colleagues at Prentice Hall. The key players in this process are respectively Jim Fegen, Dennis Hogan, Janet Schmid, and Colleen Brosnan. Many Prentice Hall professionals have made significant contributions to this project, however; some deserve special recognition: Gary June, Rob Dewey, Alice Dworkin, Maureen Eide, Lisa Garboski, Barbara Kittle, and Debbie Kesar. We are forever indebted to our Prentice Hall family for their contribution and their ongoing commitment to education.

Literally hundreds of companies have in some way participated in the compilation of this book and its support package. A grateful academic community would like to thank them, one and all, for their ongoing commitment to education.

The imagination and hard work of our colleagues Ted Kalmon (co-author of the *Lab Manual*) and Marty Chamberlain are liberally sprinkled throughout the "Micro" teaching/learning system.

Larry Long, Ph.D.
Nancy Long, Ph.D.

ABOUT THE AUTHORS

Dr. Larry Long and Dr. Nancy Long, both of Long and Associates, are lecturers, authors, consultants, and educators in the computer and information services fields. Their many books cover a broad spectrum of computer and MIS-related topics from micros to programming to MIS strategic planning.

Larry has served as a computer/MIS consultant to all levels of management in virtually every major type of industry. Over the past twenty years, he has taught a variety of courses on computer-related topics both in the private sector and at the University of Oklahoma and Lehigh University, where he continues to be an active lecturer. Larry received his Ph.D., M.S., and B.S. degrees in Industrial Engineering at the University of Oklahoma.

Nancy has a decade of teaching and administrative experience at all levels of education: elementary, secondary, college, and continuing education. Nancy received a Ph.D. in Reading Education and Educational Psychology, an M.S. in Personnel Services, and B.S. in Elementary Education at the University of Oklahoma. Her wealth of knowledge in the areas of pedagogy and reading education is evident throughout the text and the supplements.

THE WORLD
OF COMPUTERS

Micros and Personal Computing

STUDENT LEARNING OBJECTIVES

- To grasp the scope of computer understanding that someone might need to become an active participant in the computer revolution.

- To describe the general function of the major categories of microcomputer productivity software: word processing, electronic spreadsheet, graphics, data management, idea processors, and communications.

- To summarize the types of services available through commercial information services.

- To describe the fundamental components and the operational capabilities of a computer system.

- To put the technological development of personal computers into historical perspective.

1–1 THE COMPUTER REVOLUTION

In a little more than three decades, *computer* technology has come a very long way. The first commercial computer was large enough to fill a gymnasium and was considered too expensive for all but the largest companies. Today, we use small computers, called **microcomputers**, for all kinds of domestic and business applications. They are thousands of times faster and more powerful than the first commercial computers. If the automobile industry had experienced similar progress, a new car would now cost less than a gallon of gas!

The *computer revolution* is upon us. This unprecedented technical revolution has made computers a *part of life*. With the rapid growth in the number and variety of computer applications, they are rapidly becoming a *way of life*. This book and its accompanying learning system will enable you to experience the adventure of computers and, at the same time, learn skills that will make you an active participant in the computer revolution, both at work and at home.

Two centuries ago, our agrarian society began to evolve into an industrial society. Today, we are rapidly transitioning to an information society where "knowledge" workers depend on their microcomputers and computer-generated information to accomplish their jobs.
(Courtesy of Xerox Corporation)

1–2 THE PERSONAL COMPUTER REVOLUTION

The First Personal Computer Boom

For the most part, a microcomputer is used by one person at a time; therefore the **micro** is also called a **personal computer**, or **PC** for short. The media attention given these desktop miracles of technology was intense during their infant years, the late 1970s and early 1980s. Fear of falling behind the competition motivated businesses to purchase personal computers by the truck load. Parents hurried to buy a personal computer so that little Johnny or Mary could march to the head of the class.

Unfortunately, businesses, parents, and others bought PCs with very little knowledge of what they do or what to do with them. In fact, the first personal computer boom was actually a bust! A great many PCs were sold, but relatively few made significant contributions in businesses, homes, or educational institutions. Because they were misunderstood and did not live up to their fanfare, the buying public cooled to PCs.

The Second Personal Computer Boom

Five years later, we are in the middle of the second personal computer boom. The capabilities of today's micros have expanded greatly. They are easier to use and people have more realistic and informed expectations of them. The second personal computer boom is more deliberate. That is, people are educating themselves about the use and application of micros; then they are buying them with purpose and direction—the result is millions of micro enthusiasts.

Personal computers are everywhere, from kindergartens to corporate boardrooms. You can see them at work, at school, and possibly in your own home. The most recent boom has made it possible for people in every walk of life to see first hand the usefulness of personal computers. Each passing month brings more power at less expense and an expansion to the seemingly endless array of microcomputer **software**. Software is a collective reference to computer programs that cause the computer to perform desired functions (for example, word processing).

At many colleges, microcomputers are strategically located throughout campus so that students and professors can have ready access to a wide variety of information and to the processing capability of a micro. The micros in the library are available on a first-come, first-serve basis. (Courtesy of Apple Computer, Inc.)

Microcomputers in factory warehouses are becoming as common as steel-toed shoes. This warehouse supervisor relies on information obtained from his portable micro to help him maintain inventory at a level that is consistent with customer demand. (Courtesy of Compaq Computer Corporation)

With microcomputers handling more and more of the routine tasks, we have more time to be creative. For this personnel manager, time-consuming summary reports are handled by the computer, thereby giving her more time to be creative in her job function.
(Photo courtesy of Hewlett-Packard Company)

Why Are Micros and Personal Computers So Popular?

The minimal cost and almost unlimited applications for the microcomputer have made it the darling of the computer industry. A little more than a decade ago, very few people had heard of a microcomputer. Now the number of microcomputers sold in one month exceeds the total number of operational computers in existence in the United States 10 years ago.

When you use a micro or personal computer, the capabilities of a complete computer system are at the tip of your fingers. Some are more powerful than computers that once handled the data processing requirements of large banks. PCs and their support software are designed so that they are easy to use and understand. The wide variety of software available for microcomputers offers something for almost everyone, from video games to word processing to education to home finances to inventory control.

A personal computer is an electronic version of a scratch pad, a file cabinet, a drawing board, a typewriter, a musical instrument, and even a friend. It can help you to think logically, to improve your spelling, to select the right word, to expand your memory, to organize data, to add numbers, and much more.

These reasons for the micro's popularity pale when we talk of the *real* reason for its unparalleled success—it is just plain fun to use, whether for personal, business, or scientific computing.

1–3   ORGANIZATION OF THIS TEXT

This text is organized in three parts.

- *Part I*. Part I, Chapters 1 and 2, provides an overview of micros and micro applications and a survey of general computer concepts.
- *Part II*. Part II, Chapters 3 and 4, contains information that provides the bridge between general understanding and the actual running of an applications software package. In Part II you will learn about interacting with microcomputer **hardware** (computing equipment composed of the computer and its peripheral devices) and the **operating system** (the software that provides the interface or link between the micro and an applications software package).
- *Part III*. The presentation in Part III, Chapters 5-13, is designed to help you acquire skills in the use and application of microcomputer productivity software: *word processing, electronic spreadsheet, graphics, database, idea processor*, and *communications software*. For each package, a conceptual discussion is followed by hands-on keystroke tutorials for a variety of commercial software packages, such as SuperCalc4, Lotus 1-2-3, and dBASE III PLUS. Tutorials are presented at the end of the chapter where the related concept is introduced or in the next chapter, depending on the depth and detail of the conceptual presentation. The purpose and function

of the various micro productivity software packages are described briefly in this chapter.

With each new slice of PC understanding, you open a new window of learning opportunities. The more you get into it, the more there is to know. Once you have a basic understanding of the function, concepts, and use of personal computers and PC software, the rate at which you learn will be accelerated with each increment of personal computer knowledge.

1–4   LEARNING ABOUT MICROCOMPUTERS

Cyberphobia.   Computers are synonymous with change, and any type of change is usually met with some resistance. We can attribute much of this resistance to a lack of knowledge about computers and, perhaps, to a fear of the unknown. People seem to perceive computers as mystical. It is human nature to fear that which we do not understand, be it extraterrestrial beings or computers. Fear of the computer is so widespread that psychologists have created a name for it: **cyberphobia**. Cyberphobia is the irrational fear of, and aversion to, computers. In truth, computers are merely machines and do not merit being the focus of such fear. If you are a cyberphobic, you will soon see that your fears are unfounded.

The Microcomputer Adventure.   A decade ago, most people were content to leave computers to computer professionals. Well, things have changed. Computers, especially personal computers, are becoming an integral part our learning experience. By the time you complete this course, you should

Can you believe that mother and daughter were at one time cyberphobics (they feared computers)? Their phobia disappeared after a few minutes of hands-on experience. Micros may be the business tools of the future, but they are also a source of enjoyment.
(Photo supplied courtesy of Epson America)

1. Feel comfortable in the use and operation of a microcomputer.
2. Be able to make the computer work for you through judicious application of microcomputer productivity software.
3. Be an intelligent consumer of computer-related products and services.

You are about to embark on an emotional and intellectual *journey* that will stimulate your imagination, challenge your every resource from physical dexterity to intellect, and perhaps, alter your sense of perspective. Learning about personal computers is more than just education—it's an adventure.

1–5   PERSONAL COMPUTING

A microcomputer sits easily on a desktop and can be controlled by one person. The growth in this kind of computing, called **personal computing**, has surpassed even the boldest forecasts of the mid-1970s. In a few years, personal computers will be as commonplace as telephones are now, both at home and at work.

Business and Domestic Applications for Personal Computing

Inexpensive microcomputers have made automation financially feasible for virtually any business environment. As a result, microcomputer software is available to support thousands of common and not-so-common business applications. There is, of course, an established need for applications such as payroll, accounting, sales analysis, project management, and inventory control. There are also hundreds of industry-specific software packages for thoroughbred breeding, for medical laboratories, for professional football, for printers, and for just about any other industry type.

Domestic applications include some of the following: maintaining an up-to-date asset inventory of household items; storing names and addresses for a personal mailing list; maintaining records for, preparing, and sending income tax returns; creating and monitoring a household budget; keeping an appointment and social calendar; handling household finances (such as checkbook balancing, bill paying, coupon refunding); letter writing; education; and, of course, entertainment. You can purchase software for all of these applications, and you can probably obtain software for your special interest, whether it be astrology, charting biorhythms, composing music, or dieting.

The Microcomputer Family of Productivity Software

Thousands of commercially available software packages run on microcomputers, but the most popular software is the family of productivity software packages. They include *word processing, electronic spreadsheet, graphics, database, idea processor,* and *communications soft-*

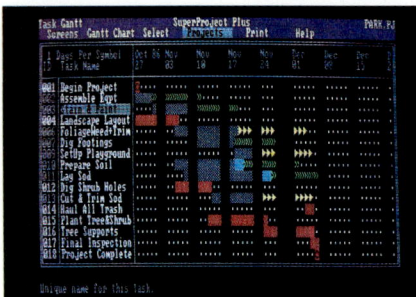

Project management is one of many timesaving applications for both business and domestic personal computing. This micro-produced Gantt chart graphically illustrates the time-phasing for the activities that comprise a landscaping project.
(Computer Associates International, Inc.)

ware. In contrast to software that is designed for a *specific* application, these software packages are *general-purpose* software and provide the framework for a great number of business and personal applications. The functions, concepts, and uses of each of these micro software tools are the focus of Part III of this text.

These software packages are often characterized as *productivity tools* because they help to relieve the tedium of many time-consuming manual tasks. Thanks to word processing software, retyping is a thing of the past. Electronic spreadsheets permit us to perform certain arithmetic and logic operations without writing programs. Say goodbye to grid paper, plastic templates, and the manual plotting of data: graphics software prepares bar, pie, and line graphs without us drawing a single line. With database software, we can format and create a data base in minutes. When brainstorming with idea processors, the result is a logical outline of conclusions, not indecipherable notes on a yellow pad. And communications software enables micro users to establish a communications link with other micros or with larger computers.

The purpose and function of each of the micro productivity software packages are described briefly below.

Word Processing.   **Word processing** is using the computer to enter text, to store it on magnetic storage media, to manipulate it in preparation for output, and to produce a hard copy. Numerous applications involve written communications: letters, reports, memos, and so on. As well as being one of the microcomputer productivity tools, word processing is also part of a set of applications collectively referred to as **office automation**. Office automation encompasses those computer-based applications associated with general office work.

If you use word processing to prepare your reports, you will only have to key in the full draft once. Revisions and corrections can be made to magnetic disk-based file before the report is printed in final form. If you forgot a word or need to add a paragraph, you do not have to retype a page or, in the worst case, the whole report. For example, the original text for this book was keyed in only once on a microcomputer. Editorial changes were then entered by the authors on a keyboard before the final manuscript was submitted to the publisher. See Chapters 5 and 6 for examples that illustrate the use of word processing software.

Microcomputers have become part of the scenery in every academic discipline. This sociology student is using her personal computer and word processing software to put the finishing touches on a term paper. This portable computer weighs less than 12 pounds, including the battery pack.
(Zenith Data Systems)

Electronic Spreadsheet.   A popular microcomputer application is the **electronic spreadsheet**. The spreadsheet contains a tabular structure of rows and columns. The user, instead of writing the entries manually in the rows and columns of a spreadsheet, has them stored in an electronic version of a spreadsheet, which can contain thousands of entries. Obviously, all entries in a large spreadsheet cannot be displayed at the same time, so the data are displayed in **windows**, or parts of the total spreadsheet. The user can display one or several windows on the screen at one time.

The applications of electronic spreadsheets are endless: think of anything that has rows and columns. For example, spreadsheet software is often used for income statement analysis, home budgeting, sales forecasting, and grade reporting.

The intersection of a row and column is called a **cell** and is referenced by its position within the matrix. In an income statement, for example, the entry in cell A1 (the first or A column, row 1) might be "Net Sales," and the entry in cell B1 might be "$183,600."

	A	B	C
1	Net Sales	$183,600	
2			

Notice that columns are lettered and rows numbered. Cell entries can be either words or numbers. See Chapters 7 through 9 for examples that illustrate the use of spreadsheet software.

Once the data are entered for a an income statement, an electronic spreadsheet permits the user to manipulate and analyze the data. For example, an accountant can use spreadsheet capabilities to forecast profit for the coming year by electronically revising the current income statement to reflect anticipated growth.

For the last several years, this product manager spent one hour each week tallying the regional sales figures. He finally spent five hours creating an electronic spreadsheet model to help with this task. Now, his weekly sales reports take only 15 minutes, and they are more accurate. In every office, there are many applications for electronic spreadsheet software. (Photo courtesy of Hewlett-Packard Company)

Graphics.   **Graphics software** enables you to create a variety of presentation graphics based on data in a data base or a spreadsheet. These graphics take the form of bar graphs, pie graphs, and line graphs.

A pie graph is easily produced from a spreadsheet containing regional sales data. Each slice of the pie might depict the sales for each region as a percentage of total sales. The slices are in proportion. For example, if sales in the northeast region are $10 million and sales in the southwest region, $5 million, the northeast region slice is shown to be twice the size of that of the southwest region. See Chapter 9 for examples that illustrate the use of graphics software.

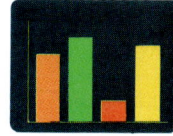

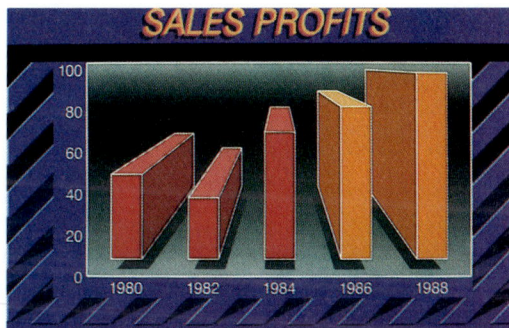

This visually pleasing three-dimensional bar graph was created in a few minutes with the aid of a graphics software package.
(Genigraphics Corporations)

Database.   **Data management software**, also called **database software**, permits the user to create and maintain a data base, and also to extract information from the data base. "Database," as one word, is commonly used to reference data management software. "Data base," as two words, refers to the highest level of the hierarchy of data organization (discussed in Chapter 2 and illustrated in Figure 2–7).

With database software, the user first identifies the format of the data, then designs a display screen format that will permit interactive entry and revision of the data. Once it is part of the data base, a record (for each salesperson, for example) can be displayed, changed, or deleted. The user can also retrieve and summarize data, based on certain criteria (such as all salespersons over quota for July). Also, data can be sorted for display in a variety of formats (for example, listing salespersons by total sales or alphabetically by last name). See Chapters 10 and 11 for examples that illustrate the use of database software.

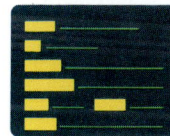

Idea Processors.   An **idea processor** is a productivity tool that helps you to organize your thoughts and ideas. Such software can be used for brainstorming, outlining project activities, developing speeches and presentations, compiling notes for meetings and seminars, and a myriad of other uses. Idea processors let you work with one idea at a time within a hierarchy of other ideas so that you can easily organize and reorganize you ideas. When you use an idea processor, you can focus your attention on the thought process by letting the computer help

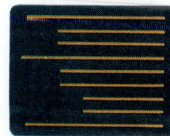

with the task of documenting your ideas. See Chapter 12 for examples that illustrate the use of idea processor software.

Communications.   **Communications software** transforms a micro into an "intelligent" **video display terminal**, or **VDT**. A VDT, or **terminal**, is a televisionlike monitor with a keyboard that enables remote communication with a computer. A micro, however, can do more than a VDT. Not only can a micro transmit and receive data from a remote computer, it can process and store data as well.

Communications software automatically "dials-up" the desired remote computer (perhaps your company's central computer system) and logs on; that is, the software establishes a communications link with the remote computer, usually via a telephone line. Once on-line, you can communicate with the remote computer or request that certain data be transmitted to your micro so that you can work with the data using the micro as a *stand-alone computer*. See Chapter 13 for examples that illustrate the use of communications software.

Productivity Software Summary.   In each productivity software category, there are dozens of commercially available software packages from which to choose. The software packages in each category accomplish essentially the same functions. They differ primarily in the scope and variety of the special features they have to offer and in their "user friendliness."

One of the beauties of micro productivity software packages is that they can work together to provide users with an even greater processing capability. For example, a manager might use several micro productivity software packages to handle a variety of administrative duties. To track product sales by region, a manager might use electronic spreadsheet software. At the end of each week the manager might summarize and plot sales data in a bar graph. Based on the results of the bar graph,

Communications software enables micro users to have access to the same time-sensitive information that is displayed for brokers on the floor of the stock exchanges. Once a communications link has been established with the information service's computer, micro users can request information for any stock. (Cromemco, Inc.)

(Copyright Viewdata Corporation of America 1984)

the manager might write a memo recommending that the top field sales representatives be considered for special recognition. Using communications software, the manager can transmit both the graph and the memo of commendation to the company's central computer systems for distribution to appropriate vice presidents. (This type of transmission—micro-to-another-computer—is called **uploading**. The reverse is called **downloading**.) As an ongoing activity, a manager might keep personal "things-to-do" notes in an outline format. This example illustrates how the capabilities of the individual software packages complement the capabilities of the others.

Many commercial software vendors offer packages that integrate two or more of the six major productivity tools. These packages are referred to as **integrated software**. A popular combination includes electronic spreadsheet, database, and graphics capabilities. Another combination includes all but idea processors. Several integrated packages include all six. Integrated software permits us to work, as we always have, on several projects at a time, but with the assistance of a computer.

Information Services

Personal computers are normally used as stand-alone computer systems, but as we have seen from earlier discussions, they can also double as remote terminals. This dual-function capability provides you with the flexibility to work with the PC as a stand-alone system or to link with a larger computer and take advantage of its increased capacity. With a PC, you have a world of information at your fingertips. The personal computer can be used in conjunction with the telephone system to transmit data to and receive data from a commercial **information service**.

A growing trend among personal computer enthusiasts is to subscribe to an information service, such as *CompuServe*, *The Source*, or *Dow Jones News/Retrieval Service*. These information services have one or several large computer systems that offer a variety of information services, from hotel reservations to daily horoscopes. Besides a micro, all you need to take advantage of these information services is a **modem** (the interface between the telephone line and a micro), a telephone line, and a few dollars. You would normally pay a one-time fee. For the fee, you get a password and personal identification number that will permit you to establish a communications link with the service. You are also given a booklet that lists the telephone numbers that you would dial to establish a link with the information service. If you are in a medium to large city, the telephone number that you would dial is usually a local number. You are billed based on how much you use the information service.

The following list summarizes the types of services available through commercial information services.

Home Banking.   Check your account balances, transfer money, and pay bills in the comfort of your home or office.

MEMORY BITS

MICROCOMPUTER PRODUCTIVITY SOFTWARE
- Word processing
- Electronic spreadsheet
- Graphics
- Database
- Idea processor
- Communications

News, Weather, Sports.   Get the latest releases directly from the wire services.

Entertainment.   Read reviews of the latest releases of movies, videos, and records. Chart your biorhythms or ask the advice of astrologers.

Games.   Hundreds of single and multiplayer games are available. You can even play a game of chess with a friend in another state! Or, you might prefer to match wits with another trivia buff.

Financial Information.   Get up-to-the-minute quotes on stocks, securities, bonds, options, and commodities. You can also use this service to help you manage a securities portfolio and to keep tax records.

Brokerage Services.   Purchase and sell securities twenty-four hours a day from your microcomputer.

Bulletin Boards.   Special-interest bulletin boards, focusing on wine, human sexuality, computer art, aviation, and many other topics, offer users a forum for the exchange of ideas and information. Besides those offered by information services, thousands of bulletin board systems (BBSs) are made available free of charge by individuals and computer clubs.

Electronic Mail.   Send mail to and receive it from other users of the information service. Each subscriber is assigned an ID and an electronic mailbox. Mail sent to a particular subscriber can be "opened" only by that subscriber.

You can use your personal computer and an information service to send flowers. To do so, you would make a selection from available arrangements, enter the name and address of the receiving party, and enter your credit card number. The system uses the destination ZIP code to search a file for the nearest participating florist. Once identified, your request is routed via data communications directly to the florist. (Photo courtesy of Hewlett-Packard Company)

Shop at Home. Select what you want from a list of thousands of items offered at discount prices. Payment is made via electronic funds transfer (EFT) and your order is delivered to your doorstep.

Reference. Look up items of interest in an electronic encyclopedia. Scan through various government publications. Recall articles on a particular subject from dozens of newspapers, trade periodicals, and newsletters. Students seeking a college might want to tap the service for information on potential colleges.

Education. Choose from a variety of educational packages, from learning arithmetic to preparing for the Scholastic Aptitude Test (SAT). You can even determine your own IQ!

Real Estate. Moving? Check out available real estate by scanning the listings for the city to which you are moving.

Home and Health. Address medical questions to a team of top physicians. Use keywords to access thousands of culinary delights (for example, entree, Spanish, rice).

Travel. Plan your own vacation or business trip. You can check airline, train, and cruise schedules and make your own reservations. You can even charter a yacht in the Caribbean, locate the nearest bed and breakfast inn, or rent a lodge in the Rockies.

These and many other timesaving applications should eventually make personal computers a "must-have" item in every home and office.

1–6 UNCOVERING THE "MYSTERY" OF COMPUTERS

What Is a Computer?

The word "computer" is an integral part of just about everyone's daily-use vocabulary, but to many people, it is some kind of miraculous "black box." Technically speaking, the **computer** is any counting device. But in the context of modern technology, we define the computer as *an electronic device capable of interpreting and executing programmed commands for input, output, computation, and logic operations.* The computer, also called a **processor**, is the "intelligence" of a *computer system.*

Computers may be technically complex, but they are conceptually simple. A computer system—any computer system, small or large—has only four fundamental components: **input**, *processing*, **output**, and *storage*. Note that a *computer system*, not a computer, has four components. The actual computer is the processing component and is combined with the other three to form a **computer system** (see Figure 1–1).

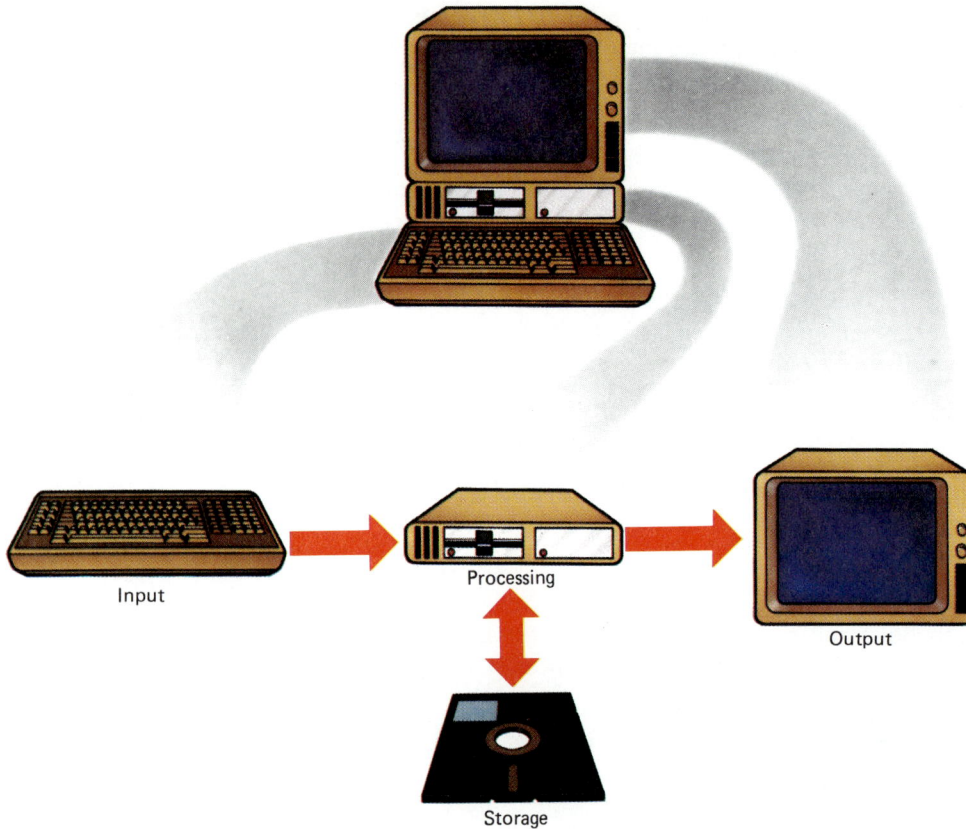

FIGURE 1–1
The Four Fundamental Components of a Microcomputer System
In a microcomputer system, the storage and processing components are
often contained in the same physical unit. In the illustration, the diskette
storage medium is inserted into the unit that contains the processor.

How a Computer System Works

A computer system can be likened to the biological system of the
human body. Your brain, which is the processing component, is linked
to the other components of the body by the central nervous system.
Your eyes and ears are input components that send signals to the
brain. If you see someone approaching, your brain matches the visual
image of this person with others in your memory (storage component).
If the visual image is matched in memory with that of a friend, your
brain sends signals to your vocal chords and right arm (output components) to greet your friend with a "Hello" and a handshake. Computer
system components interact in a similar way.

(Courtesy of Unisys Corporation)

(Courtesy of Unisys Corporation)

(Courtesy of AT&T Bell Laboratories)

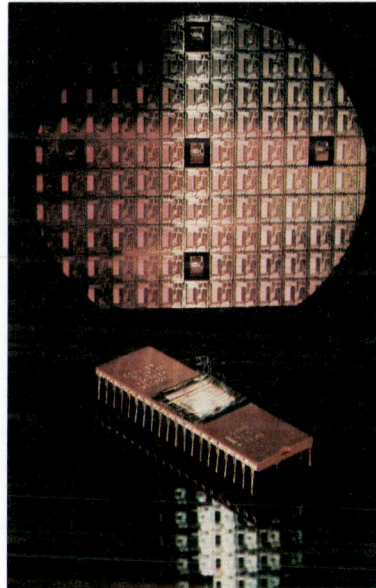

(Courtesy Intel Corporation)

The electronic circuitry for microcomputers is embedded in a variety of tiny silicon chips. These photos illustrate the four phases of the chip manufacture process: design, fabrication, testing, and packaging. Chips are designed (top left) to accomplish a particular function (for example, a processor or memory). During fabrication (top right), the circuitry of several hundred chips is etched into these silicon wafers. The chips are tested (bottom left) while they are still part of the wafer. The chips are separated from the wafer and packaged (bottom right) in protective carriers that can be plugged into circuit boards. The completed circuit boards are installed in computers.

The payroll system in Figure 1–2 illustrates how data are entered and how the four computer system components interact to produce information (such as, a "year-to-date overtime report") and the payroll checks. The hours-worked data are *input* to the system and are *stored* on the personnel master file. Note that the storage component of a computer system stores data, not information!

The payroll checks are produced when the *processing* component, or the computer, executes a program. In this example, the employee record is recalled from storage, and the pay amount is calculated. The *output* is the printed payroll checks. Other programs extract data from the personnel master file to produce a year-to-date overtime report and any other information that might help in the decision-making process.

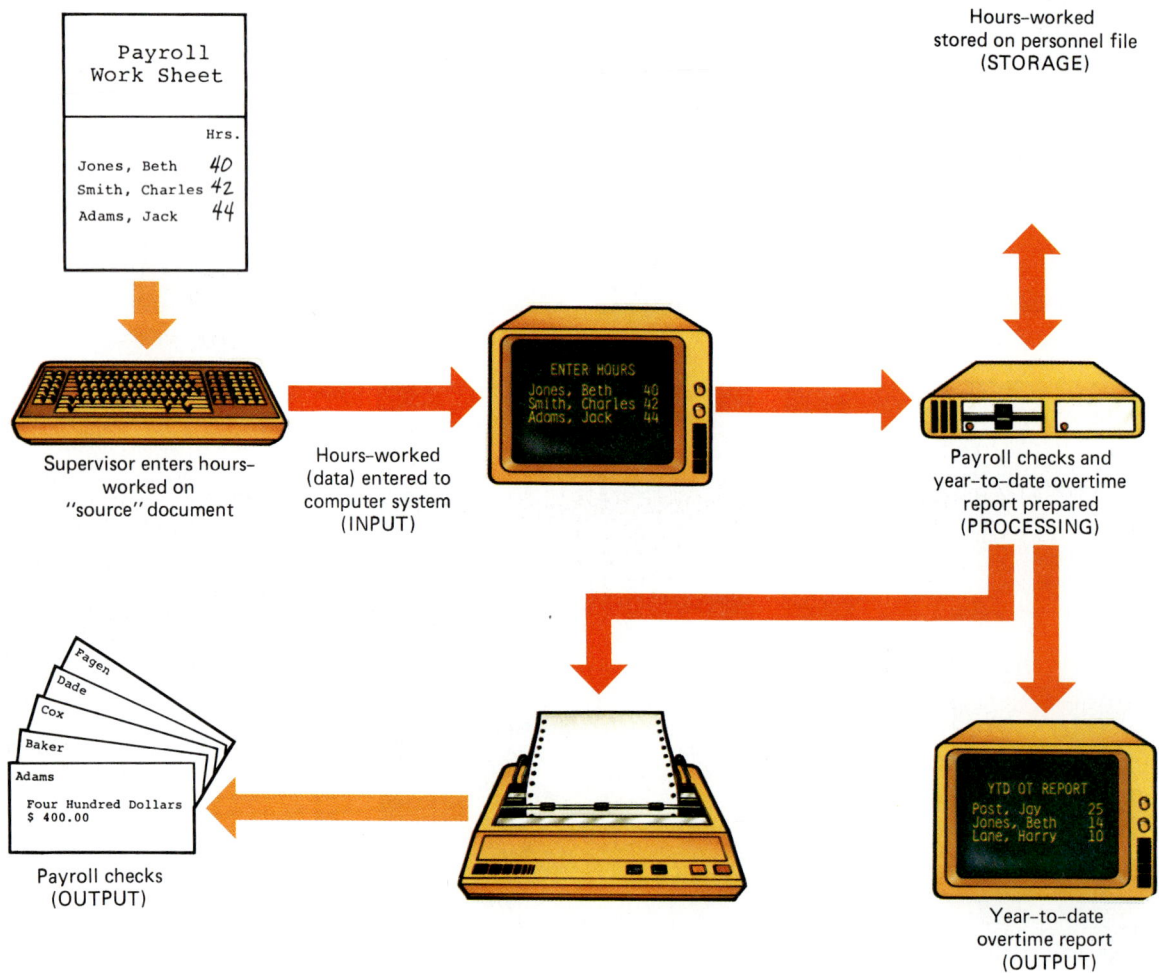

FIGURE 1–2
Payroll System
This microcomputer-based payroll system illustrates input, storage, processing, and output.

The Hardware

In the microcomputer-based payroll example, data are entered (input) on a typewriterlike **keyboard** and displayed (output) on a televisionlike (video) screen, called a **monitor**. The payroll checks are then output on a device called a **printer**. Data are stored for later recall on **magnetic disk**. There are a wide variety of input/output (**I/O**) and storage devices. The variety of hardware devices that make up a microcomputer system are discussed in detail in Chapter 2.

The principles discussed above apply equally to microcomputers and the larger **mainframe computers**. Each has the four components

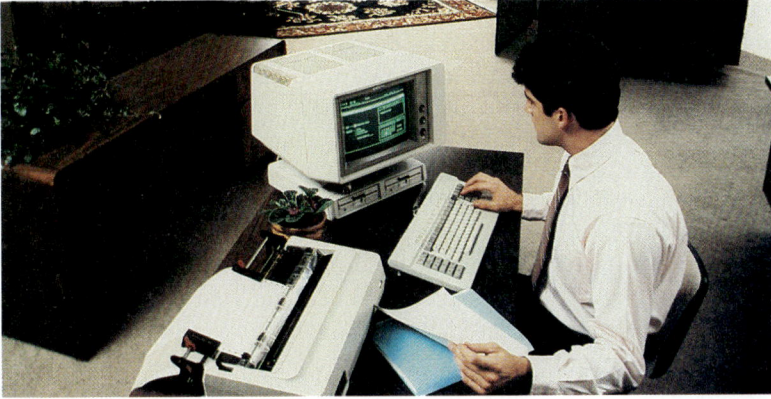

This credit manager's micro is configured with a keyboard for input, a video monitor and a printer for output, and two disk drives for storage of data and programs.
(Courtesy of Unisys Corporation)

The components of a mainframe computer system are not as apparent as those of a microcomputer. The processing component is the box in the middle. The printer (output) is on the right. Input is on the operator consoles in the foreground. The other boxes are for permanent and temporary storage of data and programs.
(Honeywell, Inc.)

and each uses data to produce information in a similar manner. The difference is that personal computers are more limited in their capabilities and are designed primarily for use by *one person* at a time. Mainframe computers can service *many users*, perhaps even thousands, all at once.

What Can a Computer Do?

The last section discussed how the *input/output* and *data storage* hardware components are configured with the *processing* component (the computer) to make up a computer system (see Figure 1–1). The focus of this section is on the the operational capabilities of a computer system.

Input/Output Operations.   The computer *reads* from input and storage devices. The computer *writes* to output and storage devices. Before data can be processed, they must be "read" from an input device or data storage device. Input data are usually entered by a user via a keyboard or some other input device or retrieved from a data storage device, such as a magnetic disk drive. Once data have been processed, they are "written" to an output device, such as a printer, or to a data storage device.

Input/output (I/O) operations are illustrated in the payroll system example in Figure 1–2. Hours-worked data are entered and read into the computer system. These data are written to magnetic disk storage for recall at a later date.

Processing Operations.   The computer is totally objective. That is, any two computers instructed to perform the same operation will arrive at the same result. This is because the computer can perform only *computation* and *logic operations*.

The computational capabilities of the computer include adding, subtracting, multiplying, and dividing. Logic capability permits the computer to make comparisons between numbers and between words, and, based on the result of the comparison, perform appropriate functions. In the payroll system example of Figure 1–2, the computer calculates the gross pay in a computation operation (40 hours at $10/hour = $400). In a logic operation, the computer compares the number of hours worked to 40 to determine the number of overtime hours that an employee worked during a given week.

Computer System Capabilities

In a nutshell, computers are fast, accurate, and reliable; they do not forget anything; and they do not complain.

Speed.   The smallest unit of time in the human experience is, realistically, the second. With the second as the only means of comparison, it is difficult for us to comprehend the time scale of computers. The operations (the execution of instructions) for personal computers are measured in **milliseconds** and **microseconds** (one thousandth and one millionth of a second, respectively). Larger processors are measured in **nanoseconds** and **picoseconds** (one billionth and one trillionth of a second, respectively). To give you a feeling for the speed of computers, a beam of light travels down the length of this page in about 1 nanosecond!

Accuracy.   You may work for years before experiencing a system error, such as an updating of the wrong record or an incorrect addition. Errors do occur, but precious few can be directly attributed to the computer system. The vast majority of these errors can be traced to a program logic error, a procedural error, or erroneous data. These are *human errors*.

Reliability.   Computer systems are particularly adept at repetitive tasks. They don't take sick days and coffee breaks, and they seldom

---

MEMORY BITS

COMPUTER OPERATIONS
- Input/output
  - Read
  - Write
- Processing
  - Computation
  - Logic

complain. Anything below 99.9 percent *uptime* is usually unacceptable. Unfortunately, *downtime* sometimes occurs at the most inconvenient times. Fortunately for microcomputer users, a *backup* micro is usually no further away than the next room.

Memory Capability.   Computer systems have total and instant recall of data and an almost unlimited capacity to store these data. A typical microcomputer will have the capacity to store and recall from one to 60 million characters and, perhaps, some graphic images. To give you a benchmark for comparison, this book contains approximately 1,000,000 characters.

Even though they have sensitive solid state electronic circuitry and high-precision moving parts, micros are very reliable. It is not unusual to find micro owners who have experienced years of trouble-free operation.
(Courtesy of Compaq Computer Corporation)

1–7   HISTORICAL PERSPECTIVE

Personal Computer Milestones

The history of microcomputers is of special significance to us because their entire history has occurred within our lifetimes. In terms of the way people live and work, John V. Atanasoff's invention of the electronic digital computer (1942) can be considered one of the most significant events in history. But not until 1975 and the introduction of the *Altair 8800* personal computer, a product of the microminiaturization of electronic circuitry, was computing made available to individuals and very small companies. This event has forever changed how we as society perceive computers. The Altair 8800, which sold for $650 ($395 as a kit), was marketed by a small electronics company called Micro Instrumentation and Telemetry Systems (MITS). After *Popular Electronics* featured the Altair 8800 on its cover, MITS received thousands of orders. People wanted their own personal computer. Within two years, 30 other companies would be manufacturing and selling personal computers.

Perhaps the most prominent entrepreneurial venture during the early years of PCs was the *Apple II* computer. It all began in 1976 when two young computer enthusiasts, Steven Jobs and Steve Wozniak (then 21 and 26 years of age, respectively), collaborated to create and build their Apple II computer. Raising $1,300 by selling Jobs' Volkswagon

The Apple II is assured of a prominent position in microcomputer history, but it continues to be a work horse for thousands of businesses. Parts inventory and customer records are maintained on this Apple II at an automobile service center.
(Courtesy of Apple Computer, Inc.)

Over three million sold. The IBM PC has been used by people in just about area of business, from architects (shown here) to zoologists.
(Courtesy of International Business Machines Corporation)

and Wozniak's programmable calculator, they opened a makeshift production line in Jobs' garage. Seven years later, Apple Computer, Inc., earned a spot on the Fortune 500, a list of the 500 largest corporations in the United States.

In 1981 International Business Machines (IBM), the giant of the computer industry, tossed its hat into the PC ring with the announcement of the *IBM PC*. In the first year, 35,000 were sold. In 1982, 800,000 were sold and the IBM PC was well on its way to becoming the "standard" for the micro industry. When software vendors began to orient their products to the IBM PC, many microcomputer manufacturers created and sold *clones* of the IBM PC. These clones, called *IBM PC compatibles*, run most or all of the software designed for the IBM PC.

Some industry analysts argue that IBM's dominance in the micro industry has helped to stabilize the growth of an industry in its infancy. Others argue that the overwhelming influence of the IBM PC tends to stifle the efforts of those entrepreneurs who want to push the limits of modern technology. In any case, whatever IBM does in the personal computer arena has immediate and far-reaching effects on the PC marketplace. The successor to the IBM PC, the IBM Personal System/

Perhaps this is the look of things to come. Just as the IBM PC series of microcomputers became the de facto industry standard during the period 1982 to 1987, industry analysts are already predicting that IBM's Personal System/2 series will carry the banner for the foreseeable future. The Personal System/2 Models 30, 50, 60, and 80 (shown here) were announced in 1987. The component that houses the processing and disk storage capabilities for PS/2 Models 60 and 80 is designed to rest on the floor.
(Courtesy of International Business Machines Corporation)

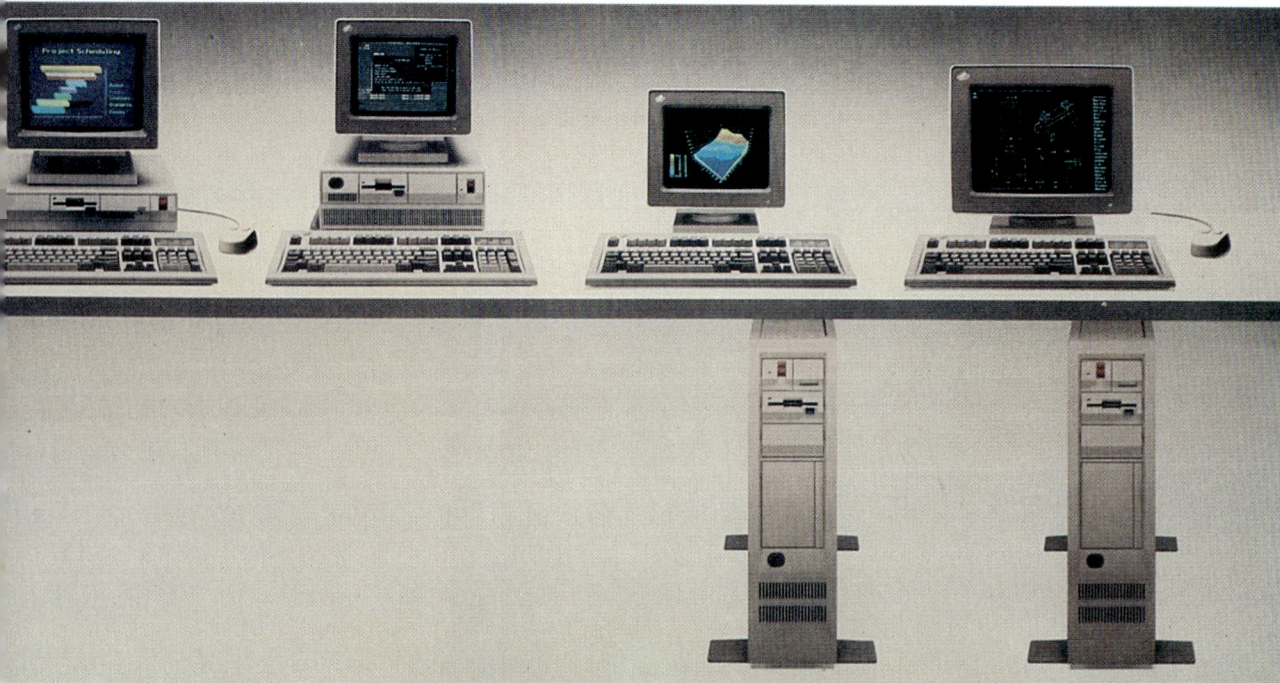

2 (introduced in 1987), will almost certainly become a milestone in PC history.

Several other personal computers have established their place in PC history. Introduced in 1982, the *Commodore-64* was significant because it signaled the buying public that powerful micros could be manufactured and sold at a reasonable cost—$599. In the same year, Compaq Computer Corporation bundled the equivalent of an IBM PC in a transportable case and named it the *Compaq Portable*: Thus began the era of the portable computer. In 1984, Apple Computer introduced the *Macintosh* with a very "friendly" graphic user interface— proof positive that computers can be easy and fun to use.

PC Software Milestones

During the early years, you had to be a programmer if you wanted to use a micro to address a particular application. During this period, the personal computer industry was waiting for the software industry to catch up. Today, it is the other way around. The software industry continues to grow at a fever pitch.

During the late 1970s, *CP/M* (Control Program for Microcomputers) was the dominant *operating system*. A micro's operating system provides the interface between the hardware and the applications software. When IBM chose *MS-DOS* from Microsoft Corporation, it, like the IBM PC, eventually became the standard for the industry. The IBM version of MS-DOS is called *PC-DOS* (both are discussed in Chapter 4, "DOS: Disk Operating System Concepts and Tutorials").

Several software packages are assured prominent places in PC history. With the introduction of *VisiCalc* in 1979, the first electronic spreadsheet program, micros became a viable business tool. Before that micros were used primarily in the educational environment and by the hobbyist. VisiCalc blazed the trail for *Lotus 1-2-3*, another electronic spreadsheet program. The success of Lotus Development Corporation's 1-2-3 is now legend. Ashton-Tate's *dBASE II*, a database software package introduced in 1979, made it possible for micro users to create their own information systems, without the aid of a professional programmer. In 1979, MicroPro International Corporation introduced *WordStar*, a word processing package that to this day enjoys an almost cultlike following. A Borland International product called *SideKick* deserves honorable mention because it did so much to introduce the concept of **memory-resident programs** to the buying public during the early 1980s. SideKick remains operational while other applications programs are running; that is, you can call up a notepad, calculator, calendar, and other application programs during a word processing or electronic spreadsheet session.

During this quick stroll through the short history of personal computers, we were only able to highlight a few of the many significant innovations and events that have occurred since the announcement of the Altair 8800. As an active participant in the microcomputer revolution you will be a part of all the history-making events of the future.

SUMMARY OUTLINE AND IMPORTANT TERMS ____

1–1   THE COMPUTER REVOLUTION.   We, as a society, are in the middle of a computer revolution. The emergence of the **microcomputer** has opened the door for virtually everyone to become an active participant in this revolution.

1–2   THE PERSONAL COMPUTER REVOLUTION.   Typically a **micro** is used by one person at a time. The first **personal computer** or **PC** boom was actually a bust because people were not prepared to cope with these new technological marvels. Today, a better educated and more deliberate buying public have spawned a very successful second personal computer boom. The powerful micro and the availability of a seemingly endless array of microcomputer **software** (the computer programs) has encouraged people in every endeavor to jump on the PC bandwagon.

1–3   ORGANIZATION OF THIS TEXT.   This text is organized in three parts. Part I, Chapters 1 and 2, provides an overview of micros and a survey of general computer concepts. Part II, Chapters 3 and 4, contains information that provides the bridge between general understanding and the actual running of an applications software package. Part III, Chapters 5-13, is designed to help you acquire skills in the use and application of microcomputer productivity software.

1–4   LEARNING ABOUT MICROCOMPUTERS.   Psychologists have created a new phobia: **cyberphobia**. Cyberphobia is the irrational fear of, and aversion to, computers. By the time you complete this course you should feel comfortable with micros, be able to make them work for you, and be an intelligent consumer of computer-related products and services.

1–5   PERSONAL COMPUTING.   **Personal computing** encompasses a broad range of applications in both the business and domestic environments. The following general purpose programs make up the microcomputer family of productivity software.

- **Word processing** software permits users to enter, store, manipulate, and print text.
- **Electronic spreadsheet** software permits users to work with the rows and columns of a matrix (or spreadsheet) of data.
- **Graphics software** permits users to create charts and line drawings that graphically portray the data in an electronic spreadsheet or data base.
- **Data management** or **database software** permits users to create and maintain a data base and to extract information from the data base.

- **Idea processor** software helps users to organize and document their thoughts and ideas.
- **Communications software** permits users to send and receive transmissions of data to and from remote computers, and to process and store the data as well.

Packages that integrate two or more of the six major productivity tools are referred to as **integrated software**.

The personal computer can be used in conjunction with the telephone system to transmit data to and receive data from a commercial **information service**. All you need to take advantage of these information services is a **modem** (the interface between the telephone line and a micro), a telephone line, and a few dollars. Some of the services available through commercial information services include home banking, news, weather, sports, entertainment, games, financial information, brokerage services, bulletin boards, electronic mail, shop at home, reference, education, real estate, home and health, and travel.

1–6 UNCOVERING THE "MYSTERY" OF COMPUTERS. The **computer** is an electronic device capable of interpreting and executing programmed commands for input, output, computation, and logic operations. A **computer system** is not as complex as we are sometimes led to believe. Micros and **mainframe computers** are computer systems, and each has only four fundamental components: **input** (the **keyboard**), processing (executing a program), **output** (a **monitor** or a **printer**), and storage.

Computer system capabilities are defined as either input/output or processing. Processing capabilities are subdivided into computation and logic operations. The computer is fast, accurate, reliable, and has an enormous memory capacity.

1–7 HISTORICAL PERSPECTIVE. The history of microcomputers is short but full of noteworthy events. Some of the more significant hardware innovations include the Altair 8800 personal computer (1975), the Apple II (1976), the IBM PC (1981), the Commodore-64 (1982), the Compaq Portable (1982), the Macintosh (1984), and the IBM Personal System/2 (1987). Software milestones in micro history include the CP/M and MS-DOS operating systems, VisiCalc (1979), Lotus 1-2-3, dBASE II (1979), WordStar (1979), and SideKick.

REVIEW EXERCISES _____

1. Which of the six components of microcomputer productivity software would be most helpful in writing a term paper?

2. What is the software capability that enables viewing of electronic spreadsheet data and a bar graph at the same time?

3. List at least six services provided by an information service.

4. What are the four fundamental components of a computer system?

5. What part of a computer system would be analogous to the central nervous system of a human being? Why?

6. Which component of a computer system executes the program?

7. In computerese, what is meant by read and write?

8. Briefly describe the function of each of the six tools known as microcomputer productivity software.

9. What device provides the interface between the telephone line system and the micro?

10. List at least five domestic applications for personal computers.

11. Contrast the first personal computer boom to the second personal computer boom.

12. What is the cure for cyberphobia?

13. In an electronic spreadsheet, what is the intersection of a row and a column called?

14. Which of the microcomputer productivity software tools would be most appropriate for brainstorming?

15. What is an integrated software package?

16. How much time elapsed between the invention of the electronic digital computer and the introduction of the first commercially available personal computer?

17. Which software package made the most significant contribution to the emergence of the personal computer as a viable business tool?

SELF-TEST (by section)

1–1. Today's microcomputers are only slightly less powerful than the first commercial computers. (T/F)

1–2. References to a microcomputer or a personal computer are often abbreviated to _____ and _____, respectively.

1–3. Computing equipment is generally referred to as software. (T/F)

1–4. The irrational fear of, or aversion to, computers is called _____.

1–5. (a) The microcomputer productivity tool that manipulates data that are organized in a tabular structure of rows and columns is called _____ software.

(b)   The transmission of data from a micro to a mainframe is called uploading. (T/F)

(c)   Bulletin board systems are synonymous with electronic mail. (T/F)

1–6.   (a)   A printer is an example of which of the four computer system components?

(b)   The two types of processing operations performed by computers are _____ and _____ .

(c)   General computer concepts that apply to a microcomputer can also be applied to a mainframe computer. (T/F)

1–7.   Which came first: the Apple II, VisiCalc, or IBM PC?

Self-Test Answers.   **1–1,** F; **1–2,** micro, PC; **1–3,** F; **1–4,** cyberphobia; **1–5 (a),** electronic spreadsheet; **(b),** T; **(c),** F; **1–6 (a),** output; **(b),** computation, logic; **(c),** T; **1–7,** Apple II.

CHAPTER 2

Hardware, Software, and Data Management

STUDENT LEARNING OBJECTIVES

- To contrast microprocessors with microcomputers.
- To describe how data are stored in a computer system.
- To identify and describe the relationships between the internal components of a computer.
- To distinguish processors by their speed, memory capacity, and word length.
- To list and describe common computer peripheral devices.
- To describe and illustrate the relationships between the levels of the hierarchy of data organization.
- To distinguish between primary and secondary storage.
- To describe the principles of operation and methods of data storage for the magnetic disk, magnetic tape, and optical laser disk.
- To discuss the fundamental terminology and concepts associated with programming languages and software.

2–1 MICROCOMPUTERS: SMALL BUT POWERFUL

Microprocessors. Here is a tough one. What is smaller than a dime and found in wristwatches, sewing machines, and jukeboxes? The answer: a **microprocessor**. Microprocessors play a very important role in our lives. You probably have a dozen or more of them at home and may not know it. They are used in telephones, ovens, televisions, thermostats, greeting cards, cars, and, of course, personal computers.

The microprocessor is a product of the microminiaturization of electronic circuitry; it is literally a "computer on a chip." The first fully operational microprocessor was demonstrated in March 1971. Since that time, these relatively inexpensive microprocessors have been integrated into thousands of mechanical and electronic devices, even elevators and ski boot bindings. In a few years, virtually everything that is mechanical or electronic will incorporate microprocessor technology into the design.

Microcomputers. The microprocessor is sometimes confused with its famous offspring, the **microcomputer**. A keyboard, video monitor, and memory were attached to the microprocessor and the microcomputer was born! Suddenly, owning a computer became an economic reality for individuals and small businesses.

In a microcomputer, the microprocessor, electronic circuitry for handling input/output signals from the peripheral devices, and memory chips are mounted on a single circuit board, called a **motherboard**.

The microprocessor in HERO JR, an educational (but functional) robot, enables it to speak "roblish" (a robot's version of English), play games, explore, wake you in the morning, and act as a security guard.
(Heath Company)

This Intel 80386 processor, which is often referred to as the "386," is the motherboard for the high-end of IBM's Personal System/2 series of micros and other state-of-the-art micros.
(Courtesy Intel Corporation)

Before being attached to the circuit board, the microprocessor and other chips are mounted to a *carrier*. Carriers have standard-sized pin connectors that permit the chips to be attached to the motherboard.

The motherboard, the "guts" of a microcomputer, is what distinguishes one microcomputer from another. The motherboard is simply "plugged" into one of several slots designed for circuit boards. The processing components of most micros have several empty **expansion slots** so that you can purchase and plug in optional capabilities in the form of **add-on boards**. Add-on boards are discussed in more detail in Chapter 3.

Microcomputer Defined.   A micro is just a small computer. Perhaps the best definition of a micro is *any computer that you can pick up and carry*. But don't be misled by the micro prefix. You can pick up and carry some very powerful computers!

Pocket, Lap, and Desktop PCs.   Personal computers come in three different physical sizes: *pocket PCs*, *lap PCs*, and *desktop PCs*. The pocket and lap PCs are light (a few ounces to 8 pounds), compact, and can operate without an external power source; so they earn the "portable" label as well. There are also a number of "transportable" desktop PCs on the market, but they are more cumbersome to move. They fold up to about the size of a small suitcase, weigh about 25 pounds, and usually require an external power source. Desktop PCs are not designed for frequent movement and are therefore not considered portable.

The power of a PC is not necessarily in proportion to its size. A few lap PCs can run circles around some of the desktop PCs. Some user conveniences, however, must be sacrificed to achieve portability. For instance, the miniature keyboards on pocket PCs make data entry and interaction with the computer difficult and slow. The display screen on some lap PCs is small and does not hold as much text as a display screen on a desktop PC.

Pocket PC's can be interfaced with other devices. In the photo, an electrical engineer is using his pocket PC for circuit testing. (Photo courtesy of Hewlett-Packard Company)

The portability of this maintenance supervisor's lab PC enables him to move his office to the field. (Photo courtesy of Hewlett-Packard Company)

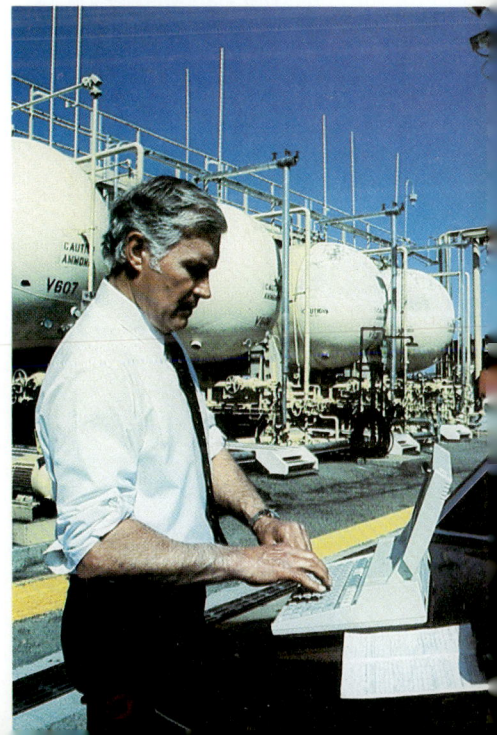

2–2   INSIDE THE COMPUTER

A Bit about the Bit

The computer's seemingly endless potential is, in fact, based on only two electrical states, *on* and *off*. The physical characteristics of the computer make it possible to combine these two electronic states to represent letters and numbers. An "on" or "off" electronic state is represented by a **bit**. Bit is short for *binary digit*. The presence or absence of a bit is referred to as *on-bit* and *off-bit*, respectively. In the **binary** numbering system (base 2) and in written text, the on-bit is a 1 and the off-bit is a 0.

Physically, these states are achieved in a variety of ways. In the micro's solid-state memory (memory chips), the two electronic states are represented by the direction of current flow. Another approach is to turn the circuit on or off. In rotating memory (disks), the two states are made possible by the magnetic arrangement of the iron oxide coating on magnetic disks.

Bits may be fine for computers, but human beings are more comfortable with letters and decimal numbers (the base-10 numerals 0 through 9). Therefore, the letters and decimal numbers that we input to a computer system must be translated to 1s and 0s for processing and storage. The computer translates the bits back to letters and decimal numbers on output. This translation is performed so that we can recognize and understand the output, and it is made possible by encoding systems.

Encoding Systems: Combining Bits To Form Bytes

Computers do not talk to each other in English, Spanish, or French. They have their own languages that are better suited to electronic communication. In these languages, bits are combined according to an **encoding system** to represent letters (**alpha** characters), numbers (**numeric** characters), and special characters (such as *, $, +, and &). One such encoding system is the seven-bit **ASCII** (*American Standard Code for Information Interchange*, pronounced *AS-key*), which is used primarily in micros and for data communications. In ASCII a B and a 3 are represented by 1000010 and 0110011, respectively.

Letters, numbers, and special characters are collectively referred to as **alphanumeric** characters. Alphanumeric characters are *encoded* to a bit configuration on input so that the computer can interpret them. The characters are *decoded* on output so that we can interpret them. This coding, which is based on a particular encoding system, equates a unique series of bits and no-bits with a specific character. Just as the words mother and father are arbitrary English-language character strings that refer to our parents, 1000010 is an arbitrary ASCII code that refers to the letter B. The combination of bits used to represent a character is called a **byte** (pronounced bite).

The seven-bit ASCII code can represent up to 128 characters (2^7). An eight-bit version of ASCII can represent up to 256 characters (2^8). The binary (and decimal) value for the codes of the first 128 characters of the eight-bit ASCII code are the same as those represented by the seven-bit code. You might ask why we need an eight-bit code when the English language has considerably fewer than 256 alphanumeric characters. The extra bit configurations are needed to communicate a variety of activities to the processor. For example, several codes cause special symbols to be displayed (such as a "happy face"), another code causes a beep sound, and another causes the blinking cursor to move one character position to the right. Many of the extra codes can be used to display graphic symbols that can be combined to display meaningful graphic images. Figure 2–1 shows the binary value (the actual bit configuration) and the decimal equivalent of commonly used ASCII characters.

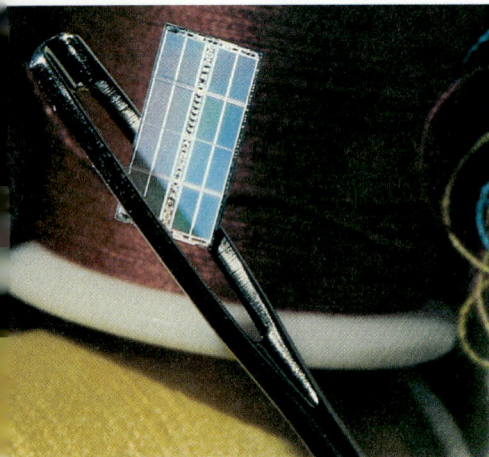

This tiny silicon chip contains one million bits of information. The awesome storage capacity of this 1-megabit chip continues to be overshadowed by the 10 trillion bit capacity of the human brain.
(Courtesy of International Business Machines Corporation)

Character	ASCII Code Binary Value	Decimal Value
A	100 0001	65
B	100 0010	66
C	100 0011	67
D	100 0100	68
E	100 0101	69
F	100 0110	70
G	100 0111	71
H	100 1000	72
I	100 1001	73
J	100 1010	74
K	100 1011	75
L	100 1100	76
M	100 1101	77
N	100 1110	78
O	100 1111	79
P	101 0000	80
Q	101 0001	81
R	101 0010	82
S	101 0011	83
T	101 0100	84
U	101 0101	85
V	101 0110	86
W	101 0111	87
X	101 1000	88
Y	101 1001	89
Z	101 1010	90
a	110 0001	97
b	110 0010	98
c	110 0011	99
d	110 0100	100
e	110 0101	101
f	110 0110	102
g	110 0111	103
h	110 1000	104
i	110 1001	105
j	110 1010	106
k	110 1011	107
l	110 1100	108
m	110 1101	109
n	110 1110	110
o	110 1111	111
p	111 0000	112
q	111 0001	113
r	111 0010	114
s	111 0011	115
t	111 0100	116
u	111 0101	117
v	111 0110	118
w	111 0111	119
x	111 1000	120
y	111 1001	121
z	111 1010	122

Character	ASCII Code Binary Value	Decimal Value
0	011 0000	48
1	011 0001	49
2	011 0010	50
3	011 0011	51
4	011 0100	52
5	011 0101	53
6	011 0110	54
7	011 0111	55
8	011 1000	56
9	011 1001	57
Space	010 0000	32
.	010 1110	46
<	011 1100	60
(	010 1000	40
+	010 1011	43
&	010 0110	38
!	010 0001	33
$	010 0100	36
*	010 1010	42
)	010 1001	41
;	011 1011	59
,	010 1100	44
%	010 0101	37
—	101 1111	95
>	011 1110	62
?	011 1111	63
:	011 1010	58
#	010 0011	35
@	100 0000	64
'	010 0111	39
=	011 1101	61
"	010 0010	34
½	1010 1011	171
¼	1010 1100	172
░	1011 0010	178
▇	1101 1011	219
▆	1101 1100	220
▌	1101 1101	221
▆	1101 1110	222
▆	1101 1111	223
√	1111 1011	251
n	1111 1100	252
2	1111 1101	253
▪	1111 1110	254
(blank)	1111 1111	255

FIGURE 2–1
ASCII Codes
This figure contains the binary and decimal values for commonly used ASCII characters.

A Closer Look at the Processor and RAM

We have discussed how data are represented inside a computer system in electronic states called bits. We are now ready to expose the inner workings of the nucleus of the computer system—the processor.

The internal operation of a computer, or processor, is interesting, but there really is no mystery about it. There are literally hundreds of different types of computers, both large and small, marketed by scores of manufacturers. The complexity of each type may vary considerably, but in the end, each processor has only two fundamental sections: the *control unit* and the *arithmetic and logic unit*. **Random access memory**, or **RAM** (pronounced ram), also plays an integral part in the internal operation of a processor. These three (RAM, the control unit, and the arithmetic and logic unit) work together. Their functions and the relationships between them are described in the following discussions and illustrated in Figure 2–2.

Random Access Memory (RAM).   Unlike **secondary storage** devices such as magnetic disk and tape, RAM, or **primary storage**, is solid state and has no moving parts. With no mechanical movement,

FIGURE 2–2
Interaction between Primary Storage and Computer System Components
All programs and data must be transferred from an input device or from secondary storage before programs can be executed and data can be processed. Output is transferred to the printer from primary storage.

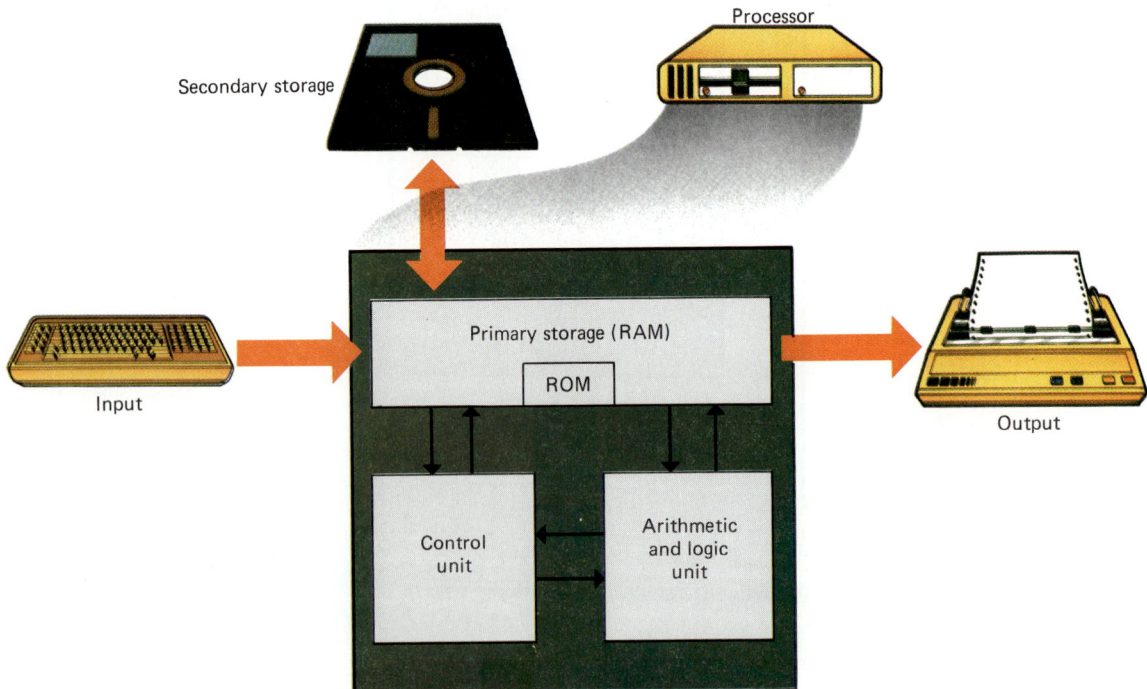

data can be accessed from RAM at electronic speeds, close to the speed of light. RAM, also called **main memory**, provides the processor with *temporary* storage for programs and data.

All programs and data must be transferred to RAM from an input device (such as a keyboard) or from magnetic storage (such as a disk) before programs can be executed or data can be processed. RAM space is always at a premium; therefore, after a program has been executed, the storage space occupied by it is reallocated to another program that is awaiting execution.

A program instruction or a piece of data is stored in a specific primary storage location called an **address**. Addresses permit program instructions and data to be found, accessed, and processed. The content of each address is constantly changing as different programs are executed and new data are processed.

A special type of RAM called **read-only memory** (**ROM**) cannot be altered by the programmer. The contents of the ROM are hard-wired (designed into the logic of a memory chip) by the manufacturer and can be "read only." When you turn on a microcomputer system, a program in ROM automatically performs diagnostic functions such as checking RAM and readies the computer system for use. Then, a ROM program loads the operating system into RAM. Some micros can be purchased with word processing software and other applications software that can be loaded from ROM rather than a disk.

The Control Unit.   Just as the processor is the nucleus of a computer system, the **control unit** is the nucleus of the processor. The control unit has three primary functions:

1. To read and interpret program instructions.
2. To direct the operation of internal processor components.
3. To control the flow of programs and data in and out of RAM.

Any program (word processing or database, for example) must first be loaded to RAM before it can be executed. During execution, the first in a sequence of program instructions is moved from RAM to the control unit where it is **decoded** and interpreted. The control unit then directs other processor components to carry out the operations necessary to execute the instruction. Productivity software programs, such as electronic spreadsheets, are made up of thousands of instructions.

Arithmetic and Logic Unit.   The **arithmetic and logic unit** performs all computations (addition, subtraction, multiplication, and division) and all logic operations (comparisons). An example of a *computation* operation is the summing of the numbers in a column of an electronic spreadsheet. In a *logic* operation, two pieces of data are compared. For example, when employee records in a data base are alphabetized, the letters in the names are compared in a logic operation (for example, "Smith" is placed before "Smyth").

The COMPAQ DESKPRO 386[tm] has a processor speed of 16 MHz, a RAM capacity of 10 megabytes, and word length of 32 bits.
(Courtesy of Compaq Computer Corporation)

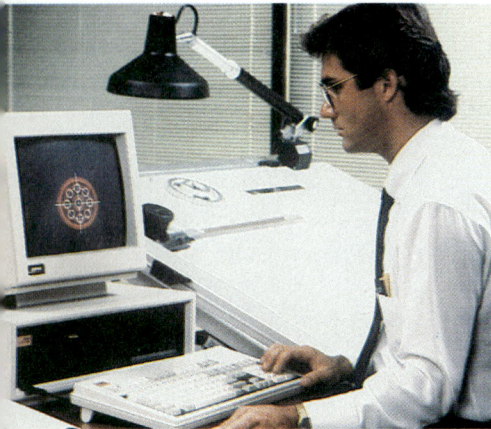

MEMORY BITS

PROCESSOR DESCRIPTION

Speed: Megahertz (clock cycles)
Capacity: K or M bytes
Word length: bits handled as a unit

Describing the Processor: Distinguishing Characteristics. We describe the processing component of microcomputers in terms of *processor speed*, *RAM capacity*, and *word length*.

Processor Speed.   Some microcomputers can sum a column of numbers in an electronic spreadsheet as much as 10 times faster than other slower micros. A *crystal oscillator* paces the execution of instructions within the processor. A micro's processor speed is rated by its frequency of oscillation or the number of clock cycles per second. Most personal computers are rated between 5 and 20 megahertz or MHz (clock cycles). The elapsed time for one clock cycle is 1/frequency (one divided by the frequency). For example, the elapsed time to complete one cycle on a 20 MHz processor is 1/20,000,000 or O.00000005 seconds or 50 nanoseconds. Normally, several clock cycles are required to *retrieve*, *interpret*, and *execute* a single program instruction. The shorter the clock cycle, the faster the processor.

We seldom think in time units smaller than a second; consequently it is almost impossible for us to think in terms of computer speeds. Imagine, today's microcomputers can execute more instructions in a minute than you have had heartbeats since the day you were born!

RAM Capacity.   The capacity of RAM is stated in terms of the number of bytes that can be stored. As we learned earlier in this chapter, a byte is roughly equivalent to a character, like A, 1, or &.

The memory capacity of microcomputers is usually stated in terms of **K** (kilo) bytes and **M** (mega) bytes, convenient designations for 1024 (2^{10}) bytes of storage and 1,048,576 (2^{20}) of bytes of storage, respectively. RAM capacities in micros range from 256K bytes (or simply 256KB) in small micros to 8M bytes (or simply 8MB) in the more powerful multiuser micros.

Word Length.   A **word** is the number of bits that are handled as a unit for a particular computer system. The word size of modern microcomputers is normally 16 or 32 bits. The newer 16- and 32-bit micros are as much as 10 times faster than the early 8-bit PCs.

Now, if anyone *ever* asks you what a 10 MHz, 1MB, 32-bit micro is, you know the answer!

2–3   INPUT/OUTPUT DEVICES: OUR INTERFACE WITH MICROCOMPUTERS _____

Data are created in many places and many ways. Before data can be processed and stored, they must be translated to a form that the computer can interpret. For this we need *input* devices. Once the data have been processed, they must be translated back to a form that we can understand. For this we need *output* devices. These **peripheral** input/output (I/O) devices enable communication between us and the computer.

Input Devices

The Keyboard.   All micros come equipped with a keyboard for input. The typical key-driven data entry device has a standard *alphanumeric keyboard* with an optional numeric keyboard, called a *10-key pad.* Some keyboards also have *special-function keys*, which can be used to instruct the computer to perform a specific operation that may otherwise require several keystrokes.

The standard QWERTY alphanumeric keyboard comes with micros unless you specifically request the alternative, the Dvorak keyboard. The layout of Dvorak keyboard places the most frequently used characters in the center. You can enter nearly 4,000 different words from the home row on the Dvorak keyboard, as opposed to 100 with the traditional QWERTY layout. With the proper software, you can electronically change a QWERTY keyboard to a Dvorak keyboard, and back again to QWERTY, by simply pressing a couple of keys.

Random Cursor Control.   For some applications the keyboard is too cumbersome. For example, you might need to "draw" a line to connect two points on the micro's display screen. Such applications call for devices that go beyond the capabilities of keyboards. These devices permit random movement of the **cursor** to create the image. A cursor, or blinking character (usually an underscore or a rectangle), indicates the location on the screen of the next input. The joystick, digitizing tablet (or pad) and pen, and mouse are among the most popular cursor movement and input mechanisms.

The **joystick** is a single vertical stick that moves the cursor in the direction in which the stick is pushed. The **digitizing tablet and pen** is a pressure-sensitive tablet with the same *X-Y* coordinates as the screen and a pen. The outline of an image drawn on a tablet is reproduced on the display screen. The **mouse**, sometimes called the "pet peripheral," is now standard equipment on some micros. The mouse, attached to the computer by a cable, is a small device that, when moved across a desktop, causes comparable movement of the cursor.

Voice Data Entry.   **Voice data entry**, or **voice recognition**, devices can be used to enter limited kinds and quantities of data. Despite being limited to the ability to interpret relatively few words, voice data entry has a number of applications. The use of voice data entry is valuable for those who require "hands-free" operation such as, for example, quality control inspectors. A computer-based audio response unit or a speech synthesizer (both covered later in this chapter) make the conversation two-way.

Optical Scanners.   **Optical scanners** bounce a beam of light off an image, and then measure the reflected light to determine the value of the image. Optical scanners can recognize printed characters and various types of codes. These scanners can "learn" to read almost

The Apple Macintosh is configured with both a keyboard and a mouse for input.
(Courtesy of Apple Computer, Inc.)

Voice recognition is in the embryonic stage of development. Although voice data entry devices are readily available on the open market, their capabilities are limited. This research team is studying speech waveforms in an attempt to advance voice recognition technology.
(Photo courtesy of Hewlett-Packard Company)

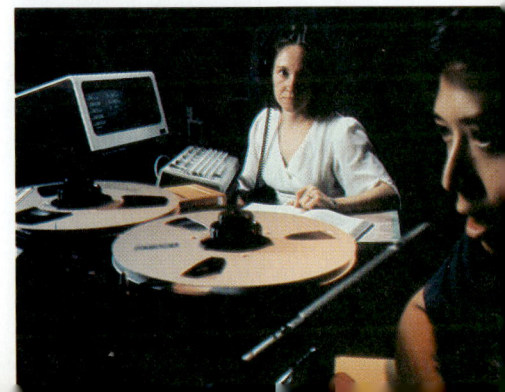

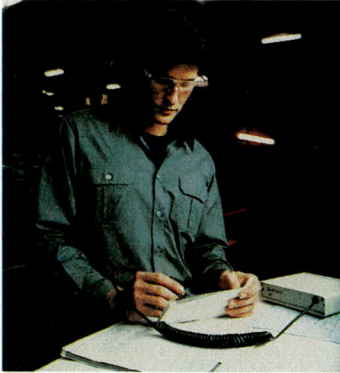

The trend in data entry is to minimize keystrokes and capture data in machine-readable form as close to the source as possible. This warehouse clerk is using an optical scanner to read information directly from a shipping order into a microcomputer.
(Courtesy of Unisys Corporation)

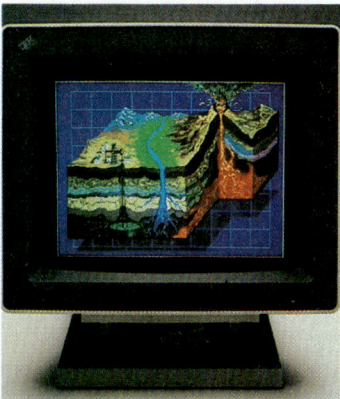

A display of a cross-section of the Earth's crust is used to demonstrate the high resolution of the monitors that accompany IBM's Personal System/2 series of micros. The user can paint up to 256 different colors on a single screen, drawing from a palette of over 256,000 possible colors.
(Courtesy of International Business Machines Corporation)

any typeface, including this book! The "learning" takes place when the structure of the character set is described to the optical scanning device. One primary application for optical scanners on microcomputers is to read printed material into a word processing document file.

Output Devices

Monitors.   Alphanumeric and graphic output are displayed on the micro's video *monitor*. Because display on the monitor's screen is temporary it is sometimes referred to as **soft copy**. The three primary attributes of monitors are the *size* of the display screen, whether the display is *color* or *monochrome* (usually white, green, or amber), and the *resolution* or detail of the display. The size of the screen varies from 5 to 25 inches (diagonal dimension).

In *RGB monitors*, the colors of red, green, and blue are combined to produce up to 64 colors. If you are willing to compromise on the quality of the display and amount of information that can be displayed, you can use an *RF modulator* to adapt a color television for use with microcomputers.

Some PC monitors have a much higher **resolution**, or quality of output. Resolution refers to the number of **pixels**, or addressable points on the screen, that is, the number of points to which light can be directed under program control. A strictly alphanumeric monitor has about 65,000 such points. A PC monitor used primarily for computer graphics may have over 250,000 points. The high-resolution monitors project extremely clear images that look almost like photographs.

Most PCs equipped with *flat panel monitors* use *liquid crystal* technology. Since liquid crystal monitors display the image by reflecting light, you must have some light to read the display. Those flat panel monitors that use *gas plasma* technology are easier to read in situations with poor lighting.

Printers and Plotters.   The most common "output only" devices are printers and plotters.

Printers.   Printers produce **hard-copy** output, such as management reports, payroll checks, and program listings. Microcomputer printers are generally classified as **character printers** or **page printers**. Printers are rated by their print speed. Print speeds for character printers are measured in *characters per second* (*cps*), and for page printers, they are measured in *pages per minute* (*ppm*). The print-speed ranges for the two types of printers are 40 to 450 cps and 8 to 20 ppm, respectively.

Character printers are the primary hard-copy output unit for microcomputers. *Impact* character printers rely on **dot-matrix** and **daisy-wheel** technology. *Nonimpact* character printers employ **ink-jet** and **thermal** technology. Regardless of the technology, the images are formed *one character at a time* as the print head moves across the paper.

The dot-matrix printer configures printed dots to form characters and all kinds of images in much the same way as lights display time

Versatile dot-matrix printers come in all shapes and sizes. This portable dot-matrix printer can produce a text chart (shown in photo) just as easily as it prints letters and reports.
(Courtesy of International Business Machines Corporation)

The daisy-wheel printer is so named because its print mechanism resembles the shape of a daisy. Each of the "petals" of the daisy-wheel contains a fully formed impression of a character. The interchangeable daisy-wheels are available in a wide variety of character sets.
(SCM Corporation)

and temperature on bank signs. One or several vertical columns of small print hammers are contained in a rectangular print head. The hammers are activated independently to form a dot character image as the print head moves horizontally across the paper (see Figures 2–3 and 2–4). Dot-matrix printers can produce graphic output as well as text output.

The daisy-wheel printer produces high-quality output for word processing applications. An interchangeable daisy wheel containing a set of fully formed characters is spun to the desired character. A print hammer strikes the embossed character on the print wheel to form the image.

Ink-jet printers squirt "dots" of ink on the paper to form images in a manner similar to that of the dot-matrix printer. The heat elements of thermal printers are activated to produce dot-matrix images on heat-sensitive paper. The big advantage that these two nonimpact character

The nozzles on the print head of a color ink-jet printer expel thousands of droplets per second to produce many different colors. The results are often amazing.
(Photo courtesy of Hewlett-Packard Company)

FIGURE 2–3
Dot-Matrix Printer Character Formation
Each character is formed in a 7 x 5 matrix as the nine-hammer print head moves across the paper. The two bottom hammers are used for lowercase letters that extend below the line (for example, g and p).

FIGURE 2–4
Letter-Quality Dot-Matrix Character Formation
The 18-hammer print head permits dots to be overlapped to increase the density and, therefore, the quality of the image.

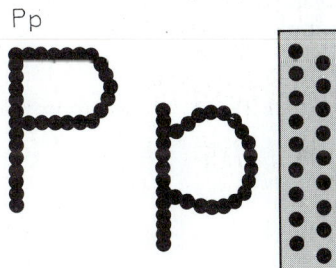

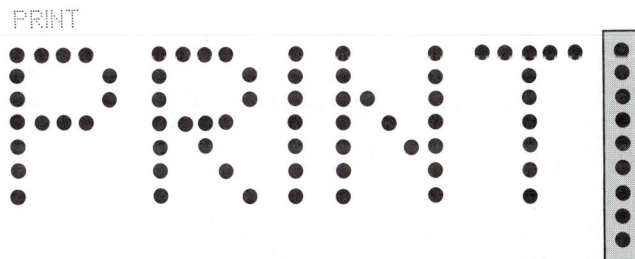

Inside this desktop laser page printer, laser beams scan across the print drum to create text and graphics at speeds of over eight pages per minute.
(Photo courtesy of Hewlett-Packard Company)

A microcomputer specialist uses this six-pen plotter to create a color-coded stacked bar chart.
(Photo courtesy of Hewlett-Packard Company)

printers have over the impact printers is that they can produce *multicolor* output.

Microcomputer page printers, often called **desktop laser printers**, use laser technology to achieve high-speed hard-copy output by printing *a page at a time*. The nonimpact laser printers have many inviting characteristics: They are quiet; they can print near-typeset-quality text and graphics; they can mix type styles and sizes on the same page, and they are much faster than character printers.

Figure 2–5 contrasts the output from a dot-matrix printer, in both normal and *near letter quality* (*NLQ*) modes, a daisywheel printer, and a laser printer.

Plotters.   A **pen plotter** is a device that converts computer-generated graphs, charts, and line drawings to high-precision hard-copy output. The plotter that is commonly used with micros has one or more pens that move concurrently with the paper to produce the image. Several pens are required to vary the width and color of the lines. Pens are selected and manipulated under computer control.

Printer or Plotter Drivers.   The various kinds of printers and plotters differ markedly in capabilities. Because of these differences, the electronic signals passed between the processor and the printer or plotter are unique for each printer and plotter. Because of this, a **driver set** for a particular printer or plotter must be used in conjunction with an applications software package (for example, an electronic spreadsheet

FIGURE 2–5
Printer Output Comparison

```
This sentence was printed on a 9-pin dot-matrix printer.
This sentence was printed in NLQ mode on a dot-matrix printer.
This sentence was printed on a daisy-wheel printer.
This sentence was printed on a desk-top laser printer.
```

package). The driver set is software that enables communication between the processor and the printer or plotter. Essentially, the driver set receives signals from the processor and relays these signals in a format that can be interpreted by the printer or plotter (or vice versa). Commercial software packages are distributed with driver sets for most of the popular printers and plotters.

Sound and Speech.   One of the standard capabilities of most micros is the ability to output sounds of varying duration and frequency. This micro output feature is used for everything from warning users of a keying error to playing the melodies of popular songs.

Speech synthesizers convert raw data to electronically produced speech. The existing technology produces synthesized speech with only limited vocal inflections and phrasing. Still, the number of microcomputer applications for speech synthesizers is growing.

2–4 DATA STORAGE DEVICES AND MEDIA

Secondary Storage: Permanent Data Storage

Within a computer system, programs and data are stored in *RAM* or *primary storage* and in *secondary storage*. Programs and data are stored *permanently* for periodic retrieval in *secondary storage*. Programs and data are retrieved from secondary storage and stored *temporarily* in high-speed RAM for processing.

The various types of **magnetic disk drives** and their respective storage media are the overwhelming choice of micro users for secondary storage. In the microcomputer environment, **magnetic tape drives** are used exclusively to backup and store disk files.

Magnetic tape is for **sequential access** only. Magnetic disks have **random-** or **direct-access** capabilities as well as sequential access capabilities. You are quite familiar with these concepts but you may not realize it. Magnetic tape is operationally the same as the one in home and car tape decks. The magnetic disk can be compared loosely to the phonograph record. When playing music on a cassette tape you have to wind the tape forward to search for the song you want. With a phonograph record, all you would have to do is move the

Programs and data are stored temporarily in RAM (primary storage) during processing and permanently on magnetic disk (secondary storage). The 5¼-inch diskette in the photo is sometimes called a floppy disk. (Protocol Computers, Inc.)

needle "directly" to the track containing the desired song. This simple analogy demonstrates the two fundamental methods of storing and accessing data, *sequential* and *random*.

Magnetic Disks

Disk Hardware and Storage Media.   Magnetic disk drives are secondary storage devices that provide a computer system with **random** *and* **sequential processing** capabilities. In random processing, the desired programs and data are accessed *directly* from the storage medium.

A variety of magnetic disk drives (the hardware device) and magnetic disks (the media) are manufactured for different user requirements. The two most popular types of *interchangeable* magnetic disks for micros are the **diskette** and the **microdisk**.

- *Diskette*. The diskette is a thin, flexible disk that is permanently enclosed within a $5\frac{1}{4}$-inch square jacket. Because the diskette is flexible, like a page in this book, it is also called a **flexible disk** or a **floppy disk**.
- *Microdisk*. The microdisk is a rigid disk that is either $3\frac{1}{4}$ or $3\frac{1}{2}$ inches in diameter.

Once inserted in a **disk drive**, the programs and data on the diskette or microdisk are said to be **on-line**. This means that the programs and data on the disk are accessible to and under the control of a computer system. Once the programs and data are no longer needed for processing, the disks can be removed for **off-line** storage. The storage capacity of diskettes and microdisks ranges from about 320K to 1.2M bytes.

Not all disk storage media are interchangeable. In fact, the trend is to permanently installed **hard** or **fixed disks**. The nickname for a microcomputer hard disk is **Winchester disk**. Most of the newer personal computers are configured with at least one diskette drive and one hard disk. The storage capacity of hard disks ranges from about

The secondary storage medium for this personal computer is the microdisk. These rigid $3\frac{1}{2}$-inch microdisks (shown in foreground) can store over a million characters of data and fit easily in a shirt pocket.
(Photo courtesy of Hewlett-Packard Company)

10M to 80M bytes, which is as much as 250 times the capacity of a diskette.

A hard disk, which may have several disk platters, spins continuously at a high speed. The floppy, however, is set in motion only when a command is issued to read from or write to disk. An indicator light near the disk drive is illuminated only when the disk is spinning. The rotational movement of the disk passes all data under or over a **read/ write head**, thereby making all data available for access on each revolution of the disk.

The manner in which data and programs are stored and accessed is very similar for both hard and floppy disks. The disk storage medium has a thin film coating of cobalt or iron oxide. The thin film coating on the disk can be electronically magnetized by the read/write head to represent the absence or presence of a bit (0 or 1). Data are recorded **serially** in concentric circles called **tracks** by magnetizing the surface to represent bit configurations (see Figure 2–6).

PC disk storage uses **sector organization** to store and retrieve data. In sector organization, the recording surface is divided into pie-shaped sectors, from 8 to 15 (see Figure 2–6). Each sector is assigned a unique number; therefore, the *sector number* and *track number* are all that is needed to comprise an **disk address** (the physical location of data or a program). To read from or write to a disk, an **access arm** containing the read/write head is moved under program control to the appropriate *track*. When the appropriate sector passes under or over the read/write head the data are read or written.

This Winchester disk, a name given to hard disk drives for microcomputers, has two read/ write heads for each recording surface. The access arms move the read/write heads to the appropriate track to retrieve the data. The Winchester drive is named after the 30-30 Winchester rifle. Early drives had two 30 megabyte disks— thus the nickname, Winchester. (Microscience International Corporation)

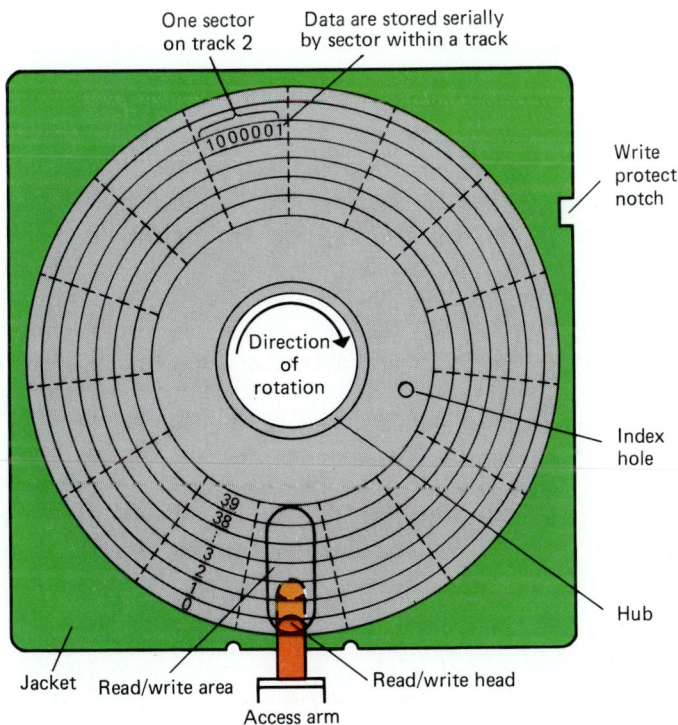

FIGURE 2–6
Cutaway of a $5\frac{1}{4}$-inch Diskette.
Photoelectric cells sense light as it passes through the index hole. This feedback enables the computer to monitor which sector is over the read/write head at any given time. Data are read or written serially in tracks, within a given sector.

The **access time** is the interval of time between the instant when a computer makes a request for a transfer of data from a secondary storage device and the instant when this operation is completed. The access time for hard disks is significantly less than for floppy disks because the hard disk is in continuous motion.

Magnetic Tape

The primary use of magnetic tape storage for micros is as a backup medium for the hard disk. For backup, a **tape cassette** is taken from off-line storage, mounted into a tape drive, and the contents of a disk file are "dumped" from the disk to the tape. The tape is removed and placed in off-line storage as a backup to the operational disk. A single tape cassette can store from 20M to 60M bytes. Approximately 60 diskettes would be needed to backup a 20M byte hard disk, but only one tape cassette would be be needed.

Optical Laser Disks

Some industry analysts have predicted that **optical laser disk** technology, now in its infant stage of development, may eventually make magnetic disk and tape storage obsolete. With this technology, the read/write head of magnetic storage is replaced with two lasers, one for read and one for write operations. Optical laser disks for micros are *write once/read only*. That is, once the data have been written to the medium, they can only be read, not updated or changed. Nevertheless, because the storage capacity of optical laser disks is many times that of a hard disk, there are many applications for this technology.

The actual optical laser disks storage media comes in three formats, 5-inch **CD ROM disk** (compact disk read-only memory) and the 8- and 12-inch **video disk**. *CD ROM readers* and *video disk readers* permit random access to the data or images stored on CD ROM and video disks, respectively. One vendor markets a CD ROM disk that contains the entire text of a 20-volume set of encyclopedias. The disk contains an index that enables users to access the text by keyword. Another vendor markets a video disk that contains images of the great works of art over the last four centuries. Video disk readers are usually used in conjunction with very high resolution monitors that can display images with a clarity that approaches that of a color photo in a magazine.

We may be approaching the technological limits of magnetic data storage. When this happens, sophisticated optics and lasers (light amplification by stimulated emission of radiation) may help to take up the slack. These newly pressed 12-inch optical laser disks are being coated with a special protective solution.
(RCA)

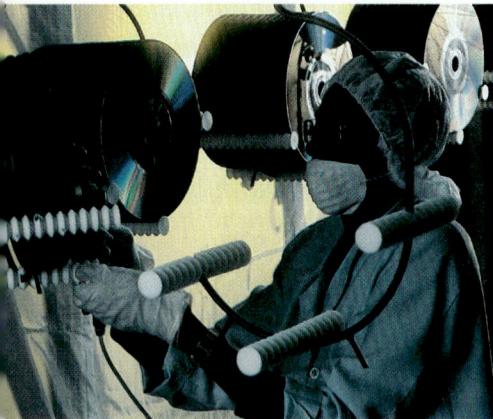

2–5   MULTIUSER MICROS

Until recently, micros were "personal" computers, that is, for individual use only. But technological improvements have been so rapid that it has become difficult for a single user to tap the full potential of state-of-the-art micros. To tap this unused potential, hardware and software vendors are marketing products that permit several users on the system at once.

These **multiuser micros**, which look very much like any other micro, can be configured with up to 10 terminals, each with a keyboard and monitor. These terminals, often located in the same office, share the microcomputer's processing and storage resources and its peripheral devices. With a multiuser micro, a secretary can be transcribing dictation at one terminal, a manager can be doing financial analysis at another terminal, and a clerk can be entering data to a data base at another terminal. All of this is taking place at the same time on the same multiuser micro.

2–6   THE HIERARCHY OF DATA ORGANIZATION_

Data (the plural of *datum*) are the raw material from which information is derived. **Information** is comprised of data that have been collected and processed into a meaningful form. Data are organized in a hierarchy that permits the data to be conceptualized by micro users and manipulated by the computer. The *hierarchy of data organization* is graphically illustrated in Figure 2–7. An understanding of the hierarchy of data organization is essential for the effective use of microcomputer productivity software, especially electronic spreadsheet and database software.

FIGURE 2–7
The Hierarchy of Data Organization

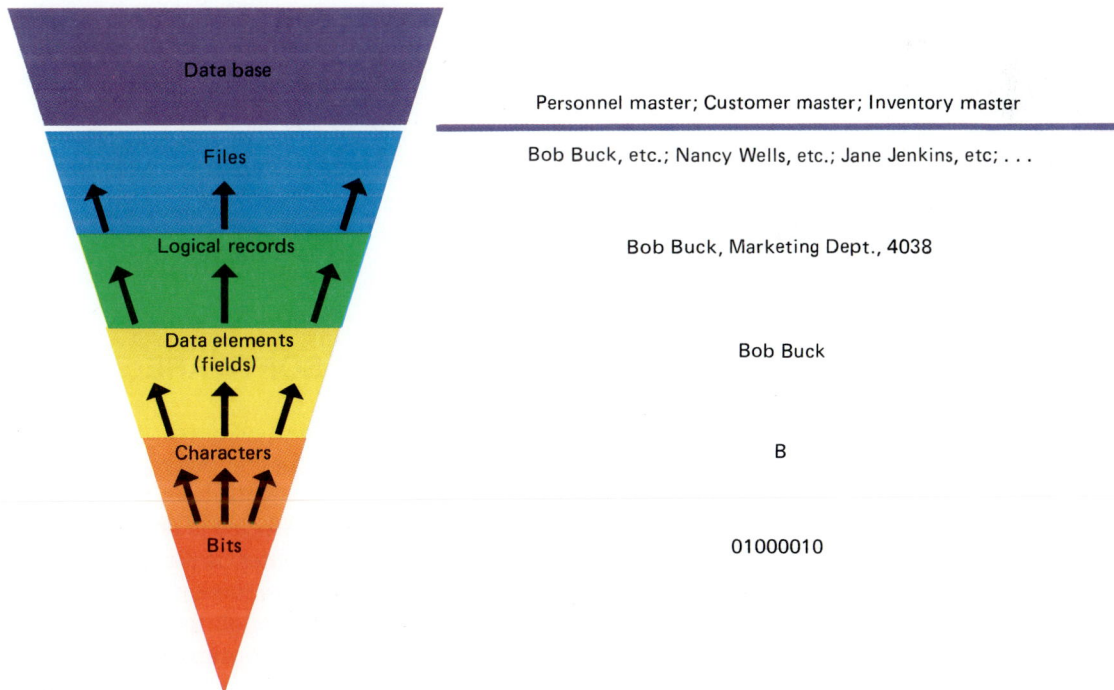

Data base	Personnel master; Customer master; Inventory master
Files	Bob Buck, etc.; Nancy Wells, etc.; Jane Jenkins, etc; . . .
Logical records	Bob Buck, Marketing Dept., 4038
Data elements (fields)	Bob Buck
Characters	B
Bits	01000010

Bits and Characters.   We learned in an earlier section that computers store data as 1s and 0s, or binary digits, called *bits*. The bit is the lowest level of the hierarchy of data organization. A series of bits can be configured to represent a *character*. (For ASCII bit configurations see Figure 2–1).

Data Elements or Fields.   At the next level of the hierarchy, characters are combined to represent the value of a **data element** or **field**, the smallest logical unit of data. Some examples of a field include name, employee number, and price.

Records.   A **record** is a description of an event (such as a sale or a hotel reservation) or a thing (such a person or a part). Related fields describing an event or a thing are logically grouped to form a record. In Figure 2–7, for example, the fields of name, department, and telephone extension number are grouped to form the employee record. The record is the lowest-level logical unit that can be accessed from a file.

Files.   At the fourth level of the hierarchy, records with the same fields are combined to form a **file**. In Figure 2–7, the file contains the name, department, telephone extension number, and other employee data for all employees in the company.

The term file is also used to refer to a named area on a secondary storage device that contains a *program* or *textual material* like a letter or a report.

Data Base.   A **data base**, the next level in the hierarchy, contains several different record types and a logical mechanism by which the different record types relate to one another. In the context of microcomputer usage, the term data base is often used to refer to a file (as described above).

Example applications of the hierarchy of data organization are contained in Chapter 9, "Electronic Spreadsheet Concepts and Tutorials: Database and Graphics Capabilities" and in Chapter 10, "Database Software Concepts."

MEMORY BITS

HIERARCHY OF DATA ORGANIZATION

- Bit
- Character (byte)
- Data element or field
- Record
- File
- Data base

2–7   PROGRAMMING AND SOFTWARE

Much of the discussion in this chapter has centered on the operation and application of computer hardware. But computer hardware is useless without software, and software is useless without hardware.

A computer system does nothing until directed to do so. A **program**, which consists of instructions to the computer, is the means by which we tell a computer to perform certain operations. These instructions are logically sequenced and assembled through the act of **programming**. **Programmers** use a variety of **programming languages**, such as **C**, *COBOL*, *Pascal*, and *BASIC* to communicate instructions to the computer.

Each computer has only *one* programming language that can be executed—the **machine language**. We talk of programming in C and BASIC, but all of these languages must be translated into the machine language of the computer on which the program is to be executed. These and other *high-level languages* are simply a convenience for the programmer.

We use the term software to refer to the programs that direct the activities of the computer system. Software falls into two general categories: applications and systems. **Applications software** is designed and written to perform specific personal, business, or scientific processing tasks, such as electronic spreadsheet processing, word processing, order entry, or financial analysis. **Systems software** is more general than applications software and is usually independent of any specific application area. The operating system, discussed in Chapter 4, "DOS: Disk Operating System Concepts and Tutorials," is classified as systems software.

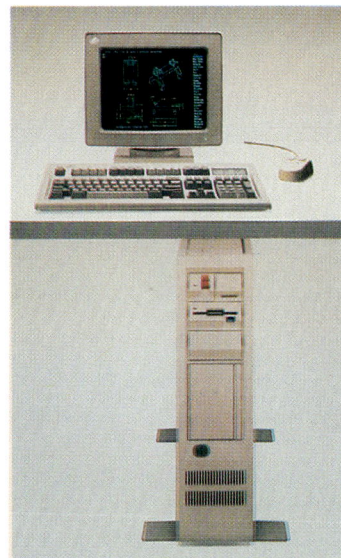

This IBM Personal System/2 Model 80 computer has more power than some mainframes of a decade ago. This added power has opened the door for micro programmers to develop sophisticated software that was previously restricted to mainframe computers.
(Courtesy of International Business Machines Corporation)

SUMMARY OUTLINE AND IMPORTANT TERMS

2–1 MICROCOMPUTERS: SMALL BUT POWERFUL. **Microprocessors** not only set the stage for **microcomputers**, but they are found in dozens of devices about the home. The **motherboard** in a microcomputer contains the electronic circuitry for processing and I/O operations, and some memory. The processing components of most micros have several empty **expansion slots** so that you can purchase and plug in optional capabilities in the form of **add-on boards**. The micro comes in pocket, lap, and desktop sizes.

2–2 INSIDE THE COMPUTER. The two electronic states of the computer are represented by a **bit**, short for **binary** digit (0,1). **Alphanumeric** characters are represented in computer storage by combining strings of bits to form unique bit configurations for each character. Characters are translated into these bit configurations, also called **bytes**, according to a particular **encoding system**. The seven- and eight-bit versions of **ASCII** are popular encoding systems for microcomputers.

Primary storage, or **RAM (random-access memory)**, provides the processor with temporary storage for programs and data. Permanent storage is provided by **secondary storage** (for example, magnetic disk). All input/output, including programs, must enter and exit RAM, also called **main memory**. Data in RAM are referenced by their **addresses**. Another variation of internal storage is **ROM (read-only memory)**.

A processor has two fundamental sections, the **control unit** and the **arithmetic and logic unit**, which work together with primary storage to execute programs. The control unit interprets instructions and directs the arithmetic and logic unit to perform computation and logic operations.

A processor is described in terms of its speed, primary storage capacity, and word length. Speed is measured in megahertz (clock cycles). Memory capacity is measured in **K** or **M** bytes. The **word** (the number of bits that are handled as a unit) length of the more recent microcomputers ranges from 16 to 32 bits.

2–3 INPUT/OUTPUT DEVICES: OUR INTERFACE WITH MICROCOMPUTERS.   A variety of **peripheral** input and output devices complement the personal computer to provide the interface between us and the computer system.

The input mechanism is usually a keyboard, and the output is normally a display screen, called a monitor. Other input devices associated with micros include the joystick, the digitizing tablet and pen, and the mouse.

Voice data entry or **voice recognition** devices can be used to enter limited kinds and quantities of data. **Optical scanners** eliminate the need for some manual data entry by encoding certain data in machine-readable format.

Output is normally displayed on a screen, called a **monitor**. The three attributes of monitors are size, color, and **resolution**.

Printers prepare hard-copy output at speeds of 40 characters per second to 20 pages per minute. Microcomputer printers can be classified as either **character** or **page** printers. Character printers can be either impact (**dot-matrix** and **daisy-wheel**) or nonimpact (**ink-jet** and **thermal**). **Desktop laser printers** are nonimpact and print a page at a time. The technologies used to produce the image vary widely from one printer to the next. **Pen plotters** convert stored data to hard-copy graphs, charts, and line drawings.

Speech synthesizers convert raw data to electronically produced speech.

2–4 DATA STORAGE DEVICES AND MEDIA.   **Magnetic disk drives** and **magnetic tape drives** are the most popular secondary storage devices for micros. Data are stored sequentially on magnetic tape (**sequential access**) and randomly on magnetic disks (**random** or **direct access**). The different types of interchangeable magnetic disks include the **microdisk** and the **diskette**, also called **floppy** and **flexible disk**. The trend is toward greater use of **fixed** or **hard disks**, often referred to as **Winchester disks**.

PC disk storage uses **sector organization**. Data are recorded **serially** in concentric circles called **tracks**. The tracks are divided into pie-shaped sectors. The sector number and track number comprise the **disk address**. An **access arm** containing the **read/write heads** is moved to the appropriate track to retrieve the data.

When used with micros, magnetic **tape cassettes** are used almost exclusively as a backup medium.

Optical laser disk storage, which has tremendous storage capacity, is write once/read only and is available in 5-inch **CD ROM disk** and 8- or 12-inch **video disk** formats.

2–5   MULTIUSER MICROS.   **Multiuser micros** can be configured with up to 10 terminals. These terminals share the microcomputer's processing and storage resources and its peripheral devices.

2–6   THE HIERARCHY OF DATA ORGANIZATION.   **Data** are the raw material from which information is derived. **Information** is comprised of data that have been collected and processed into a meaningful form.

A string of **bits** is combined to form a character. Characters are combined to represent the values of **data elements**, also called **fields**. Related data elements are grouped to form **records**. Records with the same fields combine to become a **file**. The term file is also used to refer to a named area on a secondary storage device. A **data base** contains several different record types and defines their relationships.

2–7   PROGRAMMING AND SOFTWARE.   A **program** directs a computer to perform certain operations. The program is produced by a **programmer** who uses any of a variety of **programming languages** to communicate with the computer.

Machine language is the only language that can be executed on a particular computer. High-level languages provide a convenience for the programmer.

Software is classified as either **applications software** or **systems software**. Applications software is designed to perform certain personal, business, or scientific processing tasks. Systems software is more general and supports the basic functions of the computer.

REVIEW EXERCISES

1. What is a motherboard?
2. Describe a multiuser micro.
3. What is the relationship between a microprocessor and a microcomputer?

4. What is the name given to printed output? Output on a monitor?

5. Name and give an example for each level of the hierarchy of data organization.

6. Describe the relationship between data and information.

7. List at least ten products that are smaller than a breadbox and use microprocessors. Select one of the ten and describe the function of its microprocessor.

8. Give two examples each of input hardware and output hardware.

9. Which two functions are performed by the arithmetic and logic unit?

10. Write your first name as an ASCII bit configuration.

11. What are the functions of the control unit?

12. Contrast the differences between a dot-matrix printer and a daisy-wheel printer.

13. Which secondary storage device is the first choice of microcomputer users? Why?

14. Give at least one alternative name for each of the following: a personal computer, RAM, a hard disk, and a diskette.

SELF-TEST (by section)

2–1. (a) The processing component of a microcomputer is a _____.

(b) The three size categories for personal computers are miniature, portable, and business. (T/F)

2–2. (a) Bit is the singular of byte. (T/F)

(b) The _____ is that part of the processor that reads and interprets program instructions.

(c) The arithmetic and logic unit controls the flow of programs and data in and out of main memory. (T/F)

(d) Some microcomputers have a word length 32 bits. (T/F)

2–3. (a) Input devices translate data to a form that can be interpreted by a computer. (T/F)

(b) The primary function of I/O peripherals is to facilitate computer-to-computer data transmission. (T/F)

(c) The input device that is rolled over a desktop to move the cursor is called a mouse. (T/F)

(d) The visual quality of output on a terminal's monitor is determined by its _____.

2–4. (a) Data are retrieved from temporary secondary storage and stored permanently in main memory. (T/F)

    (b) The flexible disk is also known as a floppy disk. (T/F)

    (c) Optical laser disks are _____ once/_____ only.

2–5. Multiuser micros can service several users simultaneously. (T/F)

2–6. **(a)** Related fields are grouped to form _____.

    (b) _____are the raw material from which _____ is derived.

2–7. _____software is more general than _____ software.

Self-Test Answers. **2–1 (a),** microprocessor; **(b),** F; **2–2 (a),** F; **(b),** control unit; **(c),** F; **(d),** T; **2–3 (a),** T; **(b),** F; **(c),** T; **(d),** resolution; **2–4 (a),** F; **(b),** T; **(c),** write, read; **2–5,** T; **2–6 (a),** files; **(b),** Data, information; **2–7** Systems, applications.

PART II

INTERACTING
WITH A
MICROCOMPUTER

Getting Acquainted
with Micros

CHAPTER 3

STUDENT LEARNING OBJECTIVES

- To understand the scope of knowledge needed to interact effectively with a personal computer.
- To describe approaches to configuring microcomputer systems.
- To describe what is entailed in the proper care and maintenance of personal computers and disk storage media.
- To describe various keyboard and data entry conventions.
- To grasp concepts related to effective interaction with and use of micros and micro software.
- To demonstrate the procedures for file backup on a personal computer.
- To describe a procedure and considerations for the evaluation, selection, and purchase of a personal computer.

3–1 INTERACTING WITH THE SYSTEM_____

To interact effectively with a personal computer you need to be knowledgeable in four areas.

1. The operation and use of microcomputer hardware
2. General microcomputer software concepts, such as windows and menus
3. **DOS**, the disk operating system
4. The specific applications programs that you are using (for example, Lotus 1-2-3)

The first three areas of understanding are prerequisites to the fourth; that is, you will need a working knowledge of micro hardware, software concepts, and DOS before you can make effective use of applications programs like dBASE III PLUS, Webster's NewWorld Writer, or any of the thousands of micro software packages.

Employees come to this in-house training facility to learn how to use word processing, electronic spreadsheet, and presentation graphics software. If the employee has little or no experience with micros, the first topic of instruction is the use and operation of microcomputer hardware. (Courtesy of International Business Machines Corporation)

3–2 CONFIGURING A MICROCOMPUTER SYSTEM_____

Normally, computer professionals are called upon to select, configure, and install the hardware associated with minicomputers and mainframe computers. But for micros, the user typically selects, configures, and installs his or her own micro; therefore, it is important that you know what makes up a microcomputer system and how it fits together.

A Typical Microcomputer Configuration

The computer and its peripheral devices are called the computer system **configuration**. The configuration of a microcomputer can vary. The most typical micro configuration consists of the following:

1. A computer
2. A keyboard for input
3. A monitor for *soft copy* (temporary) output
4. A printer for *hard copy* (printed) output
5. One or two disk drives for permanent storage of data and programs

In some microcomputer systems these components are purchased as separate physical units then linked together. Micros that give users the flexibility to configure the system with a variety of peripheral devices (input/output and storage) are said to have an **open architecture**. A component stereo system provides a good analogy to illustrate the concept of open architecture. In a stereo system, the tuner is the central component to which record turntables, equalizers, tape decks, compact disk players, speakers, and so on can be attached. A microcomputer system with an open architecture is configured by linking any of the many peripheral devices discussed in Chapter 2 to the processor component. The IBM PC, IBM PC compatibles, and the IBM Personal System/2 are the focus of this book and all have an open architecture. As a rule of thumb, if there is a need for a special type of input/output or storage device, then someone markets it. In a **closed architecture**, the system is fully configured when it is sold.

In keeping with conversational computerese, we will drop the "system" from "microcomputer system." Therefore, all future references to a personal computer or a microcomputer imply a microcomputer *system*.

Linking Micro Components

An open architecture, also called a **bus architecture**, is made possible because all micro components are linked via a common electrical **bus**. In Chapter 1, we likened the processing component of a microcomputer

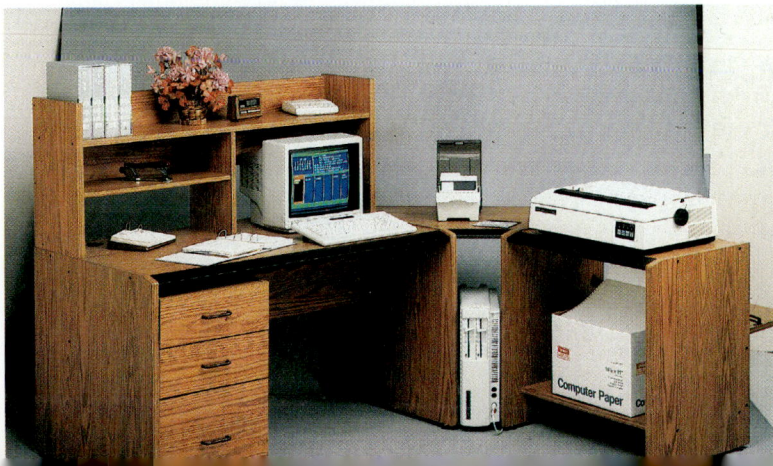

This upright micro has an open architecture and is currently configured with a color monitor, two 5¼-inch disk drives, a Winchester disk, and a dot-matrix printer.
(Courtesy of Radio Shack, A Division of Tandy Corporation)

to the human brain. Just as the brain sends and receives signals through the central nervous system, the processor sends and receives electrical signals through the bus. The bus is the path through which the processor sends data and commands to RAM and all peripheral devices. Data and commands are transmitted between the processor and its peripheral devices in the form of electronic signals. In short, the bus is the vehicle by which the processor communicates with its peripherals and vice versa. The processor, RAM, and disk storage devices are usually connected directly to the bus, that is, without cables.

In an open architecture, external input/output devices (that is devices external to the processor cabinet) and some storage devices are plugged into the bus in much the same way that you would plug a lamp into a electrical outlet. The receptacle, called a **port**, provides a direct link with the micro's common electrical bus.

External peripheral devices are linked or *interfaced* with the processor through either a **serial port** or a **parallel port**. Serial ports facilitate the *serial transmission* of data, *one bit at a time*. Serial ports provide an interface for low-speed printers and modems. The defacto standard for micro serial ports is the 25-pin (male or female) **RS-232C port**. Parallel ports facilitate the *parallel transmission* of data, *usually one byte (eight bits) at a time*. Parallel ports provide the interface for devices like high-speed printers (e.g., laser printers), magnetic tape backup units, and other computers.

Also connected to the common electrical bus are *expansion slots*, which are usually housed in the processor cabinet. These slots enable a micro owner to enhance the functionality of a basic micro configuration with a wide variety of special-function *add-on boards*, also called **add-on cards**. These ''add-ons'' contain the electronic circuitry for a wide variety of computer-related functions. The number of available expansion slots varies from computer to computer. Some of the more popular add-on boards are listed below.

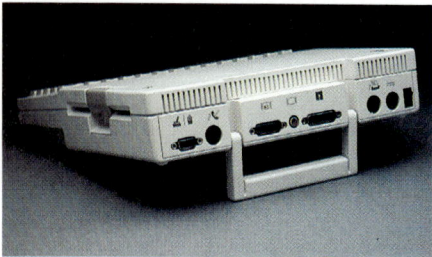

The processor unit is at the center of a microcomputer system. Cables from each device are interfaced to the input/output ports at the rear of the processor unit. From left to right, this portable micro has ports to interface with a joystick or mouse, modem, monitor 1, monitor 2, auxiliary disk, and printer. The connector on the far right is for the power supply.
(Courtesy of Apple Computer, Inc.)

- *RAM*. Expands memory, usually in increments of 64K bytes.
- *Color and graphics adapter*. Permits the interfacing of video monitors that have graphics and/or color capabilities. The *EGA* or *enhanced graphic adapter* board enables the interfacing of high resolution monitors (e.g., 640 x 350). The EGA boards usually come with at least 256K bytes of dedicated RAM or RAM that is not available to the user.
- *Modem*. Permits communication with remote computers via a telephone line link.
- *Internal battery-powered clock/calendar*. Provides continuous and/or on-demand display of, or access to, the current date and time (e.g., Monday, Dec. 18, 1989, 9:35 a.m.).
- *Serial port*. Installation of the board provides access to the bus via another serial port.
- *Parallel port*. Installation of the board provides access to the bus via another parallel port.

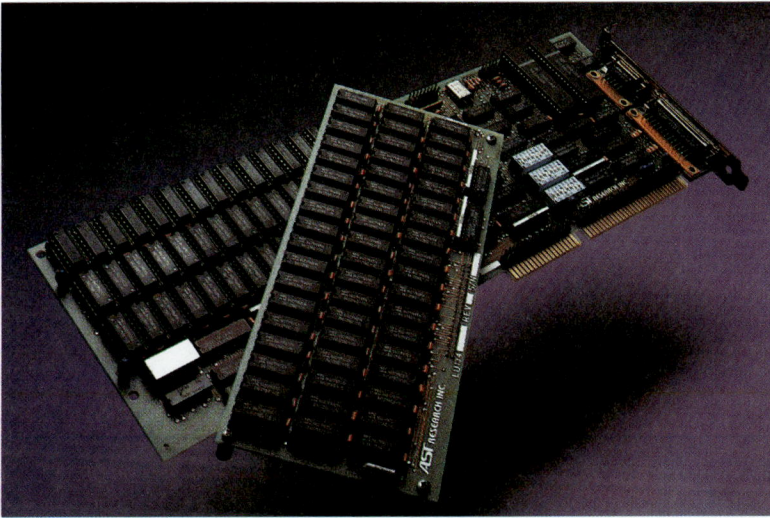

The capabilities of a microcomputer can be enhanced with the addition of a memory expansion add-on board (top) and/or a multifunction add-on board (bottom).
(AST Research Inc.)

- *Printer spooler*. Enables data to be printed while the user continues with other processing activities. The data are transferred (spooled) at high speed from RAM to a *print buffer* (an intermediate storage area) and then routed to the printer from the buffer.
- *Hard disk*. Hard disks with capacities of as much as 20M bytes can be installed in expansion slots.
- *Coprocessor*. These "extra" processors, which are under the control of the main processor, help to relieve the main processor of certain tasks, such as arithmetic functions. This sharing of duties helps to increase system **throughput**, the rate at which work can be performed by the microcomputer system.
- *VCR backup*. This board enables an ordinary Beta or VHS video cassette recorder to be used as a tape backup device. One ordinary video cassette tape can hold up to 80M bytes of data.

Most of the add-on boards are *multifunction*: that is, they include two of more of these capabilities. For example, one popular **multifunction add-on board** comes with a serial port, a modem, and an internal battery-powered clock/calendar.

Expansion slots are at a premium. To make the most efficient use of these slots, circuit board manufacturers have created half-size expansion boards that fit in a "short slot" (half of an expansion slot). These half-size boards effectively double the number of expansion slots available for a given microcomputer.

3–3 CARE AND MAINTENANCE OF MICROS AND THEIR STORAGE MEDIA

Micros, peripheral devices, and storage media are very reliable. Apply the dictates of common sense to their care and maintenance and they will give you months, even years, of maintenance free operation. A few helpful hints are listed below.

■ Avoid excessive dust and extremes in temperature and humidity.

■ Avoid frequent movement of desktop micros.

■ Install a *surge protector* between the power source and the micro. Micros, as well as other electronic devices, can be seriously damaged by a sudden surge of power caused by such things as a bolt of lightening striking a power line.

Costing only a few dollars, a blank diskette has a very modest value. But once you begin to use the diskette, its value, at least to you, increases greatly. Its value includes the many hours of work that you have spent entering data, preparing spreadsheets, or writing programs. Such a valuable piece of property should be handled with care. The following are a few guidelines for diskette handling.

Do

■ *Do* label each diskette and use a soft-tipped pen on the label.

■ *Do* cover the *write-protect notch* on all important diskettes that are intended for read-only use, such as the program diskettes for micro software packages.

■ *Do* store diskettes in their envelopes so that the exposed surface is covered.

■ *Do* store diskettes vertically, or, if stored flat, place no more than ten in a stack.

■ *Do* store diskettes at temperatures ranging from 50–125 degrees Fahrenheit.

■ *Do* keep a backup of diskettes containing important data and programs.

■ *Do* remove diskettes from disk drives before you turn off the computer.

Don't

■ *Don't* fold, spindle, or mutilate diskettes.

■ *Don't* force a diskette into the disk drive. It should slip in with little or no resistance.

■ *Don't* touch the diskette surface.

■ *Don't* place diskettes near a magnetic field, such as magnetic paperclip holders, tape demagnetizers, or electric motors.

■ *Don't* expose diskettes to direct sunlight for a prolonged period.

■ *Don't* insert or remove a diskette from a disk drive if the red "drive active" light is lit.

3–4   MICROCOMPUTER OPERATION

Getting Started

Once all micro components have been installed and connected to the processor unit, DOS has been installed (hard disk systems), and the

Microcomputers and magnetic storage media are designed for durability. Apply the dictates of common sense to their care and you will realize years of maintenance-free operation.
(Courtesy of Compaq Computer Corporation)

various components are connected to an electrical power source, you are ready to begin processing. Micros are similar to copy machines, toasters, and other electrical devices—you must turn them on by applying electrical power. If you have a micro with a hard disk, all you have to do is turn on the computer and, perhaps, the monitor and printer. After a short period, a beep signals the end of the *system check* and DOS is loaded automatically from disk to RAM. If your micro does not have a hard disk and is configured with one or two diskette drives, you must insert the DOS diskette before turning on the system. Interaction with DOS and procedures for running an applications program are covered in detail in Chapter 4, "DOS: Disk Operating System Concepts and Tutorials."

Entering Commands and Data

Micros Can Be Very Picky.   A personal computer is responsive to your commands, but it does *exactly* what you tell it to do—no more, no less. If you do something wrong it tells you, and then gives you another chance.

When entering a command in DOS or in an applications program such as word processing, you must be explicit. For example, if you wish to copy a word processing document file from one disk to another, you cannot just enter "copy", or even "copy MYFILE". You must enter the command that tells the micro to copy MYFILE from disk A to disk B (copy a:myfile b:). If you omit needed information in a command or the format of the command is incorrect, an error message will be displayed and/or an on-screen prompt will request that you reenter the command correctly.

Micros are not always so picky. You can enter DOS commands and filenames as either uppercase or lowercase characters. For example, the system interprets the command "copy a:myfile b:" and "COPY A:MYFILE B:" to be the same command. Some software packages do not distinguish between uppercase and lowercase *commands*; however, all software packages do make the distinction between uppercase and lowercase entries for *keyed-in data*.

The Keyboard

A microcomputer's *keyboard* is normally the primary input and control device. You enter data and issue commands via the keyboard. Besides the standard typewriter keyboard, most micro keyboards have **function keys**, also called **soft keys**. When pressed, these function keys trigger the execution of software, thus the name "soft" key. For example, pressing a particular function key might call up a *menu* of possible activities that can be performed. Another function key might rearrange a paragraph in a word processing document for right and left justification. Some function keys are permanently labeled: copy, find, save, and so on. Others are numbered and assigned different functions for different software packages. The software packages are usually distributed with **keyboard templates** that designate which commands are

Micros throughout this bank help loan officers provide customers with quick turnaround on loans, letters of credit, guarantees, and other customer documents. However, before officers can process applications, DOS must be loaded to memory.
(Photo courtesy of Hewlett-Packard Company)

Keyboards, the primary input device for micros, vary considerably in design. Besides the alphanumeric keyboard (not shown), this keyboard has a 10-key pad, function keys (top row), and a special area for the cursor control keys. This system is also configured with a mouse.
(Courtesy of Unisys Corporation)

assigned to which function keys. For example, "help" is often assigned to F1 or function key number 1. The templates are usually designed to be fitted over the keyboard or attached with an adhesive.

Most keyboards are equipped with a *10-key pad* and *cursor control keys*. The 10-key pad permits rapid numeric data entry. It is normally positioned to the right of the standard alphanumeric keyboard. The cursor control keys or "arrow" keys allow you to move the cursor up and down (usually a line at a time) and left and right (usually a character at a time). To move the cursor rapidly about the screen, simply hold down the desired cursor control key.

For many software packages, you can use the cursor control keys to view parts of a document or worksheet that extend past the bottom, top or sides of the screen. This is known as **scrolling**. Use the up and down cursor control keys to *scroll vertically* and the left and right keys to *scroll horizontally*. For example, if you wish to scroll vertically through a word processing document, move the up or down cursor control key to the edge of the current screen and continue to press the key to view more of the document, one line a time. Figure 3–1 graphically illustrates vertical and horizontally scrolling.

In summary, there are three basic ways to enter a command from the keyboard:

- *Key in* the command using the alphanumeric portion of the keyboard.
- Press a *function key*.
- Use the *cursor control keys* to select a *menu option* from the display of a menu. Menus are discussed in detail in the next section.

Other important keys common to most keyboards are the *enter or*

FIGURE 3–1
Electronic Spreadsheet: Scrolling
Scroll vertically and horizontally to view those portions of an electronic spreadsheet or word processing document that do not fit on a single screen.

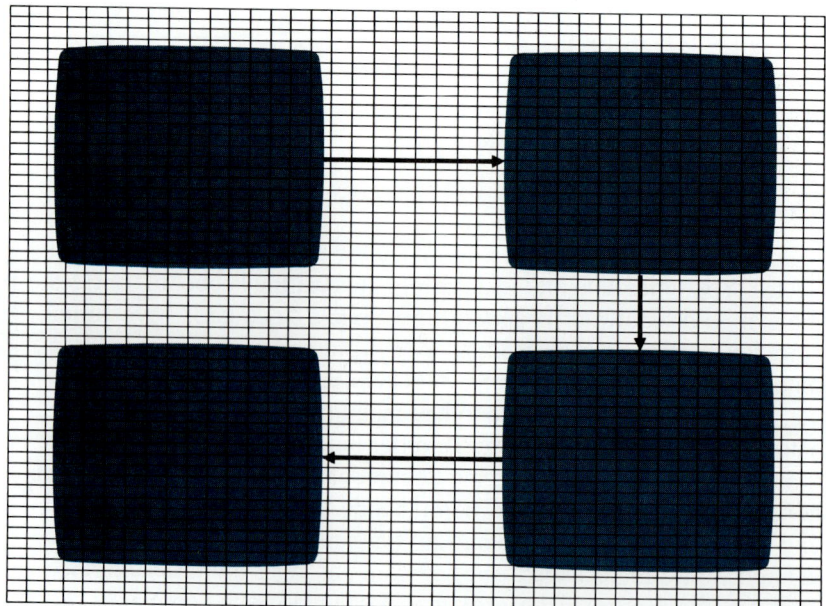

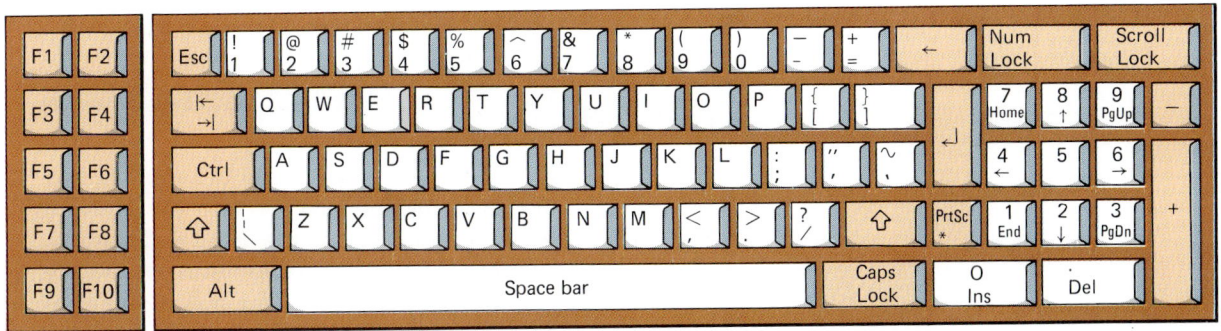

carriage return (ENTER or RETURN), *home* (HOME), *page up* and *page down* (PGUP and PGDN), *delete* (DEL), *insert-overstrike toggle* (INS), *backspace* (BKSP), *escape* (ESC), *space* (SPACE), *control* (CTRL), and *alternate* (ALT) keys (see Figure 3–2).

FIGURE 3–2
A Microcomputer Keyboard
This is a representative microcomputer keyboard. In this figure, the alphanumeric characters follow the commonly-used Qwerty layout. The positioning of the function keys, cursor control keys, and the ten-key pad may vary substantially among keyboards.

ENTER
Normally the ENTER key is used to send keyed-in data or a selected command to RAM for processing. For example, when you want to enter data to a spreadsheet cell, the characters that you enter are displayed in an edit area until you press ENTER, also called the *carriage return* or RE-TURN. When you press ENTER, the data are displayed in the appropriate spreadsheet cell. When you highlight a menu option with the cursor control keys, press ENTER to select that option. Like most of the special keys, ENTER has other meanings, depending on the type of software package you are using. In word processing, for example, you would designate the end of a paragraph by pressing the ENTER key.

HOME
Pressing the HOME key results in different actions for different packages, but often the cursor is moved to the beginning of a work area (the beginning of the screen or document in word processing, the upper left corner of the spreadsheet, or the first record in a data base).

END
With most software packages, press END to move the cursor to the end of the work area (the end of the screen or document in word processing, the lower right corner of the spreadsheet, or the last record in a data base).

PGUP PGDN
Press PGUP (*page up* or previous) and PGDN (*page down* or next) to scroll vertically *a page (screen) at a time* to view parts of the document or spreadsheet that extend past the top or bottom of the screen, respectively. PGUP and PGDN are also used to position the cursor at the

previous and next record, respectively, when using database software.

DEL — Press DEL to *delete* the character at the cursor position.

INS — Press INS to **toggle** (switch) between the two modes of entering data and text—*insert and replace*. Both modes are discussed and illustrated later in the word processing discussion. The term toggle is used to describe the action of pressing a single key to rotate between two or more modes of operation (insert and replace), functions (underline on or off), or operational specifications (for type of database field: character, numeric, date, memo).

BKSP — Press the BKSP, or *backspace*, key to move the cursor one position to the left and delete the character in that position.

ESC — The ESC, or *escape*, key may have many functions, depending on the software package, but in most situations you can press the ESC key to negate the current command.

SPACE — Press the SPACE bar at the bottom of the keyboard to key in a space at the cursor position.

CTRL ALT — The CTRL, or *control*, and ALT, or *alternate*, keys are used in conjunction with another key to expand the functionality of the keyboard. You hold down a CTRL or ALT key to give another key new meaning. For example, on some word processing systems you press HOME to move the cursor to the top left corner of the screen. When you press CTRL and HOME together, the cursor is positioned at the beginning of the document.

This laboratory technician uses the keyboard's 10-key pad and the keystroke buffer to expedite the entry of numeric data into an electronic spreadsheet.
(Courtesy of Compaq Computer Corporation)

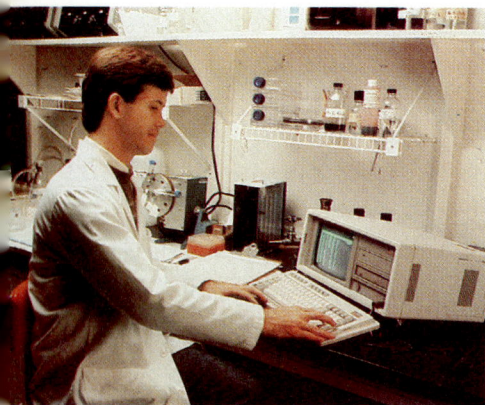

Each keystroke that you enter is first sent to an intermediate *keystroke buffer* that can save from 15 to 256 keystrokes. Under normal processing conditions, the keystroke is sent immediately from the buffer to the processor; however, there are many instances (such as disk reads or preparation of a graphics display) where you can key ahead. For example, if you know that the next prompt to be displayed is "Enter filename:" you can enter the desired filename in anticipation of the prompt. When the prompt appears, the filename that you entered is loaded from the keystroke buffer and displayed after the prompt. Judicious use of the keystroke buffer can make your interaction with micro software packages much more efficient.

Another device used for input and control is the *mouse*. The hand-held mouse is connected to the computer by an electrical cable (the mouse's tail) and rolled over a desktop to move the cursor. Buttons on the mouse are activated to select a menu item or to perform certain tasks, such as moving blocks of data from one part of the screen to another.

Issuing Commands to Micro Software Packages

You can interact with software packages, such as electronic spreadsheet and database, at several different levels of sophistication: the *menu level*, the *macro level*, and the *programming level*. These three levels of command interaction are discussed in the following sections.

Menus

The Hierarchy of Menus. When using productivity software, you issue commands and initiate operations by selecting activities to be performed from a hierarchy of **menus**. These hierarchies are sometimes called menu trees. When you select an item from the **main menu**, you are often presented with another menu of activities, and so on. Depending on the items you select, you may progress through as few as one and as many as eight levels of menus before processing is initiated for the desired activity.

Let's use graphics software to illustrate how you might use a hierarchy of menus. The main menu of a graphics software package might give you the choice of what type of graph you want produced:

    Bar   Pie   Line

If you select *bar graph*, another menu lets you choose whether you wish to create a new one, revise an existing one, or view an existing one.

    Create   Revise   View

If you select *create*, more menus are presented that permit you to describe the appearance of the graph (using labels) and to identify what data are to be graphed.

Types of Menus. A menu can appear as a **bar menu** in the *user interface* portion of the display, a **pull-down menu**, or a **pop-up menu**. The user interface is from one to six lines at the bottom and/ or top of the screen. The menu options in a bar menu are displayed across the screen. To select an item in a bar menu, use the left and right cursor control keys to highlight the desired menu option and press ENTER.

The result of a menu selection from a bar menu at the top of the screen is often a pull-down menu. The subordinate menu is "pulled-down" from the selected menu option and displayed as a vertical list of menu options. The entire menu is shown in a **window** directly under the selected menu option and over whatever is currently on the screen. A window is a rectangular display that is temporarily super-imposed over whatever is currently on the screen. Use the up and down cursor control keys to highlight the desired menu option and press ENTER to select the menu option.

The menu options for Webster's NewWorld Writer, a popular word processing program, are displayed in a bar menu (Search, Block, Appearance, and so on) at the top of the screen. If the user hesitates in selecting an option, an explanation of the currently highlighted option (Appearance) is superimposed over the document in a window.

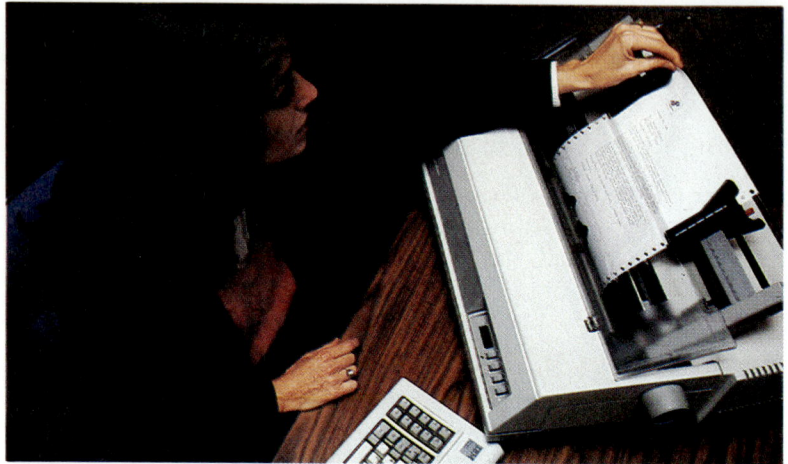

The default for output document size on most word processing packages is $8\frac{1}{2}$ by 11 inches, a common size for letterhead paper.
(Dataproducts Corporation)

Like the pull-down menu, the pop-up menu is superimposed over the current screen in a window. A pop-up menu can be called up in a variety of ways, including function keys or as the result of a selection from a higher-level pop-up menu.

Defaults. As you progress through a series of menus, you are eventually asked to enter the specifications for data to be graphed (graphics software), the size of the output paper (word processing software), and so on. As a convenience to the user, many of the specification options are already filled in to reflect common situations. For example, word processing packages set output document size to be $8\frac{1}{2}$ by 11 inches. If the user is satisfied with these **default options**, no further specifications are required. The user can easily revise the default options to accommodate the less common situations. So, to print a document on legal-size paper, the default paper length of 11 inches would need to be revised to 14 inches.

Menu Summary.   During any given point in a work session, *the options available to the user of a micro productivity software tool are displayed somewhere on the screen*. For example, in word processing, the instructions for calling up the main menu or a help screen are prominently displayed above or below the document work area. If you are ever confused about what to do next, the available user options are usually displayed on the current screen.

Macros and Programming.   At the menu level of command interaction you are initiating individual commands. At the macro and programming levels of interaction you can string together commands and even introduce logic operations.

A handy feature available with most micro software packages is the **macro**. A macro is a sequence of frequently used operations or keystrokes that can be recalled as you need them. You create a macro by entering the sequence of operations or keystrokes and storing them on disk for later recall. To *invoke* or execute the macro, you either refer to it by name (perhaps in the text of a word processing file) or enter the series of keystrokes that identify the desired macro (e.g., ALT-8, CTRL-F4). Three common user-supplied macros in word processing could be the commands necessary to format the first-, second- and third-level headings in a report. For example, the user might want the first level heading to be centered, boldfaced, and followed by two spaces; the second level to be flush left, boldfaced, and followed by an indented paragraph; and the third level to be flush left, underlined, and followed on the same line by the beginning of the first paragraph. In electronic spreadsheets, macros are commonly used to produce graphs automatically from spreadsheet data.

Some software packages permit users the flexibility to do their own *programming*. That is, micro software users can create logical sequences of instructions. For example, a database software program can be written that will retrieve records from a particular data base depending on preset criteria, process the data according to programmed instructions, and print out a report. The programming capability enables users to create microcomputer-based information systems for an endless number of applications from payroll processing to inventory control. Programming with a database software package is explained and illustrated in Chapter 10, "Database Software Concepts."

> **MEMORY BITS**
>
> **COMMAND FORMATS FOR MICRO SOFTWARE**
> - Menus (individual commands)
> - Macros (command sequence)
> - Programming (command sequence with logic operations)

3–5   USER FRIENDLY SOFTWARE

Virtually all vendors of micro software tout their product as being **user friendly**. Software is said to be user friendly when someone with relatively little computer experience has little difficulty using the system. User-friendly software communicates easily understood words and phrases to the end user, thus simplifying the user's interaction with the computer system. A central focus of the design of any micro productivity software is user friendliness.

Icons and Help Commands.   Some software packages use **icons** or pictographs (a graphic rendering of a file cabinet, a diskette, and so on), rather than words or phrases, to communicate with the end user.

A handy feature available on most software packages is the **help command**. When you find yourself in a corner, you can press the help key, which is often assigned to a numbered function key, to get more explanation or instruction on how to proceed. When you are finished reading the help information, you can return to your work at the same point that you left it.

Not all micro software packages are as user friendly as vendors would have us believe. Vendors are sometimes overzealous in their use of the phrase "easy to learn." However, millions of computer

The buying public is demanding that user-friendliness be one of the primary design considerations in microcomputer productivity software packages. In the photo, a personnel administrator is creating an organization chart with a user-friendly graphics package.
(Photo courtesy of Hewlett-Packard Company)

novices and experts have mastered the use of these valuable productivity tools, and with a little study and practice, you will, too.

Windows.   *Windows* allow users to "look through" several windows on a single display screen; however, you can only manipulate text or data in one window at a time. This is called the current window. Windows can overlap one another on the display screen. For example, some integrated software packages permit users to view a spreadsheet in one window, a bar chart in another window, and a word processing document in a third window. With windows, you can work the way you think and think the way you work. Several projects are at your fingertips and you can switch between them with relative ease.

You can perform work in one of several windows on a display screen or you can **zoom** in on a particular window. That is, the window you select is expanded to fill the entire screen. Press a key and you can return to a multiwindow display. A multiwindow display permits you to view how a change in one window affects another window. For example, as you change the data in a spreadsheet, you can view how an accompanying pie graph is revised to reflect the new data.

You can even create **window panes**! As you might expect, a window is divided into panes so that you can view several parts of the same window subarea at a time. For example, if you are writing a long report in a word processing window, you might wish to write the conclusions to the report in one window pane while viewing portions of the report in another window pane.

3–6   BACKUP: BETTER SAFE THAN SORRY

The safeguarding of software and your data may be more important than the safeguarding of micro hardware. The first commandment in personal computing is BACKUP YOUR FILES. If data and program files are destroyed, it may be impossible for them to be re-created within a reasonable period of time. If, on the other hand, the hardware is destroyed, it can be replaced fairly quickly. The impact of losing critical software or files makes **backup** a major concern.

When you create a document, a spreadsheet, or graph and you wish to recall it at a later time, you *store* the file on disk. You can, of course, store many files on a single disk. If the disk is in some way destroyed (scratched, demagnetized, and so on), you have lost your files unless you have a backup disk. To minimize the possibility of losing valuable files, you should periodically back up (make a copy of) your work disk.

The frequency with which a work disk is backed up depends on its *volatility*, or how often you use the files on the disk. If you spend time *every* day working with files on a work disk, you should back it up each day. Others are backed up no more often than they are used. Since some updating will occur between backup runs, the re-creation of lost files means that subsequent updates and changes must be redone from the point of the last backup.

Figure 3–3 illustrates the backup procedure for a work diskette that

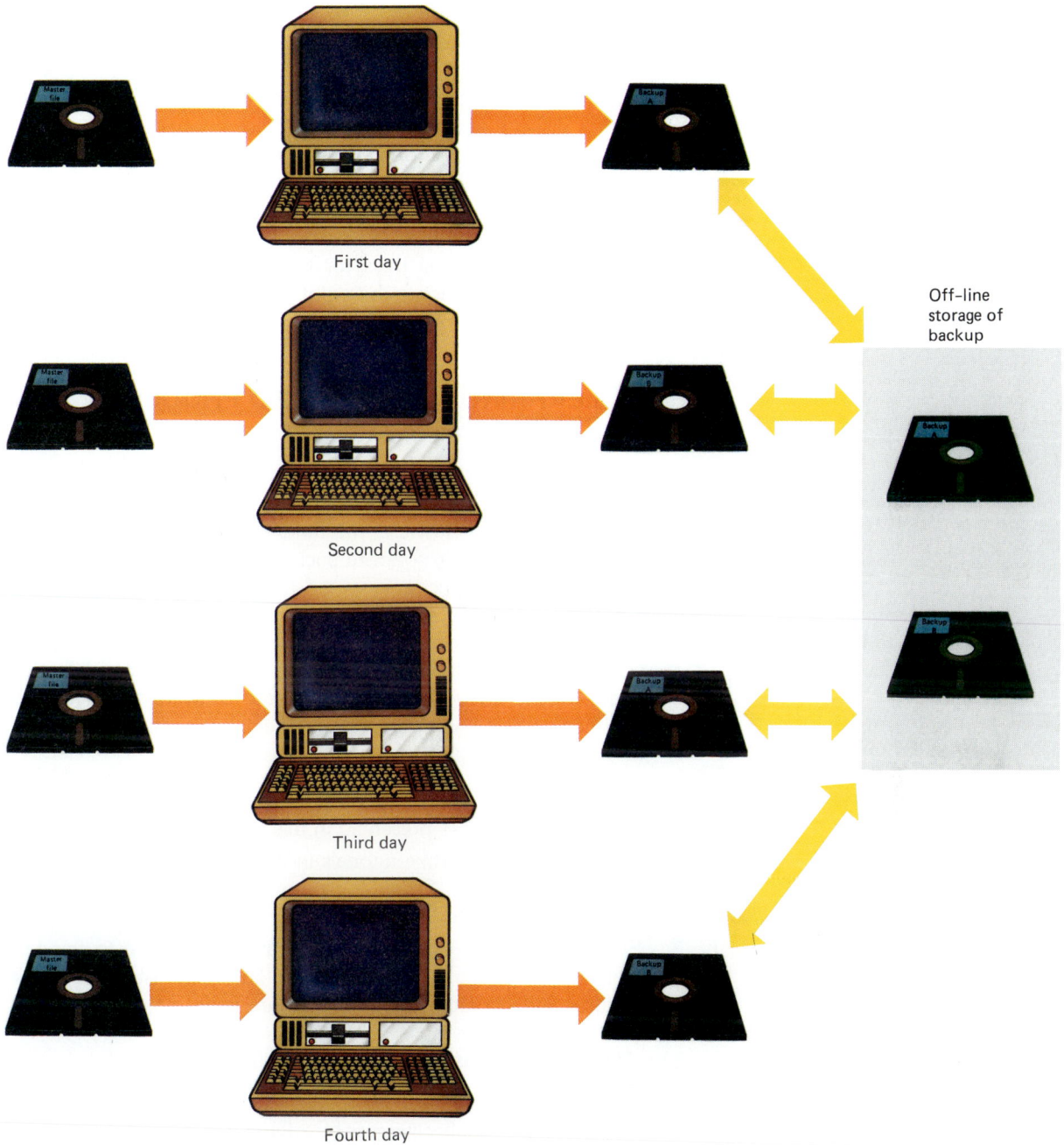

FIGURE 3–3
Backup Procedure for a Diskette-based Master File
The master file is backed up alternately to diskette A or B at the end of
each day so that one backup file is always current within one day's
processing.

is used daily. Two *generations* of backup are maintained on backup diskettes A and B. After each day's processing, the contents of the work diskette are copied (or dumped) alternately to diskette A or B. In this manner, one backup is always current within a day's processing. If the work diskette and the most recent backup are accidentally destroyed, a third backup is current within two days' processing. Diskettes A and B are alternated as the most current backup.

At one time or another, just about every computer specialist has experienced the trauma of losing work for which there was no backup. It is no fun seeing several days (or weeks!) of work go down the drain, but it does drive home the point that it is well worth the effort to make backup copies of your work.

3–7   LEARNING TO USE MICRO PRODUCTIVITY SOFTWARE

An Approach to Learning

At the intermediate level of use, the fundamental concepts embodied in the various productivity software packages are essentially the same, be it word processing, electronic spreadsheet, or something else. Their differences are primarily in the way the software interacts with the user and in their advanced features. This book is designed around an educational approach that should enable you to develop skills that will make it easy for you to use any of the software packages that you might encounter at your college or place of business. This approach to learning includes

1. In-class lectures
2. The conceptual base presented in this text
3. The hands-on keystroke tutorials in the text and the *Lab Manual* (DOS, WordPerfect, SuperCalc4, Lotus 1-2-3, dBASE III PLUS, The OUTLINER, and many others)
4. SuperSoftware: an educational software supplement to this text that includes, among other things, on-line demonstrations of the features and operation of micro software tools

The Method of Presentation in this Text

The presentation in Part III, "Microcomputer Productivity Software," optimizes pedagogical effectiveness by adhering to the following premise: *If you understand the fundamental concepts embodied in word processing, spreadsheet, graphics, database, idea processor, and communications software, you can easily apply your knowledge to the use of any of a variety of commercial productivity software packages.* That is, once you grasp the concepts, you can learn to use any of the available software packages with a little hands-on practice.

Each of the conceptual discussions of the various software packages is followed by keystroke tutorials for popular commercial software packages. The keystroke tutorials illustrate how these software packages would be used to develop the examples presented in the conceptual discussion. Educational versions of WordPerfect, The TWiN, dBASE III PLUS, The OUTLINER, and Crosstalk XVI are made available to the colleges and businesses using this text so that students can reinforce their understanding of the concepts with some hands-on experience. The *Lab Manual* that accompanies this text contains follow-on keystroke tutorials for these and other popular software packages.

Throughout the special skills sections in Part III, microcomputer software concepts are discussed and illustrated within the context of Zimco Enterprises, a fictitious medium-size manufacturer of handy consumer products: the Stib, Farkle, Tegler, and Qwert.

Additional Help

When you purchase a software package, you will usually receive at least one manual, the software on diskettes, and often a *tutorial disk*. It is a good idea to go over the tutorial disk to get a feeling for the menu options and how the software interacts with the user. When you load the tutorial disk on the micro, an instructional program interactively walks you through a simulation (demonstration) of the features and use of the software. Once you have an overview understanding of the features and how the components fit together, it is easier to go to the manual for specific operational questions.

During the learning stages, keep a list of error messages handy; you will probably need them. A word of warning: Manuals and disk tutorials tell you everything you *can* do but say very little about what you *cannot* do. That may take a bit of experimentation and trial and error to learn.

3–8 BUYING A MICRO

Retail Sales

Where to Buy. Microcomputers and personal computers can be purchased at thousands of convenient locations. Retail chains, such as ComputerLand, ENTRE Computer Center, 20/20, and MicroAge, market and service a variety of small computer systems. Radio Shack stores carry and sell their own line of computers. Micros are also sold in the computer department of most department stores. The demand for micros has encouraged major computer system manufacturers to open retail stores.

There is an alternative to buying a computer at a retail store. If you know what you want, you can call any of several mail order services, give them a credit card number, and your PC will be delivered to your doorstep.

The Perks of Employment. You might be able to acquire a micro through your employer. Many companies offer their employees a "com-

Just a few years ago, college courses and curriculums devoted to the study of micros and micro software did not exist. Today, most colleges offer (and sometimes require) micro-oriented courses. A growing number of colleges offer degree programs in the micro field.
(Courtesy of Radio Shack, A Division of Tandy Corporation)

Salespeople at computer retail stores are usually happy to show you what options are available for a particular microcomputer. Available in most retail stores are "demo disks" that, when loaded to a PC, demonstrate the features of the hardware or a software package.
(Courtesy of International Business Machines Corporation)

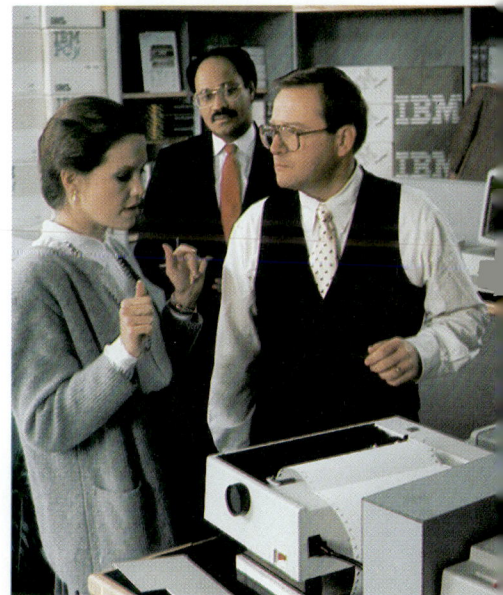

puter perk." In cooperation with vendors, companies make volume purchases of PCs at discount rates, and then offer them to employees at substantial savings. Many colleges sponsor similar programs to benefit students and professors.

Micro Manufacturers

Visions of tremendous profit opportunities have lured scores of companies into developing products to meet the growing demand for personal computers. The number of personal computer manufacturers may have peaked in 1983, with over 150 companies manufacturing about 700 PCs. Recent failures of both small and large companies have caused potential entrepreneurs to think twice before going head-to-head with dozens of established, well-financed companies. Industry analysts are predicting that at least half of the existing micro vendors will not survive the decade.

Commodore Business Machines, Apple, Tandy, Compaq, Eagle, Leading Edge, Epson, Zenith, Panasonic, and Kaypro are just a few of many manufacturers of microcomputers. Computer giants such as IBM and DEC did not enter the microcomputer market until 1981. The giants may have had a late start, but they have been making up for lost time by taking substantial shares of the micro market. Almost immediately after it was announced, the IBM PC became an industry phenomenon. During most of the 1980s it has been the industry standard. At one time, over 30 companies manufactured *IBM PC-compatible micros*. These supposedly would run the same software and accomplish the same functions as the IBM PC. A few IBM PC-compatible micros are indeed completely compatible, but others are only partially compatible. If history repeats itself, the new IBM Personal System/2, which is compatible with the IBM PC series, may well be the standard bearer in the 1990s.

Choosing a Microcomputer

Buying a microcomputer can be a harrowing experience or it can be a thrilling and fulfilling one. If you approach the purchase of a micro haphazardly, expect the former. If you go about the acquisition methodically and with purpose, expect the latter. This section contains some hints for the evaluation and selection of a microcomputer.

Steps to Buying a Micro

1. *Achieve computer literacy.* You don't buy an automobile before you learn how to drive, and you shouldn't buy a microcomputer without a good understanding of its capabilities and limitations. By the time you finish this course, you will have the knowledge to make informed decisions when buying a micro.

2. *Determine your information and computer usage needs.* There is an old adage, "If you don't know where you are going, any road will get you there." The statement is certainly true of choosing a

PC. Knowing where you are going can be translated to mean "How do you plan to use the PC?"

Do you wish to develop your own software or purchase commercially available software packages? Or perhaps do both? If you want to write your own programs, you must select the programming language that is best suited to your application needs. The only programming language that is supported by all microcomputers is BASIC. If you plan on purchasing the software, determine which general application areas you wish to have supported on the proposed PC (spreadsheet, accounting, word processing, home banking, or others).

3. *Assess availability of software and information services.* Determine what software and information services are available to meet your prescribed needs. Good sources of this type of information include a wide variety of periodicals (*PC*, *Byte*, *Creative Computing*, *Computerworld*, and *Personal Computing*, to name a few), salespersons at computer stores, and acquaintances who have knowledge in the area.

Several hundred micro productivity software packages are available commercially. Commercially available software packages vary greatly in capabilities and price. Software with essentially the same capabilities may be priced with differences of as much as several hundred dollars. Some graphics software creates displays of graphs in seconds, while others take minutes. Some software packages are easy to learn and are accompanied by good documentation, others are not. Considering the amount of time that you might spend using micro software, any extra time you spend in evaluating the software will be time well spent.

4. *Investigate hardware options.* If you select a specific software product or an information service, your selection may dictate the general computer system configuration requirements and, in some cases, a specific microcomputer system. In all likelihood, you will have several, if not a dozen, hardware alternatives available to you. Become familiar with the features and options of each system.

5. *Determine features desired.* You can go with a minimum system configuration or you can add a few "bells and whistles." Expect to pay for each feature in convenience, quality, and speed that you add to the minimum configuration. For example, people are usually willing to pay a little extra for the added convenience of a two-disk system, even though one disk will suffice. On the other hand, a color monitor may be an unnecessary luxury for some applications. The peripherals that you select depend on your specific needs and volume of usage. For example, the type of printer that you choose will depend on the volume of hard copy output that you anticipate, whether or not you need graphics output, whether or not you need letter-quality print, and so on.

6. *"Test drive" several alternatives.* Once you have selected several software and hardware alternatives, spend enough time to gain

In the process of selecting micros for his staff, this credit manager decided that it was not economically feasible to configure each micro with a letter-quality printer. As an alternative, he purchased one high-speed desktop laser printer that would be shared by all of the micros in his department. (Photo courtesy of Hewlett-Packard Company)

some familiarity with them. Do you prefer one keyboard over another? Does a word processing system fully use the features of the hardware? Is one system easier to understand and use than another? Use these sessions to answer any questions that you might have about the hardware or software. Salespersons at most retail stores are happy to give you a test drive—just ask.

7. *Select and buy*. Apply your criteria, select, and then buy your hardware and software.

Factors to Consider

1. *Future computing needs*. What will your computer and information processing needs be in the future? Make sure the system you select can grow with your needs.

2. *Who will use the system*? Plan not only for yourself but for others in your home or office who will also use the system. Get their input and consider their needs along with yours.

3. *Availability of software*. Software is developed for one or several microcomputers, but not for all microcomputers. As you might expect, a more extensive array of software is available for the more popular micros. However, do not overlook some of the less visible vendors if their products, in your mind, are superior to the other alternatives.

4. *Service*. Computing hardware is very reliable. Even so, the possibility exists that one or several of the components will eventually malfunction and have to be repaired. Before purchasing a micro, identify a reliable source of hardware maintenance. Most retailers service what they sell. If a retailer says that the hardware must be returned to the manufacturer for repair, choose another retailer or another system.

   Most retailers or vendors will offer a variety of maintenance contracts. Maintenance contract options range from on-site repair that covers all parts and service to carry-in service that does not include parts. Most domestic users elect to treat their micros like their televisions and autos: When the warranty runs out, they pay for repairs as they are needed. Under normal circumstances, this strategy will prove the least expensive.

   Service extends beyond hardware maintenance. Service is also an organization's willingness to respond to your inquiries, before *and* after the sale. Some retailers and vendors offer classes in programming and in the use of the hardware and software that they sell.

5. *Hardware Obsolescence*. "I'm going to buy one as soon as the price goes down a little more." If you adopt this strategy, you may never purchase a computer. If you wait another six months, you will probably be able to get a more powerful micro for less money. But what about the lost opportunity?

   There is, however, a danger in purchasing a micro that is near or at the end of its life cycle. Focus your search on micros with

Portability was a key consideration when this production scheduling supervisor purchased his microcomputer because he spends at least one day a week in transit between plants.
(Photo courtesy of Hewlett-Packard Company)

state-of-the-art technology. Even though you may get a substantial discount on the older micro, you will normally get more for your money with the newer one.

6. *Software Obsolescence*. Software can become obsolete as well. Software vendors are continually improving their software packages. Each packages is assigned a **version number**, the first *release* being 1.0 (referred to as one point zero). Subsequent updates to version 1.0 become version 1.1, version 1.2, and so on. The next major revision to the package is released as version number 2.0. Make sure that you are buying the most recent release of a particular software package.

7. *Other costs*. The cost of the actual microcomputer system is the major expense, but there are numerous incidental expenses that can mount up that may influence your selection of a micro. If you have a spending limit, consider these costs when purchasing the hardware (the cost ranges listed are for a first-time user): software ($100–$1,500), maintenance (0–$500/year), diskettes and tape cassettes ($50–$200), furniture (0–$350), insurance (0–$40), and printer ribbons or cartridges, paper, and other supplies ($40–$400).

3–9 SUMMARY

With Chapters 1 through 3 under your belt, you are ready to embark on a journey toward becoming a power user, a euphemism for a technically-oriented user that uses software and hardware to its full potential, and then demands more. Perhaps the best way to learn micro software is to use it. Anticipate some frustrations, but before you know it, you will be a software wizard. What you do with the software is 10 percent skills and 90 percent imagination.

SUMMARY OUTLINE AND IMPORTANT TERMS

3–1 INTERACTING WITH THE SYSTEM. To interact effectively with a personal computer you need to know the operation and use of microcomputer hardware, general microcomputer software concepts, **DOS** (the disk operating system), and the specific applications programs that you are using. The first three areas of understanding are prerequisites to the fourth.

3–2 CONFIGURING A MICROCOMPUTER SYSTEM. The computer and its peripheral devices are called the computer system **configuration**. A typical micro configuration would be comprised of a computer, a keyboard, a monitor, a printer, and one or two disk drives. Micros that give users the flexibility to configure the system with a variety of peripheral devices are said to have an **open architecture** or **bus architecture**.

In a **closed architecture**, the system is fully configured when it is sold.

The electrical **bus** is the path through which the processor sends data and commands to RAM and all peripheral devices. A **port** provides a direct link with the micro's bus. External peripheral devices are interfaced with the processor through either a **serial port** or a **parallel port**. The defacto standard for micro serial ports is the **RS-232C port**.

Expansion slots can house a wide variety of special-function add-on boards or **add-on cards**. The add-ons can include one of more of the following functions: RAM, color/graphics adapter, modem, internal battery-powered clock/calendar, serial port, parallel port, printer spooler, hard disk, coprocessor, and VCR backup. Most are **multifunction add-on boards**.

3–3 CARE AND MAINTENANCE OF MICROS AND THEIR STORAGE MEDIA.   Apply the dictates of common sense to the care and maintenance of micros, peripheral devices, and storage media. For example, avoid excessive dust, extremes in temperature and humidity, and don't fold, spindle, or mutilate the diskettes.

3–4 MICROCOMPUTER OPERATION.   A personal computer is responsive to your commands, but it does exactly what you tell it to do. A micro's keyboard is the primary input and control device. Most micro keyboards have a 10-key pad, cursor control keys, and **function keys** or **soft keys**. **Keyboard templates** show you which commands are assigned to which function keys. Use the cursor control keys for vertical and horizontal **scrolling** and for menu selection. Another device used for input and control is the mouse.

You can interact with software packages at several different levels of sophistication: the menu level, the macro level, and the programming level. Issue individual commands and initiate operations by selecting activities to be performed from a hierarchy of **menus**, starting with the **main menu**. A menu can appear as a **bar menu** in the user interface portion of the display, a **pull-down menu**, or a **pop-up menu**. Menus are sometimes displayed in a **window**.

As a convenience to the user, many of the specification options are already filled in to reflect common situations. These are called **default options**.

At the menu level of command interaction you are initiating individual commands. At the macro and programming levels of of interaction you can string together commands and even introduce logic operations. A **macro** is a sequence of frequently used operations or keystrokes that can be recalled as you need them. Micro software users can create logical sequences of instructions called programs.

3–5 USER FRIENDLY SOFTWARE.   Software is said to be **user friendly** when someone with relatively little computer experience has little difficulty using the system. Some software packages use **icons** or pictographs to communicate with the end user. Issue the **help command** to get more explanation or instruction on how to proceed. You can perform work in one of several windows on a display screen or you can **zoom** in on a particular window or create **window panes**.

3–6 BACKUP: BETTER SAFE THAN SORRY.   The safeguarding of software and your data may be more important than the safeguarding of micro hardware. The impact of losing critical software or files makes **backup** a major concern. The frequency with which a work disk is backed up depends on its volatility. It is common practice to maintain two generations of backup.

3–7 LEARNING TO USE MICRO PRODUCTIVITY SOFTWARE.   This book is designed around an educational approach that should enable you to develop skills that will make it easy for you to use any of the software packages that you might encounter at your college or place of business. In the text, each of the conceptual discussions of the various software packages is followed by keystroke tutorials for popular commercial software packages.

When you purchase a software package, you will usually receive at least one manual, the software on diskettes, and a *tutorial diskette*.

3–8 BUYING A MICRO.   Micros and PCs can be purchased computer and traditional retail stores everywhere. A number of computer vendors, such as Apple and Tandy Corporation, specialize in microcomputers, but in recent years the vendors of mainframe computers, such as DEC and IBM, have made micros a major segment of their product lines.

Buying a microcomputer, whether for home or business, should be approached methodically and with purpose. Factors to consider when buying a micro include: future computing needs; who will use the system, availability of software, service, obsolescence, and other costs.

3–9 SUMMARY.   Perhaps the best way to learn micro software is to use it. What you do with the software is 10 percent skill and 90 percent imagination.

REVIEW EXERCISES _____

1. What is the purpose of soft keys? Of cursor control keys?
2. Describe the attributes of user-friendly software.

3. Contrast a bar menu and a pull-down menu.

4. Most word processing packages have a default document size. What other defaults would a word processing package have?

5. Briefly describe a typical configuration for a microcomputer system.

6. List five functional enhancements that can be made to a microcomputer by inserting one or more optional add-on boards into available expansion slots.

7. What is a printer spooler?

8. List those costs that might be associated with owning a personal computer that do not involve hardware or software.

9. Briefly describe three ways that you can use a keyboard to enter commands to a microcomputer software package.

10. During a micro software session, what key would you commonly press to move to the beginning of the work area? To negate the current command?

11. What do you look for when you ''test drive'' a microcomputer before purchasing it?

12. When would use the zoom feature of a microcomputer software package?

13. How is a pop-up menu displayed?

14. Why are some microcomputers sold with empty expansion slots?

15. What is a macro and how can the use of macros save time?

16. What do you look for when buying a microcomputer software package?

SELF-TEST (by section)

3–1. DOS is an acronym for disk operating system. (T/F)

3–2. (a) The computer and its peripheral devices are called the computer system _____.

(b) The RS-232C connector provides the interface to a parallel port. (T/F)

3–3. You should cover the write-protect notch on a diskette on those disks that are intended for read-only use. (T/F)

3–4. (a) Use the _____ for rapid numeric data entry.

(b) When interacting with microcomputers, you must wait until the execution of one command is finished before issuing another. (T/F)

(c) A sequence of frequently used operations or keystrokes that can be activated by the user is called a: (a) menu, (b) macro, or (c) program.

3–5. Pictographs, called _____, are often associated with user-friendly software.

3–6. The frequency with which a work disk is backed up depends on its data integrity. (T/F)

3–7. Manuals and disk tutorials for micro software tend to emphasize that which cannot be done, not that which can be done. (T/F)

3–8.   **(a)** The most important consideration in buying a microcomputer is whether or not a long-term service contract is available. (T/F)

   (b) Not all "IBM PC compatible" microcomputers are 100 percent compatible. (T/F)

3–9. A technically-oriented user who uses the full potential of micro hardware and software is called a _____ user.

Self-Test Answers.   **3–1,** T; **3–2,** configuration; **(b),** F; **3–3,** T; **3–4 (a),** 10-key pad; **(b),** F; **(c),** b; **3–5,** icons; **3–6,** F; **3–7,** F; **3–8 (a),** F; **(b),** T; **3–9,** power.

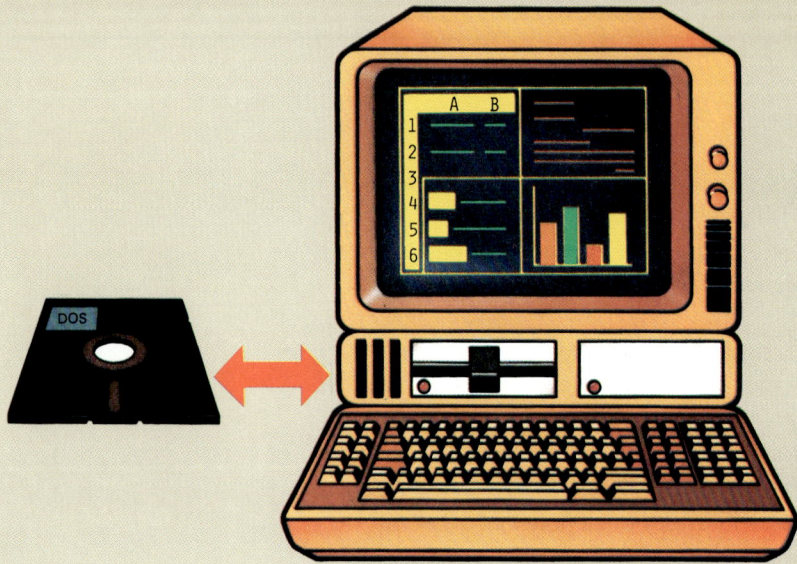

CHAPTER 4

DOS: Disk Operating System Concepts and Tutorials

STUDENT LEARNING OBJECTIVES

- To describe the function and purpose of a microcomputer's disk operating system (DOS).
- To load and run both DOS and microcomputer applications software.
- To name and reference files.
- To describe the use of directories and paths.
- To identify and use common DOS commands.
- To identify and use common DOS keyboard functions.
- To create batch files and self-booting applications diskettes.
- To acquire the ability to apply the DOS skills demonstrated in the hands-on tutorials.

HANDS-ON TUTORIALS for *MS-DOS* and *PC-DOS*

1. Loading DOS
2. Running an Applications Program
3. Working with DOS Commands

ADVANCED AND SPECIAL FEATURES TUTORIAL: *DOS*

Creating a File Using EDLIN (the DOS line editor)
Modifying a File Using EDLIN
Using DOS Batch Files

4–1 THE DISK OPERATING SYSTEM (DOS) _____

The nucleus of a microcomputer system is its **operating system**. The operating system monitors and controls all input/output and processing activities within a computer system. All hardware and software, including micro productivity software, are under the control of the operating system. Micro users need a working knowledge of their micro's operating system because they must use it to interface their applications programs with the microcomputer hardware.

Some of the more popular micro operating systems are MS-DOS, CP/M, UNIX, and Operating System/2. You may encounter spin-offs of these operating systems. For example, PC-DOS for the IBM PC is based on Microsoft Corporation's MS-DOS. Unfortunately, the logic, structure, and nomenclature of the different operating systems vary considerably. Our emphasis will be on PC-DOS, the operating system used with the IBM PC series of computers and the IBM Personal System/2 series of computers, and on MS-DOS, the operating system used with IBM PC-compatible computers. The discussions in this chapter apply to both MS-DOS and PC-DOS. In practice, these operating systems, which are essentially the same, are referred to simply as DOS (rhymes with boss), an acronym for disk operating system. DOS is a "disk" operating system because the operating system is stored on disk.

DOS Is the BOSS. Just as the processor is the center of all hardware activity, DOS is the center of all software activity. The operating system is a family of *systems software* programs that are usually, though not always, supplied by the computer system vendor. Because all hardware, software, and input/output are controlled by DOS, you might even call DOS the "boss."

One of the DOS family of programs is always *resident* in RAM during processing. This program, called COMMAND.COM, loads other operating system and applications programs into RAM as they are needed or as directed by you, the user. COMMAND.COM is usually referred to as COMMAND "dot" COM (rhymes with mom).

Besides controlling the ongoing operation of the microcomputer systems, DOS has two other important functions.

- *Input/output control.* DOS facilitates the movement of data between peripheral devices, the processor, RAM, and programs.
- *File and disk management.* DOS and its file and disk management utility programs enable users to perform such tasks as making backup copies of work disks, erasing disk files that are no longer needed, making inquiries about the number and type of files on a particular diskette, and preparing new diskettes for use. DOS also handles many file and disk oriented tasks that are transparent to the end user. For example, DOS keeps track of the physical location of disk files so that we, as users, need only to refer to them by name (for example, myfile) when loading them from disk to memory.

The band director at this high school uses a micro to maintain a data base for the music library and to keep track of all school-owned musical instruments. In college he studied music theory, applied music, conducting, music history, and DOS.

The DOS commands needed to perform user-oriented input/output tasks and file and disk management tasks are discussed and illustrated later in this chapter.

Booting the System. Before you can use a microcomputer you must load DOS, or **boot** the system. The procedure for booting the system on most micros is simply to load the operating system from disk storage into random access memory. In most micros this is no more difficult than inserting a DOS disk in a disk drive, closing the disk drive door, and flipping the switch on. On micros with hard disks, all you have to do is turn on the system and DOS is automatically loaded from the hard disk to RAM.

Micros configured with an internal clock-calendar have time and date data available to the user and user programs at all times. If your micro is not configured with an internal clock-calendar, DOS will give you the option of entering the date and time. See "Hands-On Tutorial 1: Loading DOS" at the end of this chapter.

4–2 RUNNING A SOFTWARE PACKAGE

The *system prompt* or the *DOS prompt* is the operating system's message to you, the user, that you can enter a *system command* (for example, copy files from one diskette to another) or the name of the program to run an applications program, such as an electronic spreadsheet. The form of the system prompt varies among operating systems. The system prompt for DOS is the greater than symbol prefaced by a disk drive specification (A> is the prompt when disk drive A is the active or default drive).

Once you have loaded the operating system to memory and the system prompt is displayed on the screen, you are ready to run a graphics package, a word processing package, or any other software package. To run a software package, you simply insert the diskette containing the software in the appropriate disk drive, close the disk drive door, then enter the name of the file that contains the applications software. For example, to run the SuperCalc4 electronic spreadsheet package on a DOS-based micro, you would load the software diskette to drive A and key in "sc4" (the name of the program file) after the DOS prompt. The next thing you see would be the opening screen, followed by the main menu for the electronic spreadsheet package.

All micro productivity tools are run in the same manner unless they are made to be *self-booting* (the operating system and the applications software are on the same diskette). By making a software package self-booting, you can bypass the step that requires you to enter the name of the program file after the prompt. To run a package on a self-booting disk, simply insert the applications software and flip the PC's switch on.

If your computer has a hard disk, you can store the program on hard disk. You can then load your program directly from the hard disk, thereby eliminating the need to insert the program diskette each

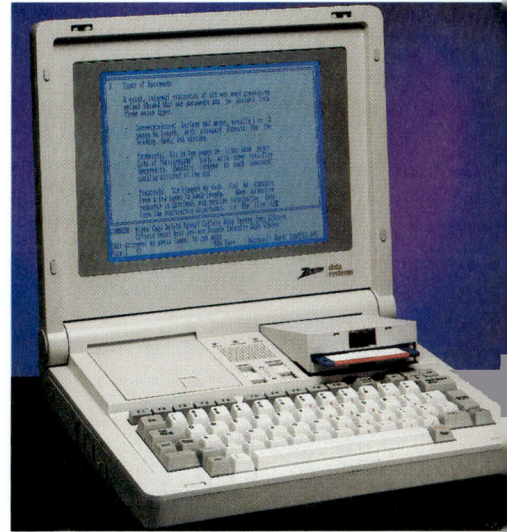

To begin a microcomputer session on a micro that is not configured with a hard disk, you will need to load DOS to main memory. Do this by manually inserting a DOS microdisk (in photo) or DOS diskette into the appropriate disk drive. On micros with hard disks, DOS is loaded to memory automatically. (Zenith Data Systems)

This micro is configured with two $5\frac{1}{4}$-inch disk drives. The top one is designated as disk drive A and the bottom is disk drive B. The system prompt for DOS is prefaced by the disk drive specification for the active drive (for example, A> or B>). (Photo courtesy of Hewlett-Packard Company)

time you run the program. See "Hands-On Tutorial 2: Running an Applications Program."

4–3   FILES

Naming Files.   On a microcomputer, a **file** is related information that is stored to disk (from memory) or retrieved from a disk (to memory) as a unit. A file can be a payroll program, sales data for an electronic spreadsheet, a database of names and addresses, the text of a progress report, or even a game. Each file is given a name, either by a user or by someone else like a software vendor. The name of a file includes

- A *filename* of up to eight characters
- An optional *extension* of up to three characters

The filename and extension are separated by a period (.). Typically, the extension identifies files that are associated with a certain application. For example, word processing packages often append the extension DOC (for document) to a user-supplied filename (REPORT.DOC). The extension appended to BASIC program filenames is BAS (PAYROLL.BAS). A spreadsheet program might use WKS (for worksheet) or a database program might use DB (for database). The following are legal filenames:

    NAMEADDR.DB   SALES.WKS   A

These are not legal:

    N+A.DB   (+ . = / \ [ ] : | < > = ; , are not
                             allowed)
    FIRSTQUARTERSALES   (more than 8 characters)
    .out   (no filename)

Referencing Files.   The *file specification* includes the filename, the extension, and a reference to the appropriate disk drive. A file (e.g., SALES.WKS) is associated with a particular disk drive. On a two disk-

Microcomputers (center), minicomputers (right), and mainframe computers (left) coexist by passing files back and forth via data communications. Data communications topic is discussed in detail in Chapter 13.
(Courtesy of Unisys Corporation)

ette system, the disk drives are labeled A and B. One of the disk drives is designated to be the *active drive*, that is, DOS commands that you issue apply to the active drive unless you state otherwise in the command. The DOS prompt indicates which drive is the active drive. For example, if the DOS prompt is B>, the active drive is B. If the desired file (SALES.WKS) is on drive B and the active drive is B, the drive specifier can be omitted. If the active drive is A (the DOS prompt is A>) and the desired file (SALES.WKS) is on the disk in drive B, the entire file specification is needed to reference the file.

ACTIVE DRIVE	FILE REFERENCE
B>	SALES.WKS
A>	B:SALES.WKS

There are many instances when you might wish to issue a DOS command that applies to several files. To perform these operations, you would use a **wildcard** or global character, in this case, the asterisk (∗). When used in a filename.extension combination, the ∗ is a generic reference to any combination of legal characters. To illustrate the use of the wildcard ∗, consider the following **directory**. A directory is simply a list of the names of the files that are stored on a particular diskette (a floppy disk) or in a named area on a hard disk (a hard disk can have several logical directories). The files on the disk in the active drive for this example are

SALES1Q.CAL	LETTER.WP	SALES3Q.CAL	MEMO2.WP
IDEA.OUT	SALES2Q.CAL	SALES4Q.CAL	THOUGHTS.OUT
NET.CAL	REPORT.WP	MEMO1.WP	NAMES.DB

WILDCARD FILE REFERENCE	FILES REFERENCED
∗.WP	LETTER.WP REPORT.WP MEMO1.WP MEMO2.WP
SALES∗.CAL	SALES1Q.CAL SALES2Q.CAL SALES3Q.CAL SALES4Q.CAL
∗.∗	all files in directory

4–4 DIRECTORIES AND PATHS

The *directory* feature of DOS enables us to form groups of related files. For example, we can create a directory into which we would store only word processing document files and another directory into which we would store only spreadsheet files. In practice, users seldom set up directories on diskettes. Therefore, when we talk of directory A:, we are referring to all files contained on the diskette in disk drive A:. However, establishing directories on a hard disk is common practice.

It is not uncommon for a hard disk to contain hundreds of files. To make file management and inquiries easier for both the user and DOS, users organize their files into a hierarchy or *tree* of directories and **subdirectories**. At the highest level of the "upside-down tree" is the **root directory**. When you load DOS, the root directory is the *active directory*. DOS reserves the drive designations A: and B: for diskette drives. The designator C: denotes the root directory for the hard disk drive.

Consider the directory tree illustrated in Figure 4–1. Two managers, Jim and Marcia, share the same personal computer. To keep their programs and files separate, they established directories as shown in Figure 4–1. Jim and Marcia created the subdirectories \JIM and \MARCIA to which they could assign subordinate subdirectories. The subdirectory \JIM\LOTUS contains the software for LOTUS 1-2-3 and all of Jim's Lotus 1-2-3 data files (SALES.WK1, BOOKFILE.WK1, etc.). The subdirectories \MARCIA\SC4, \MARCIA\NWW, and \MARCIA\DBASE contain the software for SuperCalc4, New World Writer, dBASE III PLUS and all of Marcia's associated data and document files (INCOME.CAL, MEMO, TRAINING.DBF, and so on).

Files of any kind can be stored in the root directory or in any subdirectory. When working with files that are stored on a disk with a hierarchy of directories, you need to specify the **path**. The path is the logical route that DOS must follow in order to locate the specified file. For example, the path to Jim's SALES.WK1 file would be *from* the root directory (C:) *to*

- Jim's subdirectory (C:\JIM) *to*
- the LOTUS subdirectory (C:\JIM\LOTUS) *to*
- the specific file (C:\JIM\LOTUS\SALES.WK1).

The filename is always the last entry in the path.

FIGURE 4–1
Example Directory Tree
The first-level subdirectories \JIM and \MARCIA have one and three second-level subdirectories, respectively.

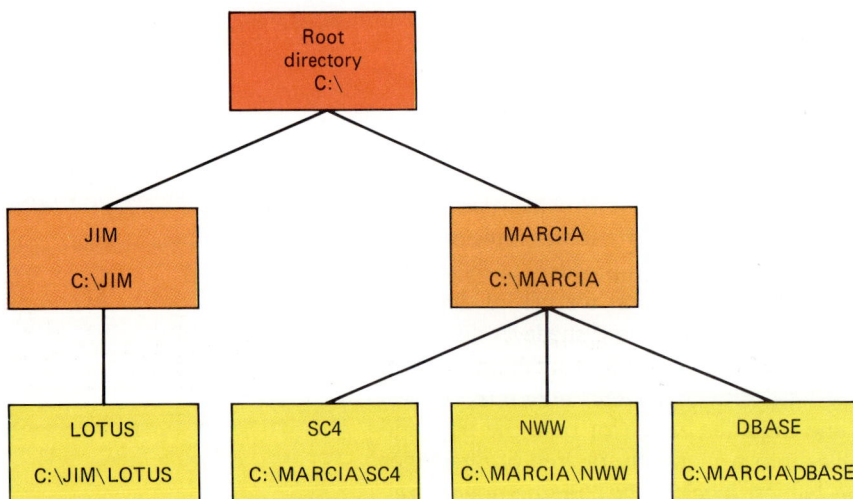

4–5   DOS COMMANDS

We use *DOS commands* to run our applications programs, make system inquiries, and manage files. This section contains a summary of the more frequently used commands.

Relative to the DOS disk, the DOS commands are of two types, *internal* and *external*. The internal commands are memory resident (they are stored in memory when you load DOS) and are available to the user at any time. The external commands must be loaded to memory from the DOS disk. If you issue an external command, such as DISKCOPY, and the DOS disk is not in the active drive, a message will be displayed asking you to insert the DOS disk in the active drive. Frequently used DOS commands are presented in four categories: disks, directories, files, and output.

Disk-related DOS Commands

- **FORMAT**. The *external* FORMAT command prepares a new disk for use. Before a disk can be used, it must be formatted; that is, the disk must be initialized with the DOS recording format of a set number of sectors per track. Formatting an already-used disk erases everything that was previously stored on it.

DOS COMMAND	RESULT
A>FORMAT B:	With DOS in drive A, the disk in drive B is formatted.

- **CHKDSK**. The *external* CHKDSK command displays a disk and RAM status report. The disk status report summarizes disk storage space in terms of the number of bytes used and the number of bytes available for use. Besides listing the number of *user files* on a disk, the CHKDSK command lists the number of *hidden files*. The hidden files are usually associated with the operating system or a software package. Hidden files are not listed when you issue a DIR (directory) command. The RAM or memory status report includes total RAM and available RAM, both in terms of bytes.

DOS COMMAND	RESULT
A>**CHKDSK B:**	With DOS in drive A, a status report for the disk in drive B and for memory is displayed.

- **DISKCOPY**. The *external* DISKCOPY command copies the entire contents of one diskette to another. In the command the source diskette is listed first and the target diskette is second. If the target diskette is a new disk, it is automatically formatted prior to the copy operation.

DOS COMMAND	RESULT
A>**DISKCOPY A: B:**	The diskette in drive A is copied to the diskette in drive B.

Microcomputer hard disks, or Winchester disks, are manufactured in clean rooms that are 1000 times cleaner than operating rooms in hospitals. Typically, micro users organize files on hard disks into directories and subdirectories.
(Seagate Technology)

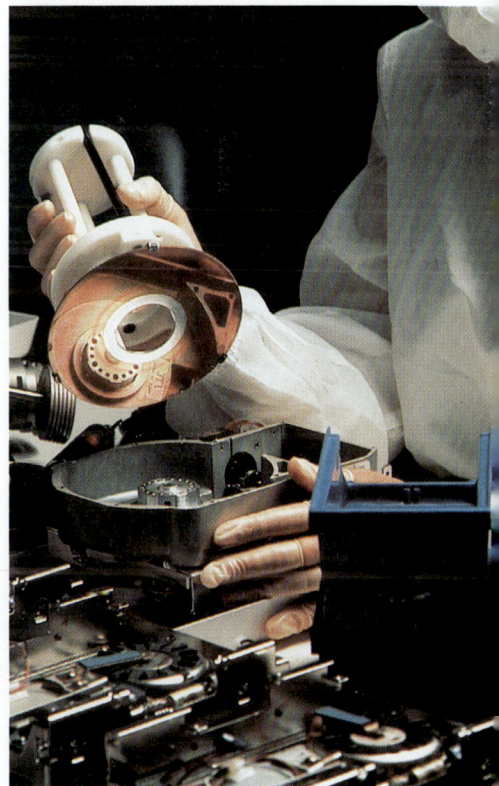

Directory-related DOS Commands

■ **DIR**. The *internal* DIR or directory command causes a list of the files on the active drive or *default directory* to be displayed on the monitor. The listing also includes such useful information as the size of each file (in bytes) and the number of bytes on the disk that are still available to the user. When the active drive is A and you want B to be the active drive/directory, enter "B:" after the A> (A>B:).

Use the /p option (A>**dir/p**) if you expect the list of files to scroll to another screen. When you specify this pause option, scrolling stops when the screen is full. Press any key to see more of the directory.

■ **MD** or **MKDIR**. The *internal* MD or MKDIR commands create a subdirectory on a specified disk.

DOS COMMAND	RESULT
C>**MD \JIM\LOTUS**	A second-level subdirectory named \JIM\LOTUS is created on the hard disk C. \JIM\LOTUS is subordinate to the subdirectory \JIM.

■ **CD** or **CHDIR**. The *internal* CD or CHDIR commands change the current directory (root or subdirectory) to the desired directory (subdirectory or root).

DOS COMMAND	RESULT
C>**CD \JIM**	The current directory is changed from the root directory to the directory \JIM on hard disk C.
C>**CD **	The current directory is changed to its root directory.

■ **RD** or **RMDIR**. The *internal* RD or RMDIR commands remove a subdirectory from a specified disk. A subdirectory must be empty (contain no user files) before it can be removed. A subdirectory is empty if only the special "." and ".." entries are displayed when the DIR command is issued.

DOS COMMAND	RESULT
C>**RD \JIM\LOTUS**	The second-level subdirectory \LOTUS is removed from the first-level subdirectory \JIM on the hard disk C.
C>**CD \JIM** C>**RD \LOTUS**	Same as above.

File-related DOS Commands

■ **COPY**. The *internal* COPY files command copies one or more files from or to the disk, directory, or device specified in the command. The *source* file(s) specification is listed first and the *target* file(s) specification is listed second. If not specified, the default drive is assumed. If you omit the filename(s) in the target specification, the file(s) that is copied to another disk is given the same name as the source file(s).

The COPY command permits copying to and from standard devices, such as the keyboard and line printer. The device names (which are DOS reserved words and cannot be user filenames) for the keyboard "console," the printer connected to the serial port, and the printer connected to the parallel port are CON, AUX, and LPT1, respectively.

DOS COMMAND	RESULT
A>**COPY SALES*.CAL B:**	Files with names beginning with SALES have the extension CAL are copied to disk B and given the same name.
A>**COPY MEMO2.WP B:MEMO3.WP**	MEMO2.WP on disk A is copied to disk B and renamed MEMO3.WP
A>**COPY CON B:NOTE** ...keystrokes...**^Z**	The keystrokes following this command and up to the end-of-file character (an F6 [function key 6] or CTRL-Z) are copied to a newly-created file on disk B called NOTE. The end-of-file is displayed as "^Z". The actual copy operation is initiated by pressing ENTER after the end-of-file.
A>**COPY MEMO2.WP LPT1**	The file MEMO2.WP is printed on the parallel printer.

When learning to use DOS or any of the micro productivity tools, it is nice to have a knowledgeable friend (or instructor) who can help you over the rough spots.
(Courtesy of Unisys Corporation)

- **ERASE** or **DEL**. The *internal* ERASE or DEL command deletes the specified file(s) from disk storage. Use the ERASE or DEL command to remove unwanted files from a directory. ERASE and DEL cause identical results.

DOS COMMAND	RESULT
Å>**ERASE B:SALESQ1.CAL**	SALESQ1.CAL on disk B is deleted.
A>**ERASE MEMO∗.WP**	All files with names that begin with MEMO and have the extension WP are deleted from the active disk (A).

- **RENAME** or **REN**. The *internal* RENAME or REN command renames an existing file.

DOS COMMAND	RESULT
A>**RENAME B:IDEA.OUT** **THOUGHT.OUT**	The name of the file IDEA.OUT on disk B is changed to THOUGHT.OUT.

Output-related DOS Commands

- **TYPE**. The *internal* TYPE command displays any standard text file. The TYPE command is handy when you want a quick preview of the contents of a particular file.

DOS COMMAND	RESULT
A>**TYPE MEMO1.WP**	Displays the contents of MEMO1.WP on the monitor.

- **PRINT**. The *external* PRINT command causes the designated file to be printed.

DOS COMMAND	RESULT
A>**PRINT MEMO1.WP**	Prints the contents of MEMO1.WP on the printer.

- **CLS**. The *internal* CLS command "clears" the screen and repositions the DOS prompt in the upper left corner of the screen.
- **GRAPHICS**. The *external* GRAPHICS command enables the printing of graphics-mode displays. After you issue the GRAPHICS command, press SHIFT-PRTSC (print screen) to print a graphics-mode screen, such as a pie chart.

4–6   DOS KEYBOARD FUNCTIONS ─────────

DOS provides you with handy internal functions that can be invoked with a single keystroke or a keystroke combination.

- ⌷SHIFT⌷ - ⌷PRTSC⌷ (*print screen*). Press SHIFT-PRTSC to print what is currently being displayed on the screen. Use this keystroke combination whenever you want a hardcopy of the current screen.

MEMORY BITS

FREQUENTLY USED DOS COMMANDS

- Disks
  - FORMAT (E)
  - CHDSK (E)
  - DISKCOPY (E)
- Directories
  - DIR (I)
  - MD, MKD (I)
  - CD, CHDIR (I)
  - RD, RMDIR (I)
- Files
  - COPY (I)
  - ERASE, DEL (I)
  - RENAME, REN (I)
- Output
  - TYPE (I)
  - PRINT (E)
  - CLS (I)
  - GRAPHICS (E)
  - I = internal command
  - E = external command

■ CTRL - PRTSC (*printer echo*). Press CTRL-PRTSC to begin echo-
   ing, or repeating, on the printer what is displayed on the screen.
   Press CTRL-PRTSC again to discontinue printer echo mode. Use
   this function to get a line by line hardcopy of your interaction
   with the computer.

■ F1 and F3 (*repeat DOS command*). Press the F3 function key
   to invoke a command that causes the last-entered line to be repeated after the DOS prompt. Edit the line, if necessary, and
   press ENTER to execute the command. Press F1 to repeat the
   first character of the last-entered line. Press F1 again to repeat
   the second character, and so on.

■ CTRL - **S** (*pause screen*). Press CTRL-S to stop the scrolling of
   the text and press any key to continue. This pause screen function is often used in conjunction with the TYPE and DIR commands when the text cannot be displayed on a single screen.

■ CTRL - BREAK (*break*). Press CTRL-BREAK to terminate a program prematurely, that is, prior to a normal and orderly finish.

■ CTRL - ALT - DEL (*restart DOS*). Make sure the DOS disk is in
   the default disk drive. Simultaneously press CTRL-ALT, then
   press DEL to reload DOS to memory. Use this keystroke combination when the computer is already on or when you are running an applications program that has no orderly *exit* (leaving the
   program) to DOS. This procedure is sometimes referred to as a
   warm boot. The *cold boot* procedure involves turning on the
   computer with the DOS diskette in place.

This accountant has just pressed
CTRL-PRTSC (the print screen
command) on the keyboard of his
portable computer. This DOS
keyboard function causes what is
currently being displayed on the
screen to be printed. This micro is
somewhat unique in that the
printer, monitor, disk drives,
processor, keyboard, and mouse
are encased in the same physical
unit. The keyboard and mouse are
detached from the unit when not in
use.
(Photo courtesy of Hewlett-Packard Company)

The hands-on DOS tutorial that parallels this discussion illustrates the
use and application of DOS commands and functions. See "Hands-
On Tutorial 3: Working with DOS Commands."

4–7 BATCH FILES AND SELF-BOOTING PROGRAM DISKS

You may want to make one or all of your program diskettes to be
self booting; that is, DOS and an applications program are stored
on the same diskette. Self-booting program diskettes are timesavers
for frequent micro users. Without a self-booting program disk, loading
a word processing or spreadsheet package is a two step process: first,
boot the system with the DOS diskette and then replace the DOS
disk with the program disk and enter the program name. With a self-
booting program diskette, it is a one-step process: simply insert the
program diskette and turn on the system.

Batch Files.   **Batch files** are needed to create a self-booting program
diskette. A batch file is a user-created disk file that contains a list of
commands and programs (program filenames) that are to be executed
immediately following the loading of DOS to RAM. One way to create
a batch file is to use the COPY command to copy from CON (the

When this sales managers flips the power switch to "on," DOS and an application software package are loaded automatically to memory from the hard disk. To do this, he created an AUTOEXEC batch file.
(Courtesy of International Business Machines Corporation)

keyboard console) to a disk file; that is, key in the commands and store these commands on a disk file.

All batch filenames must have the extension BAT (for example, BATCHFIL.BAT). If you want to execute the commands and/or programs in BATCHFIL.BAT, a batch file on disk A, you simply key BATCHFIL at the A> prompt (the .BAT is optional on input). The commands and/or programs listed in BATCHFIL are executed in the order in which they appear. See the "Advanced and Special Features Tutorial" at the end of this chapter for creating and using batch files.

As soon as DOS is loaded to RAM, DOS searches for a special batch file called AUTOEXEC.BAT. If such a file exists, the commands and/or programs listed in AUTOEXEC are executed automatically. This special file makes the creation of self-booting program diskettes possible.

Creating a Self-Booting Program Diskette.   Creating a self-booting program diskette is a three step process.

1. *Format a blank diskette using the /S option.* Follow the normal procedure for formatting a new diskette, as given in the "DOS Commands" section of this chapter, but use the /S option.

   A>**FORMAT B:/S**

   This version of the FORMAT command formats a new disk in drive B. The /S option causes COMMAND.COM and other *hidden* DOS control files to be transferred from the DOS diskette in drive A to the newly formatted diskette. Of course, the hidden files and COMMAND.COM take up disk space; therefore, those applications programs that require all or almost all of a diskette's storage space cannot be made to be self-booting.

2. Insert your program diskette in drive A and use the COPY command to copy all program files to the specially formatted diskette.

   A>**COPY *.* B:*.***

3. Set up an AUTOEXEC.BAT batch file that contains the name of the program (the name you would enter at the A> prompt to run the program, for example, dbase). The "DOS Commands" section of this chapter explained how the COPY command can be used to create a text file on disk.

> **A>COPY CON B:AUTOEXEC.BAT**
> **DBASE ˆZ**

If your micro is not configured with an internal clock-calendar and you want to enter the date and time, you must place the DATE and TIME commands in the batch file.

4–8   USER-FRIENDLY DOS INTERFACES

Most applications software packages would be considered more user friendly than DOS. Nevertheless, we need to attain at least rudimentary DOS skills before we can effectively interface our microcomputer with the plethora of applications software packages available to us. It is ironic, but to use micros effectively, we must learn DOS first, before using the more user-friendly applications packages.

There are, however, programs that make DOS as user friendly as any other applications program. These programs are sometimes called "DOS shells" or "DOS helpers" and provide users with a *user-friendly interface* between DOS, applications software, and user files. The term **operating environment** is sometimes used to describe the use of a user-friendly DOS interface. Instead of entering DOS commands at the A> prompt, you interact with DOS by selecting options from pull-down menus or by identifying the appropriate symbolic icon (a file cabinet for file operations, for example).

These RAM-resident DOS interface software packages are accompanied by a variety of helpful RAM-resident programs. These include such programs as the on-line calendar, scratch pad, calculator, and clock.

These user-friendly DOS interfaces have effectively eliminated the need for users to memorize and enter the sometimes cryptic DOS commands. This user-friendly concept is being applied to future enhancements of personal computer operating systems. In fact, the IBM Operating System/2, the successor to IBM's ubiquitous PC-DOS, provides an operating environment for the IBM Personal System/2 series of computers.

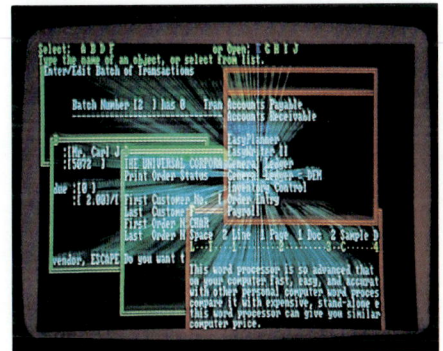

Windows enable users to view and work with several applications programs at the same time. Most of the new micro productivity software packages include windowing capabilities.
(Computer Associates International, Inc.)

SUMMARY OUTLINE AND IMPORTANT TERMS

4–1   THE DISK OPERATING SYSTEM (DOS).   The **operating system** is a family of systems software programs that monitors and controls all input/output and processing activities within a computer system. The COMMAND.COM program, which is always resident in RAM, loads other operating system and applications programs to RAM. Besides controlling the ongoing operation of a microcomputer system, DOS controls all input/output and handles the file and disk management duties.

Before you can use a microcomputer, you must **boot** the system; that is, load the operating system from disk storage into RAM.

4–2   RUNNING A SOFTWARE PACKAGE.   A system or DOS prompt is a signal to the user to enter a system command. To run a software package, you simply insert the diskette containing the software in the appropriate disk drive, close the disk drive door, then, and enter the name of the file that contains the applications software at the prompt.

4–3   FILES.   On a microcomputer, a **file** is related information stored to a disk (from memory) or retrieved from a disk (to memory) as a unit. The file specification includes the filename, the extension, and a reference to the appropriate disk drive. DOS commands that you issue apply to the active drive unless you state otherwise in the command.

When used in a filename.extension combination, the more commonly used **wildcard** character, the asterisk (∗), can provide a generic reference to a group of files on a particular **directory**. A directory is a list of the names of the files that are stored on a particular diskette or in a named area on a hard disk.

4–4   DIRECTORIES AND PATHS.   Users organize their files into a hierarchy or tree of directories and **subdirectories**. At the highest level of the hierarchy is the **root directory**. When working with files that are stored on a disk with a hierarchy of directories, you will need to specify the **path**. The path is the logical route that DOS must follow to locate the specified file.

4–5   DOS COMMANDS.   Internal DOS commands are memory resident, and external commands must be loaded to memory from the DOS disk. A summary of commonly used disk, directory, file, and output commands follows.

Disk   The **FORMAT** command prepares a new disk for use. The **CHKDSK** command displays a disk and RAM status report. The **DISKCOPY** command copies the entire contents of one diskette to another.

Directory   The **DIR** or directory command causes a list of the files on the active drive or default directory to be displayed on the monitor. The **MD** or **MKDIR** commands create a subdirectory on a specified disk. The **CD** or **CHDIR** commands change the current directory to the desired directory. The **RD** or **RMDIR** commands remove a subdirectory from a specified disk.

File   The **COPY** files command copies one or more files from or to the disk, directory, and/or device specified in the command. The **ERASE** or **DEL** command deletes the specified file(s) from disk storage. The **RENAME** or **REN** command renames an existing file.

Output   The **TYPE** command displays any standard text file. The **PRINT** command causes the designated file to be printed. The **CLS** command clears the screen and repositions the DOS prompt in the upper left corner of the screen. The **GRAPHICS** command enables the printing of graphics-mode displays.

4–6   DOS KEYBOARD FUNCTIONS.   The following DOS internal functions can be invoked with a single keystroke or a keystroke combination: **SHIFT-PRTSC** (print screen), **CTRL-PRTSC** (printer echo), **F1** and **F3** (repeat DOS command), **CTRL-S** (pause screen), **CTRL-BREAK** (break), and **CTRL-ALT-DEL** (restart DOS).

4–7   BATCH FILES AND SELF-BOOTING PROGRAM DISKS. Program diskettes can be made to be **self booting**. **Batch files**, that are needed to create a self-booting program diskette are user-created disk files that contain a list of commands and programs to be executed immediately following the loading of DOS to RAM.

When loaded, DOS searches for a special batch file called AUTOEXEC.BAT. If such a file exists, the commands and/or programs listed in AUTOEXEC are executed automatically.

4–8   USER-FRIENDLY DOS INTERFACES.   "DOS shells" or "DOS helpers" provide users with a user-friendly interface between DOS, applications software, and user files. The term **operating environment** is sometimes used to describe the use of a user-friendly DOS interface. RAM-resident DOS interface software packages are often accompanied by a variety of helpful RAM-resident programs, such as on-line calendar, scratch pad, calculator, and clock.

REVIEW EXERCISES

1.   What is meant by booting the system?

2.   Name two external and two internal DOS commands.

3.   Explain why the following could not be valid DOS filenames?
NAME.LAST   firstname   I/O   <filenm>.ext

4.   What are the major functions of a microcomputer operating system?

5.   List and describe one DOS command for each of these command categories: disk, directory, file, and output.

6.   What happens if you omit the filename in the target specification of a COPY file command?

7.   The files on the disk in the active drive contain word processing (WP) and database (DB) files.

LETTER1.WP	LETTER2.WP	INVENTORY.DB	DRAFT.WP
NAMEADDR.DB	REPORT.WP	BIO.WP	LETTER3.WP

What wildcard reference would refer to
(a) All files.
(b) Only word processing files.
(c) Only database files.
(d) Only LETTER word processing files.

8. Briefly describe what is meant by an operating environment.

9. Briefly describe the general procedure that a user at a two-diskette microcomputer would follow to run a word processing program and begin a session.

10. Just after DOS is loaded into a two-diskette micro, which directory is the active directory? Which would be the active directory on a micro with a hard disk?

11. Create three filenames that would be included within EXAMPLE*.*.

12. Describe circumstances that might encourage you to use the DOS pause screen (CTRL-S) function.

13. What makes batch files named AUTOEXEC.BAT unique?

SELF-TEST (by section)

4–1. (a) The name of the DOS program that is always resident in RAM during microcomputer operations is _____.

(b) A micro user must "kick the system" to load DOS to RAM prior to processing. (T/F)

4–2. DOS displays a system _____ to signal the user that it is ready to accept a system _____.

4–3. DOS.DOS is a legal DOS filename. (T/F)

4–4. The logical route that DOS would follow to locate a specified file is called a (a) road, (b) path, or (c) sidewalk.

4–5. (a) All user files are deleted from a diskette when the diskette is formatted. (T/F)

(b) The DOS command that clears the screen is _____.

4–6. Before initiating the warm boot procedure for loading DOS, the micro must be turned off. (T/F)

4–7. The first step in creating a self-booting program diskette is to copy COMMAND.COM and the DOS hidden files to the original program diskette. (T/F)

4–8. A user-friendly interface between DOS, the applications program, and user files is sometimes called an operating environment. (T/F)

Self-Test Answers.   **4–1 (a)**, COMMAND.COM; **(b)**, F; **4–2**, prompt, command; **4–3**, T; **4–4**, b; **4–5 (a)**, T; **(b)**, CLS; **4–6**, F; **4–7**, F; **4–8**, T.

HANDS-ON EXERCISES

1. Complete DOS Hands-On Tutorials 1 through 3 and the Advanced and Special Features Tutorial in the tutorials section of this chapter.

2. (a) Format a new or blank disk. After formatting is complete, examine the directory on your work disk to confirm that no files exist on the disk. Print the screen image.

(b) Clear the screen, then use the COPY CON command (see Hands-On Tutorial 3) to create the following text file on your work disk.

This is a "hands-on exercise" text file.

Name the file "one.txt" and store it on your newly formatted work disk. Confirm that one.txt is stored on your disk by displaying the contents of the file. Print the screen image and clear the screen.

(c) Create a duplicate copy of "one.txt" and call it "two.txt". Confirm that the copy was successful by examining the directory of your work disk.

(d) Rename "one.txt" as "three.txt". Confirm that only two files, two.txt and three.txt, are stored on the disk. Print the screen image.

(e) Use a wildcard file reference to delete both of the files on the work disk. Confirm that the files were deleted by examining the directory. Print the screen image and clear the screen.

3. (a) You will need two blank disks for this exercise. Use the DISKCOPY command to make a backup of a work disk that contains at least one file.

(b) With the printer on, activate the printer echo and display the directory for the backup diskette. Deactivate the printer echo.

(c) Use a newly formatted diskette to make another backup of the same work disk, but this time use the COPY command. (You can reformat the backup diskette used in [a].)

(d) With the printer on, activate the printer echo and display the directory for the backup diskette. Deactivate the printer echo.

(e) Compare the printed directories to ensure that the contents of the backup diskettes are the same.

(f) You used the DISKCOPY and COPY commands to accomplish the same task, but the function and purpose of the commands are very different. Describe these differences.

KEYSTROKE TUTORIALS IN THE *LAB MANUAL*

The *Lab Manual* that accompanies this text contains additional advanced DOS keystroke tutorials. The keystroke tutorials illustrate DOS commands that are not presented in the text.

DOS TUTORIAL

QUICK REFERENCE GUIDE
DOS

COMMANDS

CD or CHDIR	Change the default directory	C>CD JIM
CHKDSK *	Check status of disk	A>CHKDSK B:
CLS	Clears screen	A>CLS
COPY	Make copy of a file	A>COPY TEST1 B:
DIR	Directory of a disk	A>DIR
DISKCOPY *	Make copy of disk	A>DISKCOPY A: B:
ERASE or DEL	Delete a specified file	A>ERASE B:TEST1
FORMAT *	Format a disk	A>FORMAT B:
GRAPHICS *	Enable graphics-mode displays	A>GRAPHICS
MD or MKDIR	Make new subdirectory	C>MD \JIM\LOTUS
PRINT *	Send file to printer	A>PRINT TEST1
RD or RMDIR	Remove a directory	C>RD \JIM\LOTUS
RENAME or REN	Rename an existing file	A>RENAME B:TEST1 TEST2
TYPE	Display contents of file	A>TYPE TEST1

*-external commands

KEYBOARD FUNCTIONS

CTRL-ALT-DEL	Reset the system (warm boot)
CTRL-BREAK	Interrupt a program
CTRL-PRTSC	Echo what is printed on screen to the printer
CTRL-S	Stop the scrolling of the text
SHIFT-PRTSC	Print current screen to printer
F1	Display last-entered line one character at a time
F3	Display last-entered line
F6	Write CTRL-Z to end of batch file

COMMON EXTENSIONS

.BAK	Backup file
.BAT	Batch file
.COM	Command file
.EXE	Executable program file
.HLP	Help file
.$$$	Temporary or incorrectly stored file

HANDS-ON TUTORIAL 1: Loading DOS

KEYSTROKE CONVENTIONS IN INTERACTIVE TUTORIALS

Included in this text of microcomputer software are keystroke tutorials. These tutorials are designed to give you hands-on experience with DOS, WordPerfect, Lotus 1-2-3, SuperCalc4, dBASE III PLUS, The OUTLINER, Crosstalk XVi, and many other packages. For any given software package, as you complete one tutorial, proceed directly to the next. Keystroke conventions are followed in the presentation of the interactive sessions so that the keystroke presentations can be made more compact and easier to follow.

Standard Type, Boldface, Outlined Keys, and Italic

Portions of the interactive session that are displayed by the program are shown in standard type. User-entered data and text commands are shown in **boldface** type.

Enter new date (mm-dd-yy): **12-14-88** ↵

For the above, you would enter "12-14-88" in response to the prompt and press the ↵ or ENTER key.

Keystroke or keystroke combination commands are shown boxed. In-line instructions or clarifications that are not displayed on the screen in response to an input are shown in italics (e.g., *Yes*). Italicized instructions or clarifications that are not extensions of commands are enclosed in parentheses, for example (*see text in Figure S-1*).

ESC **A***ppearance* **U***nderline* → (*15 times*) ↵

For the above, you would press the escape (ESC) key, "A", "U", the right cursor control key 15 times, and ↵.

Summary of Keystroke Conventions

KEYSTROKE(S)	ACTION
↵	Press ENTER, RETURN, CR (carriage return)
← → ↑ ↓	Press the left, right, up, or down cursor control (arrow) key indicated.
F1	Press function key number 1 (or the number indicated). Boxed keys refer to particular keys (F5, ESC).
/**F**ile **S**ave	Press " /", then "F", then "S". Clarifications and instructions displayed by the program are in standard print.
ESC **E***nd* **Q***uit*	Press ESC, then "E", then "Q". Clarifications and instructions not displayed by the program are in italics.
CTRL - PRTSC	Press hyphenated keys simultaneously (press and hold CTRL, then press PRTSC).

General Format of the Margin Tutorials

HANDS-ON TUTORIAL #: Descriptive Title

Overview description of this tutorial, if needed.

■ Brief description of the current bullet activity followed by the keystroke depiction of the interactive session.

Enter new date (mm-dd-yy): **12-14-88** ↵

Follow-up clarification and additional remarks regarding commands and/or idiosyncracies of the package.

■ A sequence of bullet activities (see above) are continued until the tutorial is complete.

This tutorial focuses on those MS-DOS features that are fundamental to the use and application of productivity software. MS-DOS and PC-DOS (the IBM version of MS-DOS) are products of Microsoft Corporation.

■ With the power off, insert the DOS disk in disk drive A (usually the disk drive on the left or top if you have two drives) and close the door.

■ Turn on the monitor, the computer, and then the printer (if needed).

■ After a short period, a beep signals the end of the system check and DOS is loaded from disk to memory.

■ At the date prompt, enter the date in the month (mm), day (dd), year (yy) format.

Enter new date (mm-dd-yy): **12-14-88** ↵

The entry above is for December 14, 1988.

To omit the date entry, press ENTER after the prompt.

- At the time prompt, enter the time in the hours:minutes format.

    Enter new time: 13:35 ↵

To omit the time entry, press ENTER after the prompt.

- The DOS prompt indicates that the system is ready to receive user commands.

    A>

```
Current date is Tue  1-01-1980
Enter new date (mm-dd-yy): 9-15-89
Current time is  0:00:12.90
Enter new time? 9:00


The IBM Personal Computer DOS
Version 3.10 (C)Copyright International Business Machines Corp 1981, 1985
            (C)Copyright Microsoft Corp 1981, 1985

A>_
```

DOS display after the completion of Hands-On Tutorial 1.

HANDS-ON TUTORIAL 2: Running an Applications Program

Refer to this tutorial when you are ready to run an applications program.

- To run an applications program, load DOS and replace the DOS disk with the program disk. Enter the program name after the DOS prompt.

    For WordPerfect:

    A>**wp** ↵

    For The TWiN:

    A>**twin** ↵

For Lotus 1-2-3:

    A>**123** ↵

For dBASE III PLUS:

    A>**dbase** ↵

For The OUTLINER:

    A>**outliner** ↵

- Use this procedure to load other applications programs in preparation for use.

HANDS-ON TUTORIAL 3: Working with DOS Commands

For this tutorial you will need a DOS disk and two blank disks.

- Load DOS (if needed) and clear the screen.

    A>**cls** ↵

- With DOS in drive A, insert one of the blank disks in drive B. Format the blank disk in drive B. From now on, we will refer to this disk as data disk #1.

    A>**FORMAT B:** ↵
    Insert new diskette for drive B:
    and strike ENTER when ready ↵

DOS should reply with the message "Formatting . . ." Answer "N" (no) when asked if you want to format another disk.

    Format another (Y/N)?**N** ↵

- To complete the tutorial, we need a file to manipulate. A quick and dirty way to create a file on disk is to use the COPY command to copy whatever you enter via the keyboard to a disk file. Use COPY to create a file on disk B called TUTOR1.TXT. The device name for the keyboard (the source of the file) is CON: (for console keyboard). We will use this form of the COPY

command only to create this file. More conventional uses of COPY are seen later in this tutorial.

    A>**COPY CON: B:TUTOR1.TXT** ↵

Key in the following sentence exactly as it appears below. Press ENTER after "created", the period, and the ^Z. The ^Z (CTRL-Z) is an end-of-file marker that is displayed when you press F6.

    This one-sentence text file is created ↵
    and manipulated in this DOS tutorial. ↵
    [F6] **^Z** ↵

- Use DIR (directory) to obtain a list of the files on disk B.

    A>**DIR B:** ↵

TUTOR1.TXT is the only file on the newly formatted disk.

- Use TYPE to display and examine the contents of TUTOR1.TXT.

    A>**TYPE B:TUTOR1.TXT** ↵
    This one-sentence text file is created
    and manipulated in this DOS tutorial.

- Use COPY to create a duplicate file called TUTOR2.TXT on disk B. The source file is

```
A)dir b:

  Volume in drive B has no label
 Directory of  B:\

TUTOR1   TXT       79  9-15-89   9:04a
        1 File(s)    361472 bytes free

A)type b:tutor1.txt
This one-sentence text file is created
and manipulated in this DOS tutorial.

A)copy b:tutor1.txt b:tutor2.txt
        1 File(s) copied

A)dir b:

  Volume in drive B has no label
 Directory of  B:\

TUTOR1   TXT       79  9-15-89   9:04a
TUTOR2   TXT       79  9-15-89   9:04a
        2 File(s)    360448 bytes free

A)_
```

DOS display just prior to the DISKCOPY operation in the Hands-On Tutorial 3.

listed first and the target file is second.

A>**COPY B:TUTOR1.TXT B:TUTOR2.TXT** ↵

Use DIR to confirm that you have two files on disk B.

A>**DIR B:** ↵

■ Now use DISKCOPY to copy the entire contents of data disk #1, now in drive B, to another blank disk. To do this you must remove, switch, and insert disks. But first, issue the external DISKCOPY command while the DOS disk is in drive A. Like files, the source disk is entered first and the target disk is second.

A>**DISKCOPY A: B:** ↵
Insert SOURCE diskette in drive A:
Insert TARGET diskette in drive B:

It is a common practice to perform a diskcopy operation with the source disk in drive A and the target disk in drive B. First, remove both the DOS disk and data disk #1. Insert data disk #1 (the source disk) in drive A and the second blank disk (the target disk) in drive B. Press any key to perform the diskcopy.

Press any key when ready . . . ↵

DOS should reply with the message "Copying . . ."

Copy another diskette (Y/N)?**N**

The target disk is automatically formatted if it is a new disk. After diskcopy is complete you will be asked to insert the DOS disk (the disk with COMMAND.COM). Remove the data disk #1 from drive A and insert the DOS disk in drive A.

Insert disk with \COMMAND.COM in drive A and strike any key when ready ↵

After inserting DOS, striking a key, and getting the A> prompt, remove the DOS disk and reinsert data disk #1. This disk swapping is necessary for external system commands such as DISKCOPY.

■ You now have two disks with exactly the same contents: two files named TUTOR1.TXT and TUTOR2.TXT. Use ERASE or DEL to delete TUTOR1.TXT from data disk #1 in drive A.

A>**ERASE TUTOR1.TXT** ↵

■ Use RENAME to change the name of the remaining file on data disk #1 from TUTOR2.TXT to TUTOR3.TXT.

A>**RENAME TUTOR2.TXT TUTOR3.TXT** ↵

Since both files are on the disk in drive A and the active drive is A, the drive specifier (A:) is not required.

■ Use DIR (directory) to confirm that you now have one file on data disk #1 in drive A (TUTOR3.TXT) and two files on data disk #2 in drive B (TUTOR1.TXT and TUTOR2.TXT).

A>**DIR** ↵

Press F3 to repeat the last DOS command, then add "B:".

A>⎡F3⎤DIR **B:** ↵

■ If your system includes a printer, print the display of the current screen.

⎡SHIFT⎤-⎡PRTSC⎤

Once you have completed the session, remove all diskettes and turn off the monitor, the printer (if used), and the computer.

ADVANCED AND SPECIAL FEATURES TUTORIAL: DOS ────────────

In this advanced DOS tutorial the following skills are introduced: creating a file using EDLIN (the DOS line editor); modifying a file using EDLIN; and using DOS batch files.

CREATING A FILE USING EDLIN

Create a text file using EDLIN, the line editor supplied with MS-DOS and PC-DOS.

- Boot the system (See Hands-On Tutorial 1).
- Insert your data diskette in drive B.
- Begin an EDLIN session and identify the file to be edited.

    A>**edlin b:practice.txt** ↵

If EDLIN does not find the file specified in the command line, it will create a new file with the filename you specified. The * indicates that EDLIN is ready to accept your input.

- Enter insert-line mode and enter the following lines of text.

    *i*insert-line mode* ↵
    1:***This is a file to be used in the advanced** ↵
    2:***DOS tutorial. It is a small file, but it will** ↵
    3:***suffice for demonstration purposes.** ↵
    4:* CTRL -**C** (*exit insert-line mode*)

- List the lines that you have entered into the file.

    *i*list* ↵

- Save the lines you have entered and exit EDLIN. EDLIN files are saved as ASCII files.

    *e*end and save* ↵

MODIFYING A FILE USING EDLIN

- Begin an EDLIN session and identify the file to be edited.

    A>**edlin b:practice.txt** ↵

- List the lines that are in the file.

    *l ↵

- Edit the first line to insert the word "text" before the word "file".

    *1 (*edit line 1*) ↵
    *1:*This is a file to be used in the advanced
    1:
    * F1 (*10 times—recreates the line one character at a time*)
    * INS (*toggle to insert mode*)
    *1:*This is a **text** SPACE F3 (*recreates the remainder of the line*) ↵

    Line 1 should now read

    This is a text file to be used in the advanced

- Create a duplicate copy of lines 1 through 3, beginning at line 4.

    *1,3 (*lines 1 through 3*), **4c**opy to line 4 ↵

- List the lines that are now in the file.

    *l ↵

- Insert a line of text before line 4 and exit the insert-line mode.

    *4i ↵
    4:***This sentence is in the middle of the text file.** ↵
    5: CTRL -**C**

- List the lines that are now in the file.

    *l ↵

- Replace all occurrences of the word "small" with "little".

    *1,7r**eplace**small F6 ^Zlittle ↵

    Your line should look like this

    *1,7rsmall^Zlittle

- List the lines that are now in the file.

    *l ↵

- Delete the first four lines of the file.

    *1,4d*elete* ↵

- List the lines that are now in the file.

    *l ↵

- Save the lines you have entered and exit EDLIN.

    *e ↵

DOS display at the completion of the section on "Modifying a File Using Edlin" in the Advanced and Special Features Tutorial: DOS.

USING DOS BATCH FILES

Batch files are files that contain DOS commands and have a .BAT filename extension. These files are executed by entering the name of the file without the extension at the DOS prompt. The result is the same as if you had manually entered each of the DOS commands in the batch file.

You will need a work disk and a newly formatted disk for this activity.

■ Boot the system (see Hands-On Tutorial 1).

■ Use EDLIN to create an ASCII batch file called "disk.bat". After creating the file, get into insert-line mode to enter the following comments and DOS commands.

```
*A>edlin b:disk.bat ↵
*i ↵
    *1:*echo off ↵
    *2:*echo This is an example batch file that
       will copy all ↵
    *3:*echo files from the disk in drive A to the
       disk in ↵
    *4:*echo drive B, and then display a directory
       of the files ↵
    *5:*echo on the disk in drive B. ↵
    *6:*echo Insert a newly formatted diskette in
       drive B: ↵
    *7:*pause ↵
    *8:*copy *.* b: ↵
    *9:*echo Here is a directory of the new
       disk: ↵
   *10:*dir b:/p ↵
   *11:* CTRL -C
```

■ After entering the above comments and DOS commands, save "disk.bat" on your work disk in drive B.

```
*e ↵
A> .
```

■ Remove your work diskette from drive B and insert it in drive A. Insert the newly formatted disk in drive B. Execute the batch file.

```
A>disk ↵
A>echo off
This is an example batch file that will copy all
files from the disk in drive A to the disk in
drive B, and then display a directory of the files
on the disk in drive B.
Insert a newly formatted diskette in drive B:
Strike a key when ready . . .
(insert a formatted disk in drive B:) ↵
(files are copied)
Here is a directory of the new disk:

Volume in drive B has no label
Directory of B:\

(disk directory is displayed here)

n File(s) n bytes free

A>
```

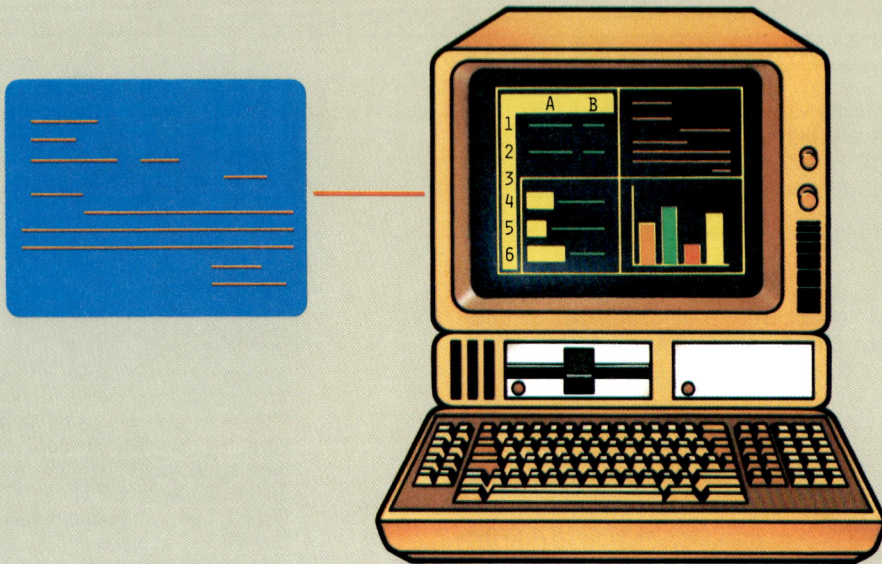

PART

III

MICROCOMPUTER PRODUCTIVITY SOFTWARE

Word Processing Concepts

CHAPTER 5

STUDENT LEARNING OBJECTIVES

- To describe the function and purpose of word processing software.
- To discuss word processing concepts associated with formatting a document, entering and editing text, block operations, and search and replace operations.
- To summarize word processing features that enhance the appearance and readability of a document.
- To explain word processing file management considerations and capabilities.
- To list common options for printing a document.
- To discuss advanced word processing features.
- To identify and describe add-on capabilities for word processing software packages.
- To identify applications for word processing software.

5-1 WORD PROCESSING _____

The Function of Word Processing

Word processing is using the computer to enter, store, manipulate, and print text for letters, reports, books, and so on. Once you have used word processing, you will probably wonder (like a million others before you) how in the world you ever survived without it!

Word processing, now the number one application for microcomputers, has virtually eliminated the need for opaque correction fluid and the need to rekey revised letters and reports. Revising a hard copy is time consuming and cumbersome, but revising the same text that is in an electronic format is quick and easy. You simply make corrections and revisions to the computer-based text before the document is displayed or printed in final form. Beginning a word processing session is as simple as booting DOS and loading the word processing software.

Categories of Word Processing Packages: Menu Driven and Command Driven

Word processing packages are generally categorized by the manner in which the user interacts with the system. In **menu-driven word processing packages**, the user interacts with the software by selecting options from a hierarchy of menus. In **command-driven word processing packages**, the user interacts with the software by *embedding* commands within the text of the document. For example, if you were using menu-driven software and wanted the output to be double spaced you would select the "double space" option in the output description menu. To double space an output document with a command-driven system you might key in an embedded command like ".si 2" (for

In 1982, the editors at *Time* chose the computer to be *Time's* "Man of the Year" because they felt it would change the way people live. Indeed it has. For example, the availability of personal computers and word processing software have redefined the way we write.
(Photo courtesy of Hewlett-Packard Company)

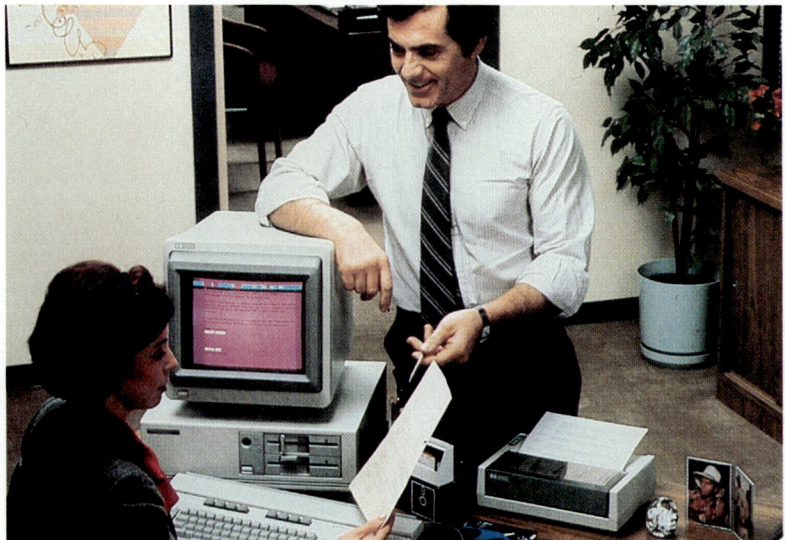

spacing interval equals double space) at the start of the document. In command-driven word processing systems, all lines that begin with a . (a period), called *dot commands*, signal the program to interpret these lines as commands.

There are, of course, advantages and disadvantages to each of the two kinds of user interfaces. Most would say that the more popular menu-driven systems are easier to learn and more user friendly. However, this user friendliness is at the expense of interactive efficiency. Most menu-driven systems are "what you see is what you get" or **WYSIWYG** (pronounced WIZ-e-wig); that is, at any given point in a word processing session, *what you see* displayed on the screen is very similar in appearance to *what you get* when the document is printed. The display is not exact because some print features, such as underlining and proportionately spaced print, cannot be displayed on the monitor.

The word "powerful" is often associated with command-driven word processing systems. As a rule, command-driven systems are preferred by sophisticated users who need expanded capabilities or power. Such systems are more difficult to learn because the user must learn scores, even hundreds, of commands. However, once a user becomes proficient with a command-driven system, system interaction is extremely efficient. Because of the embedded commands, what you see is on the monitor is *not* what you get when the document is printed. However, command-driven word processing packages usually have a *preview* feature that permits you to format and display the document on the monitor as it would appear when printed.

The word processing discussion that follows is oriented toward menu-driven word processing systems. However, the concepts presented are equally applicable to command-driven systems. See "Hands-on Tutorial 4: Using Word Processing Software" in the next chapter.

At this company, the public relations department puts out a bi-monthly newsletter. They use WYSIWYG word processing software to create the two-column format for the newsletter. (AST Research Inc.)

5–2   CREATING A DOCUMENT

Formatting a Document

Before you begin keying in the text of a document (for example, a letter or report), it is always a good idea to *format* the document. When you format a document, you are describing the size of the print page and how you want the document to look when it is printed. To format the document, you either accept the system default settings or enter new settings for the following elements:

- *Left and right margins*. The default settings for left and right margins are often one inch or 10 character positions for pica type. The blank space between the left edge of the paper and the beginning of the lines of print is known as the **page offset**.

- *Top and bottom margins*. The default settings for top and bottom margins are often one inch or six line spaces for standard vertical spacing.

- *Tabs*. The tab settings represent the character positions to which

Word processing is a popular application on both microcomputers and mainframe computers. This secretary's workstation is one of a 150 workstations that are linked to the company's mainframe.
(Photo courtesy of Hewlett-Packard Company)

Vendors must assume that any micro they make and sell will be used extensively. It is not unusual for the keystroke count to reach one million a month on micros that are used primarily for word processing; therefore, keyboards must be built for durability. In the photo, a keyboard in production is put through its paces by a robotic tester.
(Courtesy of International Business Machines Corporation)

the cursor will move when you press the TAB key. For a given line, the cursor will be positioned at the first setting (e.g., column 6) the first time you press TAB and at the second setting (e.g., column 11) the second time, and so on. The default TAB settings are often preset at 5-, 6-, 7-, or 8-position intervals.

- *Vertical or line spacing.* The default vertical line spacing is usually six lines per inch. Some printers, however, print only at six lines per inch and cannot accept other settings. Double spacing results in three printed lines per inch and triple spacing produces two printed lines per inch.

- *Horizontal or character spacing.* The default horizontal spacing is usually 10 characters per inch. Horizontal spacing is also referred to as the **pitch**. Most printers can print at 10 (pica) and 12 (elite) characters per inch. Some printers also have the capability to print at lower pitches (5 and 6 per inch) and at higher pitches (15 and 20 per inch). **Proportional spacing** is an option on many printers. In proportional spacing, the spacing between characters remains relatively constant. For example, characters like m take up proportionately more space than characters like i.

- *Paper size.* The default output document size is almost always $8\frac{1}{2}$ by 11 inches.

Depending on the software package, some or all of these specifications are made in a **layout line**. At a minimum, the layout line would graphically illustrate the settings for the *left* and *right margins* and the *tab settings* with appropriately positioned indicators (an L, an R, and Ts). For example, a layout line with the tabs set at 5-position intervals might look like this.

```
L----T----T----T----T----T----T----T----T----T----T---R
```

Generally, you can have as many layout lines as you want in a single document. Text is printed according to specifications in the most recent layout line until another layout line is defined.

You must also specify the size of the output document, then set margins for the top and bottom of the text. See "Hands-on Tutorial 5: Creating and Formatting a Document."

Entering Text

Replace and Insert Mode.   Text is entered in **replace mode** or **insert mode**. When in replace mode, the character that you enter *overstrikes* the character at the cursor position. For example, suppose that you typed the word "the" but you wanted to type "and". To make the correction in replace mode, you would position the cursor at the t and type a n d, thereby replacing "the" with "and".

On most word processing systems you toggle or switch between replace and insert mode by pressing a key. When in insert mode, you can enter *additional* text. Let's use a memo written by George Brooks, the Northern Regional Sales Manager for Zimco Enterprises, to illustrate the effects of insert mode data entry. George often uses word processing to generate memos to his staff. The first draft of one of George's memos is shown in Figure 5–1. George wanted to emphasize that an upcoming meeting was to be on Thursday, so he decided to insert "See you Thursday! " just before the last sentence. To do this, he selected the insert mode, placed the cursor on the W in "We'll", and entered "See you Thursday! " (see Figure 5–2).

Word Wrap.   On most word processing packages, text that extends past the defined margins automatically *wraps around* to the next line. That is, words that are pushed past the right margin are moved into the next line, and so on, to the end of the paragraph. This capability is known as **word wrap**. In Figures 5–1 and 5–2, compare how the words "conference room." (in the last sentence) are wrapped around

FIGURE 5–1
Word Processing: Memorandum
This first-draft memo is revised for illustrative purposes in Figures 5–2 through 5–6.

```
To:     Field Sales Staff
From:   G. Brooks, Northern Sales Manager
Re:     Weekly Briefing Session

     The Sales Department's weekly briefing session will be
held at 9:00 a.m. this Thursday.  Last month's sales figures
and new sales strategies for the Tegler and Qwert will be
discussed.  We'll meet in the second floor conference room.
```

FIGURE 5–2
Word Processing: Insert Mode
This memo is the result of the sentence "See you Thursday! " being inserted before the last sentence of the memo of Figure 5–1. Notice how the text wraps around to make room for the addition of a sentence.

```
To:     Field Sales Staff
From:   G. Brooks, Northern Sales Manager
Re:     Weekly Briefing Session

     The Sales Department's weekly briefing session will be
held at 9:00 a.m. this Thursday.  Last month's sales figures
and new sales strategies for the Tegler and Qwert will be
discussed.  See you Thursday!  We'll meet in the second floor
conference room.
```

to the next line when "See you Thursday! " is inserted. On some packages, you must *reformat* the document if you wish to see the document within the predefined margins.

To end a paragraph and begin another, press ENTER. Whenever you press ENTER you insert a **hard carriage return** in your document. Most word processing systems denote a hard carriage return by displaying a special character, sometimes a solid arrow. When "See you Thursday! " is inserted, the word wrap is only to the next hard carriage return.

The word processing software automatically inserts **soft carriage returns**. These soft carriage returns are placed after the last full word that is within the right margin in all but the last line in a paragraph. For example, in the memo of Figure 5–1, invisible soft carriage returns are automatically placed after "be", "figures", "be", and "room." After the insertion of "See you Thursday! " in Figure 5–2, the paragraph is automatically reformatted to fit within the prescribed margins. In reformatting the memo, the soft carriage return after "room" is removed and another soft carriage return is inserted after "floor". The insertion and deletion of software carriage returns is *transparent* to the end user; that is, it is done automatically without any action on the part of the user.

Full-Screen Editing. Word processing permits *full-screen editing*. That is, you can move the cursor to any position in the document to insert or replace text. You can browse through a multiscreen document by *scrolling* a line at a time or a "page" (a screen) at a time. You can edit any part of any screen.

Text Entry Summarized. When you enter text, *press the ENTER key only when you wish to begin a new line of text*. As you enter text in replace mode, the computer automatically moves the cursor to the next line. In insert mode, the computer manipulates the text such that it wraps around to the next hard carriage return, usually the end of a paragraph. See "Hands-on Tutorial 6: Entering and Adding Text."

5–3 BLOCK OPERATIONS

The *block* operations are among the handiest of word processing features. They are the block *move*, the block *copy*, and the block *delete* commands. These commands are the electronic equivalent of "cut and paste."

Moving Blocks. With the *move block* feature, you can select a block of text (a word, a sentence, a paragraph, a section of a report, or as much contiguous text as you desire) and move it to another portion of the document. To do this, follow these steps.

1. Issue the move command (select the "move" menu option or press the "move" function key).

At many companies, all office workers, including executives, are trained to use word processing. Executives at this company save time and money by using word processing to edit their reports. They find this approach more effective than having a secretary key in their red-pencil revisions from a hard copy.
(AST Research Inc.)

2. Indicate the start and end positions of the block of text to be moved (*mark* the text).

3. Move the cursor to the destination location (where the text is to be moved).

4. Press the ENTER (or the appropriate function key) to complete the move operation.

At the end of the move procedure, the marked block of text is moved to the location that you designate, and the original is deleted. The text is adjusted accordingly.

The following example demonstrates the procedure for marking and moving a block of text. After reading over the memo (of Figure 5–2), George decided to edit his memo to the field staff to make it more readable. He did this by moving the last sentence from the end of the memo to just after the first sentence. To perform this block move operation, he first selected the move option (a function key on his word processing system) and marked the beginning (W in "We'll") and end (the position following the . at end of paragraph) of the block. On most word processing systems, the portions of text that are marked for a block operation are usually displayed in *reverse video* (see Figure 5–3). After marking the block, George then positioned the cursor at the destination location (just after the first sentence) and pressed the appropriate key (a function key) to complete the operation (see Figure 5–4).

Copying Blocks.   The *copy block* command works similarly to the move block command, except that the text block you select is copied to the location that you designate. To perform a copy operation, follow these steps:

1. Issue the copy command (select the "copy" menu option or press the "copy" function key).

FIGURE 5–3
Word Processing: Marking Text for a Block Operation
The last sentence of the memo of Figure 5–2 is marked to be moved.

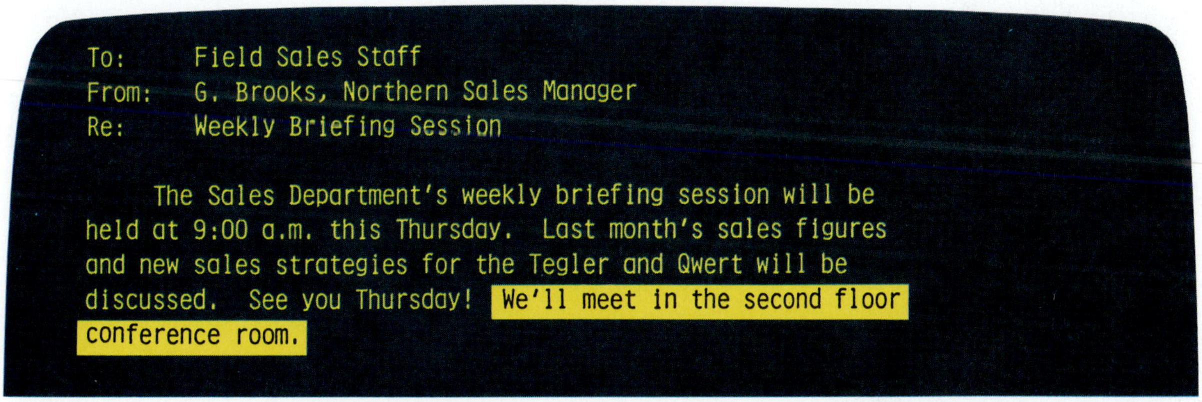

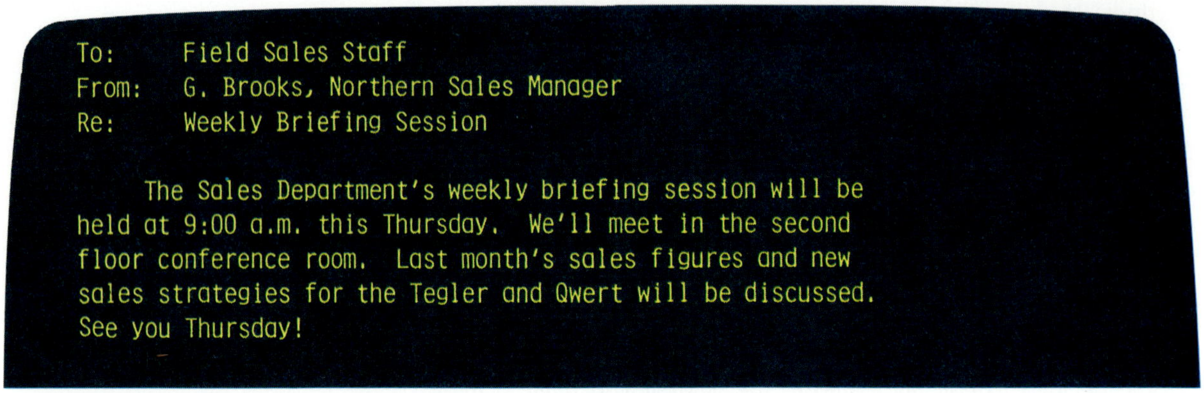

```
To:     Field Sales Staff
From:   G. Brooks, Northern Sales Manager
Re:     Weekly Briefing Session

    The Sales Department's weekly briefing session will be
held at 9:00 a.m. this Thursday.  We'll meet in the second
floor conference room.  Last month's sales figures and new
sales strategies for the Tegler and Qwert will be discussed.
See you Thursday!
```

FIGURE 5–4
Word Processing: Move Text
This memo is the result of the marked block in Figure 5–3 being moved to
a position following the first sentence.

2. Indicate the start and end positions of the block of text to be copied (*mark* the text).
3. Move the cursor to the destination location (where the copied text is to be placed).
4. Press the ENTER (or the appropriate function key) to complete the copy operation.

At the completion of the operation, two exact copies of the text are present in the document.

Deleting Blocks.   The *delete block* command works similarly to the the move and copy block commands. To perform a delete operation, follow these steps:

1. Issue the delete command (select the "delete" menu option or press the "delete" function key).
2. Indicate the start and end positions of the block of text to be deleted (*mark* the text).
3. Press the ENTER (or the appropriate function key) to complete the delete operation.

Of the three block commands, move, copy, and delete, the delete command is the most dangerous. If you make an error when performing a move or copy block operation, the marked text is still in the document. However, if you accidentally delete the wrong block of text, that text is removed permanently from the document unless your word processor has an *undo* command. When you issue an undo command, the last line (or block) of text that was added to the undo stack (text that has been deleted) is retrieved from intermediate buffer area in memory and restored to the document. Take special care when performing delete operations because word processing packages without the undo capability are unforgiving when you accidentally delete a block of text. See "Hands-On Tutorial 7: Moving Text."

5–4   THE SEARCH FEATURES _____

Just as George Brooks was about to print his memo (Figure 5–4), he learned that an important client was coming to town on Thursday, so he decided to switch the meeting from Thursday to Friday. He can make the necessary revisions to the memo by using any of several word processing features. One option is to use the *search* or *find* feature. This feature permits George to search through the entire document and identify all occurrences of a particular character string. For example, if George wanted to search for all occurrences of "Thursday" in his memo of Figure 5–4, he would simply initiate the search command and type in the desired *search string*, "Thursday" in this example. The cursor is immediately positioned at the first occurrence of the character string "Thursday" so he can easily edit the text to include the new meeting day. From there, he can "find" other occurrences of "Thursday" by pressing the appropriate key.

As an alternative approach to making the Thursday-to-Friday change, George could use the *search and replace* feature. This feature enables George to selectively replace occurrences of "Thursday" (the search string) in his memo with "Friday" (the replacement string). Since he knows that he wants *all* occurrences of "Thursday" to be replaced by "Friday", he performs a *global search and replace* (see Figure 5–5).

FIGURE 5–5
Word Processing: Search and Replace
With the search and replace command, the two occurrences of "Thursday" in Figure 5–4 are located and replaced automatically (option A) with "Friday",

```
To:        Field Sales Staff
From:      G. Brooks, Northern Sales Manager
Re:        Weekly Briefing Session

     The Sales Department's weekly briefing session will be
held at 9:00 a.m. this Friday.  We'll meet in the second floor
conference room.  Last month's sales figures and new sales
strategies for the Tegler and Qwert will be discussed.  See you
Friday!
------------------------------------------------------------
Search for:  Thursday
Replace with:  Friday
Manual or Automatic (M/A): A
Number of replacements:  2
```

Since the global search and replace command automatically replaces occurrences of the search string with the replacement string throughout the entire document, you should check your work carefully before selecting the global option. For example, if you accidentally replaced all commas with periods in a long report, you would have to read through the entire report to identify and then change the erroneous periods back to commas. See "Hands-on Tutorial 8: Search and Replace."

5–5   FEATURES THAT ENHANCE APPEARANCE AND READABILITY

George used several commonly-used word processing features to enhance the appearance and readability of his memo before distributing it to his staff.

Centering a Line of Text.   George decided to enter the word "MEMORANDUM" at the top of his memo and use the *automatic centering* feature to position it such that it is equally spaced between the left and right margin. On his word processing system, all he has to do to center whatever is on a particular line is to move the cursor to that line and press the "center" function key. The rest is automatic (see Figure 5–6).

Emphasizing Text with Boldface Type and Underlining.   Word processing provides the facility to *boldface* and/or *underline* parts of the text for emphasis. Like block operations, you must first mark the text to be underlined or boldfaced. In the memo of Figure 5–6a, the word "MEMORANDUM" is marked at the beginning and end with a reverse video b. The marked text appears in boldface print on output (see Figure 5–7). The reverse video u before and after the sentence "See you Friday!" (see Figure 5–6a) causes it to be underlined on output (see Figure 5–7).

Some word processing systems display text that is to be in boldface type or underlined on output in reverse video. The distinction can be made by displaying the text in different colors on color monitors or in shades of gray on monochrome monitors (see Figure 5–6b). Systems with high-resolution monitors permit text to be displayed in boldface and underlined directly on the display screen (see Figure 5–6c).

Right and Left Justification.   To enhance the appearance of a document, some people like to *justify* (make even) both the left margin (*flush left*) and the right margin (*flush right*), like the print in newspapers and this book. The default justification for most word processing packages is to justified left and ragged right (lines of uneven length at the right margin). When you select the "justify" option, the word processing software produces even margins on both sides of the output document by adding small spaces between characters and words in a line. George issued the "justify" command to produce the memo of Figure 5–7.

The memo of Figure 5–6 is displayed as it was prepared by two popular word processing packages: WordPerfect (WordPerfect Corporation) and Webster's NewWorld Writer (Simon and Schuster). Hands-on tutorials for these and other word processing packages are contained in Chapter 6.

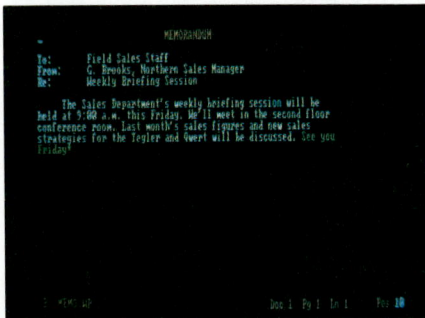

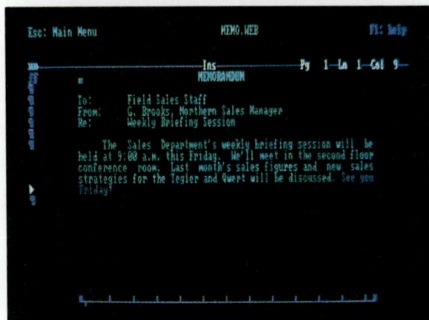

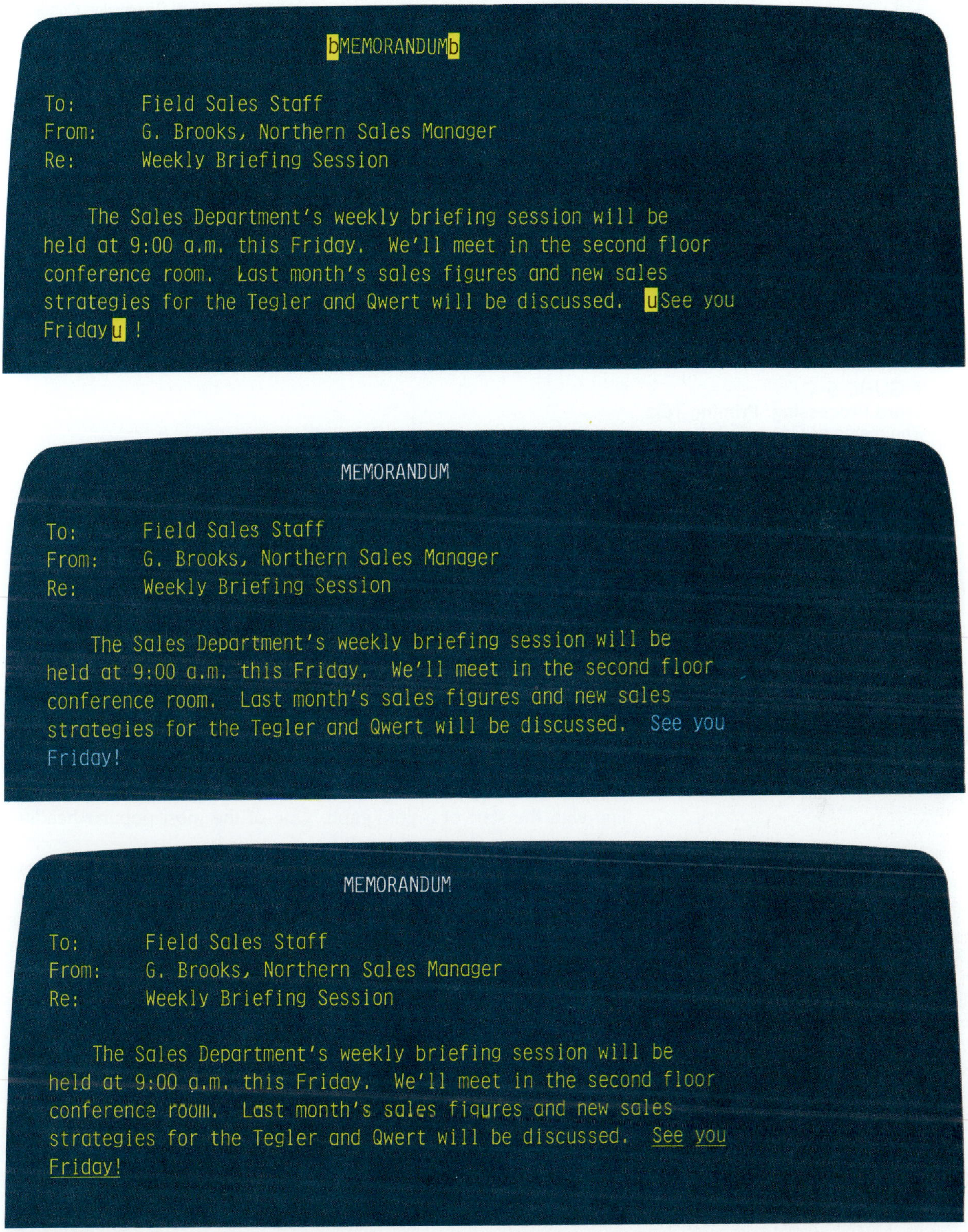

bMEMORANDUMb

To: Field Sales Staff
From: G. Brooks, Northern Sales Manager
Re: Weekly Briefing Session

    The Sales Department's weekly briefing session will be
held at 9:00 a.m. this Friday. We'll meet in the second floor
conference room. Last month's sales figures and new sales
strategies for the Tegler and Qwert will be discussed. uSee you
Fridayu !

MEMORANDUM

To: Field Sales Staff
From: G. Brooks, Northern Sales Manager
Re: Weekly Briefing Session

    The Sales Department's weekly briefing session will be
held at 9:00 a.m. this Friday. We'll meet in the second floor
conference room. Last month's sales figures and new sales
strategies for the Tegler and Qwert will be discussed. See you
Friday!

MEMORANDUM

To: Field Sales Staff
From: G. Brooks, Northern Sales Manager
Re: Weekly Briefing Session

    The Sales Department's weekly briefing session will be
held at 9:00 a.m. this Friday. We'll meet in the second floor
conference room. Last month's sales figures and new sales
strategies for the Tegler and Qwert will be discussed. See you
Friday!

FIGURE 5–6
Word Processing: Boldface and Underline
Text to be in boldface type or underlined is displayed differently,
depending on the word processing system and the color or resolution of
the monitor.

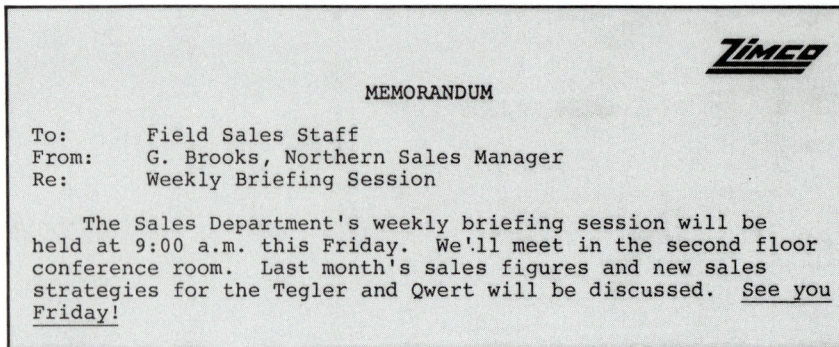

```
                                                              Zimco
                        MEMORANDUM

To:       Field Sales Staff
From:     G. Brooks, Northern Sales Manager
Re:       Weekly Briefing Session

   The Sales Department's weekly briefing session will be
held at 9:00 a.m. this Friday.  We'll meet in the second floor
conference room.  Last month's sales figures and new sales
strategies for the Tegler and Qwert will be discussed.  See you
Friday!
```

FIGURE 5–7
Word Processing: Printing Text
The memo of Figure 5–6 is printed on letterhead paper.

See "Hands-on Tutorial 9: Centering, Boldfacing, Underlining, and Justifying Text."

George right justifies all of his text documents except his personal letters. He, like the majority of word processing users, believes that the ragged right option makes the letter appear more personal and not so much a product of automation.

Creating Headings in Word Processing Documents.   The readability of any document in excess of a page and a half in length can be improved with the addition of judiciously-placed headings and subheadings. This is especially true of reports. The best way to create headings is to use various combinations of upper and lower case letters, boldface type, underlining, centering, justification, and running the heading in line with the start of a paragraph. One of the most popular heading combinations is illustrated below.

Level one and two headings are normally separated from the text by a blank line.

Some word processing systems allow users to mark headings as first, second, third, and fourth level headings so that on output the headings are automatically numbered to show subordination of headings (1, 1.1, 1.1.1, 1.1.2, 1.2, 1.3, and so on).

LEVEL 1:   BOLDFACE—UPPER CASE—CENTERED

Level 2:   Boldface—Upper & Lower (U & L) Case—Left Justified

Level 3:   Boldface—U & L Case—Left Justified—In Line. The third-level heading is inserted in line at the start of the first line of a paragraph.

Level 4:   Underlined—U & L Case—Left Justified—In Line. Like the third-level heading, the fourth-level heading is inserted at the start of the first line of a paragraph.

Indentation.   In creating the memo of Figure 5–7, George Brooks used many, but not all of the features that enhance appearance and readability. These and other word processing features are illustrated in Figure 5–8. One popular word processing feature permits you to *indent* a line or a block of text. The indentation feature is often used to set a line or block of text apart from the running text. For example, in Figure 5–8 a quote from a book is indented from both the left and right margins. The indentation of a block of text on most word processing systems is a four step process.

FIGURE 5–8
Word Processing:
Features Overview
Many of the more common capabilities of word processing software are illustrated in this example printout of a text file.

Left header label	**Tips**	Word Processing	Right header label

CHOOSING WORD PROCESSING SOFTWARE → Centered heading

Block indenting →
"Word processing is using the computer to enter, store, manipulate, and print text in letters, reports, books, and so on. Once you have used word processing, you will probably wonder (like a million others before you) how in the world you ever survived without it!"* → Hyphenation / Footnote marker

Paragraph indenting →
As more word processing packages come on the market, choosing the right software can become very confusing. Nevertheless, there is probably a word processing package that will serve your needs. As you begin looking, ask yourself these questions:

Numbered list →
1. What <u>types</u> <u>of</u> <u>documents</u> am I now producing or planning to produce? → Underline

2. What types of <u>features</u> do I need and want?

Boldface →
Documents types can range from **simple letters** and **memos** to **proposals, reports, legal documents, books, newsletters, scientific papers, form letters,** and so on. The point is, match the features you need with the features in the software package. For example, if you write articles that require references, you will need the **footnoting** feature; if you develop a newsletter, having the **multicolumn** layout feature would be handy; and if you send "personalized" form letters, the **mail-merge** feature is a necessity.
What you can do with word processing is limited only by your imagination and willingness to learn the system. Good luck in your computer-assisted writing adventure! → Right justification

Footnoting →
* Long, Larry, <u>Computers</u> <u>in</u> <u>Business</u> (Englewood Cliffs, NJ: Prentice-Hall, Inc. 1987).

Pagination →   - 1 -

1. Move the cursor to the beginning of the text to be indented. All text between the cursor and the next hard carriage return (ENTER) will be indented according to your specifications.

2. Select the "indent" option from the appropriate menu.

3. When prompted, enter the number of spaces that the block is to be indented from the left margin. If your word processing system permits indentation from the right margin as well (as shown in Figure 5–8), enter the number of spaces from the right margin that the text line should stop.

Headers, Footers, and Pagination.   Most word processing software packages have the capability to print automatically *headers*, *footers*, and/or *page numbers* (**pagination**) on each page of a document. George Brooks usually repeats the report title at the top of each page (header) and the company name at the bottom of each page (footer), and he numbers each page at the bottom. Headers, footers, and page numbers are separated from the running text by at least one blank line.

The procedure for adding headers and/or footers to a document is straightforward.

1. Select the header or footer option from the appropriate menu.

2. Enter the text to be added to each page (for example, "Annual Sales Summary Report", "Zimco Enterprises", "Chapter 1").

3. Designate whether the header or footer is to be left justified, centered, or right justified. On some word processing systems, you can select an option that causes the printing of the headers and footers to alternate between left justification and right justification. This option is used when you print on both sides of the paper and plan to bind the document or put it in a three-ring binder. The alternating format results in a consistent positioning of the the header or footer relative to the binding (next to or away from the binding).

The *pagination* feature, which is usually a print option, automatically numbers the pages of a document. Depending on the sophistication of the word processing systems, page numbers can be left justified, centered, or right justified at either the top or bottom of the page.

The laser printer in the foreground provides users with the flexibility to create word processing documents that contain a variety of fonts, from 10-point Dutch italic to 24-point Swiss bold.
(Photo courtesy of Hewlett-Packard Company)

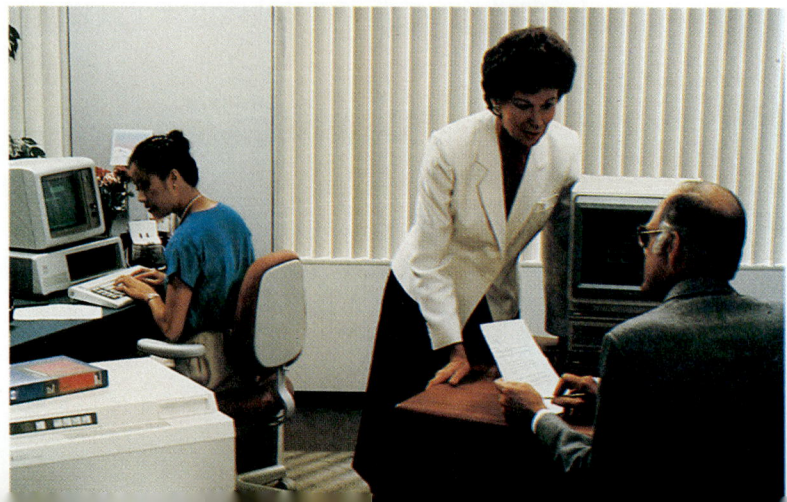

Mixing Type Fonts.   Depending on the type of software and printer you have, you may even be able to mix the size and style of type fonts in a single document. For example, you could print key words in *italics*, major headings in larger letters, and footnotes in smaller letters. George Brooks could even print MEMORANDUM in 48-point (about ½-inch high) old English print if he wanted to.

5–6   FILE FEATURES

Save, Retrieve, and Delete Files.   Certainly, one of the most important features of a word processing package is the ability to store a document on disk storage for later recall (files and file management are discussed in detail in Chapter 4, "DOS: The Disk Operating System Concepts and Tutorials"). The *file* feature permits you to *save, retrieve,* and *delete* a file that contains a word processing document. This is the minimum that most word processing systems provide. No matter which option you choose, you are asked by the system to identify the file (document). To create a document file, you enter a descriptive name that in some way identifies the document (such as MEMO). The document is saved to the default disk drive unless you specify otherwise by prefacing the filename with a drive specifier (B:MEMO). To retrieve or delete an existing file, select the appropriate menu option and enter the file name of an existing file.

George Brooks saved his memo by storing it on disk under the file name MEMO. He stored it on disk because he knew that he was planning a similar meeting next week at the same time and place to discuss sales and strategies for Zimco's other two products, the Farkle and Stib. All that he will have to do to prepare a memo to announce next week's meeting will be to retrieve the MEMO file and change the phrase "Tegler and Qwert" to "Farkle and Stib". See "Hands-on Tutorial 10: Saving and Retrieving a Document."

Merging Files.   As you continue to use and build expertise in word processing, you will surely come across many circumstances that call for merging the contents of an existing document file with the current document (the one in memory). Most word processing packages have the capability to *merge files.* The procedure for merging files is similar for all word processing packages. First, move the cursor to the position in the current document to where the file is to be added or included. Select the "merge file" option from the appropriate menu, then enter the name of the file to be merged. The contents of the file are inserted at the cursor position. See the "Advanced and Special Features Tutorial for WordPerfect" in the next chapter for an activity using the merge feature.

File Backups.   Under normal circumstances, an existing file is overwritten on disk storage when a revised document is saved to disk under the same name. Some word processing programs give you the option of storing the most recent revision of a file while retaining the earlier version as a backup or **BAK** file. To create the backup file, the program alters the name of the original file by attaching the extension BAK (for backup) to the filename (e.g., MEMO.DOC to MEMO.BAK). If you select this option, the following file activities occur when a document file is saved to disk.

1. If a BAK file exists for the saved filename, it is deleted; that is, MEMO.BAK is deleted.
2. The original file is renamed and becomes a BAK file; MEMO.DOC becomes MEMO.BAK.
3. The current document is saved under the user-defined filename (MEMO.DOC).

Of course, retaining a BAK file takes extra processor time and disk storage space. However, if you accidentally delete a critical segment of your document during editing, the BAK file can be a life saver.

ASCII Files.   Issuing a normal save command causes the text of the current document and a variety of hidden program-specific control characters (to center a line of text, for example, or cause a page break) being saved to a disk file. Each word processing package interprets these control characters differently. Therefore, if you wish to modify a document, you must retrieve and manipulate the document with the same word processing package that you used to create it. In practice, however, there are many instances where you might want a colleague or friend to review and edit your word processing document. With literally scores of word processing packages being used, the chances are slim that you and your colleague or friend will use the same word processing package.

Fortunately, there is a way to save files with a word processing program that can be retrieved and manipulated by a different word processing program. Most word processing packages allow you to save your document to an **ASCII file**. An ASCII file is a generic file that is stripped of program-specific control characters. To create an ASCII file, select the "ASCII save" option. ASCII files are sometimes referred to as *text files*.

With a line of over 500 products, this manufacturing sales representative keeps product information handy in the form of word processing documents. He uses onscreen displays of product information during customer presentations.
(Photo courtesy of Hewlett-Packard Company)

5–7   PRINTING A DOCUMENT

When your document is ready for distribution, use the print function to transform your electronic document into a *hard copy* document. When you select the print option from the main menu, most word processing systems will present you with a few final options. For example, you can chose to

- Print the document as single (the default), double, or triple spaced.
- Print the whole document (the default) or only specific pages (for example, pages 3-5).
- Print one page after another on continuous-feed paper (the default)

or pause at the end of each page for printing on individual sheets of paper.

- Print one copy (the default) or multiple copies.
- Print the document with or without page numbers. The default varies among word processing packages, but for many, numbering begins on the second page unless the "without pagination" option is selected.

If you are willing to accept all of the print defaults, all you have to do is ready the printer (turn it on and align the paper) and select the print option on the main menu.

Page Breaks.   During the printing of a multipage document, the word processing software automatically breaks the pages so that text spills over from one page to the next. The only time that a page is not filled is when the program detects a user-supplied or hard **page break** or if it is the last page printed. When the word processing program detects a hard page break, the text following the page break is printed on a new page. For example, if you were writing a four-part report, you might wish to begin each part on a new page.

Cumbersome page breaks can deter from the overall appearance of the document and make the it more difficult to read. For example, a bad page break results in a *widow* or an *orphan*. A widow is the last line of a paragraph that is printed as the first line on a page and an orphan is the first line of paragraph that is printed as the last line of a page. Some word processing programs give you the option of allowing widows and orphans or eliminating them. The program eliminates them by forcing widows to the next page and accompanying orphans with a line from the previous page. See "Hands-on Tutorial 11: Printing a Document and Terminating a Session."

Chain Printing.   The size of a word processing document is limited either by the characteristics of the software or the amount of available RAM. A long report that exceeds the software or RAM limitations may need to be created as two or more separate document files. To print such a report, you will need to *chain* the files together. To do this, select the "chain printing" option and enter the names of the files to be printed in the order in which they are to be printed. The files will then be printed as if they were merged into one big file; even the page numbering will be consecutive from one file to the next.

While attending a conference on presentation techniques, this information center director used his portable micro and word processing software to take notes. On his way home, he edited his notes, highlighting key points with boldface and underlining.
(Photo courtesy of Hewlett-Packard Company)

5—8 ADVANCED WORD PROCESSING FEATURES

The features that have been discussed and illustrated in previous sections are common to most word processing software packages. The more sophisticated word processing packages have some or all of the following advanced features.

- *Footnoting.* One of the most tedious typing chores, footnoting, is done automatically (see Figure 5–8). Footnote spacing is resolved electronically before anything is printed. Footnotes can be printed at the bottom of the page on which they are referenced or as a group at the end of a document.

■ *Hyphenation.* The hyphenation feature automatically breaks and hyphenates long words that fall at the end of the line on output (see Figure 5–8).

■ *Numbered lists.* Another advanced feature—numbered lists—is illustrated in Figure 5–8. When using the numbered list feature, all you have to do is enter the items in the list. The spacing and the insertion of the numbers are automatic.

■ *Table of contents.* A simple command creates a table of contents with page references for the first-level headings. This feature is very helpful in the compilation of reports, strategic plans, doctoral theses, and other sectionally-organized documents.

■ *Indexing.* An alphabetical index of keywords can be created that lists the page numbers for each occurrence of designated words. In preparation for creating the index, you will need to flag those words or phrases that are to be included in the index in a manner similar to the way you would highlight words for underlining or boldface.

■ *Multicolumn output.* Another feature permits multicolumn output (one or more columns of text on a single page). This feature is often used to produce *camera ready copy* (ready for reproduction) for internal newsletters.

■ *Subscripts and superscripts.* **Subscripts** and **superscripts** are characters that are positioned slightly below or above the line of type, respectively. They are commonly used in mathematical formulas ($Y = X_1^2 + X_2^3$), in notations for chemical compounds (H_2O), and as a crossreference to footnotes. To print a subscript on a character printer, the software advances the platen by half a line, prints the subscript, then returns the platen to the original line of print. The procedure is reversed for superscripts.

■ *Windows.* Some word processing packages permit the concurrent display of up to four documents. Each document is displayed in a separate window. Besides being able to view several documents at once, you can use this feature to move and copy blocks of text from one document file to another.

5–9   WORD PROCESSING ADD-ON CAPABILITIES

A number of software programs are designed to enhance the functionality of word processing programs. These add-on capabilities are usually in the form of stand-alone programs. That is, they are programs that either come with a word processing package or are purchased separately.

Electronic Dictionary and Spelling Checker

If spelling and typos are a problem, then word processing is the answer. Once you have entered the text and formatted the document the way you want it, you can call on the **spelling checker**. This add-on program checks every word in the text against an **electronic dictionary** that contains from 75,000 to 150,000 words and alerts you if a word is not in the dictionary. Upon finding an unidentified word, the spelling checker program will normally give you several options.

1. *Request possible spellings.* When you request possible spellings, the spelling checker displays a list of similarly spelled words in a window that is superimposed over your document. For example, upon finding the nonword ''compte'', the spell function might suggest compete, compote, and compute. For short nonwords such as spead, the list of possible spellings can be substantial: speak, spear, sped, speed, spend, spread, and stead. If the correct spelling is among the list of alternative spellings, you use you cursor control keys to highlight and select the correct spelling so that it can replace the misspelled word in your document.

2. *Edit the word.* If the correct spelling is not among the list of alternative spellings, you can edit the word and correct the spelling error.

3. *Ignore the word.* You can ignore the word and continue scanning the text. Normally, you do this when a word is spelled correctly but is not in the dictionary (for example, a company name such as Zimco).

4. *Add the word to a personal dictionary.* George Brooks would probably add Zimco to his **personal dictionary** and continue scanning. The spelling checker loads your personal dictionary to RAM along with the main dictionary. Words not found in the main dictionary are matched against words in your personal dictionary. In this way, a possible misspelling is brought to your attention only if it is not found in either dictionary.

On-Line Thesaurus

Have you ever been writing along and been unable to put your finger on the right word? If so, what you need is an **on-line thesaurus**! Suppose that you have just written, ''The Grand Canyon certainly is beautiful.'' But ''beautiful'' is not quite the right word. Position the cursor over the word ''beautiful'' and call the on-line thesaurus. An on-line thesaurus is always ready with possible synonyms: pretty, elegant, exquisite, angelic, pulchritudinous, ravishing, ... Pulchritudinous? Oh, well.

An on-line thesaurus can be a valuable writing tool. Use it to find that word that makes your sentence flow or clarifies what you are trying to say. You can choose to replace a word with one of the synonyms that is displayed in a window by the on-line thesaurus.

See the ''Advanced and Special Features Tutorial for WordPerfect'' in the next chapter for activities using the spelling checker and on-line thesaurus features.

The display shows what happens when WordPerfect's spelling checker detects a misspelled word (''Sals''). Alternative spellings are listed below the word processing document.

The display shows what happens when synonyms are requested from the on-line thesaurus that accompanies Webster's NewWorld Writer. Displayed are synonyms for ''note'' and, on the right, an alternate entry page for ''write down.''

Grammar and Style Checkers

Grammar and style checkers are the electronic version of a copy editor. A **grammar checker** highlights grammatical concerns and deviations from conventions. For example, it highlights split infinitives, phrases with redundant words (very highest), misuse of capital letters (JOhn or MarY), subject and verb mismatches (they was), double words (and and), and punctuation errors. A **style checker** alerts users to such writing concerns as sexist words or phrases (chairman), long or complex sentence structures, hackneyed cliches (the bottom line), and sentences that are written in the passive rather than active voice.

Grammar and style checkers analyze the document, point out potential problem areas, and when possible, suggest alternatives. Notations and comments are included in an edited version of the document, not the original.

Some style checkers are able to determine the *reading level* of a document. The reading level is usually represented by grade level. For example, the reading level of a document evaluated at 13.4 would be appropriate, on the average, for someone who has completed the fourth month of the freshman year of college (the thirteenth year of schooling). The reading level is determined by examining such variables as the average number of words per sentence, the number of three and four syllable words, the number of compound or complex sentences, and the number of predefined "difficult" words.

5–10   WORD PROCESSING IN PRACTICE

You can create just about any kind of text-based document with word processing software: letters, reports, books, articles, forms, memos, theses, newsletters, brochures, tables, and so on. In a few short years word processing has revolutionized the manner in which we put pen to paper.

Merging Text with a Data Base.   The features of some word processing packages go beyond the generation of text documents. Besides providing a faster and easier way to type, some word processing packages have the facility to merge the text generated by word processing with data from a data base. For example, a typical word processing application could involve the preparation of the same letter to be sent to a number of people.

When Zimco Enterprises announced the enhanced version of the Qwert, all regional sales managers sent personal letters to every Zimco customer in their respective regions. There were thousands of customers in each region. The secretary with a regular typewriter would have only two choices: either type thousands of separate letters or type one letter and photocopy it. In the business world in general, the latter is not desirable. Using word processing, a secretary can type the letter once, store it on the disk, and then simply merge the customer name-

and-address file (also stored on the disk) with the letter. The letters will be printed with the proper addresses and salutations.

Figure 5–9 illustrates how the Qwert announcement letter is merged with the customer name-and-address data base to produce a personalized letter. In the example, the variables (for example, *First Name* or *Zip*) in the text of the letter take on selected values from the record of Marty E. Chambers in Zimco's customer master file.

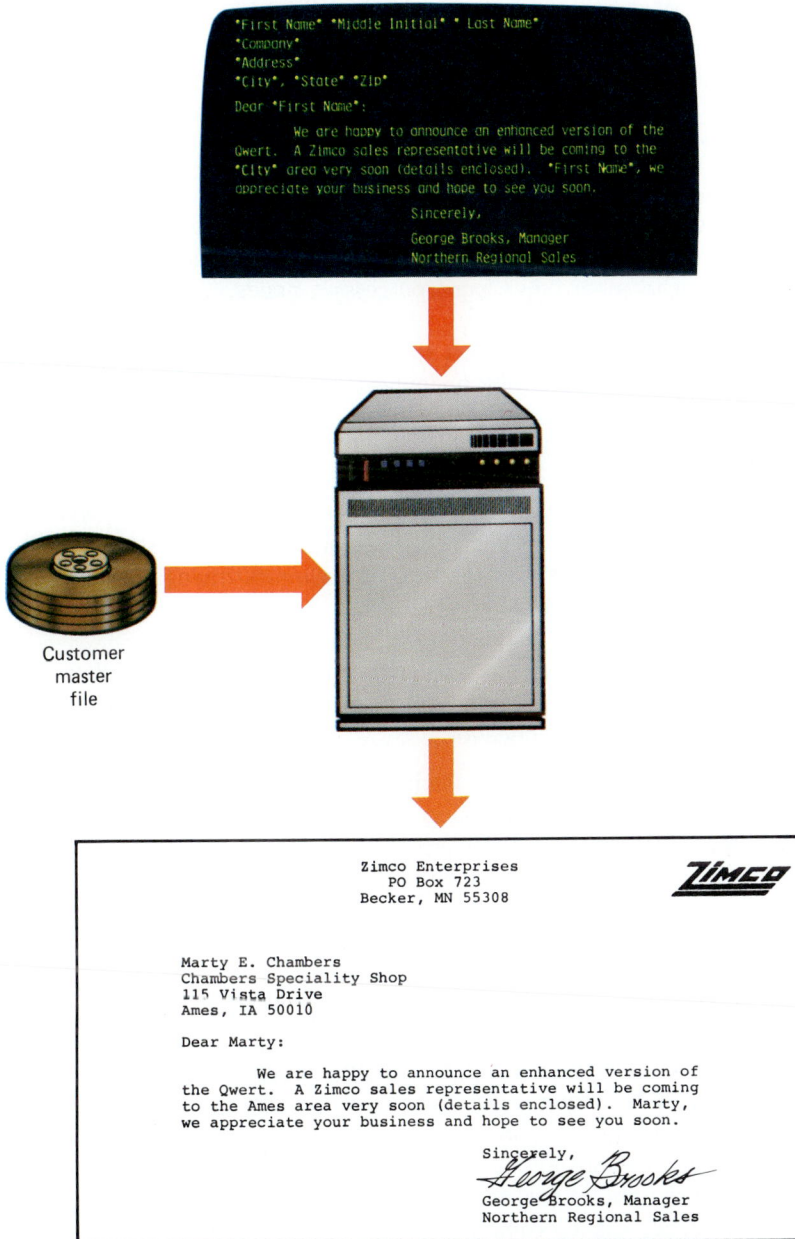

FIGURE 5–9
Merging Data with Word Processing
The names and addresses from a customer master file are retrieved from secondary storage and merged with the text of a letter. In the actual letter, the appropriate data items are inserted for *First Name*, *Company*, *Address*, *City*, and so on. In this way, a "personalized" letter can be sent to each customer.

Marty	→	*First Name*
E.	→	*Middle Initial*
Chambers	→	*Last Name*
Chambers Specialty Shop	→	*Company*
115 Vista Drive	→	*Address*
Ames	→	*City*
Iowa	→	*State*
50010	→	*Zip*

In the next letter, the variables will take on the values from the record of another customer.

Boilerplate Text.   The mail merge example in the preceding section is a good example of the use of **boilerplate**. Boilerplate is existing text that can in some way be customized to be applicable to a variety of word processing applications. One of the beauties of word processing is that you can accumulate text on disk storage that will eventually help you to meet other word processing needs. You can even buy boilerplate.

The legal profession offers some of the best examples of the use of boilerplate. Simple wills, uncontested divorces, individual bankruptcies, real estate transfers, and other straightforward legal documents may be as much as 95% boilerplate. Even more complex legal documents may be as much as 80% boilerplate. Once the appropriate boilerplate has been merged into a document, the lawyer edits the document to add transition sentences and the variables, such as the names of the litigants. Besides the obvious improvement in productivity, lawyers can be relatively confident that their documents are accurate and complete when they use boilerplate.

Lawyers, of course, do not have a monopoly on boilerplate. The use of boilerplate is common in all areas of business, education, government, and personal endeavor.

Desktop Publishing.   The ultimate extension of word processing is **desktop publishing**. Desktop publishing refers to the capability of producing *near typeset-quality copy* from the confines of a "desktop." The concept of desktop publishing is changing the way companies, government, and individuals approach the printing of newsletters, brochures, user manuals, pamphlets, restaurant menus, periodicals, greeting cards, and thousands of other printed items.

Traditionally, drafts of documents to be printed were delivered to commercial printers to be typeset. Desktop publishing has made it possible to eliminate this expensive typesetting process for those printed documents that required only near typeset quality. In a typical company, near typeset-quality copy is acceptable for most printed documents. Relatively few documents need to be prepared using the expensive commercial phototypesetting process. The output of the desktop publishing process is the *camera-ready copy*. The document is reproduced from the copy by any of a variety of means, from copy machines to commercial processing.

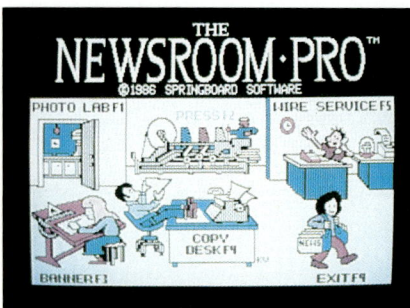

The main menu for this desktop publishing software package is presented in the form of icons. This approach is consistent with the user-friendly philosophy of desktop publishing.
(Aldus Corporation)

This full WYSIWYG desktop publishing system is configured with an image processor (right) and mouse. The image processor enables photographs, line art, handwriting, text, and anything else that can be rendered on paper to be scanned and then edited on the computer. The final copy is produced on a laser printer (left).
(AST Research Inc.)

The primary components required for desktop publishing are *desktop publishing software*, a *microcomputer*, and a *laser printer*. The more sophisticated desktop publishing environments include *scanners* that can be used to digitize images, such as photographs. Desktop publishing software is essentially sophisticated word processing software (all of the capabilities described in this chapter) plus *page-composition software*. The page composition software enables the users to design and make up pages. The page make-up process involves the integration of graphics, photos, text, and other elements into a visually appealing *page layout*. Besides the positioning of the elements, the user must also select the desired mix of type sizes and fonts. Desktop publishing software may be the next generation of word processing software.

Keyboarding Skills—the Key to Successful Word Processing. When working with word processing software, you are likely to enter long, continuous strings of text, rather than short commands and data for the other types of micro software. Therefore, if you expect to use word processing capabilities frequently, you might consider acquiring a solid foundation in keyboarding skills, if you have not already done so. SuperSoftware, one of the software supplements that accompanies this text, includes a comprehensive keyboarding tutorial.

One of the word processing add-on programs uses a keystroke shorthand to help you to increase the speed at which you enter text. The program works like this. First you associate shorthand abbreviations with words and phrases that you use frequently in word processing. For example, for "word processing software" you might use the abbreviation "WP+". The file containing the words and phrases and associated shorthand symbols is loaded to memory with your document. When you enter a keystroke combination that is contained in the memory resident file, the abbreviation is immediately expanded to the full word or phrase; that is, "WP+" becomes "word processing software."

Word Processing Is for Everybody—Managers, Too.   Word processing can make any person's professional and personal life a little easier, even managers with secretaries. Managers have begun to embrace word processing. Many draft their own correspondence on their micros and give diskettes to their secretaries for proofreading and printing. In fact, more managers are using word processing than dictation machines. They have found that it is much less time consuming to edit a draft letter themselves on a display screen than it is to ask a secretary to make corrections from a marked-up hard copy. Word processing has redefined the working relationship between secretaries and managers.

In Summary.   Word processing is the perfect example of how automation can be used to increase productivity and foster creativity. It minimizes the effort that you must devote to the routine aspects of writing, so that you can focus you attention on the creative aspects of writing. Most word processing users will agree that their writing style has improved measurably. The finished product is less verbose, better organized, devoid of spelling errors, and of course, more visually appealing.

SUMMARY OUTLINE AND IMPORTANT TERMS

5–1   WORD PROCESSING.   *Word processing* is using the computer to enter, store, manipulate, and print text in letters, reports, books, and so on. Word processing software packages are generally categorized by the manner in which the user interacts with the system. In **menu-driven word processing packages**, the user interacts with the software by selecting options from a hierarchy of menus. Most menu-driven systems are "what you see is what you get" or **WYSIWYG**. In **command-driven word processing packages**, the user interacts with the software by embedding commands within the text of the document.

5–2   CREATING A DOCUMENT.   When you format a document, you are describing the size of the print page and how you want the document to look when it is printed. Some or all of these specifications are made in a **layout line**: left margin (**page offset**) and right margin, top and bottom margins, tabs, vertical spacing, horizontal spacing (**pitch**), **proportional spacing**, and paper size.

Text is entered and edited in **replace mode** or **insert mode**. **Word wrap** is when text that extends past the defined margins automatically wraps around to the next line. Word processing permits full-screen editing.

5–3   BLOCK OPERATIONS.   The block move, the block copy, and the block delete commands are collectively known as block operations, the electronic equivalent of "cut and paste." A block of text is a word, a sentence, a paragraph, a section of a report, or as much contiguous text as you desire. Before a block can be moved, copied, or deleted, it must be marked.

5–4   THE SEARCH FEATURES.   The search or find feature permits the user to search through the entire word processing document and identify all occurrences of a particular character string. The search and replace feature enables the user to selectively replace occurrences of the search string with the replacement string.

5–5   FEATURES THAT ENHANCE APPEARANCE AND READABILITY.   Word processing has several features that enable users to enhance the appearance and readability of their documents. These include automatic centering, boldface, underlining, right and left justification, section headings, indentation, headers, footers, **pagination**, and mixing type fonts.

5–6   FILE FEATURES.   All word processing packages permit users to save, retrieve, and delete files that contain word processing documents. Most word processing packages have the capacity to merge files; that is, the contents of one file can be inserted into another. Many word processing packages can create **ASCII files**. ASCII files can be retrieved and manipulated by different word processing programs.

5–7   PRINTING A DOCUMENT.   The print function transforms your electronic document into a hard copy document. Typical print options include single, double, or triple spacing; printing the whole document or specific pages; printing continuously or with a pause at the end of each page; printing one copy or multiple copies; and printing the document with or without page numbers. Pages in a word processing document are always filled unless the program detects a hard **page break** or it is the last page. Use chain printing to print documents that span more than one file.

5–8   ADVANCED WORD PROCESSING FEATURES.   The more sophisticated word processing packages have some or all of the following advanced features: footnoting, hyphenation, numbered lists, table of contents, indexing, multicolumn output, **subscripts** and **superscripts**, and windows.

5–9   WORD PROCESSING ADD-ON CAPABILITIES.   Several add-on programs are designed to enhance the functionality of word processing programs. The **spelling checker** program checks every word in the text against an **electronic dictionary** and alerts the user when a word is not in the dictionary. An **on-line thesaurus** is always ready with possible synonyms for any word in a word processing document. A **grammar checker** highlights grammatical concerns and deviations from conventions. A **style checker** alerts users to such writing concerns as sexist words and hackneyed cliches. Some style checkers have the capability to determine the reading level of a document.

5–10   WORD PROCESSING IN PRACTICE.   Any kind of text-based document can be created with word processing software. Some word processing packages have the ability to merge the text generated by word processing with data from a data base (for example, merging a form letter with a name and address file).

Boilerplate is existing text that can in some way be customized so that it is applicable to a variety of word processing applications.

The ultimate extension of word processing is **desktop publishing**. Desktop publishing refers to the capability of producing near typeset-quality copy from the confines of a "desktop." The primary components required for desktop publishing are desktop publishing software, a microcomputer, and a laser printer. The more sophisticated desktop publishing environments include scanners that can be used to digitize images, such as photographs.

REVIEW EXERCISES

1. What is the function of word processing software?
2. What must be specified when formatting a document?
3. What is meant when a document is formatted to be right and left justified?
4. Text is entered in either of what two modes? What mode would you select to change "the table" to "the long table"? What mode would you select to change "pick the choose" to "pick and choose"?
5. What causes text to wrap around?
6. What are the three primary components of a desktop publishing system?
7. Name and briefly describe three programs that provide add-on capabilities to word processing software.
8. Describe two word processing applications that would involve the use of boilerplate.
9. Give an example of when you might issue a global search and replace command.
10. When running the spelling function, what options does the system present to the user upon encountering an unidentified word?
11. Briefly describe how the indexing feature works.
12. Describe circumstances that may dictate the need to chain print a word processing document.
13. A word processing document that is saved as an ASCII file provides the user with the flexibility to do what?
14. What options can be presented to the user when a spelling checker program finds an unidentified word?
15. When a word processing document is printed, some words are in boldface type or underlined. How can these words be displayed on the monitor?

SELF-TEST (by section)

5–1. Command-driven word processing systems are usually WYSIWYG. (T/F)

5–2. **(a)** The _____ line in a word processing document provides information on format specifications.

(b) A hard carriage return is inserted to (a) begin, (b) delete,
or (c) end a paragraph in a word processing document.

(c) To add a word in the middle of an existing sentence,
you would use insert mode. (T/F)

5–3. Use the _____ command to reinsert previously deleted
text.

5–4. The search string can contain any combination of letters or
numbers, but it cannot contain punctuation marks, such as a
colon or a comma. (T/F)

5–5. Which word processing feature enables the automatic numbering of the pages of a document: (a) pagination, (b) page break-
ing, or (c) footers?

5–6. **(a)** The filename extension BAK is normally associated with
backup files. (T/F)

(b) Since ASCII files contain program-specific control characters, they can be used only by the originating word processing program. (T/F)

5–7. A _____ is the first line of a paragraph that is printed as
the last line on a page.

5–8. The advanced word processing feature that automatically
breaks long words that fall at the end of a line is called

_____.

5–9. **(a)** A personal dictionary is associated with which word processing add-on program: (a) spelling checker, (b) style
checker, or (c) grammar checker?

(b) An on-line thesaurus can be used to suggest possible
synonyms for a word in a word processing document.
(T/F)

5–10. **(a)** _____ is existing text that can be customized to meet
a variety of word processing needs.

(b) The type of printer normally associated with desktop publishing is the daisy-wheel printer. (T/F)

Self-Test Answers.   **5–1,** F; **5–2 (a),** layout; **(b),** c; **(c),** T; **5–3,** undo;
5–4, F; **5–5,** a; **5–6 (a),** T; **(b),** F; **5–7,** widow; **5–8,** hyphenation;
5–9 (a), a; **(b),** T; **5–10 (a),** Boilerplate; **(b),** F.

HANDS-ON EXERCISES

1. Complete Hands-On Tutorials 4 through 11 and the Advanced
and Special Features Tutorial (if appropriate) in Chapter 6,
"Word Processing Tutorials."

2. **(a)** Enter the following text into your word processing system:

Too Much Paper!

Last year, the Public Relations Department's paper budget was overrun by
$350. Therefore, Public Relations personnel are requested to learn word

processing. It is apparent that Public Relations has not taken full advantage of the word processing capabilities of its microcomputers.

> Use the default layout line options (normally 8½- by 11-inch document size, 1-inch right and left margins, 6 lines per inch, and so on). Justify the right margin. Print the document.
>
> In the remaining portion of Hands-On Exercise 2, make the changes cumulative; that is, revise whatever text is left after the previous revision. Each part of the exercise builds on the results of the previous part.

(b) In insert mode, insert the word "all" before "Public" in the second sentence. In replace mode, replace the lowercase letters in the title with capital letters. Print the document.

(c) Center the title. Print the document.

(d) At the end of the second sentence, add "by the end of the month". Observe how words at the end of the line wrap around to the next line. Print the document.

(e) Use the move command to move the second sentence to the end of the document. Print the document.

(f) Designate the word "all" to be underlined and the title to be in boldface when printed. Print the document.

(g) Place the "page" (new page) marker at the end of the document and use the copy command to produce another copy of the entire document just below the original. Print the document.

(h) Use the search and replace command to replace all occurrences of "Public Relations" in the second document with "Research and Development". Revise $350 in the second document to be $525. Print the document.

(i) Run the spell function. Print the document. If you performed all the exercises a through h, your printed output should be similar to the examples that follow. Since the default margins vary among word processing systems, the lines in your printouts may break differently from those of the following example outputs.

TOO MUCH PAPER!

Last year, the Public Relations Department's paper budget was overrun by $350. It is apparent that Public Relations has not taken full advantage of the word processing capabilities of its microcomputers. Therefore, *all* Public Relations personnel are requested to learn word processing by the end of the month.

TOO MUCH PAPER!

Last year, the Research and Development Department's paper budget was overrun by $525. It is apparent that Research and Development has not taken full advantage of the word processing capabilities of its microcomputers. Therefore, *all* Research and Development personnel are requested to learn word processing by the end of the month.

3. (a) Design and compile a personal resume using word processing software. Use appropriate word processing features to enhance the presentation of the resume. At a minimum, include these elements: your name, address, telephone number, education history (dates, school, degree), work history (dates, position title and brief description of work, employer, employer address), and a personal section (interests, special achievements, and so on).

   (b) Use a spelling checker (if available) to check your resume for misspelled words and typographical errors.

   (c) Print the resume.

4. (a) Write a cover letter to accompany the resume you created in Hands-On Exercise 3. Address the letter to Mrs. Peggy Peoples, VP of Personnel, Zimco Enterprises, P.O. Box 923481, Dallas, TX, 75208. In the letter, inform Mrs. Peoples of your availability, describe the type of work you are seeking, mention that your resume is enclosed, and state that references will be supplied upon request.

   (b) Use a spelling checker (if available) to check your cover letter for misspelled words and typographical errors.

   (c) Print the cover letter.

5. (a) If your word processing program has mail merge capabilities, create an employer name and address file that contains Zimco's address (see Hands-On Exercise 4) and the addresses of three companies in your local area.

   (b) Modify the cover letter created in Hands-On Exercise 4 so that the salutation reads "To the Director of Personnel:" and so that it can be merged with the employer name and address file.

   (c) Use the mail merge capability to print a cover letter to each company in the employer name and address file.

KEYSTROKE TUTORIALS IN THE *LAB MANUAL*

The *Lab Manual* that accompanies this text contains keystroke tutorials for

- WordPerfect (© WordPerfect Corporation)
- Webster's NewWorld Writer (© Simon & Schuster, Inc.)
- WordStar Professional (© MicroPro International Corporation)
- MultiMate Advantage II (© Ashton-Tate, Inc.)
- PFS:Professional Write (© Software Publishing Corporation)

These keystroke tutorials illustrate the use of particular word processing software package in a domestic and a business application. The more advanced features of the packages are introduced in the business application tutorials.

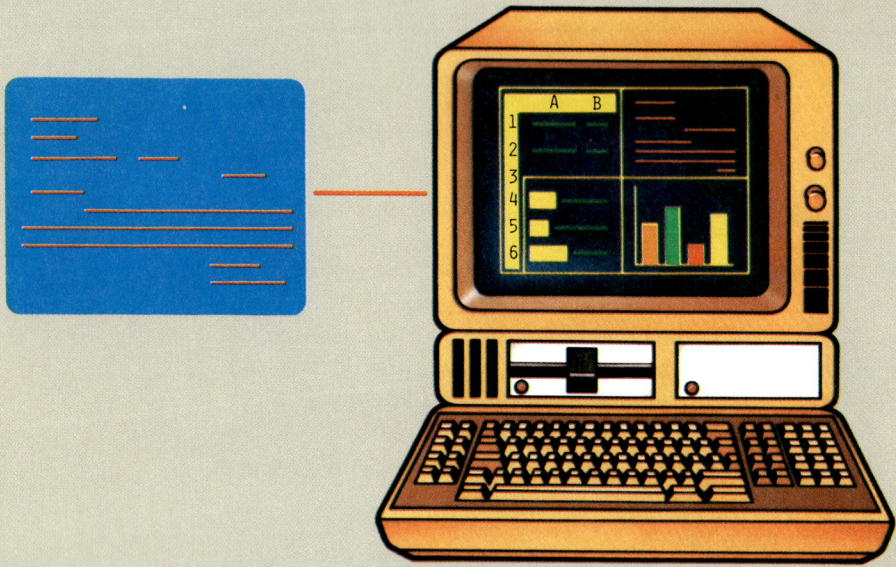

CHAPTER **6**

Word Processing Tutorials

STUDENT LEARNING OBJECTIVES

■ To become familiar with the use and application of one or more of the following word processing software packages:
- ■ WordPerfect
- ■ Webster's NewWorld Writer
- ■ WordStar Professional
- ■ MultiMate Advantage II
- ■ PFS:Professional Write
■ To acquire the ability to apply the word processing skills demonstrated in the hands-on tutorials.

HANDS-ON TUTORIALS for *WordPerfect, Webster's NewWorld Writer, WordStar Professional, MultiMate Advantage II*, and *PFS:Professional Write*

4. Using Word Processing Software
5. Creating and Formatting a Document
6. Entering and Adding Text
7. Moving Text
8. Search and Replace
9. Centering, Boldfacing, Underlining, and Justifying Text
10. Saving and Retrieving a Document
11. Printing a Document and Terminating a Session

ADVANCED AND SPECIAL FEATURES TUTORIALS: *WordPerfect* and *Webster's NewWorld Writer*

Merging (Combining) Files
Formatting by Using Page Breaks, Double Spacing, and Boxes
Using the On-line Thesaurus
Using the Spelling Checker

WORD PROCESSING TUTORIAL: WORDPERFECT

QUICK REFERENCE GUIDE
WordPerfect
(Version 4.2)
A>wp ↵

FUNCTION KEYS

Line 1 = CTRL-Fn
Line 2 = SHIFT-Fn
Line 3 = ALT-Fn
Line 4 = Fn

Shelf			Spell
Super/Subscript			◀Search
Thesaurus			Replace
Cancel	F1	F2	▶Search
Screen			Move
Switch			▶Indent◀
Reveal Codes			Block
Help	F3	F4	▶Indent
Text In/Out			Tab Align
Date			Center
Mark Text			Flush Right
List Files	F5	F6	Bold
Footnote			Print
Print		FORMAT	Line
Math/Columns			Page
Exit	F7	F8	Underline
Merge/Sort			Macro Def
Merge E			Retrieve
Merge Codes			Macro
Merge R	F9	F10	Save

CURSOR MOVEMENT

By word right/left	CTRL-→	CTRL-←
To margin right/left	HOME HOME →	HOME HOME ←
	(or END)	
To screen end/beg.	HOME ↓	HOME ↑
To document end/beg.	HOME HOME ↓	HOME HOME ↑

OTHER

ESC DEL	Delete a line

HANDS-ON TUTORIAL 4: Using WordPerfect

WordPerfect, a product of WordPerfect Corporation, is a popular menu-driven word processing package. This tutorial is based on WordPerfect Version 4.2.

Most of the commands in WordPerfect are entered using the function keys. WordPerfect supplies a handy template for quick reference that fits over the function keys. Ask your instructor if there is one available or refer to the key assignments presented in the Quick Reference Guide.

The Keystroke Conventions box in Hands-On Tutorial 1 explains and illustrates the keystroke format used for the interactive tutorials.

- Boot the system (see Hands-On Tutorial 1).
- Load WordPerfect to memory. Insert the

WordPerfect Program Disk in drive A.

A>**wp** ↵

■ When the WordPerfect work screen appears you will see a blank screen with the cursor in the top left corner. The cursor position indicators are in the bottom right corner: document 1 (Doc 1), page

1 (Pg 1), line 1 (Ln 1), and position 10 (Pos 10). WordPerfect automatically sets the page offset (left margin) at about one inch (Pos 10).

■ Insert your data disk in drive B. You are now ready to begin your word processing session.

HANDS-ON TUTORIAL 5: Creating and Formatting a Document

In Hands-On Tutorials 5 through 11, we will create and print the memo in Figure 5–7. Figures 5–1 through 5–6 illustrate steps in the creation and development of the Figure 5–7 memo.

■ Before entering text, familiarize yourself with WordPerfect's function-key-based command structure (see the Quick Reference Guide). Each function key is assigned four functions, depending on whether it is press alone or in conjunction with the CTRL, SHIFT, or ALT keys.

■ Set up the layout line.

SHIFT - F8 (*format line menu*)

The format line menu appears at the bottom of the screen.

■ Change the right margin from 74 (the default) to 71 and accept the other default settings (tab settings at 5, 10, 15, and so forth and single spacing).

3 (*margins*)
[Margin Set] 10 74 to Left = **10** ↵ Right = **71**
↵

HANDS-ON TUTORIAL 6: Entering and Adding Text

■ If WordPerfect is in insert mode, there is no indication on the work screen status line; but in overstrike mode the word "Typeover" appears in the bottom left corner of the screen. Toggle between insert and replace (or typeover) mode with the INS key and observe the indicator. Finish in insert mode.

INS INS INS INS

■ Enter the first three lines of the text of the memo (Figure 5–1). To correct typographical errors, use the cursor control keys in combination with the DEL and BKSP keys.

To: TAB TAB **Field Sales Staff** ↵
From: TAB **G. Brooks, Northern Sales**
Manager ↵
Re: TAB TAB **Weekly Briefing Session**
↵ ↵

The second ENTER adds a blank line. The status line should indicate Ln 5, Pos 10.

■ Key in the text of the memo in Figure 5–1. Since the lines wrap automatically, *press ENTER only at the end of the paragraph!*

TAB **The Sales Department's** . . . (*see text in Figure 5–1*) **conference room.** ↵

■ Add the sentence "See you Thursday!" (see Figure 5–2).

(*position cursor in Ln 8 on the "W"*)
See you Thursday! SPACE

If text extends beyond the right margin, as it does in this instance, move the cursor and the document will be reformatted to fit the defined margins.

Save option: If at anytime you cannot continue with the tutorials, save your work so that you can pick up where you left off. To do this, see "Hands-On Tutorial 10: Saving and Retrieving a Document." When you return, retrieve your document and continue the tutorials.

WordPerfect display after the completion of Hands-On Tutorial 6.

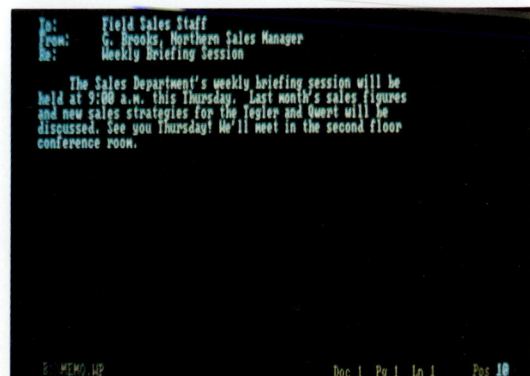

HANDS-ON TUTORIAL 7: Moving Text

Move the last sentence in the current memo to be the second sentence in a revised memo (see Figures 5–3 and 5–4).

■ Position the cursor at the beginning of the last sentence and mark the beginning of the block to be moved.

> (*position cursor in Ln 8 on the "W"*)
> CTRL - F4 (*move and retrieve menu*)
> **1** (*move sentence*)
> **1** (*cut*)

Swoosh! The sentence has been stored in memory.

■ Indicate the destination of the block (sentence) move by positioning the cursor at the beginning of the second sentence. Execute the move (retrieve and insert the "cut" sentence).

> (*position cursor in Ln 6 on the "L"*)
> CTRL - F4
> **5** (*retrieve text*)

■ Separate the second and third sentences with a space.

> (*position cursor in Ln 7 on the "L"*)
> SPACE

WordPerfect display just prior to the block move in Hands-On Tutorial 7.

HANDS-ON TUTORIAL 8: Search and Replace

Search for all occurrences of the word "Thursday" in the memo of Figure 5–4 and replace them with the word "Friday". The memo should be similar to Figure 5–5.

■ Position the cursor at the beginning of the document.

> HOME ↑ (*position cursor in first line of screen*)
> HOME ← (*position cursor at beginning of line*)

■ Initiate the search and replace sequence.

> ALT - F2 (*search and replace key*)

w/Confirm? (Y/N) N (*replace without confirmation*) ↵

Answering "N" or No to the prompt causes all occurrences of the search string to be replaced without confirmation for each occurrence.

■ Enter the search and replace patterns.

> --> Srch: **Thursday** F2 (*search forward*)
> Replace with: **Friday** F2

WordPerfect uses the F2 key, not the ENTER key, to signify the end of the search pattern. This allows the user to include a hard carriage return in the search string, if necessary.

HANDS-ON TUTORIAL 9: Centering, Boldfacing, Underlining and Justifying Text

Center, add, and boldface the title "MEMORANDUM". Underline the sentence "See you Friday!"

■ Add two blank lines at the top of the memo, then reposition the cursor to "home."

> HOME ↑
> HOME ←
> ↵ ↵ HOME ↑

■ Center the title on the first line.

> SHIFT - F6 (*center*)

The cursor moves to the center of the line.

■ Enter the title "MEMORANDUM".

> **MEMORANDUM**

■ Mark then boldface the title.

> ALT - F4 (*block marker*)
> ← (*11 times, highlight the title*)
> F6 (*boldface*)

The title changes color or intensity to indicate bold (e.g., white to amber on a color monitor).

- Underline "See you Friday!"

    (*position cursor in Ln 10 on the "S"*)
    ALT - F4
    ! (*cursor moves to the "!"*)
    F8 (*underline block*)

The sentence changes color or intensity to indicate underlining (e.g., white to green on a color monitor).

- The default value for right justification in WordPerfect is "on." Although the right justification does not appear on the screen, the document will be right justified when printed.

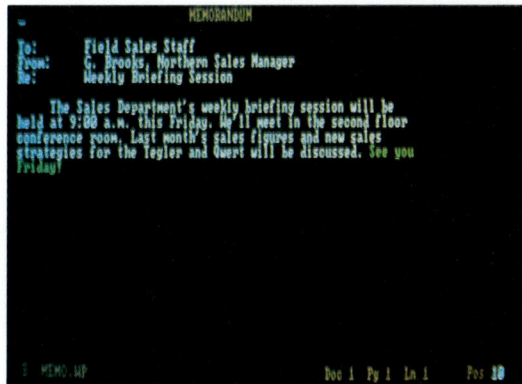

WordPerfect display after the completion of Hands-On Tutorial 9.

HANDS-ON TUTORIAL 10: Saving and Retrieving a Document

Do the following to save then retrieve the document "memo".

- Name and save "memo" to disk storage.

    F10 (*save*)
    Document to be Saved: **b:memo** ↵

- Clear the screen before retrieving "memo".

    F7 (*exit key*)
    Save Document? (Y/N) **N**
    Exit WP? (Y/N) N ↵

Because the text had not been modified, you do not need to save the memo.

- Retrieve "memo".

    SHIFT - F10 (*retrieve a document from disk storage*)
    Document to be Retrieved: **b:memo** ↵

The "memo" document should now be on the screen with its name listed in the lower left corner.

HANDS-ON TUTORIAL 11: Printing a Document and Terminating a Session

Turn on the printer and produce a hardcopy of the memo (see Figure 5–7) and exit Word-Perfect.

- Open the simple print menu (not the format print menu).

    SHIFT - F7 (*simple print menu*)
    1 (*print the full text*)

- Exit WordPerfect.

    F7 (*exit*)

As a safety precaution, you are prompted to save the document on which you are working. If any revisions have been made since the document was last saved, answer "**Y**" to the prompt; otherwise the revisions will be lost.

    Save Document? (Y/N) **N**
    Exit WP? (Y/N) **Y**

ADVANCED AND SPECIAL FEATURES TUTORIAL: WordPerfect

In this advanced WordPerfect tutorial the following skills are introduced: setting tabs; combining files; setting page breaks; double spacing; drawing boxes; using WordPerfect's On-line Thesaurus; and using WordPerfect's Spelling Checker.

George Brooks, Zimco's Northern Sales

Manager, wanted to create product descriptions for the Tegler and Qwert to hand out at an upcoming meeting (see Figure 5–7). He wants to add these descriptions to the previously created "memo" (from Hands-On Tutorials 4-11). To do this, he plans to use a variety of WordPerfect's features.

GETTING STARTED

WordPerfect's program disk (Training Version) and your data disk are all that you will need to complete most of this advanced tutorial. However, you will need the full-function version of WordPerfect (with Thesaurus and Speller disks) for the last two parts.

■ Load WordPerfect's program to memory differently than was explained in Hands-On Tutorial 4. Insert the WordPerfect program disk in drive A.

> A>**wp/s** ↵

The /s calls up the Set-up menu so you can ensure that the Thesaurus and Speller will function correctly.

■ In the Set-up menu, select option 1 to set the drive designations for the dictionary and thesaurus files.

> **1** (*set drives for dictionary and thesaurus files*)
> Where do you plan to keep the dictionary (LEX.WP)?
> Enter full pathname: **b:lex.wp** ↵
> Where do you plan to keep the supplementary dictionary file?
> Enter full pathname: **b:lex.sup** ↵
> Where do you plan to keep the thesaurus (TH.WP)?
> Enter full pathname: **b:th.wp** ↵

■ End the Set-up menu and continue to WordPerfect's work screen.

> **0** (*end set-up*)

■ Insert your data disk in drive B.

CREATING THE PRODUCT DESCRIPTION FILE

Create a new file that will contain descrip-

tions of the two Zimco products, the Tegler and the Qwert.

■ Reset the margins to match the "memo" margins (see Hands-On Tutorial 5).

> SHIFT - F8 (*format line*)
> **3** (*margins*)
> [Margin Set] 10 74 to Left = **10** ↵ Right = **71** ↵

ENTERING THE PRODUCT DESCRIPTIONS

Key in the name of each product (boldfaced and centered), followed by its description.

■ Boldface and center the product title "TEGLER" (see Hands-On Tutorial 9).

> SHIFT - F6 (*center*)
> F6 (*boldface on*)
> **TEGLER**
> F6 (*boldface off*)

■ Key in the rest of the text (see Hands-On Tutorial 6. Center and boldface the Qwert title, center the subheadings, leave lines blank as shown, and use the TAB key to indent text where necessary.

> The default tab setting for WordPerfect is 5. If this is not the case (press SHIFT-F8, option 1 to see the layout line), follow these directions in resetting the first 3 tabs to intervals of 5.
>
> SHIFT - F8 **1** (*display layout line*)
> (*follow directions on screen for arrows/space bar*)
> (*put tabs in columns 15, 20, and 25*)
> F7 (*return to document*)

Now enter the remainder of the text.

> (*insert 2 line spaces after TEGLER and after QWERT*)

WordPerfect display after the completion of the section on "Creating the Product Description File" in the Advanced and Special Features Tutorial (HOME position).

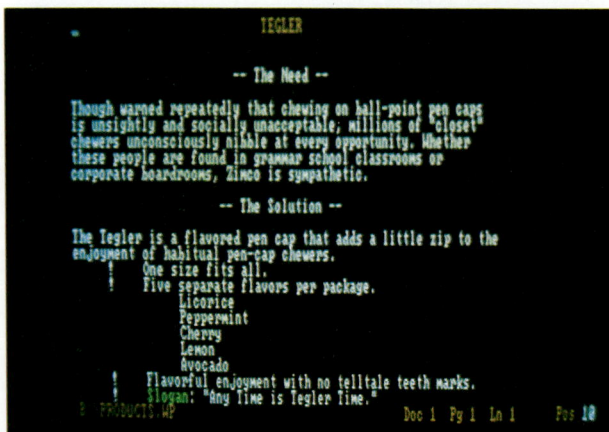

-- The Need --

Though warned repeatedly that chewing on ball-point pen caps
is unsightly and socially unacceptable, millions of "closet"
chewers unconsciously nibble at every opportunity. Whether
these people are found in grammar school classrooms or
corporate boardrooms, Zimco is sympathetic.

-- The Solution --

The Tegler is a flavored pen cap that adds a little zip to the
enjoyment of habitual pen-cap chewers.
  ! One size fits all.
  ! Five separate flavors per package.
    Licorice
    Peppermint
    Cherry
    Lemon
    Avocado
  ! Flavorful enjoyment with no telltale teeth marks.
  ! Slogan: "Any Time is Tegler Time."

(insert 2 line spaces here)

QWERT

-- The Need --

Have you ever been at a loss when asked, "How are you today?"
Have you ever wanted to know exactly how on-top-of-it you are
before taking a test, meeting the boss, or going on a date?
Now you can answer these important questions and more, such as
"How difficult an opponent can I manage today in tennis?",
"Can I tackle that big project now?", or "Is it time for
lunch?"

-- The Solution --

Zimco's Qwert is a watch-like biofeedback mechanism that, when
placed around the wrist, measures variations in galvanic skin
response and heart rate. A tiny computer inside the Qwert
collects and analyzes these data to provide a continuous
readout of a person's physical and, to some extent, emotional
well-being. The readout varies from 1 (extreme lethargy) to 10
(extreme anxiety). Qwert users can learn to adjust their body
chemistry to optimize their mental acuity and reduce stress
and tension.
     Slogan: "Do Smart Work with a Qwert."

SAVING THE "PRODUCTS" FILE
AND EDITING THE "MEMO" FILE

Save "products" to disk storage, then open
and edit the "memo" file (see Hands-On Tutorial 10).

■ Save the "products" file.

> [F7] (*exit*)
> Save Document? (Y/N) **Yes**
> Document to be saved: **b:products** ↵
> Exit WP? (Y/N) **N**

The "products" file disappears, leaving
WordPerfect's clean screen.

■ Retrieve the "memo" file.

> [SHIFT] - [F10] (*retrieve*)
> Document to be Retrieved: **b:memo** ↵

■ Add an additional paragraph to the
memo.

> [PGDN] (*move cursor to end of document*)

You should now be at the beginning of
line 12. Key in the following:

[TAB] **Attached are the latest descriptions of our products from the Marketing Department. Please note your comments on the descriptions so that we can discuss them at the meeting.**

↵ ↵

COMBINING THE "PRODUCTS" FILE AND THE "MEMO" FILE

Add the contents of the "products" file to the end of "memo".

■ Combine the "products" file, starting at the current cursor position (beginning of line 16). After the combining operation, the "products" file remains intact on your disk.

[SHIFT] - [F10]
Document to be Retrieved: **b:products** ↵

■ Move the cursor to the end of the document to confirm that all was transferred, then return to the current position. The line of hyphens (---) indicates a page break.

[HOME] [HOME] ↓ *(move to end of document)*
[CTRL] - [HOME] [CTRL] - [HOME] *(return to previous position)*

FORMATTING THE COMBINED FILE: PAGE BREAKS, DOUBLE SPACING, AND BOXES

Insert page breaks, double space the product descriptions, and draw a box around the To:/From:/Re: area.

■ Insert page breaks so that the memo is on the first page, the Tegler description on the second page, and the Qwert description on the third page.

(position cursor at beginning of line with TEGLER heading)
[CTRL] - ↵ *(inserted page break)*
(position cursor at beginning of line with QWERT heading)
[CTRL] - ↵ *(inserted page break)*

Notice that an inserted page break is signified by a line of equals signs (===).

■ George Brooks decided to double space the product descriptions so that salespeople could insert their comments directly on the descriptions.

(position cursor at beginning of line with TEGLER heading)
[SHIFT] - [F8] 4 *(spacing)*
[Spacing Set] 2 ↵

■ Draw a box around the "To:/From:/Re:"

area of "memo". Insert three spaces in front of "To:", "From:", and "Re:" to make room for the left border of the box.

(position cursor in Ln 3, Pos 10)
[SPACE] *(3 times)*
(position cursor in Ln 4, Pos 10)
[SPACE] *(3 times)*
(position cursor on the "G" in Ln 4)
[SPACE] *(4 times)*
(position cursor in Ln 5, Pos 10)
[SPACE] *(3 times)*
(position cursor in Ln 2, Pos 10 to draw box)
[CTRL] - [F3] *(screen menu)* 2 *(line draw)*
1 *(select single line draw)*

Use the cursor control keys to draw the box. Corners will be inserted automatically when the direction changes. To erase mistakes, select option 5 (erase) and erase the mistake, then select option 1 to continue drawing single lines.

→ *(press repeatedly to draw horizontal line to Ln 2 Pos 59)*
↓ *(press repeatedly to draw vertical line to Ln 6 Pos 59)*
← *(press repeatedly to draw horizontal line to Ln 6 Pos 10)*
↑ *(press repeatedly to draw vertical line to Ln 2 Pos 10)*
[F7] *(exit line draw)*

If you need to correct line errors, press INS to toggle to overtype mode so that the lines and text inside the box are not altered. Return to insert mode when you finish editing the lines.

■ Add a blank line above and below the box.

(position cursor in Ln 2, Pos 10)
↵
(position cursor in Ln 8, Pos 10)
↵

WordPerfect display after the completion of the section on "Formatting the Combined File: Page Breaks, Double Spacing, and Boxes" in the Advanced and Special Features Tutorial (HOME position).

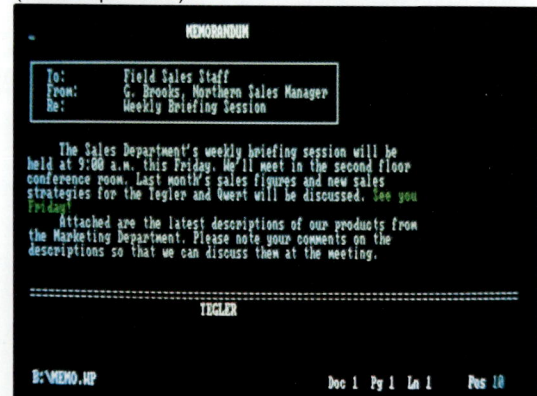

USING THE ON-LINE THESAURUS

George Brooks was not satisfied with the word "note" in the last sentence of the memo and wants to examine some other possibilities.

■ Using the full-function version of WordPerfect's Thesaurus Disk, employ the on-line thesaurus feature to find another word for "note". The cursor must be on the desired word before opening the thesaurus.

> (*position cursor in Ln 15 on the "n" in "note"*)
> (*replace your data disk in drive B with the thesaurus disk*)
> ALT - F1 (*thesaurus*)

■ The program reads the word at the cursor (i.e., note) and suggests alternative synonyms. Not satisfied with the options, Mr. Brooks wants to see more. Select the verb "record" in the second column.

> → (*move to column two*)
> **A** (*select the verb "record"*)

■ After examining the new set of options, Mr. Brooks decides to replace "note" with the word "indicate".

> **1** (*word replacement key*)
> Press letter for word **K**

You are returned to the work screen.

The display shows what happens when synonyms for "note" are requested from the on-line thesaurus that accompanies WordPerfect during the section on "Using the On-Line Thesaurus" in the Advanced and Special Features Tutorial.

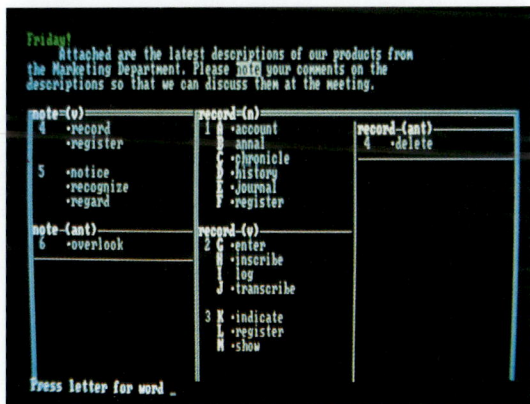

USING THE SPELLING CHECKER

Using the full-function version of WordPerfect's Speller Disk, employ the spelling checker feature to ensure that all words in "memo" are spelled correctly.

In all likelihood you will have at least one spelling error, but just in case, alter the spelling of "Sales" in the To: line (line 4) memo to "Sals".

■ Insert the Speller disk in drive B and initiate the spell function.

> CTRL - F2 (*spell*)

■ Select the "document" option to spell-check the entire document.

> **3** (*document*)

■ WordPerfect highlights the first unrecognized word (probably "Sals"), suggests optional spellings, and displays a menu. Press the letter next to the correct spelling to replace "Sals" with "Sales".

> **E** (*sales*)

As you spell-check the remainder of the document, you may need to select options from the spell menu. The options are

Skip Once	Spell-checking continues; the Speller stops at the next occurrence of the word.
Skip	Spell-checking continues; the word is ignored for the rest of the document.
Add Word	The word is saved in the supplementary dictionary and spell-checking continues (*do not use this option at this time*).
Edit	You can correct the spelling, then press the Enter key to continue spell-checking.
Look Up	You can look up a word in the main dictionary that matches a pattern and replace the word not found with the correct spelling.

Continue the above procedure for each misspelled word until you reach the end of the document.

■ When the spell-check is complete, replace the Speller disk in drive B with your data disk and press any key to continue.

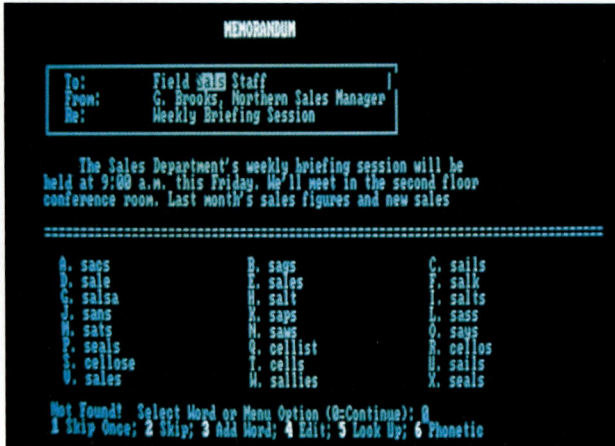

The display shows what happens when the spelling checker that accompanies WordPerfect detects a misspelled word ("Sals") during the section on "Using the Spelling Checker" in the Advanced and Special Features Tutorial.

PRINTING THE EXTENDED MEMO AND TERMINATING THE SESSION

■ Save the current memo before attempting to print.

> F10
>
> Document to be Saved: B:MEMO ↵
> Replace B:MEMO (Y/N) **Y**es

■ Print the memo.

> SHIFT - F7
>
> **1** (*full text*)

■ Terminate the session (see Hands-On Tutorial 11).

> F7
>
> Save Document? (Y/N) **N**o
> Exit WP? (Y/N) **Y**es

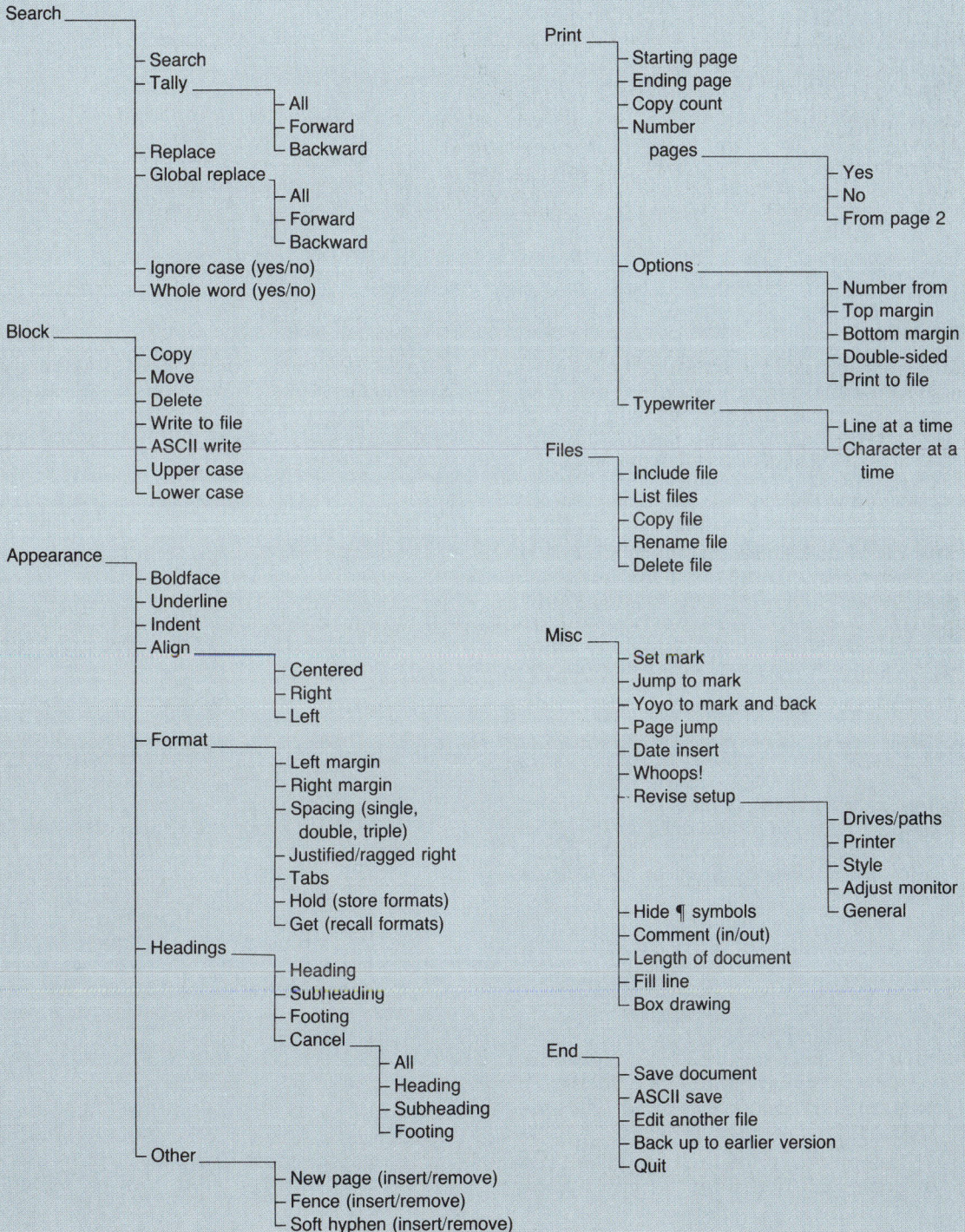

QUICK REFERENCE GUIDE
Webster's NewWorld Writer
(Version 1.06)
A>wwp ↵

MENU

Search
- Search
- Tally
  - All
  - Forward
  - Backward
- Replace
- Global replace
  - All
  - Forward
  - Backward
- Ignore case (yes/no)
- Whole word (yes/no)

Block
- Copy
- Move
- Delete
- Write to file
- ASCII write
- Upper case
- Lower case

Appearance
- Boldface
- Underline
- Indent
- Align
  - Centered
  - Right
  - Left
- Format
  - Left margin
  - Right margin
  - Spacing (single, double, triple)
  - Justified/ragged right
  - Tabs
  - Hold (store formats)
  - Get (recall formats)
- Headings
  - Heading
  - Subheading
  - Footing
  - Cancel
    - All
    - Heading
    - Subheading
    - Footing
- Other
  - New page (insert/remove)
  - Fence (insert/remove)
  - Soft hyphen (insert/remove)

Print
- Starting page
- Ending page
- Copy count
- Number pages
  - Yes
  - No
  - From page 2
- Options
  - Number from
  - Top margin
  - Bottom margin
  - Double-sided
  - Print to file
- Typewriter
  - Line at a time
  - Character at a time

Files
- Include file
- List files
- Copy file
- Rename file
- Delete file

Misc
- Set mark
- Jump to mark
- Yoyo to mark and back
- Page jump
- Date insert
- Whoops!
- Revise setup
  - Drives/paths
  - Printer
  - Style
  - Adjust monitor
  - General
- Hide ¶ symbols
- Comment (in/out)
- Length of document
- Fill line
- Box drawing

End
- Save document
- ASCII save
- Edit another file
- Back up to earlier version
- Quit

QUICK REFERENCE GUIDE Continued
Webster's NewWorld Writer
(Version 1.06)
A>wwp ↵

CURSOR MOVEMENT		
By word right/left	SHIFT-→	SHIFT-←
To margin right/left	CTRL-→	CTRL-←
To screen end/beg.	END	HOME
To document end/beg.	CTRL-END	CTRL-HOME

FUNCTION KEYS			
Recalls/removes help window	F1	F2	Topic index
Main Command Menu	F3	F4	Cursor keys
Insert/delete keys	F5	F6	Alt keys
Screen symbols	F7	F8	System status
Setup summary	F9	F10	ASCII table

HANDS-ON TUTORIAL 4: Using Webster's NewWorld Writer

Webster's NewWorld Writer, word processing software from Simon & Schuster, Inc., has redefined the meaning of "user friendly." The easy-to-use menu-driven user interface of Webster's NewWorld Writer is designed to display instructional prompts in windows if the user hesitates when selecting an option from a menu.

Take time to read the windows that explain the various menu options. This is a good way to learn more about this package. Often, there is more than one way to accomplish a task. However, while working through the tutorials, follow what is presented in the text so that you stay synchronized with the tutorial. This tutorial is based on Webster's NewWorld Writer Educational Version 1.06.

The Keystroke Conventions box in Hands-On Tutorial 1 explains and illustrates the keystroke format used for the interactive tutorials.

■ Boot the system (see Hands-On Tutorial 1).
■ Load Webster's to memory. Insert the Webster's program disk in drive A.

    A>**wwp** ↵

■ Insert your data disk in drive B. You are now ready to begin your word processing session.

HANDS-ON TUTORIAL 5: Creating and Formatting a Document

In Hands-On Tutorials 5 through 11, we will create and print the memo in Figure 5–7. Figures 5–1 through 5–6 illustrate steps in the creation and development of the Figure 5–7 memo.

■ The first screen after the Webster's title screen allows us to name and create a new file (document) or call up an existing one. Name the new file "memo".

    Filename? B:**memo** ↵

Now, whatever text you enter becomes part of the document "memo". But before entering text, become familiar with the display.

Instructions in the top corners tell you to press ESC to call up the main menu and F1 for help. The status line above the document work area indicates that the current file is an ASCII file (A); that you are in insert (Ins) mode, not overstrike mode (Ovr); and that the cursor is located at page (Pg) 1, line (Ln) 1, and column (Col) 1 of the document. The layout line at the bottom of the screen shows the current tab settings (upward tick marks) and current position of the cursor (downward tick mark).

■ Change the left margin from 1 (the default) to 9 and accept the other default settings (for example, tab settings and single spacing). To reset the left margin, select the main menu (ESC). In Webster's, you select an option from a bar menu by highlighting the desired option with the left/right cursor control keys and pressing ENTER. Or, press the first letter of the desired menu option. Select the "Appearance" option by pressing "A", the "Format" option with an "F", the left margin option with an "L", and use the right cursor control key to set Col in the status line to 9.

> ESC Appearance Format Left → (8 times) ↵ ↵

The first ENTER confirms the new margin and the second ENTER causes the document to be reformatted.

HANDS-ON TUTORIAL 6: Entering and Adding Text

■ Notice that the insert mode (Ins) cursor is a blinking square and the overstrike mode (Ovr) cursor is a blinking underscore. Toggle between the two with the INS key and observe the changes to the status line and the cursor. Finish in insert mode.

> INS INS INS INS

■ Enter the first three lines of the text of the memo. To correct typographical errors, use the cursor control keys in combination with the DEL and BKSP keys.

> **To:** TAB TAB **Field Sales Staff** ↵
> **From:** TAB **G. Brooks, Northern Sales Manager** ↵
> **Re:** TAB TAB **Weekly Briefing Session** ↵ ↵

The second ENTER adds a blank line. The status line should now indicate Pg 1, Ln 5, and Col 9.

■ Key in the text of the memo in Figure 5–1. Since the lines wrap automatically, *press ENTER only at the end of the paragraph!*

> TAB **The Sales Department's** . . . (*see text in Figure 5–1*) **conference room.** ↵

■ Add the sentence "See you Thursday!" (see Figure 5–2).

> (*position cursor in Ln 8 on the "W"*)
> **See you Thursday!** SPACE

If the text runs off the right side of the screen, as it will in this instance, just keep entering text, or move the cursor, and the document will be reformatted to fit in the defined margins.

Save option: If at anytime you cannot continue with the tutorials, save your work so that you can pick up where you left off. To do this, see "Hands-On Tutorial 10: Saving and Retrieving a Document." When you return, retrieve your document and continue the tutorials.

Webster's NewWorld Writer display after the completion of Hands-On Tutorial 6.

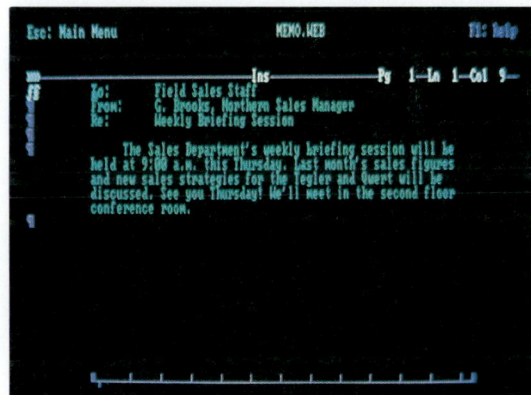

HANDS-ON TUTORIAL 7: Moving Text

Move the last sentence in the current memo to be the second sentence in a revised memo (see Figures 5–3 and 5–4).

■ Position the cursor at the beginning of the last sentence and mark the beginning of the block to be moved.

> (*position cursor in Ln 8 on the "W"*)

> ESC **B**lock

■ Move the cursor to the position following the period (.) at the end of the last sentence and mark the end of the block.

> (*position cursor in Ln 9 following the "."*)
> ↵

■ Select the "Move" (block) option.

Move

- Indicate the destination of the block move by positioning the cursor at the beginning of the second sentence (the L in "Last"). Execute the move.

  (position cursor in Ln 6 on the "L")
  ↵

- Separate the second and third sentences with a space.

  (position cursor in Ln 7 on the "L")

  SPACE

Webster's NewWorld Writer display just prior to the block move in Hands-On Tutorial 7.

HANDS-ON TUTORIAL 8: Search and Replace

Search for all occurrences of the word "Thursday" in the memo of Figure 5–4 and replace them with the word "Friday". The memo should appear as shown in Figure 5–5.

- Position the cursor to the beginning of the document.

  HOME

  Pressing HOME moves the cursor to the top of the current screen. Use CTRL-HOME to position the cursor to the beginning of the document if your document is more than one screen in length. Pressing the END key positions the cursor at the end of the text of the current screen. Use CTRL-END to position the cursor at the end of the document when your document is more than one screen in length.

- Select the global replace option of the search command series.

  ESC **S**earch **G**lobal replace

- Enter the search and the replace patterns.

  Enter search pattern: **Thursday** ↵
  Enter replacement pattern: **Friday** ↵ **A**ll

HANDS-ON TUTORIAL 9: Centering, Boldfacing, Underlining, and Justifying Text

Add, then boldface and center the title "MEMORANDUM". Underline the sentence "See you Friday!" (see various word processing examples in Figure 5–6).

- Add two blank lines at the top of the memo, then reposition the cursor to "home."

  HOME ↵ ↵ HOME

- Enter "MEMORANDUM" and designate as boldface.

  MEMORANDUM CTRL-←
  ESC **A**ppearance **B**oldface → (10 times) ↵

  The CTRL-← and CTRL-→ keystroke combinations reposition the cursor to the beginning and end of the current line.

- Center the text on the first line.

  ESC **A**ppearance **A**lign **C**enter

- Underline "See you Friday!"

  (position cursor in Ln 10 on the "S")

  ESC **A**ppearance **U**nderline → (15 times, to the "!") ↵

- Right justify the document.

  ESC **A**ppearance **F**ormat **J**ustify/ragged **U**se

  The sequence above would be repeated to change back to a ragged right margin.

Webster's NewWorld Writer display after the completion of Hands-On Tutorial 9.

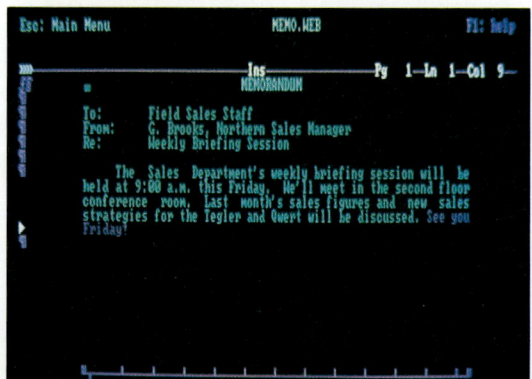

144

HANDS-ON TUTORIAL 10: Saving and Retrieving a Document

Do the following to save then retrieve the document named "memo".

- Save "memo" to disk storage.

    [ESC] *E*nd *S*ave ↵ *R*esume

    The ENTER saves the current document ("""memo") to disk storage. "Resume" returns you to the document. If you wanted to save the document under another name, such as "memo1", you would have entered a new name following the prompt, "Filename?" Remember to include the disk specifier (for example, B:memo1), if necessary.

- Retrieve "memo" from disk storage.

    [ESC] *E*nd *E*dit another file
    Filename? B:**memo** ↵

    This command sequence causes Webster's to search disk B for a file named "memo". If such a file exists, it is loaded to memory and displayed on the screen. If no such file exists, the screen will be cleared and "memo" will be the name of the document to be created.

HANDS-ON TUTORIAL 11: Printing a Document and Terminating a Session

Turn on the printer and produce a hard copy of the memo (see Figure 5–7), then exit Webster's.

- Select the "Print" option from the main menu.

    [ESC] *P*rint *P*rint

    Notice that the Print bar menu gives you several options, such as selecting the pages to be printed, numbering the pages, and selecting other options such as revising the top or bottom margin.

- If you have not made any revisions to "memo" since the last save command, issue the following sequence to exit Webster's.

    [ESC] *E*nd *Q*uit
    A>

- If you have made revisions to "memo" since the last save command, issue the following sequence to exit Webster's.

    [ESC] *E*nd *Q*uit *Y*es ↵
    A>

    All software productivity tools ask for exit confirmation if the most current revisions have not been saved to disk storage. If you respond "Yes", you are given an opportunity to change the name of the document to be saved. Even though you get a last chance, it is good practice to save your work before exiting the program.

ADVANCED AND SPECIAL FEATURES TUTORIAL: Webster's NewWorld Writer

In this advanced Webster's tutorial the following skills are introduced: setting tabs; merging (including) files; setting page breaks; double spacing; drawing boxes; using Webster's fences; using Webster's On-line Thesaurus; using Webster's Spelling Checker; and adjusting pagination.

George Brooks, Zimco's Northern Sales Manager, wants to create product descriptions for the Tegler and Qwert to hand out at an upcoming meeting (see memo of Figure 5–7). He wants to add these descriptions to the previously created "memo" (from Hands-On Tutorials 4 through 11). To do this, he plans to use a variety of Webster's features.

GETTING STARTED
To complete this tutorial, you will need Webster's program disk, the Thesaurus Dictionary disk, the Spelling Checker disk, and your data disk.

- Load the Webster's word processing program (master disk 1) to memory (see Hands-On Tutorial 4). Insert the Webster's program disk in drive A.

    A>**wwp** ↵

- Insert your data disk in drive B.

CREATING THE PRODUCT DESCRIPTION FILE

Create a new file that will contain descriptions of the two Zimco products, the Tegler and the Qwert.

- Name and create a file called "products".

Filename? B:**products** ↵

■ Reset the left margin to match the "memo" margin of 9 (see Hands-On Tutorial 5).

> ESC **A**ppearance **F**ormat **L**eft → (*8 times*)
> ↵ ↵

ENTERING THE PRODUCT DESCRIPTIONS

Webster's has several paragraph symbols with which you should be familiar.

¶ First line of a paragraph
ƒ Formatted (fenced) paragraph
§ Paragraph with a heading change
▶ Line containing position marker

The second and third symbols above should appear on the screen of the "products" file that you just created. Webster's lets you change the format of any portion of your document. One of the ways it does this is through the fences that are automatically placed at the beginning of a formatted paragraph. The same format will be followed until the next fence is reached. To revise a fence setting, use the ESC-Appearance-Other menu option.

Now key in the name of each product (boldfaced and centered), followed by its description.

■ Boldface and center the product title "TEGLER" (see Hands-On Tutorial 9).

> TEGLER   CTRL -←
> ESC **A**ppearance **B**oldface CTRL -→ ↵
> ESC **A**ppearance **A**lign **C**enter ↵ ↵

■ Key in the rest of the text (see Hands-On Tutorial 6). Center and boldface the Qwert title, center the subheadings, leave lines blank as shown, and use the TAB key to indent text where necessary.

> The default tab setting for Webster's is 5. If this is not the case (see the layout line at the bottom of the screen), follow these directions in resetting the first 3 tabs to intervals of 5.
>
> ESC **A**ppearance **F**ormat **T**abs
> (*follow directions on screen for arrows/space bar*)
> (*put tabs in columns 6, 11, and 16*)
> ↵ ↵

Now enter the remainder of the text.

(*insert 2 line spaces after TEGLER and after QWERT*)

-- The Need --

Though warned repeatedly that chewing on ball-point pen caps is unsightly and socially unacceptable, millions of "closet" chewers unconsciously nibble at every opportunity. Whether these people are found in grammar school classrooms or corporate boardrooms, Zimco is sympathetic.

-- The Solution --

The Tegler is a flavored pen cap that adds a little zip to the enjoyment of habitual pen-cap chewers.
! One size fits all.
! Five separate flavors per package.
Licorice
Peppermint
Cherry
Lemon
Avocado
! Flavorful enjoyment with no telltale teeth marks.
! Slogan: "Any Time is Tegler Time"

(*insert 2 line spaces here*)

QWERT

-- The Need --

Have you ever been at a loss when asked, "How are you today?" Have you ever wanted to know exactly how on-top-of-it you are

before taking a test, meeting the boss, or going on a date?
Now you can answer these important questions and more, such as
"How difficult an opponent can I manage today in tennis?",
"Can I tackle that big project now?", or "Is it time for
lunch?"

-- The Solution --

Zimco's Qwert is a watch-like biofeedback mechanism that, when
placed around the wrist, measures variations in galvanic skin
response and heart rate. A tiny computer inside the Qwert
collects and analyzes these data to provide a continuous
readout of a person's physical and, to some extent, emotional
well-being. The readout varies from 1 (extreme lethargy) to 10
(extreme anxiety). Qwert users can learn to adjust their body
chemistry to optimize their mental acuity and reduce stress
and tension.
Slogan: "Do Smart Work with a Qwert."

■ Right justify the document, but first return to the top of the document.

  CTRL - HOME ESC Appearance Format
  Justify/ragged Use

The above sequence would be repeated to change back to a ragged right margin.

Webster's NewWorld Writer display after the completion of the section on "Creating the Product Description File" in the Advanced and Special Features Tutorial (HOME position).

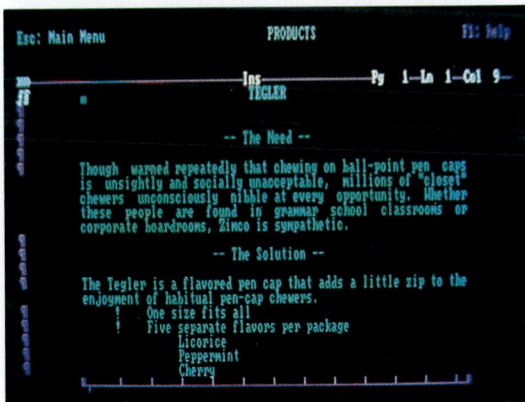

SAVING THE "PRODUCTS" FILE AND EDITING THE "MEMO" FILE

Save "products" to disk storage, then open and edit the "memo" file (see Hands-On Tutorial 10).

■ Save the "products" file.

  ESC End Save ↵

■ Do not return to the "products" file.

Choose the command "Edit another file" and open the "memo" file.

  Edit another file
  Filename B:memo ↵

■ Add an additional paragraph to the memo.

  END (move cursor to end of document)

You should now be in line 12, column 1 before you key in the following:

TAB Attached are the latest descriptions of our products from the Marketing Department. Please note your comments on the descriptions so that we can discuss them at the meeting. ↵ ↵

MERGING (INCLUDING) THE "PRODUCT" FILE INTO THE "MEMO" FILE

Add the contents of the "products" file to the end of "memo".

■ The products file will be merged, or included, starting at the current cursor position. After the merge, the "products" file still remains on your disk, but its content will have been copied to the "memo" file.

  ESC Files Include file B:products ↵

■ Mark the current cursor position because we will return here shortly

  ESC Misc Set mark

The Miscellaneous menu is in two parts. If "Set mark" is not in the initial menu display, press M for More.

■ Move the cursor to the end of the document to confirm that all was transferred; then return to the marked position. The line of periods (. . .) indicates the position of the page break.

[CTRL]-[END]
[ESC] **M**isc **J**ump to mark

FORMATTING THE COMBINED FILE: PAGE BREAKS, DOUBLE SPACING, AND BOXES

Insert page breaks, double space the product descriptions, and draw a box around the To:/From:/Re: area.

■ Insert page breaks so that the memo is on the first page, the Tegler description on the second page, and the Qwert description on the third page.

> (*position cursor in line 16 with "TEGLER"*)
> [ESC] **A**ppearance **O**ther **N**ew *page insert*
> [PGDN]
> (*position cursor in line 27 with "QWERT"*)
> [ESC] **A**ppearance **O**ther **N**ew *page insert*

■ George Brooks decided he wanted to leave room for the salespeople to write their comments directly on the descriptions. Return to the marked position so that you can enter commands to double space the product descriptions.

> [ALT]-**J** (*return to the marked position*)
> [ESC] **A**ppearance **F**ormat **S**pacing **D**ouble **U**se

Page down to confirm that the remainder of the document is now double spaced.

■ Draw a box around the To:/From:/Re: area of "memo". Insert two spaces in front of "To:", "From:", and "Re:" to make room for the left border of the box.

> (*position cursor in Ln 3, Col 9*) [SPACE] [SPACE]
> (*position cursor in Ln 4, Col 9*) [SPACE] [SPACE]
> (*position cursor in Ln 5, Col 9*) [SPACE] [SPACE]

Use the default border that looks like a wicket (⌐¬). The following box characters are assigned to keys on the 10-key pad.

> (*position cursor in Ln 2, Col 9 to draw box*)
> [ESC] **M**isc **B**ox

To draw the box, use the SHIFT key in conjunction with the numeric 10-key pad, and the + (plus) and - (minus) keys.

> [SHIFT]-**7** (*draw upper left corner*)
> [SHIFT]-**-** (*press repeatedly to draw horizontal line to Ln 2 Col 55*)
> [SHIFT]-**9** (*draw upper right corner*)
> [SHIFT]-**+** (*press repeatedly to draw vertical line to Ln 6 Col 55*)
> [SHIFT]-**3** (*draw lower right corner*)
> [SHIFT]-**-** (*press repeatedly to draw horizontal line to Ln 6 Col 9*)
> [SHIFT]-**1** (*draw lower left corner*)
> [SHIFT]-**+** (*press repeatedly to draw vertical line to Ln 2 Col 9*)
> [ESC]

If you need to correct errors, press INS to toggle to overstrike mode so that the box lines and text inside the box are not altered. Return to insert mode when you finish editing.

■ Add a blank line below and above the box.

> (*position cursor in Ln 2, Col 9*)
> ↵
> (*position cursor in Ln 8, Col 9*)
> ↵

Webster's NewWorld Writer display after the completion of the section on "Formatting the Combined File: Page Breaks, Double Spacing, and Boxes" in the Advanced and Special Features Tutorial (HOME position).

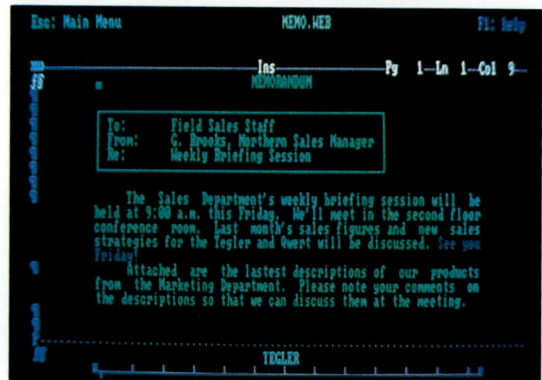

Drawing Boxes	
Keys	Description
[SHIFT]- numeric keypad	Produce box characters shown here
[ENTER]	Select line style
↑↓ ←→	Position cursor in text

USING THE ON-LINE THESAURUS

George Brooks was not satisfied with the word "note" in the last sentence of the memo and wanted to examine some other possibilities.

■ Use Webster's On-Line Thesaurus to find another word for "note". The cursor must be at the beginning of the word before opening the thesaurus.

> (*position cursor in Ln 15 on the "n" in "note"*)
> ESC *Thesaurus*

■ At the prompt, replace your data disk with the Thesaurus Dictionary disk.

> (*remove data disk from drive B*)
> (*insert Thesaurus Dictionary disk in drive B*)
> ↵

■ The program reads the word at the cursor (i.e., note) and suggests possible alternative synonyms. Not satisfied with the options, Mr. Brooks wants to see more. Use the cursor keys to highlight the verb "record" in the last line of the window display for "note" (see entry 2). Select record for more possibilities.

> ↓ (*8 times*) ↵

■ After examining the new set of options, Mr. Brooks decides to replace "note" with the phrase "write down".

> F2 (*press F2 to toggle between thesaurus windows*)
> (*highlight "write down"*)
> F10 (*word replacement key*)
> F10 (*confirmation of replacement*)

The display shows what happens when synonyms for "note" are requested from the on-line thesaurus that accompanies Webster's NewWorld Writer during the section on "Using the On-Line Thesaurus" in the Advanced and Special Features Tutorial.

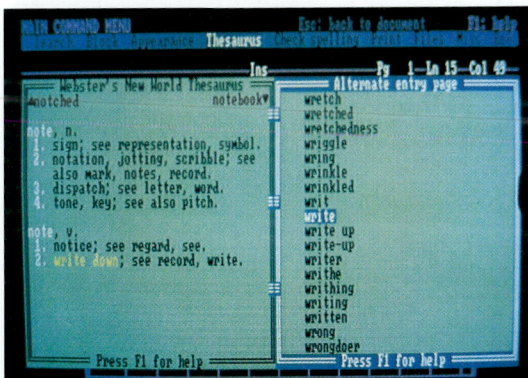

USING THE SPELLING CHECKER

Use Webster's Spelling Checker to ensure that all words are spelled correctly. In all likelihood you will have at least one spelling error, but just in case, alter the spelling of "Sales" in the To: line (line 4) of the memo to "Sals."

■ Select the "Check spelling" option from the main menu.

> ESC *Check spelling* **Yes**
> (*at the prompt, reinsert the data disk*)
> ↵

■ The document "memo" is saved and the next prompt asks that you insert the Spelling Checker disk.

> (*remove system disk from drive A*)
> (*insert Spelling Checker disk*)
> (*press any key*)

■ After "memo" is checked for spelling, press ESC to preview questionable words.

> ESC

■ The list of words at the top of the screen includes "qwert," "tegler," "zimco," and any misspelled words. Mark the words to tell Webster's Spelling Checker whether the spelling is "ok" or should be changed (see instructions in the lower left box). Use the arrow keys to highlight an incorrect word then press ENTER to toggle between the three options. For example, change the symbol in front of "qwert", "tegler", and "zimco" from "?" (word is not in dictionary) to "−" (minus), to indicate that the words are acceptable as is. If any other words appear in the list, leave the preceding "?" and Webster's will stop at the word during the edit scan and suggest possible correct spellings.

Do *not* change the "?" symbol to the "+" symbol in these tutorials because we do not want to add any new words to the auxiliary dictionary.

■ When all of the words have been marked, press ESC to edit the document.

> ESC

■ At a minimum, you will need to correct the spelling of "Sals". When the edit scan highlights "Sals" as the "Word in question:", ask Webster's to suggest possible spellings.

> F6 (*suggest spellings*)

Notice the other functional options at the lower-left portion of the screen.

■ Select the correct spelling from the list of "Possible spellings:" by using the up/down cursor keys to select "Sales."

> ↓ *(3 times to "Sales")* ↵
> ↵ *(confirmation)*

■ Continue the above procedure for each misspelled word until the edit scan is complete.

■ When the edit scan is complete, insert the Word Processor program disk in drive A and press any key to return to the document.

The display shows what happens when the spelling checker that accompanies Webster's NewWorld Writer detects a misspelled word ("Sals") during the section on "Using the Spelling Checker" in the Advanced and Special Features Tutorial.

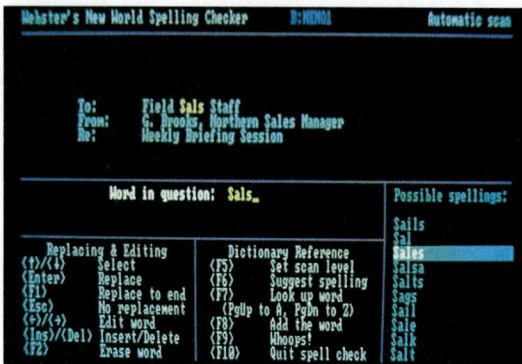

PRINTING THE EXTENDED MEMO AND TERMINATING THE SESSION

George Brooks does not want the memo page numbered and he wants the product descriptions to begin on page 2. This is the default option for Webster's.

■ Save the current memo before attempting to print.

> ESC **E**nd **S**ave ↵ **R**esume

■ Print the memo.

> ESC **P**rint ↵

■ Check that the words "from pg. 2" appear under the heading "Number pages" and give the command to print.

> *Print*

■ Terminate the session (see Hands-On Tutorial 11).

> ESC **E**nd **Q**uit

Webster's New World Spelling Checker   B:MEMO1   Automatic scan

```
To:      Field Sals Staff
From:    G. Brooks, Northern Sales Manager
Re:      Weekly Briefing Session


        Word in question:  Sals_           Possible spellings:
                                            Sails
                                            Sal
     Replacing & Editing      Dictionary Reference    Sales
  (↑)/(↓)   Select         <F5>    Set scan level     Salsa
  (Enter)   Replace        <F6>    Suggest spelling   Salts
  (F1)      Replace to end <F7>    Look up word       Sags
  (Esc)     No replacement   (PgUp to A, PgDn to Z)   Sall
  (+)/(→)   Edit word      <F8>    Add the word       Sale
  (Ins)/(Del) Insert/Delete <F9>   Whoops!            Salk
  (F2)      Erase word     <F10>   Quit spell check   Salt
```

WORD PROCESSING TUTORIAL: WORDSTAR PROFESSIONAL

QUICK REFERENCE GUIDE
WordStar Professional
(Release 4)
A>ws ↵

MENUS

OPENING MENU

D	open a document	L	change logged drive/directory
N	open a nondocument	C	protect a file
P	print a file	E	rename a file
M	merge print a file	D	copy a file
I	index a document	Y	delete a file
T	table of contents	F	turn directory off
X	exit WordStar	Esc	shorthand
J	help	R	run a DOS command

The edit menu appears after opening a file.

EDIT MENU

CURSOR		SCROLL		ERASE		OTHER		MENUS	
^E	up	^W	up	^G	char	^J	help	^O	onscreen format
^X	down	^Z	down	^T	word	^I	tab	^K	block & save
^S	left	^R	up screen	^Y	line	^V	turn insert off	^P	print controls
^D	right	^C	down screen	Del	char	^B	align paragraph	^Q	quick functions
^A	word left			^U	unerase	^N	split the line	Esc	shorthand
^F	word right					^L	find/replace again		

Use CTRL-O to see the following menu:

ONSCREEN FORMAT MENU

MARGINS		TYPING		DISPLAY	
L	set left	W	turn word wrap off	D	turn print controls off
R	set right	J	turn right justify off	H	turn hyphen help on
X	release	E	enter soft hyphen	P	turn preview on
T	turn ruler off	G	temporary indent	B	turn soft space dots on TABS
F	ruler from text	S	set line spacing	I	set tab stop
O	ruler to text	C	center line	N	clear

Use CTRL-K to see the following menu:

BLOCK & SAVE MENU

SAVE		BLOCK				FILE			
S	save & resume edit	B	mark begin	C	copy	O	copy	P	print
D	save document	K	mark end	V	move	E	rename		
X	save & exit WordStar	H	turn display on	Y	delete	J	erase		
Q	quit without saving	W	write to disk	M	math	L	logged drive/dir		
	CURSOR	N	turn column mode on			R	insert a file		
0–9	set/remove marker	I	turn column replace on			F	run a DOS command		

Quick Reference Guide (*continued*)

QUICK REFERENCE GUIDE Continued
WordStar Professional
(Release 4)
A>ws ↵

Use CTRL-P to see the following menu:

PRINT CONTROLS MENU

BEGIN & END			OTHER		
B bold	X strike out		H overprint char	O binding space	
S underline	D double strike		↵ overprint line	C print pause	
V subscript	Y italics/color		F phantom space	I column tab	
T superscript	K indexing		G phantom rubout	@ fixed position	
	Q W E R custom		N normal pitch	
	L form feed		A alternate pitch	

Use CTRL-Q to see the following menu:

QUICK MENU

CURSOR		FIND		OTHER		SPELL	
E upper left	P previous	F find text	U align paragraphs	L check rest
X lower right	V last find	A find/replace	M math Q repeat	N check word
S left side	B beg block	G char forward	ERASE	O enter word
D right side	K end block	H char back	Y line to right	SCROLL
R beg doc	0–9 marker	I find page	Del line to left	W up, repeat
C end doc	? char count	(or line)	T to character	Z down

Use ESC to see the following menu:

SHORTHAND MENU

?   display and/or change definitions   ^J   help

=   result from last ^QM or ^KM math   @   today's date
$ formatted result from last ^QM or ^KM math   !   current time
#   last ^QM math equation ﹨

CURSOR MOVEMENT

By word right/left	CTRL-→	CTRL-←
To margin right/left	CTRL-F10	CTRL-F9
To screen and/beg.	END	HOME
To document end/beg.	CTRL-END	CTRL-HOME

FUNCTION KEYS

Line 1 = Fn
Line 2 = CTRL-Fn
Line 3 = SHIFT-Fn
Line 4 = ALT-Fn

Help				Undo
Find				Find and Replace
Display On/Off				Center
Draw |	F1		F2	Draw –
Underline Beg/End				Boldface Beg/End
Find Again				Go to Page
Check Spelling				Check Spelling
in Rest of File				of Word
Draw ⌈	F3		F4	Draw ⌉
Delete Line				Delete Word Right
Left Margin				Right Margin
Delete Block				Hide Block
Draw ⌊	F5		F6	Draw ⌋
Align Paragraph				Insert Ruler
Paragraph Margin				Insert Page Break
Move Block				Copy Block
Draw ⊤	F7		F8	Draw ⊥
Save/Continue				Save/Done
Left End of Line				Right End of Line
Begin Block				End Block
Draw ⊢	F9		F10	Draw ⊣

HANDS-ON TUTORIAL 4: Using WordStar Professional _____

WordStar Professional, a product of MicroPro International Corporation, is a popular word processing menu-driven word processing package. WordStar Pro is a descendant of the classic WordStar package that was release in 1979. This tutorial is based on WordStar Professional Release 4.0.

WordStar Professional, a state-of-the-art update of the earlier versions of WordStar, is referred to throughout the tutorials as WordStar. It allows you to work on two types of files: document files and nondocument files. The focus of the tutorials is on document files.

The Keystroke Conventions box in Hands-On Tutorial 1 explains and illustrates the keystroke format used for the interactive tutorials.

■ Boot the system (see Hands-On Tutorial 1).

■ Load WordStar to memory. Insert the WordStar program disk in drive A.

   A>**ws** ↵

The title screen is followed automatically by the Opening Menu.

■ Insert your data disk in drive B. You are now ready to begin your word processing session.

HANDS-ON TUTORIAL 5: Creating and Formatting a Document _____

In Hands-On Tutorials 5 through 11, we will create and print the memo in Figure 5–7. Figures 5–1 through 5–6 illustrate steps in the creation and development of the Figure 5–7 memo.

■ Before entering text, familiarize yourself with WordStar's hierarchy of menus. WordStar commands are entered using codes. These codes are listed in the menus in the top part of the WordStar screen or by function keys. Look over the Opening Menu and review available commands. The directory of disk A is shown just below the Opening Menu.

■ Drive A is now the active drive. Change the active drive to B.

   L (*change logged disk drive*)
   What would you like the new logged drive to be? **b:** ↵

■ Name and create a new file (document) named "memo".

   D (*open a document file*)
   Document to open? **memo** ↵
   Can't find that file. Create a new one (Y/N)? **Y**

The current menu is the Edit Menu. The top line, the status line, contains the name of the current file, the cursor location (page, line, and column), an edit mode indicator (insert or replace), and the alignment indicator.

■ In the Edit Menu, commands are entered using keystroke combinations. The first keystroke is always CTRL, which is indicated by a carat (for example, ^G). When indicated, press and hold CTRL and press the appropriate alpha key to initiate the desired command.

Four submenus are listed in the rightmost column of the Edit Menu (onscreen format, block & save, print controls, and quick functions). These submenus can be called only from the Edit Menu.

The bottom two lines of the screen contain the function key assignments. For functions on the first of the two lines, use the SHIFT key in combination with the function key (for example, to mark the beginning of a block, press SHIFT-F9). In this tutorial, we generally will initiate commands from the menu rather than from the function keys.

■ Change the right margin from 65 (the default) to 62 and accept the other default settings (tab settings at 6, 11, 16, and so forth, single spacing, and right justification). WordStar automatically sets the page offset (left margin) at about one inch. Call up the onscreen format menu to revise the right margin.

   CTRL -**O** (*onscreen format menu*)
   R (*set right margin*)
   New right margin? **62** ↵

The Edit Menu reappears and you are ready to enter text.

HANDS-ON TUTORIAL 6: Entering and Adding Text

■ When "Insert" is displayed in the status line, you are in insert mode. Toggle between insert and replace (or overstrike) mode with the INS key and observe the indicator. Finish in insert mode.

INS   INS   INS   INS

■ Enter the first three lines of the text of the memo (Figure 5–1). To correct typographical errors, use the cursor control keys in combination with the DEL and BKSP keys.

> To: TAB TAB **Field Sales Staff** ↵
> From: TAB **G. Brooks, Northern Sales**
>   **Manager** ↵
> Re: TAB TAB **Weekly Briefing Session**
>   ↵ ↵

The second ENTER adds a blank line. The status line should indicate line 5 (L05) and column 1 (C01).

■ Key in the text of the memo in Figure 5–1. Since the lines wrap automatically, *press ENTER only at the end of the paragraph!* Your final result will look slightly different from Figure 5–1 because WordStar adds extra spaces between words to right justify each line.

> TAB **The Sales Department's** . . . (*see text in Figure 5–1*) **conference room.** ↵

■ Add the sentence "See you Thursday!" (see Figure 5–2).

> (*position cursor in line 8 on the "W"*)
> **See you Thursday!** SPACE

Adding the new sentence pushes part of the last sentence to the right of the screen.

■ Reformat, or align, the paragraph.

> CTRL -**B** (*align paragraph*)

WordStar reformats from the position of the cursor forward to the end of the paragraph. The F7 key can also be used for aligning text.

Save option: If at anytime you cannot continue with the tutorials, save your work so that you can pick up where you left off. To do this, see Hands-On Tutorial 10, Saving and Retrieving a Document. When you return, retrieve your document and continue the tutorials.

WordStar display after the completion of Hands-On Tutorial 6.

HANDS-ON TUTORIAL 7: Moving Text

Move the last sentence in the current memo to be the second sentence in a revised memo (see Figures 5–3 and 5–4).

■ Position the cursor at the beginning of the last sentence. Call the "block and save" menu to mark the beginning of the block to be moved.

> (*position cursor in line 8 on the "W"*)
> CTRL -**K** (*block and save menu*)
> **B** (*mark beginning of block*)

The block marker (<B>) appears in front of the sentence and you are returned to the Edit Menu. The SHIFT-F9 key can also be used to mark the beginning of the block.

■ Move the cursor to the position following the period at the end of the last sentence and mark the end of the block.

> (*position cursor in line 9 following the "."*)
> CTRL -**K**
> **K** (*mark end of block*)

The marked sentence appears in reverse video and you are returned to the Edit Menu. The SHIFT-F10 key can also be used to mark the end of the block.

■ Indicate the destination of the block move by positioning the cursor at the beginning of the second sentence. Execute the move.

(position cursor in line 6 on the "L")

CTRL -**K**

V *(move block)*

The SHIFT-F7 key can also be used to move a block.

■ Separate the second and third sentences with a space.

(position cursor in line 7 on the "L")

SPACE

■ Unmark the marked sentence.

CTRL -**K**

H *(turn display off/on)*

■ Reformat (align) the paragraph.

(position cursor at the beginning of the paragraph, line 5)

CTRL -**B**

WordStar display just prior to the block move in Hands-On Tutorial 7.

HANDS-ON TUTORIAL 8: Search and Replace

Search for all occurrences of the word "Thursday" in the memo of Figure 5–4 and replace them with the word "Friday". The memo should be similar to Figure 5–5.

■ Position the cursor at the beginning of the document.

HOME *(position cursor to top of screen)*

CTRL-HOME moves the cursor to the beginning of the file. END moves the cursor to the right end of the current screen and CTRL-END moves the cursor to the end of the file.

■ Use the Quick Menu to begin the search (find) and replace sequence.

CTRL -**Q** *(Quick Menu)*

A *(find/replace)*

Find what? **Thursday** ↵
Replace with? **Friday** ↵
Option(s)? **g** *(start from beginning or end)* ↵

Keying in "g" selects the global replace option, although the search will stop at each occurrence.

■ Respond "Yes" to the prompt in the top-right corner of screen for both occurrences of "Thursday".

Replace (Y/N): **Y** *(2 times)*
Press Esc to continue. ESC

You are returned to the Edit Menu.

■ Reformat the paragraph.

(position cursor at beginning of paragraph, line 5)

CTRL -**B**

HANDS-ON TUTORIAL 9: Centering, Boldfacing, Underlining and Justifying Text

Add, boldface, and center the title "MEMO-RANDUM". Underline the sentence "See you Friday!"

■ Add two blank lines at the top of the memo, then reposition the cursor to "home."

HOME ↵ ↵ HOME

■ Mark the beginning of boldface, enter the title "MEMORANDUM", and mark the end of boldface.

CTRL -**P** *(Print Controls Menu)*
Bold **MEMORANDUM** CTRL -**P** **B**old

The "^B" on the screen marks the beginning and end of boldface type. The F4 key can also be used to mark boldface. To remove the boldface markers, use the backspace or delete keys.

■ Center the title on the first line by selecting the "center line" option from the On-screen Format Menu.

CTRL-O
Center line

The SHIFT-F2 keys can also be used to center a line.

■ Underline "See you Friday!"

　　　(*position cursor in line 10 on the "S"*)
　　　CTRL-P
　　　S (*underline*)
　　　(*position cursor in line 11 on the "!"*)
　　　CTRL-P
　　　S (*underline*)

The "^S" on the screen marks the beginning and end of underlining. The F3 key can also be used to mark text for underlining.

■ Right justification is the default setting for WordStar.

WordStar display after the completion of Hands-On Tutorial 9.

HANDS-ON TUTORIAL 10: Saving and Retrieving a Document

Do the following to save then retrieve the document named "memo".

■ Save "memo" to disk storage through options in the Block and Save Menu.

　　　CTRL-K
　　　D (*save document*)

This save option returns you to the Opening Menu.

■ Now retrieve the document "memo" from disk storage. To do this, follow the procedure described in Hands-On Tutorial 5.

　　　D (*open a document file*)
　　　Document to open? **memo** ↵

HANDS-ON TUTORIAL 11: Printing a Document and Terminating a Session

Turn on the printer and produce a hardcopy of the memo (see Figure 5–7); then exit WordStar. If you have made revisions to "memo" since the last save command, be sure to save your revisions before printing.

■ Call the Block and Save Menu and select the print option.

　　　CTRL-K
　　　Print

If you are in the Opening Menu, press "P" to print a file.

■ Key the file name in response to the prompt.

　　　Merge print (Y/N)? **N**
　　　Document to print? **memo** ↵

■ Accept the default values for all of the print settings by pressing ENTER.

　　　Number of copies? ↵
　　　Pause between pages (Y/N)? ↵
　　　Use form feeds (Y/N)? ↵
　　　Starting page? ↵
　　　Ending page? ↵
　　　Nondocument (Y/N)? ↵

■ Check that the printer is on and print the document.

　　　Name of printer? ↵

You will be returned to the Edit Menu.

■ Exit WordStar through the Block and Save Menu. Select the "save & exit WordStar" option.

　　　CTRL-K
　　　X (*save and exit WordStar*)

To exit WordStar from the Opening Menu, select the "exit WordStar" option. Be careful with this option because all unsaved work will be erased.

WORD PROCESSING TUTORIAL: MULTIMATE ADVANTAGE II

QUICK REFERENCE GUIDE
MultiMate Advantage II
(Version 1.0)
A>mm ↵

FUNCTION KEYS

Line 1 = SHIFT-F*n*
Line 2 = F*n*

Help			Page combine
Go to	F1	F2	Page break
Column mode			Decimal tab
Center	F3	F4	Indent
Attach a library			Replace
Create a library	F5	F6	Search
			Copy from a document
Hyphen-soft			
Move	F7	F8	Copy
Insert current format line			Save
Change format	F9	F10	Save and Exit

CURSOR MOVEMENT

By word right/left	CTRL-→	CTRL-←
To margin right/left	ALT-F3	ALT-F4
To screen end/beg.	END	HOME
To document end/beg.	F1 END	F1 HOME

OTHER

ALT-3	Print a document
ALT-L	Access Pull-Down Menu functions
ALT-Z	Boldface

HANDS-ON TUTORIAL 4: Using MultiMate Advantage II

MultiMate, a product of Ashton-Tate, is a popular word processing package. This tutorial is based on MultiMate Advantage II Version 1.0.

Most of the commands in MultiMate are entered using the function keys and key combinations using the ALT, CTRL, and SHIFT keys. MultiMate supplies a handy keyboard template for quick reference that fits on top of the keyboard. Ask your instructor if there is one available or refer to the key assignments presented in the Quick Reference Guide.

The Keystroke Conventions box in Hands-On Tutorial 1 explains and illustrates the keystroke format used for the interactive tutorials.

■ Boot the system (see Hands-On Tutorial 1).

■ Load MultiMate to memory. Insert the MultiMate Boot disk in drive A.

   A>mm ↵

On the opening screen, select the "Professional Word Processing" option.

   Press desired number **1**

Switch the MultiMate boot and system disks in drive A as directed by the program and press any key to continue.

■ When the MultiMate main menu appears, insert your data disk in drive B. You are now ready to begin your word processing session.

HANDS-ON TUTORIAL 5: Creating and Formatting a Document _____

In Hands-On Tutorials 5 through 11, we will create and print the memo in Figure 5–7. Figures 5–1 through 5–6 illustrate steps in the creation and development of the Figure 5–7 memo.

■ Select the option "Create a Document" from the main menu.

> Press desired number **2**

■ Key in the name "memo".

> Document : **memo** `F10`

■ The Document Summary Screen that appears allows you to add information that will help identify the document. For now, do not key in any information, just press F10 to continue to the next screen.

> `F10`

■ MultiMate displays the default settings and gives you the opportunity to change them. Accept the default settings; press F10 to continue.

`F10`

■ Familiarize yourself with the work screen before entering text. The status line at the top of the screen indicates that the cursor is positioned on page 1, line 1, column 1 of the document "memo". The number 1 on the format line indicates single spacing. Tabs are set at columns 5, 10, and 15. The return symbol at the end of the format line marks the right margin. The SHIFT (S) and numeric (N) key indicators are in the lower right corner.

■ Change the right margin to 62 and exit the format line. The words "FORMAT CHANGE" appear on the status line after you press F9.

> `F9` (*move cursor to format line*)
> → (*position cursor at column 62*)
> ↵
> `F9` (*exit format line*)

Pressing ENTER sets the new right margin.

HANDS-ON TUTORIAL 6: Entering and Adding Text _____

■ MultiMate Advantage is currently in strikeover (replace) mode. Toggle between strikeover and insert modes with the INS key and observe the indicator in the status line. Finish in insert mode.

> `INS` `INS` `INS`

■ Enter the first three lines of the text of the memo (Figure 5–1). During text entry, use the cursor control keys in combination with the DEL and BKSP keys to correct typographical errors.

> To: `TAB` `TAB` **Field Sales Staff** ↵
> From: `TAB` **G. Brooks, Northern Sales**
> **Manager** ↵
> Re: `TAB` `TAB` **Weekly Briefing Session**
> ↵ ↵

The second ENTER adds a blank line. The status line should indicate line 5, column 1.

■ Key in the text of the memo in Figure 5–1. Since the lines wrap automatically, *press ENTER only at the end of the paragraph!*

> `TAB` **The Sales Department's** . . . (*see text in Figure 5–1*) **conference room.** ↵

■ Add the sentence "See you Thursday!" (see Figure 5–2).

(*position cursor in line 8 on the "W"*)
See you Thursday! `SPACE`

Notice that the paragraph is automatically reformatted.

Save option: If at anytime you cannot continue with the tutorials, save your work so that you can pick up where you left off. To do this, see "Hands-On Tutorial 10: Saving and Retrieving a Document." When you return, retrieve your document and continue the tutorials.

MultiMate Advantage II display after the completion of Hands-On Tutorial 6.

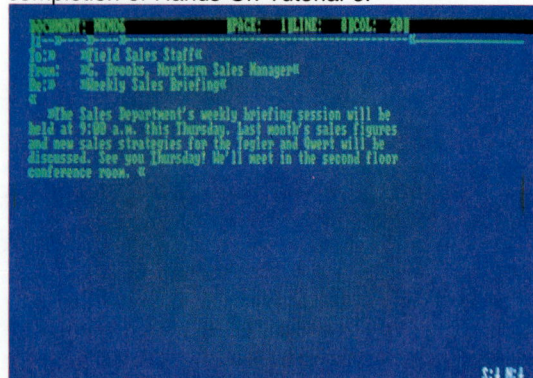

HANDS-ON TUTORIAL 7: Moving Text

Move the last sentence in the current memo to be the second sentence in a revised memo (see Figures 5–3 and 5–4).

■ Position the cursor at the beginning of the last sentence and mark the beginning of the block to be moved.

> (position cursor in line 8 on the "W")
> F7 (mark beginning of block)

The message "MOVE WHAT?" appears on the status line. MultiMate moves the cursor to the first occurrence of the next key pressed; so press the period, which highlights the entire sentence.

> . (highlight from the mark to the period)
> F7 (mark end of block)

The message "TO WHERE?" appears in the status line.

■ Indicate the destination of the block move by positioning the cursor at the beginning of the second sentence.

> (position cursor in line 6 on the "L")
> F7

■ Separate the second and third sentences with a space.

> (position cursor in line 7 on the "L")
> SPACE

MultiMate Advantage II display just prior to the block move in Hands-On Tutorial 7.

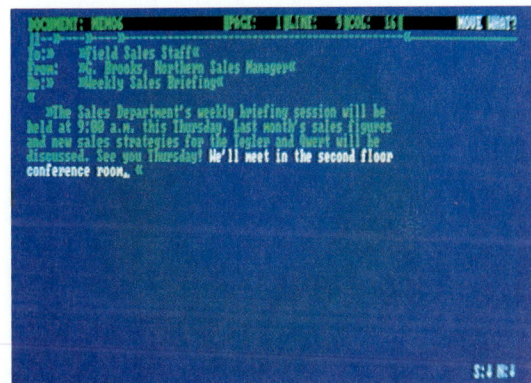

HANDS-ON TUTORIAL 8: Search and Replace

Search for all occurrences of the word "Thursday" in the memo of Figure 5–4 and replace them with the word "Friday". The memo should be similar to Figure 5–5.

■ Position the cursor at the beginning of the document.

> HOME

If there was more than one page of the document, you would use F1, HOME.

■ Initiate the search and replace sequence.

> SHIFT - F6 (search and replace)
> ALT -3 (toggle to "Global" replace option)

■ Enter the search and replace patterns.

> REPLACE WHAT? **Thursday** F10
> REPLACE WITH? **Friday** F10

MultiMate uses the F10 key, not the ENTER key, to signify the end of the search pattern. This allows the user to include a hard carriage return in the search string, if necessary.

HANDS-ON TUTORIAL 9: Centering, Boldfacing, Underlining and Justifying Text.

Center, boldface, and add the title "MEMORANDUM". Underline the sentence "See you Friday!"

■ Add two blank lines at the top of the memo and reposition the cursor to "home."

> HOME ↵ ↵ HOME

■ Center the title on the first line.

> F3 (center)

The cursor moves to the center of the line and adds a screen symbol.

■ Mark the beginning of boldface.

> ALT -Z (boldface)

A screen symbol for bolding appears.

■ Enter the title "MEMORANDUM".

MEMORANDUM

- Mark the end of boldface.

  ALT -Z

- Underline "See you Friday!"

  (position cursor in line 10 on the "S")
  SHIFT -- *(14 times to underline the sentence)*

- Right justification is toggled on and off in the Print Parameters Menu. We address justification in "Hands-On Tutorial 11: Printing a Document and Terminating a Session."

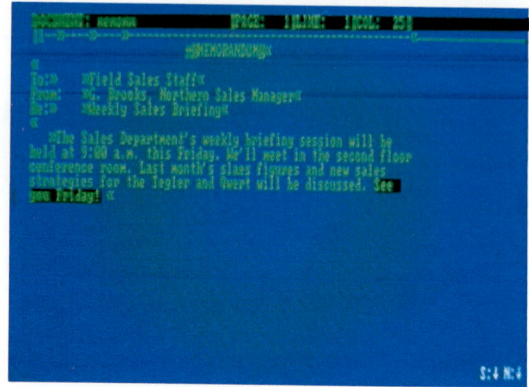

MultiMate Advantage II display after the completion of Hands-On Tutorial 9.

HANDS-ON TUTORIAL 10: Saving and Retrieving a Document

Do the following to save and retrieve the document "memo".

- Save "memo" to disk storage and exit to the Main Menu.

  F10 *(save and exit)*

If you want to save the document and then continue working it, press SHIFT-F10.

- Select option 1 from the Main Menu to edit an existing document.

  1 ↵ *(edit a document)*
  memo ↵
  F10 *(bypass the Document Summary Screen)*

The "memo" document should now be on the screen.

HANDS-ON TUTORIAL 11: Printing a Document and Terminating a Session

Before printing "memo" set the print parameters so that the memo will be printed with a left margin of one inch (10 character positions), a top margin of one inch, and with right justification. Turn on the printer and produce a hardcopy of the memo (see Figure 5–7), then exit MultiMate Advantage.

- Press ALT-3 to bypass the Main Menu and go directly to the Document Print Options.

  ALT -3 *(Document Print Options)*

- Change the left margin from the default value (000) to 010 (10 positions).

  → *(3 times to "Left margin")*
  010

- Change the top margin from the default value (000) to 006. Because we have ac-

cepted the default of 6 lines per inch, this will give a one-inch margin.

(cursor should be at the 000 in Top margin)
006

- Change justification from the default value (No) to Yes.

  ↓ *(6 times to "justification")*
  Y *(turn justification on)*

- Press F10 to accept the other default values, exit from the menu, and print the document.

  F10 *(exit the menu and print)*

- Exit MultiMate Advantage by choosing the appropriate number.

  9 *(return to MultiMate Menu)*
  9 *(return to DOS)*

WORD PROCESSING TUTORIAL: PFS:PROFESSIONAL WRITE

QUICK REFERENCE GUIDE
PFS:Professional Write
(Version 1.0)
A>pw ↵

MAIN MENU

Create/Edit
- Help
- File/Print
  - Get file
  - Save working copy
  - Delete file
  - Insert file
  - Print working copy
  - Erase working copy
  - Use macros
- Edit
  - Insert blank line
  - Delete word
  - Delete line
  - Mark text
  - Paste
  - Boldface word
  - Underline word
  - Draw lines
  - Find and replace
- Format
  - Set margins/page length
  - Set header/footer
  - Set tabs
  - Turn indent on/off
  - Turn double-spacing on/off
  - Center line
  - Left justify line
  - Right justify line
- Dictionary
  - Proof word
  - Proof document
  - Find synonyms
- Addresses
  - Select address book
  - Add an address
  - Find an address
  - Specify copy format
- Setup
  - Select printer 1
  - Select printer 2
  - Specify printer control codes
  - Change data directory
  - Change work drive
  - Change screen colors
  - Change screen update speed
- Exit

CURSOR MOVEMENT

By word right/left	CTRL-→	CTRL-←
To margin right/left	END	HOME
To document end/beg.	CTRL-END	CTRL-HOME

FUNCTION KEYS

				File/
Help	F1	F2		Print
Edit	F3	F4		Format
Dictionary	F5	F6		Addresses

HANDS-ON TUTORIAL 4: Using PFS:Professional Write

PFS:Professional Write, a product of Software Publishing Corporation, is a popular word processing package. This tutorial is based on PFS:Professional Write 1.0.

■ Boot the system (see Hands-On Tutorial 1).
■ Load PFS:Professional Write to memory.

Insert the PFS:Professional Write Program Disk in drive A.

   A>**pw** ↵

■ Insert your data disk in drive B. You are now ready to begin your word processing session.

HANDS-ON TUTORIAL 5: Creating and Formatting a Document

In Hands-On Tutorials 5 through 11, we will create and print the memo in Figure 5–7. Figures 5–1 through 5–6 illustrate steps in the creation and development of the Figure 5–7 memo.

■ Before entering text, familiarize yourself with PFS:Professional Write's menu-based command structure. Most of the commands in PFS:Professional Write are entered using the function keys to select a pull-down menu and to make a selection from the menu. Press F1 (for help) to get an on-screen explanation of the various menu options. Functions key assignments are displayed in the first line of the work screen.

■ Set up the layout line.

   1 (*create/edit from the Main Menu*)

When the PFS:Professional Write work screen appears you will see a blank screen with a blinking cursor. The cursor position indicators are in the bottom right corner (line 1 (Ln 1), page 1 (Pg 1)) and in the layout line (currently at position 10) in the work area. PFS:Professional Write automatically sets the page offset (left margin) at about one inch (e.g., position 10).

   F4 (*format menu*)

Add a tabstop at position 20. The default tabstop (which is position 15) and one at position 20 are needed to enter the text for the example memo.

   3 (*set tabs*)
   → (*9 times to position 20*)
   T ↵

HANDS-ON TUTORIAL 6: Entering and Adding Text

■ If PFS:Professional Write is in overstrike mode, there is no indication on the work screen status line. In insert mode the word "Inserting" appears in the bottom left corner of the screen. Toggle between insert and replace (or typeover) mode with the INS key and observe the indicator. Finish in insert mode.

   INS   INS   INS   INS

■ Enter the first three lines of the text of the memo (Figure 5–1). To correct typographical errors, use the cursor control keys in combination with the DEL and BKSP keys.

   To: TAB TAB **Field Sales Staff** ↵
   From: TAB **G. Brooks, Northern Sales Manager** ↵
   Re: TAB TAB **Weekly Briefing Session** ↵ ↵

The second ENTER adds a blank line. The status line should indicate line 5 of page 1.

■ Key in the text of the memo in Figure 5–1. Since the lines wrap automatically, *press ENTER only at the end of the paragraph!*

   TAB **The Sales Department's** . . . (*see text in Figure 5–1*) **conference room.** ↵

■ Add the sentence "See you Thursday!" (see Figure 5–2).

   (*position cursor in line 8 on the "W"*)
   See you Thursday! SPACE

Save option: If at anytime you cannot continue with the tutorials, save your work so that you can pick up where you left off. To do this, see "Hands-On Tutorial 10: Saving and Retrieving a Document." When you return, retrieve your document and continue the tutorials.

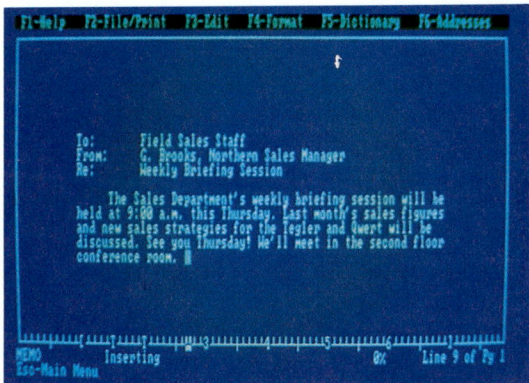

PFS:Professional Write display after the completion of Hands-On Tutorial 6.

HANDS-ON TUTORIAL 7: Moving Text

Move the last sentence in the current memo to be the second sentence in a revised memo (see Figures 5–3 and 5–4).

■ Position the cursor at the beginning of the last sentence and mark the beginning of the block to be moved.

   (position cursor in line 8 on the "W")
   F3 *(edit)*
   4 *(mark text)*
   (position cursor in line 9 on the ".")
   F10
   1 *(cut)*

Swoosh! The sentence has been stored in memory.

■ Indicate the destination of the block move by positioning the cursor at the beginning of the second sentence. Execute the move (retrieve and insert the "cut" sentence).

   (position cursor in line 6 on the "L")
   F3
   5 *(paste)*

■ Realign the text after inserting the block.

   (position cursor in line 9 after the ".")
   DEL   SPACE

PFS:Professional Write display just prior to the block move in Hands-On Tutorial 7.

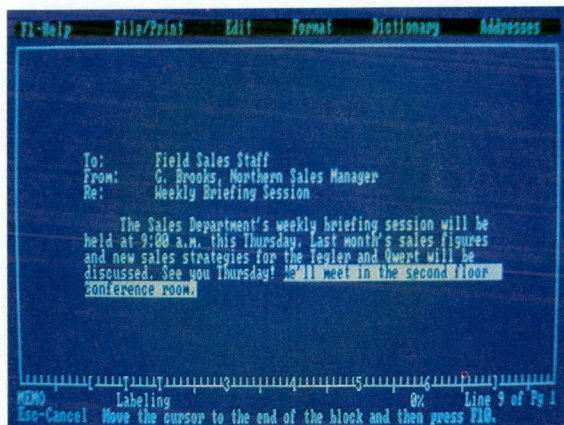

HANDS-ON TUTORIAL 8: Search and Replace

Search for all occurrences of the word "Thursday" in the memo of Figure 5–4 and replace them with the word "Friday". The memo should be similar to Figure 5–5.

■ Position the cursor at the beginning of the document.

   CTRL - HOME *(position cursor in line 1)*

■ Initiate the search and replace sequence.

   F3 *(edit)*
   9 *(find and replace)*

■ Enter the search and replace patterns.

   Find: **Thursday**   TAB
   Replace with: **Friday**   TAB
   Manual or automatic (M/A): **a** ↵ ↵

HANDS-ON TUTORIAL 9: Centering, Boldfacing, Underlining, and Justifying Text

Center, add, and boldface the title "MEMO-RANDUM". Underline the sentence "See you Friday!"

■ Add two blank lines at the top of the memo, then reposition the cursor to "home."

CTRL - HOME
↵ ↵ CTRL - HOME

■ Enter the title "MEMORANDUM".

MEMORANDUM

■ Center the title on the first line.

F4 (*format*)
6 (*center line*)

■ Boldface the title.

(*position cursor in line 1 on the first "M"*)
F3 (*edit*)
6 (*boldface word*)

The title changes intensity to indicate bold (for example, white to high intensity white).

■ Underline "See you Friday!"

(*position cursor in line 10 on the "S"*)
F3
7 (*underline word and cursor moves to the next word*)
F3 **7**
F3 **7**

The sentence changes color or intensity to indicate underlining (for example, white to yellow on a color monitor).

■ Right justification in PFS:Professional File is a "Print Option" so justification is initiated in "Hands-On Tutorial 11: Printing a Document and Terminating."

PFS:Professional Write display after the completion of Hands-On Tutorial 9.

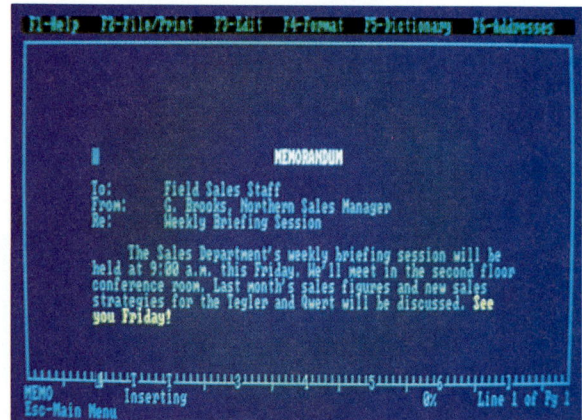

HANDS-ON TUTORIAL 10: Saving and Retrieving a Document

Do the following to save then retrieve the document "memo".

■ Name and save "memo" to disk storage.

F2 (*file/print*)
2 (*save working copy*)
Filename: B:**memo** ↵

■ Clear the screen before retrieving "memo".

F2
6 (*erase working copy*)

■ Retrieve "memo".

F2 **1** (*get file*)
Filename: B:**memo** ↵

The "memo" document should now be on the screen with its name listed in the lower left corner.

HANDS-ON TUTORIAL 11: Printing a Document and Terminating a Session

Turn on the printer and produce a hardcopy of the memo (see Figure 5–7), then exit PFS:Professional Write.

■ Open the File/Print menu.

F2
5 (*print working copy*)

■ Change the "Print style" in the Print Options menu to "Justified".

TAB (*7 times*)
2 (*justified*)

■ Print the memo.

↵

■ Exit PFS:Professional Write after the memo is printed.

ESC (*to reach Main Menu*)
e (*exit*)

If any revisions have been made since the document was last saved, you are warned and given the option to return to the menu and save your work.

CHAPTER 7

Electronic Spreadsheet Concepts: Spreadsheet Capabilities

STUDENT LEARNING OBJECTIVES

- To describe the function and purpose of electronic spreadsheet software (spreadsheet capabilities).
- To demonstrate a working knowledge of the tabular format of an electronic spreadsheet.
- To be able to identify and define spreadsheet cells and ranges.
- To distinguish between text, numeric, and formula entries.
- To create spreadsheet formulas that involve relative cell addressing, absolute cell addressing, arithmetic operations, predefined functions, logical operations, and/or character strings.
- To describe the mechanics of manipulating and modifying an electronic spreadsheet to meet the information needs of a particular application.
- To describe how electronic spreadsheet software can be use for "what if" analysis.
- To identify applications for electronic spreadsheet software.

7–1 THE ELECTRONIC SPREADSHEET _____

The Function of an Electronic Spreadsheet. The name electronic spreadsheet describes the software's fundamental application. The spreadsheet has been a common business tool for centuries. Before computers, the ledger (a spreadsheet) was the accountant's primary tool for keeping the books. Grade books, for example, are set up in spreadsheet format.

Electronic spreadsheets are simply an electronic alternative to thousands of traditionally manual tasks. No longer are we confined to using pencils, erasers, and hand calculators for applications that deal with rows and columns of data. Think of anything that has rows and columns of data and you have identified an application for spreadsheet software. For example, how about income (profit and loss) statements (see Figure 7–1), personnel profiles, demographic data, and budget summaries, to mention a few? Because electronic spreadsheets so closely resemble many of our manual tasks, they enjoy widespread acceptance.

Differences between Electronic Spreadsheet Packages. All commercially available electronic spreadsheet packages provide the facility to manipulate rows and columns of data. However, the *user interface*, or the manner in which the user enters data and commands, differs from one package to the next. The conceptual coverage that follows is generic and is applicable to all commercial electronic spreadsheets. The examples, however, are oriented to SuperCalc4 (a product of Computer Associates), Lotus 1-2-3 and Symphony (both products of Lotus Development Corporation).

The Income Statement Example. The primary example that we will use to illustrate and demonstrate electronic spreadsheet concepts is the Zimco Enterprises *income statement* (see Figure 7–1). The income statement and the *balance sheet* (discussed and illustrated in Figure 7–16) are the primary documents that describe a business's financial position. Monroe Green, the vice-president of Finance and Accounting at Zimco, often uses an electronic spreadsheet **template** of Zimco's

For the last several years, this stock broker spent hours analyzing the stock portfolios of his clients. He finally spent five hours creating a spreadsheet template to help with this task. Now, computations that used to take hours are completed in minutes. Electronic spreadsheet software can be a real timesaver in this and many other applications.
(AST Research Inc.)

C4: 153000

	A	B	C	D
1	==============================	======	======	======
2	ZIMCO INCOME STATEMENT ($1000)	Next Year	This Year	Last Year
3				
4	Net sales	$183,600	$153,000	$144,780
5	Cost of sales & op. expenses			
6	Cost of goods sold	116,413	115,260	117,345
7	Depreciation	4,125	4,125	1,500
8	Selling & admin. expenses	19,875	19,875	15,000
9		----------	----------	----------
10	Operating profit	$43,187	$13,740	$10,935
11	Other income			
12	Dividends and interest	405	405	300
13		----------	----------	----------
14	TOTAL INCOME	$43,592	$14,145	$11,235
15	Less: interest on bonds	2,025	2,025	2,025
16				
17	Income before tax	41,567	12,120	9,210
18	Provision for income tax	18,777	5,475	4,160
19		----------	----------	----------
20	NET PROFIT FOR YEAR	$22,790	$6,645	$5,050

A34: 'FORECAST VARIABLES FOR NEXT YEAR'S PRO RATA INCOME STATEMENT

	A	B	C	D
21	==============================	======	======	======
22				
23				
24	==============================	======	======	======
25	Shares outstanding	6,300,000	6,000,000	6,000,000
26	Market price	$21.25	$14.00	$13.00
27	Earnings per share	$3.62	$1.11	$0.84
28		----------	----------	----------
29	Price-earnings ratio	5.87	12.64	15.45
30	==============================	======	======	======
31				
32				
33	==============================	======	======	======
34	FORECAST VARIABLES FOR NEXT YEAR'S PRO RATA INCOME STATEMENT			
35				
36	Projected change in sales		20.00%	
37	Projected change in cost of goods sold		1.00%	
38	Projected change in administrative expenses		0.00%	
39	==============================	======	======	======
40				

FIGURE 7–1
Electronic Spreadsheet: A Pro Rata Income Statement Template
This electronic spreadsheet template (both screens) is the basis for the explanation and demonstration of spreadsheet concepts. The "Next Year" pro rata income statement is extrapolated from the data in the "This Year" income statement and the values of forecast variables. The price-earnings ratio is calculated for each year.

income statements of the past two years to do financial planning. The template, which is simply a spreadsheet model, contains a column that allows him to produce a *pro rata income statement* for next year (see column B in Figure 7–1). A pro rata income statement is a projected income statement that is based on the figures in the income statement for the preceding year(s).

An income statement, also called a *profit and loss statement* or an *earnings report*, is the origin of the phrase "the bottom line," which has come to mean the final result. The bottom line in the income statement of Figure 7–1 is "NET PROFIT FOR THE YEAR" (row 20). Zimco's past, current, and projected profits are all positive, but profits can also be negative (losses).

The income statement is essentially a record of a company's operating activities over an entire year. Some companies compile quarterly income statements to determine profit during a three month period. The income statement reflects the amount of money received from the sale of goods and services ("Net sales" in row 4) and other incomes ("Dividends and interest" in row 12) against all costs ("Cost of goods sold" and so forth in rows 6, 7, and 8) and other outlays ("Interest on bonds" in row 15 and "Provisions for income tax" in row 18). Income statements are formatted differently for different types of companies; however, the Zimco income statement in Figure 7–1 is representative for manufacturing companies.

In Figure 7–1, the actual income statement is shown on the first screen. The second screen contains the calculations for the price-earnings ratio (rows 25–29) and the display of the variables used to produce the pro rata income statement for next year (rows 34–38). The computation of the price-earnings ratio is discussed in a later section. In the example of Figure 7–1, Monroe Green projected that sales and cost of goods sold would increase by 20 percent and 1 percent, respectively, and that administrative expenses would hold steady (0 percent) for the coming year.

The income statement spreadsheet of Figure 7–1 is the basis for the explanation of spreadsheet principles used in this chapter. Preparation of this spreadsheet involves the application of many common spreadsheet features and capabilities.

7–2   SPREADSHEET ORGANIZATION

Rows and Columns.   Electronic spreadsheets are organized in a *tabular structure* with **rows** and **columns**. The intersection of a particular row and column designates a **cell**. As you can see in Figure 7–1, the *rows are numbered* and the *columns are lettered*. Single letters identify the first 26 columns and double letters are used thereafter (A, B, . . ., Z, AA, AB, . . ., AZ, BA, BB, . . ., BZ). The number of rows or columns available to you depends on the size of your micro's RAM (random access memory). Most spreadsheets permit hundreds of columns and thousands of rows.

Data are entered and stored in cells. During operations, data are referenced by their **cell addresses**. A cell address identifies the location of a cell in the spreadsheet by its column and row, with the column designator first. For example, in the income statement example of Figure 7–1, C2 is the address of the column heading "This Year," and C4 is the address of net sales amount for this year ($153,000).

In the spreadsheet work area (the rows and columns), sometimes referred to as the *worksheet*, a movable highlighted area "points" to the *current cell* (location of the pointer). This highlighted area, which is appropriately called the **pointer**, can be moved around the spreadsheet with the cursor control keys to any cell address. To add or edit (revise the content) an entry at a particular cell, the pointer must be located at the desired cell.

The address and contents of the current cell are displayed in the *user interface* portion of the spreadsheet, the area above and/or below the spreadsheet work area. Specifically, this information is displayed in a *cell status line* (C4 and A34 in Figure 7–1). The contents or resultant value (from a formula) of each cell is shown in the spreadsheet work area. The current cell, however, is displayed in reverse video (e.g., black on white or, for color monitors, black on a color). See "Hands-On Tutorial 12: Using SuperCalc4 (Spreadsheet Capabilities)" or "Using Lotus 1-2-3 (Spreadsheet Capabilities)" in Chapter 8, "Electronic Spreadsheet Tutorials." All tutorials referenced in this chapter can be found in Chapter 8.

Astronauts are conducting more and more scientific experiments while in space. They take microcomputers and electronic spreadsheet software along so they can analyze the data from certain experiments while they are still in orbit.
(NASA)

Viewing Data in a Spreadsheet.   *Scrolling* through a spreadsheet is much like looking through a magnifying glass as you move it around a page of a newspaper. Scrolling is discussed and illustrated in Chapter 3 (see Figure 3-1). You *scroll* left and right (horizontal scrolling) and up and down (vertical scrolling) to view various portions of a large spreadsheet. For example, since only 20 lines of the spreadsheet template in Figure 7–1 can be displayed at one time, Monroe Green must page up or page down to see all of this spreadsheet.

What if the spreadsheet template of Figure 7–1 reflected data for the past five years? Since the screen on the monitor can display only a certain amount of information, Monroe would need to scroll horizontally through the spreadsheet to view the first three years.

7–3   CELL ENTRIES

Making a Cell Entry.   To make an entry in the spreadsheet, use the cursor control keys to move the pointer to the appropriate cell and key in the data. To *edit* or *replace* an existing entry, you also move the pointer to the appropriate cell. The new or revised entry appears first in the status line beside the cell address (see Figure 7–1). Once you have completed work on a particular entry, press ENTER or a cursor control key to make the entry in the actual spreadsheet. For example, let us say that "Net sales" in A4 was incorrectly entered

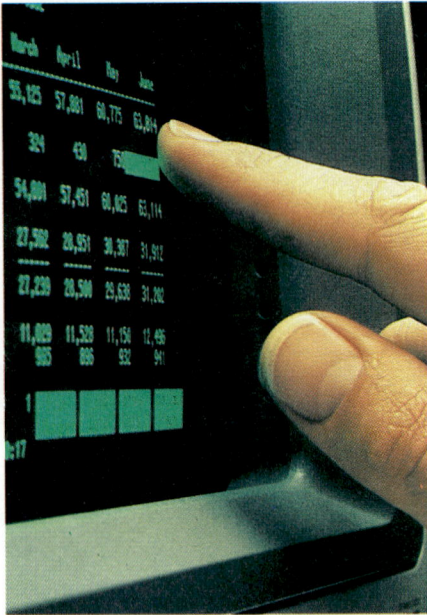

People naturally point at what they want. With this touchscreen system, there is less worry about pressing keys or moving a mouse around. All you do to reposition the pointer in a spreadsheet is to point to the desired cell.
(Photo courtesy of Hewlett-Packard Company)

initially as "New sales". To make the correction, the user would move the pointer to A4, switch to *edit mode* (from *entry mode*), delete the "w", insert a "t", and press ENTER. Normally you would press the designated edit key (usually a function key) to switch to edit mode. When in edit mode, revise the entry in a manner similar to the way you would revise the text in a word processing document (using the left and right cursor keys, backspace, or delete key).

Setting the Column Width.   The standard or default column width for most spreadsheet packages is nine positions. The column width, however, does not limit the length of the entry. Most spreadsheet packages permit entries of at least 200 character positions. An entry that exceeds the column width will spill over into any blank cell(s) to the immediate right. If the adjacent cell(s) already contains an entry, that portion of the entry that extends past the original cell is hidden from view. Spreadsheet packages permit the user to vary the column width to improve readability. The column width for column A in Figure 7–1 is set at 30 positions, and the column width for columns B, C, and D is set at 15 positions.

7–4   CELL RANGES

Types of Ranges.   Many electronic spreadsheet operations ask you to designate a **range** of cells. The four types of ranges are highlighted in Figure 7–2.

1.   A single cell (example range is B12)
2.   All or part of a column of adjacent cells (example range is A17..A20)
3.   All or part of a row of adjacent cells (example range is B2..D2)
4.   A rectangular block of cells (example range is B6..D8)

A particular range is depicted by the addresses of the endpoint cells and separated by two periods (some packages use only one period or a colon: C6.D8, C6:D8). Any cell can comprise a single cell range. The range for the total income amounts in Figure 7–2 is B14..D14 and the range for the row labels is A4..A20. The range of the dollar amounts in the three income statements for "Next Year", "This Year", and "Last Year" data is depicted by any two opposite corner cell addresses (B4..D20 or D4..B20).

Defining and Entering a Range.   Many spreadsheet operations require users to designate ranges. Spreadsheet programs provide two ways to define and enter a range.

1.   *Key the addresses of the endpoint cells* (C6..D8).
2.   *Use the cursor keys and the anchor.* First, move the pointer to an endpoint cell. Then *anchor* the pointer (to that cell) by pressing a particular key, often a tab key or a period. Once you have set the anchor (C6), move the pointer to the other endpoint (D8)

	A	B	C	D
1	==			
2	ZIMCO INCOME STATEMENT ($1000)	Next Year	This Year	Last Year
3	--			
4	Net sales	$183,600	$153,000	$144,780
5	Cost of sales & op. expenses			
6	Cost of goods sold	116,413	115,260	117,345
7	Depreciation	4,125	4,125	1,500
8	Selling & admin. expenses	19,875	19,875	15,000
9				
10	Operating profit	$43,187	$13,740	$10,935
11	Other income			
12	Dividends and interest	405	405	300
13				
14	TOTAL INCOME	$43,492	$14,145	$11,235
15	Less: interest on bonds	2,025	2,025	2,025
16				
17	Income before tax	41,567	12,120	9,210
18	Provision for income tax	18,777	5,475	4,160
19				
20	NET PROFIT FOR YEAR	$22,790	$6,645	$5,050

FIGURE 7–2
Electronic Spreadsheet: Ranges
The four types of ranges are highlighted: cell (B12), column (A17..A20), row (B2..D2), and block (B6..D8).

and press ENTER (or use a follow-on command). This procedure defines the range (C6..D8) without having to key in the endpoint cells.

Many of the spreadsheet operations involve ranges. When you issue a command you may be prompted to enter one or more ranges. The spreadsheet copy operation requires users to define a "copy from" range and a "copy to" range. For example, when the operating profit formula in C10 of Figure 7–1 was copied to the adjacent cell in the "Last Year" column, C10 was defined as the "copy from" range and D10 was the "copy to" range. When you want to erase a portion of the spreadsheet, you first define the range that you wish to erase. For example, if you wish to erase the line of equals signs (=) on row 1, you define the range to be A1..D1, and then issue the erase command. See "Hands-On Tutorial 13: Formatting the Column Width."

7–5 TEXT, NUMERIC, AND FORMULA ENTRIES

An entry to a cell is classified as a *text* entry (also called *label*), a *numeric* entry, or a *formula* entry. Strictly *numeric* entries fall under the formula heading in some spreadsheet programs.

Text Entries.   A text entry, or a label, is a word, phrase, or string of alphanumeric text (spaces included) that occupies a particular cell. In the example of Figure 7–1, "This Year" in cell C2 is a text entry, as is "Net Sales" in A4, and "FORECAST VARIABLES FOR NEXT YEAR'S PRO RATA INCOME STATEMENT" in A34. Notice that the label in A34 extends across columns B and C. If an entry were made in B34, only the first 30 positions, or the width of column A, would be visible on the spreadsheet ("FORECAST VARIABLES FOR NEXT YE").

Unless otherwise specified, text entries are left justified. You can specify that entries be left or right justified or centered in the column. Note that the column heading in A2 is left justified (the default) and that the column headings in B2, C2, and D2 are right justified to improve the appearance of the spreadsheet.

A special form of text entry is the *repeating text* entry. For example, the entries in rows A1 and A3 are repeated text. To create this type of entry, the user designates the cell as repeated text,and then enters a character string that is repeated in that cell and all consecutive empty cells to the right of the current cell. In Figure 7–1, the text string repeated in A1 is = (an equals sign) and the string repeated in A3 is a - (a hyphen). Repeating text entries are used primarily to enhance the appearance and readability of the spreadsheet.

Numeric Entries.   A numeric entry is any number. In Figure 7–1, the values in C4 and D4 are numeric. Numeric entries are automatically right justified unless you specify that the entry is to be left justified. The formatting of numeric entries to show currency (153000 as $153,000 in C4) and percent (.2 as 20.00% in C36) is discussed in a later section. See "Hands-On Tutorial 14: Entering Text Data" and "Hands-On Tutorial 15: Entering Numeric Data."

Sideways, a commercial software package, lets you print spreadsheets that are too wide for a printer. Shown is a 30-year financial projection.
(Funk Software)

Formula Entries.   Cells C10 and C14 contain formulas, but it is the numeric results ($13,740 and $14,145) that are displayed in the spreadsheet. The formula value of C10 (see Figure 7–3) computes the operating profit (net sales minus the cost of sales and operating expenses or +C4-C6-C7-C8). With the pointer positioned at C10, the formula appears in the cell contents line in the user interface panel and the actual numeric value appears in the spreadsheet work area. When the pointer is positioned at C4, the actual numeric value (153000) is displayed as the cell contents in the user interface and an optional *edited* version (with $ and comma) is displayed in cell C4 (see Figure 7–3).

Spreadsheet formulas use standard programming notation for **arithmetic operators**: + (add), − (subtract), * (multiply), / (divide), ^ (raise to a power, or exponentiation). The formula contained in C10 (top of Figure 7–3) computes the operating profit for "This Year". Compare this formula

+C4−C6−C7−C8

to the formula in cell D10

+D4−D6−D7−D8

The formulas are similar, but the first formula references those amounts in column C and the second formula references those amounts in column D.

7–6   RELATIVE AND ABSOLUTE CELL ADDRESSING

The distinction between the way the dollar amounts (net sales in C4) and the forecast variables (projected change in sales in C36) are represented in the formulas highlights a very important concept of electronic

FIGURE 7–3
Electronic Spreadsheet:
Formulas
The actual content of C10 is the formula in the user interface panel in the upper left-hand part of the screen. The result of the formula appears in the spreadsheet at C10.

C10: +C4-C6-C7-C8

	A	B	C	D
1	===
2	ZIMCO INCOME STATEMENT ($1000)	Next Year	This Year	Last Year
3	---
4	Net sales	$183,600	$153,000	$144,780
5	Cost of sales & op. expenses			
6	Cost of goods sold	116,413	115,260	117,345
7	Depreciation	4,125	4,125	1,500
8	Selling & admin. expenses	19,875	19,875	15,000
9				
10	Operating profit	$43,187	$13,740	$10,935

spreadsheets, that of **relative cell addressing** and **absolute cell addressing**.

The relative cell address is based on its position relative to the cell containing the formula. When you copy or replicate a formula to another cell, the relative cell addresses in the formula are revised so that they retain the same position relative to the new location of the formula. The dollar signs ($), which preface both the column and row in an absolute cell address, distinguish it from a relative cell address (for example, C4 versus $C$36). *When a formula is copied, the absolute cell addresses in the formula remain unchanged.*

Examples of Relative and Absolute Cell Addressing.   The two types of cell addressing are illustrated in the spreadsheet in Figure 7–4. Suppose that the formula B3*$E$1 is in cell A1. In the formula, B3 is a relative cell address that is one column to the right of and two rows down from A1, the location of the formula. If the formula, B3*$E$1, is copied to C2, the formula in C2 is D4*$E$1. Notice that D4 has the same relative position to the formula in cell C2: one column to the right and two rows down. The absolute cell address ($E$1) remains the same in both formulas.

Monroe Green references the values of the forecast variables in formulas with absolute cell addresses ($C$36, $C$37, and $C$38). The formulas that compute the "Next Year" values for net sales (B4), cost of goods sold (B6), and selling and administrative expenses (B8) are

    B4:   +C4*(1+$C$36)
    B6:   +C6*(1+$C$37)
    B8:   +C8*(1+$C$38)

Monroe was thinking ahead. The absolute cell reference would not be required if he did not intend to alter the current form of the spreadsheet template. But later on, the absolute cell references will be needed when Monroe adds an "After Next" year column (see Section 7–10). Through judicious use of absolute cell addressing, Monroe has added some flexibility to his spreadsheet template.

Copying Formulas.   In creating the spreadsheet template for the income statement of Figure 7–1, Monroe Green entered the operating

FIGURE 7–4
Electronic Spreadsheet: Relative and Absolute Cell Addressing
When the formula in A1 is copied to C2, the formula in C2 becomes D4*$E$1.

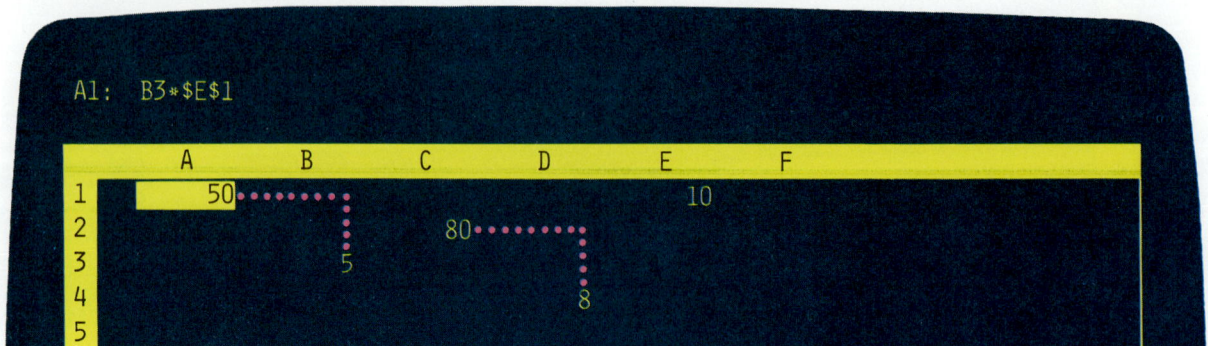

Many companies have information centers. Typically an information center will have several micros, a variety of software and specialized input/ output devices, and most important, information center specialists. The specialists assist users in the use and application of hardware and software until they can become self sufficient.
(Photo courtesy of Hewlett-Packard Company)

profit formula only once—in C10 (see Figure 7–3). Then spreadsheet commands were selected that *copied* or *replicated* the formula into cell D10. You can see from the results in Figure 7–1 that the exact formula was not copied. Instead, the formula in D10 (+D4−D6−D7−D8) manipulates the data in the cells for "Last Year", not "This Year" (as in the formula in C10: +C4−C6−C7−C8). The same is true of other formulas that were copied from the "This Year" column to the "Last Year" column.

The formula in C10 references cells that have a relative position to C10, the location of the formula. When the formula in C10 is copied to D10, the electronic spreadsheet software revises these *relative cell addresses* so that they apply to a formula that is located in D10. As you can see, the formula in D10 references cells that contain the data for "Last Year"

Each of the three forecast variables (C36..C38) is assigned an abso- lute cell address. The absolute cell address does not change when a formula in which it appears is copied from row to row or from column to column. The formula in B4 will always reference the forecast variable in cell C36, even if copied to any other location in the spreadsheet.

7–7   CREATING SPREADSHEET FORMULAS _____

This section expands on the use and application of formulas—the es- sence of spreadsheet operations. A formula causes the spreadsheet software to perform numeric and/or string calculations and/or logic operations that result in a numeric value (for example, 13740) or an alphanumeric character string (for example., "ABOVE 25% LIMIT"). A formula may include one or all of the following: *arithmetic operations*, *functions*, *logic operations*, and *string operations*, such as joining or concatenating character strings. Each is discussed below in more detail.

When you design a spreadsheet, keep in mind where you want to place the formulas and what you want them to accomplish. Since formulas are based on relative position, you will need a knowledge of the layout and organization of the data in the spreadsheet. When you define a formula, you must first determine what you wish to achieve (for example, calculate net profit). Then, you select a cell location for the formula (C20) and create the formula by connecting relative and absolute cell addresses with operators, as appropriate. In many instances, you will copy the formula to other locations, as C20 was copied to D20 in Figure 7–1.

Spreadsheet applications begin with a blank screen and an idea. The spreadsheet that you create is a product of skill and imagination. What you get out of a spreadsheet is very dependent on how effectively you use formulas.

Arithmetic Operations

Formulas containing arithmetic operators are resolved according to a hierarchy of operations. That is, when more than one operator is included in a single formula, the spreadsheet software uses a set of rules to determine which operation to do first, second, and so on. In the hierarchy of operations, illustrated in Figure 7–5, exponentiation has the highest priority, followed by multiplication and division and then by addition and subtraction. In the case of a tie between * and / or + and −, the formula is evaluated from *left to right. Parentheses*, however, override the priority rules. Expressions placed in parentheses have priority and are evaluated innermost first, and left to right.

The formula that results in the value in B4 (183600) of Figure 7–1 is shown below.

+C4*(1+$C$36)

The parentheses in the cell B4 formula cause the expression inside the parentheses to be evaluated first; then the value of the expression and the value in cell C4 are multiplied. All of the formulas in the spreadsheet of Figure 7–1 are listed in Figure 7–6.

Remember, once entered, these formulas can be copied so that they apply to a different set of data. For example, the earnings-per-share formula was entered in B27 and copied to the range C27..D27. Compare these three formulas in Figure 7–6. See "Hands-On Tutorial 16: Entering Formulas."

Creating arithmetic expressions to represent more complex spreadsheet formulas, such as the future value of an annuity (see Figure

FIGURE 7–5
Hierarchy of Operations

The Hierarchy of Operations	
OPERATION	**OPERATOR**
Exponentiation	∧
Multiplication-Division	* /
Addition-Subtraction	+ −

	A	B	C	D
1	==			
2	ZIMCO INCOME STATEMENT ($1000)	Next Year	This Year	Last Year
3	--			
4	Net sales	+C4*(1+$C$36)	153000	144780
5	Cost of sales & op. expenses			
6	Cost of goods sold	+C6*(1+$C$37)	115260	117345
7	Depreciation	+C7	4125	1500
8	Selling and admin. expenses	+C8*(1+$C$38)	19875	15000
9		---		
10	Operating profit	+B4-B6-B7-B8	+C4-C6-C7-C8	+D4-D6-D7-D8
11	Other income			
12	Dividends and interest	+C12	405	300
13		---		
14	TOTAL INCOME	+B10+B12	+C10+C12	+D10+D12
15	Less: interest on bonds	+C15	2025	2025
16		---		
17	Income before tax	+B14-B15	+C14-C15	+D14-D15
18	Provision for income tax	(C18/C17)*B17	5475	4160
19		---		
20	NET PROFIT FOR YEAR	+B17-B18	+C17-C18	+D17-D18
21	==			
22				
23				
24	==			
25	Shares outstanding	6300000	6000000	6000000
26	Market price	21.25	14	13
27	Earnings per share	(B20*1000)/B25	(C20*1000)/C25	(D20*1000)/D25
28		---		
29	Price-earnings ratio	+B26/B27	+C26/C27	+D26/D27
30	==			
31				
32				
33	==			
34	FORECAST VARIABLES FOR NEXT YEAR'S PRO RATA INCOME STATEMENT			
35	--			
36	Projected change in sales		0.2	
37	Projected change in cost of goods sold		0.01	
38	Projected change in administrative expenses		0	
39	==			

FIGURE 7–6

Electronic Spreadsheet: Actual Content of Spreadsheet Cells
This figure illustrates the actual content of all cells in Figure 7–1. In an
actual spreadsheet display, the formulas would be resolved when
displayed (for example, C10 would appear as $13,740) and the values
would be displayed according to a preset format (C36 would appear as
20%).

7–7), can be cumbersome. In our handwritten calculations, we put
the numerator physically over the denominator (½) and denote exponentiation with superscripts (A^2). In spreadsheets and in programming,
however, we have to put the numerator, denominator, and superscripts
on the same level, on one continuous line.

Because the formulas in the income statement example are relatively
straightforward, the future worth of an annuity formula in Figure 7–7
is used to illustrate the presentation of a more complex formula. Assume
that a spreadsheet contains the value of an annuity (an amount of
money deposited at the end of each year), the annual percentage
rate, and the number of years in cells A1, A2, and A3, respectively.

$$\text{Future worth} = \text{Annuity} \left[\frac{(1 + I)^N - 1}{I} \right]$$

Given
A1: Annuity = \$10
A2: I = 12% (.12)
A3: N = 5 years
    Computed
A4: Future worth = \$63.53

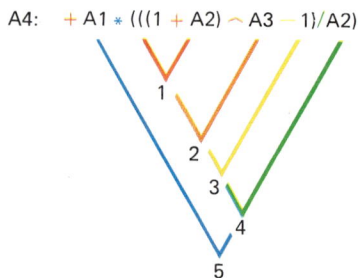

A4:   + A1 * (((1 + A2) ^ A3 — 1)/A2)

1	$1 + .12 = 1.12$
2	$1.12^5 = 1.762$
3	$1.762 - 1 = .762$
4	$\frac{.762}{.12} = 6.353$
5	$10 \times 6.353 = 63.53$

Future worth of a \$10 annuity
for 5 years at 12% = \$63.53

FIGURE 7–7
Evaluation of an Arithmetic Expression
The formula for the future worth of an annuity is shown algebraically and
as a spreadsheet formula. The expression is resolved by the computer in
stages, according to the hierarchy of operations.

Once data have been entered into an electronic spreadsheet, it is easy to create a variety of graphs from the data. In the photo, a credit manager has just created a stacked-bar graph. Creating graphs from spreadsheet data is covered in Chapter 9, "Electronic Spreadsheet Concepts and Tutorials: Database and Graphics Capabilities."
(Courtesy of Unisys Corporation)

The formula for the future value of an annuity is entered in A4. Notice that the numerator, denominator, and superscript are entered on the same level. Figure 7–7 illustrates the order in which the formula in A4 would be resolved by a spreadsheet program.

Functions

Electronic spreadsheets offer users a wide variety of predefined operations called **functions**. These functions can be used to create formulas that perform mathematical, logical, statistical, financial, and character-string operations on spreadsheet data. To use a function, simply enter the desired function name (AVG for average) and enter the **argument**. Some spreadsheet programs require the user to prefix the function with a symbol such as @. The argument, which is placed in parentheses, identifies the data to be operated on. The argument can be one or several numbers, character strings, or ranges that represent data.

In the spreadsheet example of Figure 7–1, the operating profit (C10) can be calculated (see the formula in Figure 7–6) by subtracting the individual cell values under the "cost of sales and operating expenses" heading (C6, C7, and C8) from the net sales (C4).

C10: +C4−C6−C7−C8

Or, the total of the "cost of sales and operating expenses" items can be computed with a function and its argument.

C10: +C4−@SUM(C6..C8)

The use of predefined functions can save a lot of time. What if the range to be summed was C6..C600? See "Hands-On Tutorial 17: Using Predefined Functions."

In the same spreadsheet template, Monroe Green created a "THREE-YEAR SUMMARY DATA" section in the range A121..D127. He did this by copying the range A1..D20 (see Figure 7–1) to the range A121..D140. He then edited the heading information to be as shown in row 122 of Figure 7–8. Monroe then deleted unneeded rows of data to end up with the spreadsheet section in Figure 7–8. In this section of the spreadsheet (the range A121..D140), Monroe used functions to calculate the overall average and to determine the minimum and maximum values for selected entries in the three-year income statement. To do this, he entered the following functions in B124, C124, and D124:

B124: @AVG(B4..D4)
C124: @MIN(B4..D4)
D124: @MAX(B4..D4)

The argument for each of these functions is the range of cells that represents the net sales for each of the three income statements. To complete the segment of the spreadsheet shown in Figure 7–8, Monroe copied the contents of B124 [@AVG(B4..D4)] to the range B125..B127 (the "average" column), thereby making every entry in this column an average of the three years. He performed the same type of operation for the other two columns. These copy operations are possible because the formulas are automatically revised relative to their new positions.

Other spreadsheet functions include trigonometric functions, square root, comparisons of values, manipulations of strings of data, computation of Julian dates, computation of net present value and internal rate of return, and a variety of techniques for statistical analysis. Vendors of spreadsheet software create slightly different names for their functions.

FIGURE 7–8
Electronic Spreadsheet: Functions
The average, maximum, and minimum spreadsheet functions are used to compute summary data in the range B124..D127.

B124: aAVG(B4..D4)

	A	B	C	D
121	===
122	THREE-YEAR SUMMARY DATA	Average	Minimum	Maximum
123	---
124	Net sales	$160,460	$144,780	$183,600
125	Operating profit	$22,621	$10,935	$43,187
126	TOTAL INCOME	$22,991	$11,235	$43,592
127	NET PROFIT FOR YEAR	$11,495	$5,050	$22,790

Logic Operations

Logic operations involve the use of **relational operators** and **logical operators** (see Figure 7–9) to compare numeric and string values. The result of a logic operation is that an expression is either *true* or *false*.

Logic operations are used primarily in defining conditions for record selection (discussed in a later section) and in formulas containing an IF function. The format of the IF function varies slightly between spreadsheet packages. One format is as follows:

@IF(*condition, result* [*condition true*], *result* [*condition false*])

The result in an IF function can be a number, a character string, or even another formula. The logical operators AND and OR (see Figure 7–9) permit us to combine relational expressions in an IF function.

Suppose that Monroe Green wanted to include some data entry validation procedures in his spreadsheet template. He could ensure that realistic values are entered for the forecast variables by displaying a warning message in C40 in Figure 7–1 if any of the values is above 25 percent. The following formula would perform the check on the data entered for the forecast variables.

@IF(C36>.25#OR#C37>.25#OR#C38>.25,"ABOVE 25% LIMIT"," ")

In the case of Figure 7–1, where all forecast variables are less than 25 percent, no message (" " represents a null entry) is displayed because the condition is false. If any of the three forecast variables exceeds 25 percent, as is the case in Figure 7–10, the message "ABOVE 25% LIMIT" is displayed in C40. See "Hands-On Tutorial 18: Using Logical Operations."

String Formulas

A character string can be a label, a user-defined group of alphanumeric characters, part of a label, or the *concatenation* (joining together) of

FIGURE 7–9
Relational and Logical Operators

Relational Operators	
COMPARISON	OPERATOR
Equal to	=
Less than	<
Greater than	>
Less than or equal to	<=
Greater than or equal to	>=
Not equal to	<>

Logical Operators AND and OR	
OPERATION	OPERATOR
For the condition to be true: Both sub-conditions must be true	AND
At least one subcondition must be true	OR

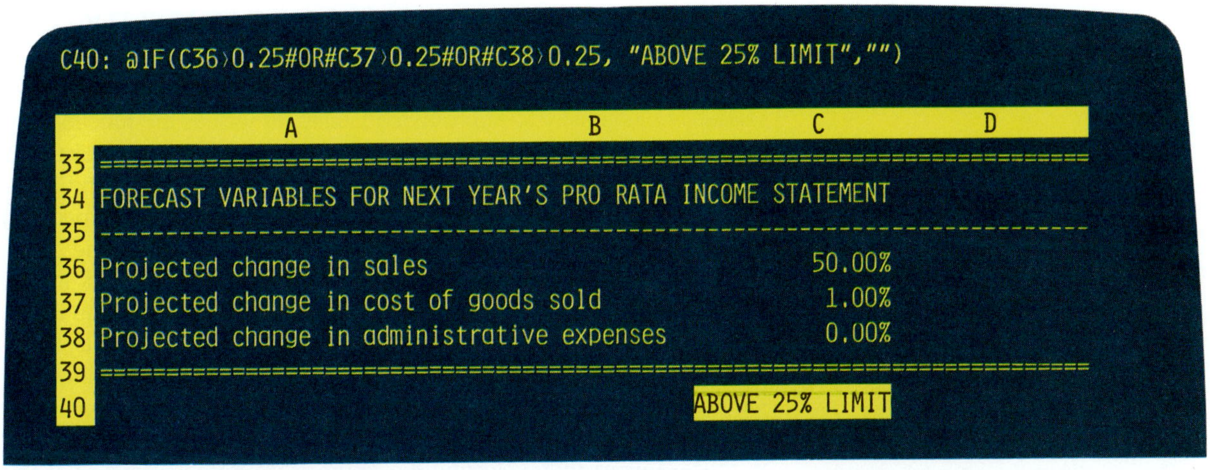

```
C40: @IF(C36>0.25#OR#C37>0.25#OR#C38>0.25, "ABOVE 25% LIMIT","")

          A                          B              C              D
33 ===================================================================
34 FORECAST VARIABLES FOR NEXT YEAR'S PRO RATA INCOME STATEMENT
35 -------------------------------------------------------------------
36 Projected change in sales                       50.00%
37 Projected change in cost of goods sold           1.00%
38 Projected change in administrative expenses      0.00%
39 ===================================================================
40                                              ABOVE 25% LIMIT
```

labels and other character strings. This is done with a *string formula*. For example, suppose Monroe Green wanted to use cell A31 of Figure 7–1 to add an explanation of price-earnings ratio. He could enter the explanation directly,

(Price-earnings ratio = Market price/Earnings per share   )

or he could use the concatenation operator, & (ampersand), to concatenate A26, A27, A29, and the necessary special characters (see Figure 7–11).

+"("&A29&" = "&A26" / "&A27&"   )"

Notice that the four leading blank spaces in A29 are part of the label and are therefore included in the result of the string formula.

FIGURE 7–10
Electronic Spreadsheet: Logical Operations
An IF function in C40 (see discussion in text) serves as a data entry validation procedure. If any of the three forecast variables exceeds 25 percent, as is the case in this figure, the message, "ABOVE 25% LIMIT", is displayed in C40.

FIGURE 7–11
Electronic Spreadsheet: String Formulas
A string formula in A31 is used to concatenate the contents of A26, A27, and A29 with several character strings.

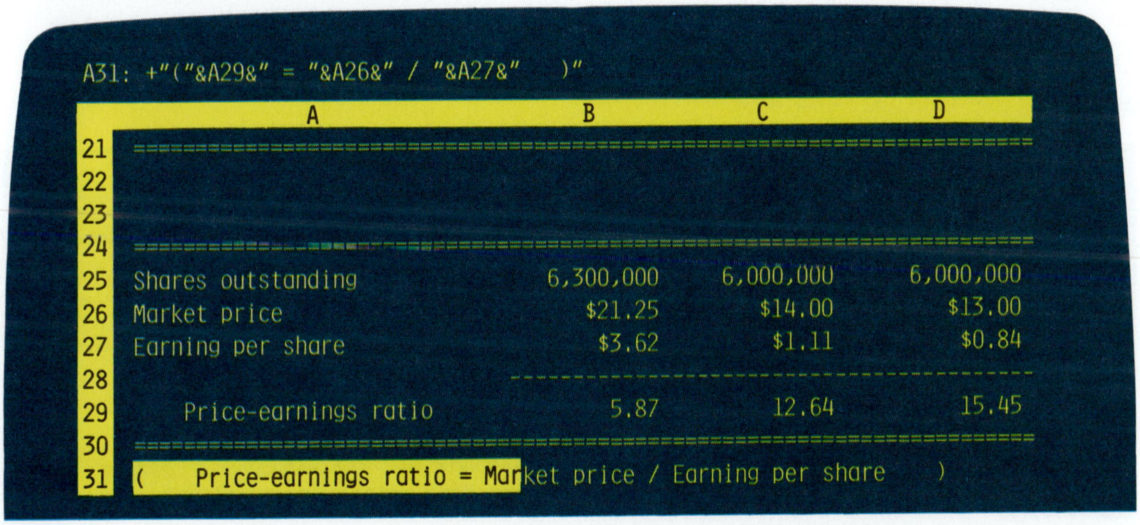

```
A31: +"("&A29&" = "&A26&" / "&A27&"    )"

          A                          B              C              D
21 ===================================================================
22
23
24 -------------------------------------------------------------------
25 Shares outstanding          6,300,000      6,000,000      6,000,000
26 Market price                   $21.25         $14.00         $13.00
27 Earning per share               $3.62          $1.11          $0.84
28 -------------------------------------------------------------------
29     Price-earnings ratio         5.87          12.64          15.45
30 -------------------------------------------------------------------
31 (    Price-earnings ratio = Market price / Earning per share    )
```

7–8   FORMATTING DATA FOR READABILITY

The appearance of data in a spreadsheet can be modified to enhance readability. One way to improve readability, as well as the functionality of a spreadsheet, is to adjust the column width. This was discussed and illustrated earlier in Section 7–3. Another way to enhancing readability is to format the individual numeric entries so that their meaning is more apparent. For example, the value .2 was entered as the "Projected change in sales" in C36 (Figure 7–1), but it appears in the spreadsheet display as a percent (20.00%). This is because the range C36..C38 was *formatted* so that the values are automatically displayed as percents rather than fractions. The procedures for formatting data vary considerably between spreadsheet software packages. The procedure usually involves identifying the range to be formatted (C36..C38 in the example) then selecting the appropriate format (percent in the example) from a menu of formatting options.

Currency amounts can be formatted so that commas and a dollar sign will be inserted. For example, in Figure 7–1 the value of "Net sales" for "This Year" was entered as 153000 in C4. Since C4 is formatted for currency, the amount is displayed as $153,000.

Numeric data can be defined so that they will be displayed with a fixed number of places to the right of the decimal point. In Figure 7–1, the format of the "Net sales" data in the range B4..D4 is defined to be currency with the number of decimal places fixed at zero. The format of the market price data in the range B26..D26 is currency with the number of decimal positions fixed at two. Numbers with more decimal digits than specified in the format are rounded when displayed. See "Hands-On Tutorial 19: Formatting the Cell Entries," "Hands-On Tutorial 20: Saving and Retrieving a Spreadsheet," and "Hands-On Tutorial 21: Printing a Document and Terminating a Session."

The photos show rows 1-20 of the income statement template of Figure 7–1 as it would be prepared using two popular electronic spreadsheet packages, Lotus 1-2-3 and SuperCalc4.

7–9 MANIPULATING ROWS AND COLUMNS_____

Adding and Deleting Rows and Columns. You can insert or delete entire rows and columns. For example, Monroe Green deleted rows in a duplicate copy of the income statement of Figure 7–1 to produce the basis for compiling the spreadsheet of Figure 7–8. If Monroe so desired, he could insert an "After Next" column (two years hence) to the spreadsheet of Figure 7–1. When rows and columns are added or deleted, the spreadsheet software automatically adjusts all cell addresses so that operation of the original spreadsheet remains intact.

Freezing Rows and Columns. If Monroe were to scroll horizontally to view data from past years, row headings (for example, Net sales, TOTAL INCOME, and so on) disappear from the screen to make room for other years of data. As you can imagine, data without labels can be very confusing. However, spreadsheet software has a solution to this dilemma: You can *freeze* selected columns or rows. In the example of Figure 7–12, Monroe has frozen the leftmost column (A), the row headings, at the left side of the screen so that they are always visible when scrolling horizontally through the income statements. When you freeze a portion of the screen, you are creating a new border with labels, and everything moves on the screen but the labels. Notice in Figure 7–12 that the "Next Year" and "This Year" columns are off the screen, but the row labels remain. These columns are returned to the screen when Monroe scrolls in the other direction.

You can also freeze the rows at the top of the screen, the ones that usually label a column. The freeze feature is particularly helpful when the spreadsheet contains many rows or columns of data and you want to work with only a few rows or columns at a time.

FIGURE 7–12
Electronic Spreadsheet: Freeze Column
When column A is frozen at the left of the screen, it is always visible when the right portion of the screen is scrolled horizontally. In the figure, column D is now adjacent to column A.

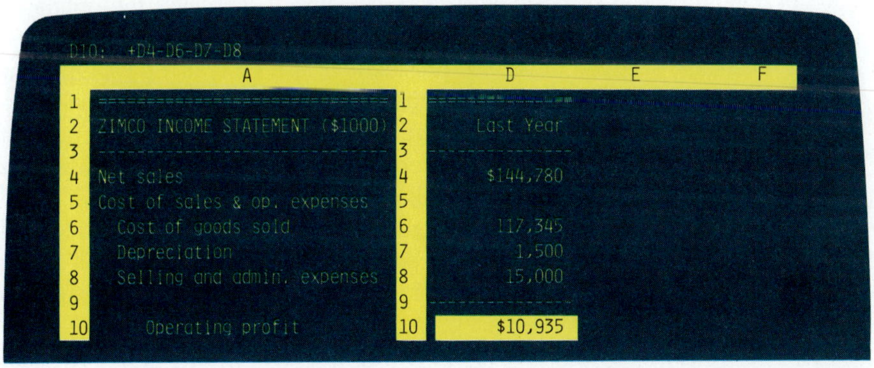

7–10   ELECTRONIC SPREADSHEETS IN PRACTICE

Spreadsheet Templates

The electronic spreadsheet of Figure 7–1 is a *template* or model of the past two years' income statements and a pro rata income statement for next year. It can be used over and over for different purposes by different people. A template is analogous to a production computer program (for printing payroll checks, for example). It can be used again and again by different people with different sets of data. Next year the data now in the "This Year" column will be moved to the "Last Year" column and a new set of data will be entered for "This Year".

With electronic spreadsheets, a template is easily modified to fit a variety of situations. Another analyst may wish to modify the template slightly to handle quarterly income statements: Only the column headings would be changed.

You can create your own templates, as Monroe Green did, or you can purchase them. A number of companies market a wide variety of spreadsheet templates, from grade book templates to templates and procedures for full-blown accounting systems (general ledger, accounts receivable, accounts payable, and so on).

"What If" Analysis

The real beauty of an electronic spreadsheet is that if you change the value of a cell in a spreadsheet, all other affected cells are revised accordingly. This capability makes spreadsheet software the perfect tool for "what if" analysis. Most of this chapter has been devoted to developing the pro rata income statement template illustrated in Figure 7–1. The following sections describe how this template can be used for "what if" analysis.

What If—the Best-Case Scenario.   Monroe Green, Zimco's vice-president of Finance and Accounting, also uses the income statement spreadsheet template of Figure 7–1 to create a variety of "what if" scenarios. The scenario illustrated in Figure 7–1 reflects the optimistic projections of two vice-presidents and the president—essentially the best-case scenario. The vice-president of the Operations Division has told Monroe that he is implementing a number of cost-cutting measures that will enable him to hold the cost of goods sold to a 1 percent increase, even though more products will be built and shipped. The vice-president of Sales and Marketing predicts that next year will be a great year and net sales will increase by 20 percent. The president of Zimco, Preston Smith, asked all managers to hold the line on all selling and administrative expenses; therefore, Monroe expects these expenses to remain about the same.

With spreadsheet software, Monroe was able to answer the question

What if sales increased by 20 percent, cost-of-goods-sold increased by 1 percent, and everything else remained the same for the coming year?

After the financial data had been enters, Monroe entered only the three forecast variables in C36, C37, and C38 (see Figure 7–1) to get the pro rata income statement (the "Next Year" column of Figure 7–1). All calculations (sales with a 20 percent increase, net profit, earnings per share, taxes) are performed automatically because the appropriate formulas are built into the spreadsheet template.

Some entries in the "Next Year" column are unchanged (depreciation, dividends, and interest); however, if Monroe wanted to reflect a change in depreciation, he would simply change the value of the "depreciation" entry in the "Next Year" column. The "provision for income tax" entry (B18) is extrapolated from the "This Year" column data by a formula that assumes the taxes will be paid at the same rate as the previous year [B18: (C18/C17)*B17].

Besides the pro rata income statement for "Next Year", Monroe wants to monitor the *price-earnings ratio*, or the relationship that exists between the *earnings per share* and the *market price* of Zimco's stock. Data and the calculations for the price-earnings ratios are in the range B25..D29 in Figure 7–1. The formulas and entries in the range B25..D29 are shown in Figure 7–6. The earnings per share is calculated by dividing the net profit by the number of shares outstanding [for "This Year", $6,645,000/6,000,000 = $1.11, which is calculated by the formula in C27: (C20*1000)/C25]. The price-earnings ratio is calculated by dividing the current market price of Zimco stock by the earnings per share [for "This Year", $14.00/$1.11 = 12.64, which is calculated by the formula in C29: +C26/C27].

In the "Next Year" column of the price-earnings (P-E) ratio section of the spreadsheet, Monroe asked

What would the P-E ratio be if Zimco issues 300,000 new shares of stock and the market price of Zimco stock reaches $21.25?

What If—the Worst Case-Scenario. The spreadsheet template of Figure 7–1 reflects the optimistic projections of Zimco vice-presidents. Over the years Zimco's president, Preston Smith, has learned to temper the optimistic projections of his vice-presidents with a touch of reality. To examine a worst-case scenario, Preston uses Monroe Green's spreadsheet template (Figure 7–1) to answer the following question:

What if sales increased by 3 percent, cost-of-goods-sold increased by 2 percent, administrative expenses increased by 4 percent, and everything else remained the same for the coming year?

Preston Smith needs only to change the three forecast variables (C36..C38) to get the worst-case results of Figure 7–13. The results confirm Preston's belief that the estimated price-earnings ratio is very sensitive to the projections for sales and expenses. Compare the price-earnings ratio of the optimistic pro rata income statement in Figure 7–1 (5.87) with the pessimistic pro rata income statement in Figure 7–13 (17.94). See "Hands-On Tutorial 22: What if. . . ."

A director of personnel in a consumer goods company uses electronic spreadsheet software to ask "what if" questions regarding a proposal for a new benefits package for the company's 1200 union workers. (Courtesy of Xerox Corporation)

A2: 'ZIMCO INCOME STATEMENT ($1000)

	A	B	C	D
1	===			
2	ZIMCO INCOME STATEMENT ($1000)	Next Year	This Year	Last Year
3	---			
4	Net sales	$157,590	$153,000	$144,780
5	Cost of sales & op. expenses			
6	Cost of goods sold	117,565	115,260	117,345
7	Depreciation	4,125	4,125	1,500
8	Selling & admin. expenses	20,670	19,875	15,000
9		---------	---------	---------
10	Operating profit	$15,230	$13,740	$10,935
11	Other income			
12	Dividends and interest	405	405	300
13		---------	---------	---------
14	TOTAL INCOME	$15,635	$14,145	$11,235
15	Less: interest on bonds	2,025	2,025	2,025
16		---------	---------	---------
17	Income before tax	13,610	12,120	9,210
18	Provision for income tax	6,148	5,475	4,160
19		---------	---------	---------
20	NET PROFIT FOR YEAR	$7,462	$6,645	$5,050

B27: (B20*1000)/B25

	A	B	C	D
21	===			
22				
23				
24	===			
25	Shares outstanding	6,300,000	6,000,000	6,000,000
26	Market price	$21.25	$14.00	$13.00
27	Earnings per share	$1.18	$1.11	$0.84
28		---------	---------	---------
29	Price-earnings ratio	17.94	12.64	15.45
30	===			
31				
32				
33	===			
34	FORECAST VARIABLES FOR NEXT YEAR'S PRO RATA INCOME STATEMENT			
35	---			
36	Projected change in sales		3.00%	
37	Projected change in cost of goods sold		2.00%	
38	Projected change in administrative expenses		4.00%	
39	===			

FIGURE 7–13
Electronic Spreadsheet: A Pro Rata Income Statement Template
This electronic spreadsheet display is the same as the one in Figure 7–1 except that the forecast variables in
C36..C38 have been changed from 20%, 1%, and 0% to 3%, 2%, and 4%, respectively.

Modifying a Spreadsheet Template

Modifying the appearance and/or function of an existing spreadsheet to meet a different purpose is common practice among spreadsheet users. For example, Monroe Green modified the template of Figure 7–1 to include an "After Next" column (two years hence). When a column is inserted at column B, what is now in columns B, C, and D is moved over one column to columns C, D, and E. The "After Next" data would be in column B. Of course, the spreadsheet software automatically adjusts the cell addresses in formulas to accommodate the new column.

After issuing the commands needed to insert a column at B, Monroe copies the "Next Year" column (now in the range C4..C20) to the "After Next" column (range B4..B20). This copy operation highlights why Monroe used absolute cell addressing for all formula references to the forecast values in the original spreadsheet template of Figure 7–1 [the formula in B4: +C4*(1+$C$36)]. The absolute cell reference is needed because the relative position of the forecast values is different for both the "After Next" and the "Next Year" columns. Figure

FIGURE 7–14
Electronic Spreadsheet:
Inserting a Column
An "After Next" (two years hence) column is inserted at column B in the income statement portion of the spreadsheet template of Figure 7–1.

A2:	'ZIMCO INCOME STATEMENT ($1000)				
	A	B	C	D	E
1	═══════════════════════════	════════	════════	════════	════════
2	ZIMCO INCOME STATEMENT ($1000)	After Next	Next Year	This Year	Last Year
3	-------------------------------				
4	Net sales	$220,320	$183,600	$153,000	$144,780
5	Cost of sales & op. expenses				
6	Cost of goods sold	117,577	116,413	115,260	117,345
7	Depreciation	4,125	4,125	4,125	1,500
8	Selling & admin. expenses	19,875	19,875	19,875	15,000
9		-------	-------	-------	-------
10	Operating profit	$78,743	$43,187	$13,740	$10,935
11	Other income				
12	Dividends and interest	405	405	405	300
13		-------	-------	-------	-------
14	TOTAL INCOME	$79,148	$43,592	$14,145	$11,235
15	Less: interest on bonds	2,025	2,025	2,025	2,025
16		-------	-------	-------	-------
17	Income before tax	77,123	41,567	12,120	9,210
18	Provision for income tax	34,839	18,777	5,475	4,160
19		-------	-------	-------	-------
20	NET PROFIT FOR YEAR	$42,284	$22,790	$6,645	$5,050

7–14 illustrates how the income statement portion of the spreadsheet would appear after being modified to accommodate an "After Next" year column. See "Hands-On Tutorial 23: Inserting a Column."

Macros

Most spreadsheet packages come with the *macro* feature (*see* Chapter 3 for an overview on macros). This feature enables you to store and recall a sequence of frequently used operations or keystrokes. Like a computer program, a spreadsheet macro can be invoked whenever you want. When you invoke a macro, the spreadsheet program reads the keystrokes and commands listed in the macro and performs the specified tasks.

The macro is very simply a user-defined range of cells that contains the keystrokes and commands needed to perform a particular spreadsheet task. The alphanumeric and special keys are entered as is. Special keys and function keys are noted in brackets ([up] for up arrow, [pgdn] for page down, and so on).

Edwina Cool, the education coordinator for Zimco, uses her spreadsheet program to maintain a "course" data base (see Figure 7–15). When used as a data management tool, electronic spreadsheet software organizes data elements, records, and files into columns, rows, and tables, respectively. Each row in the spreadsheet of the course data base of Figure 7–15 contains the data items for each individual course record (CS11, Business COBOL, college, and so on). All of the records are combined in a table of rows (records) and columns (fields) to make a file. Using spreadsheet programs for data management is discussed in detail in Chapter 9, "Electronic Spreadsheet Concepts and Tutorials: Database and Graphics Capabilities."

Edwina created a macro to sort the course data base in Figure 7–15 in ascending sequence by TITLE. The macro that accomplishes this sort is contained in B16..B19 of Figure 7–15 and is invoked by referencing its name "\s". A line-by-line description of the macro is contained in C16..C19. Macros depend on the command structure of the program being used. The macro in Figure 7–15 is for the Lotus 1-2-3 spreadsheet program. Edwina created the macro so that she could sort the records in the data base in other ways (by ID, by TYPE) and return them quickly to the sequence shown in Figure 7–15.

As you become more familiar with spreadsheets you will see 1001 time-saving uses for macros.

Spreadsheet Summary

The possibilities of what Monroe Green, Preston Smith, you, and others can do with electronic spreadsheet software and micros are endless.

```
A1:  'ID

       A              B                C         D           E          F
1    ID      TITLE              TYPE      SOURCE      DURATION
2    VC44    4th Generation Lang.  media     VidCourse      30
3    3223    BASIC Programming     media     Takdel Inc     40
4    CIS11   Business COBOL        college   St Univ        45
5    7771    Data Base Systems     media     Takdel Inc     30
6    VC10    Elec. Spreadsheet     media     VidCourse      20
7    2535    Intro to Info. Proc.  media     Takdel Inc     40
8    EX15    Local Area Networks   vendor    HAL Inc        30
9    MGT10   Mgt. Info. Systems    college   St Univ        45
10   201     Micro Overview        in-house  Staff           8
11   100     MIS Orientation       in-house  Staff          24
12   310     Programming Stds.     in-house  Staff           6
13   VC88    Word Processing       media     VidCourse      18
14
15   Name    Macro                         Description
16   \s      /dsr                  call main menu, select Data, Sort, Reset
17           da2..e13~             select Data-Range, enter range
18           pb1~a~                select Primary-Key (TITLE), ascending
19           g                     select Go (perform sort)
```

FIGURE 7–15
Electronic Spreadsheet: Database Capabilities and Macros
This spreadsheet is organized as a data base. The data base contains a record for each of the 12 courses that Zimco offers to its employees. The labels for the fields are listed in the first row. Each subsequent row contains one record. A macro named "\s" in B16..B19 can be invoked to sort the data base in ascending sequence by TITLE.

For example, Monroe can add the Zimco balance sheets for the last two years (see Figure 7–16) to the spreadsheet of Figure 7–1 to create even more "what if" scenarios. With the income statement and the balance sheet in the same spreadsheet, he can change values in Zimco's financial statements to see how various financial indices, such as the net working capital (current assets minus current liabilities), the current ratio (current assets divided by current liabilities), and the inventory turnover (net sales divided by inventories), are affected. The formulas for the "This Year" balance sheet in in Figure 7–16 are listed in Figure 7–17 to give you one more example of how formulas are used in an electronic spreadsheet template.

C53: @SUM (C47..C51)

	A	B	C	D
41	==			
42	ZIMCO BALANCE SHEET ($1000)		This Year	Last Year
43	--			
44	ASSETS			
45	--			
46	Current assets			
47	Cash		$6,750	$4,500
48	Marketable securities @ cost		$12,750	$6,900
49	Accounts receivable			
50	Less: bad debt allowance		$30,000	$28,500
51	Inventories		$40,500	$45,000
52			---------------	
53	Total current assets		$90,000	$84,900
54				
55	Fixed assets			
56	Land		6,750	$6,750
57	Building		$55,500	$52,500
58	Machinery		$14,250	$12,750
59	Office equipment		$1,500	$1,425
60			---------------	

C71: +C53+C64+C67+C69

	A	B	C	D
61			$78,000	$73,425
62	Less: accum. depreciation		$27,000	$22,500
63			---------------	
64	Net fixed assets		$51,000	$50,925
65				
66				
67	Prepayments & deferred charges		$1,500	$1,350
68				
69	Intangibles (goodwill, patents)		$1,500	$1,500
70			---------------	
71	TOTAL ASSETS		$144,000	$138,675
72			===============	
73				
74			---------------	
75	LIABILITIES			
76			---------------	
77	Current liabilities			
78	Accounts payable		$15,000	$14,100
79	Notes payable		$12,750	$15,000
80	Accrued expenses payable		$4,950	$4,500

```
C100: +C89+C98
                     A                    B           C           D
 81    Federal income taxes payable                $4,800      $4,350
 82                                               -----------------------
 83       Total current liabilities              $37,500     $37,950
 84
 85    Long-term liabilities
 86       First mortgage bonds;
 87       9% interest, due 2000                   $40,500     $40,500
 88                                               -----------------------
 89       Total liabilities                       $78,000     $78,450
 90    --------------------------------------------------------------
 91    STOCKHOLDERS' EQUITY
 92    --------------------------------------------------------------
 93    Common stock, $5 par;
 94       6,000,000 shares outstanding            $30,000     $30,000
 95    Capital surplus                            $10,500     $10,500
 96    Retained earnings                          $25,500     $19,725
 97                                               -----------------------
 98       Total stockholders' equity              $66,000     $60,225
 99                                               -----------------------
100    TOTAL LIABILITIES & STOCKHOLDERS' EQUITY  $144,000    $138,675
```

FIGURE 7–16
Electronic Spreadsheet: A Balance Sheet Template
This electronic spreadsheet representation of the Zimco balance sheets
for the last two years is included in rows 41 through 100 of a spreadsheet
template. The income statement template of Figures 7–1 and 7–13 is on
rows 1 through 40 of the same spreadsheet.

SUMMARY OUTLINE AND IMPORTANT TERMS ____

7–1   THE ELECTRONIC SPREADSHEET.   Electronic spreadsheets are simply an electronic alternative to thousands of manual tasks that involve rows and columns of data. Commercially
available electronic spreadsheet packages are organized similarly but differ in their user interfaces. The primary example
used in this chapter to illustrate and demonstrate electronic
spreadsheet concepts is an electronic spreadsheet **template**
of a pro rata income statement. An income statement is essentially a record of a company's operating activities over a entire
year.

7–2   SPREADSHEET ORGANIZATION.   Electronic spreadsheets
are organized in a tabular structure with **rows** and **columns**.
The intersection of a particular row and column designates a
cell. Rows are numbered and the columns are lettered. During
operations, data are referenced by their **cell addresses**. The

FIGURE 7–17
**Electronic Spreadsheet:
Formulas in Balance Sheet
Template of Figure 7–16**
These are the formulas for the
"This Year" column of the
balance sheet spreadsheet in
Figure 7–16.

Cell	Formula
C53	@ SUM (C47 . . C51)
C61	@ SUM (C56 . . C59)
C64	+C61—C62
C71	+C53+C64+C67+C69
C83	@ SUM (C78 . . C81)
C89	+C83+C87
C98	@ SUM (C94 . . C96)
C100	+C89+C98

pointer can be moved around the spreadsheet with the cursor control keys to any cell.

Scroll left and right (horizontal scrolling) and up and down (vertical scrolling) to view various portions of a large spreadsheet.

7–3 CELL ENTRIES.   To make an entry or edit or replace an entry in a spreadsheet, move the pointer to the appropriate cell. When in edit mode, revise the entry in a manner similar to the way you would revise the text in a word processing document. Spreadsheet packages permit the user to vary the column width to improve readability.

7–4 CELL RANGES.   The four types of **ranges** are a single cell, all or part of a column of adjacent cells, all or part of a row of adjacent cells, and a rectangular block of cells. A particular range is depicted by the addresses of the endpoint cells (for example, C6..D8). Many spreadsheet operations involve ranges.

7–5 TEXT AND FORMULA ENTRIES.   An entry to a cell is classified as text (or label), numeric, or formula. A text entry is any string of alphanumeric text (spaces included) that occupies a particular cell. The repeating text entry is a special form of the text entry that can be used to enhance the appearance and readability of the spreadsheet. A numeric entry is any number. Unless specified otherwise, numeric entries are automatically right justified.

A cell may contain a formula, but it is the numeric results that are displayed in the spreadsheet. Spreadsheet formulas use standard programming notation for **arithmetic operators**: +, −, ∗, /, and ^. Strictly numeric entries fall under the formula heading in some spreadsheet programs.

7–6 RELATIVE AND ABSOLUTE CELL ADDRESSING.   The **relative cell address** is based on its position relative to the cell containing the formula. When you copy or replicate a formula to another cell, the relative cell addresses in the formula are revised such that they retain the same relative position to the new location of the formula. When a formula is copied, the **absolute cell addresses** in the formula remain unchanged.

7–7 CREATING   SPREADSHEET   FORMULAS. A formula causes the spreadsheet software to perform numeric and/or string calculations and/or logic operations that result in a numeric value or an alphanumeric character string. A formula may include one or all of the following: arithmetic operations, functions, logic operations, and string operations.

When you design a spreadsheet, keep in mind where you want to place the formulas and what you want them to accomplish. Since formulas are based on relative position, you will need a knowledge of the layout and organization of the data in the spreadsheet.

Formulas containing arithmetic operators are resolved according to a hierarchy of operations. Predefined **functions** can be used to create formulas that perform mathematical, logical, statistical, financial, and character-string operations on spreadsheet data. Logic operations involve the use of **relational operators** and **logical operators** to compare numeric and string values.

7–8 FORMATTING DATA FOR READABILITY.   The appearance of data in a spreadsheet can be modified to enhance readability by adjusting the column width. Another way to enhance readability is to format the individual numeric entries so that their meaning is more apparent (for example, currency, percent).

7–9 MANIPULATING ROWS AND COLUMNS.   Entire rows and columns can be inserted or deleted. When rows and columns are added or deleted, the spreadsheet software automatically adjusts all cell addresses so that operation of the original spreadsheet remains intact. Selected columns or rows can be frozen so that labels remain in position while data are scrolled.

7–10 ELECTRONIC SPREADSHEETS IN PRACTICE.   A template is a model that can be used over and over for different purposes by different people. If you change the value of a cell in a spreadsheet, all other affected cells are revised accordingly. This capability makes spreadsheet software the perfect tool for "what if" analysis.

The macro feature of spreadsheet packages enables the user to store and recall a sequence of frequently used operations or keystrokes. Like a computer program, a spreadsheet macro can be invoked whenever it is needed.

REVIEW EXERCISES

1. Describe the layout of an electronic spreadsheet.
2. Give an example cell address. Which portion of the address depicts the row and which portion depicts the column?
3. On what is a relative cell address based?
4. Give an example of each of the four types of ranges.
5. Give examples of the three types of entries that can be made in an electronic spreadsheet.
6. What types of operators are used to compare numeric and string values?
7. Write the equivalent formula for @AVG(A1..D1) without the use of functions.
8. If the formula B2∗$B$1 is copied from C1 to E3, what is the formula in E3? If the formula in E3 is copied to D45, what is the formula in D45?

9. What is the difference between the pointer and the cursor in an electronic spreadsheet?

10. List three alternatives descriptors for the range A4..P12.

11. When do you anchor the pointer?

12. What would you use in a formula to override the priority rules for arithmetic operators?

13. What formula would be entered in A5 to sum all numbers in the range A1..A4?

14. When would you need to scroll horizontally? Vertically?

15. What is a spreadsheet template?

16. The column width for all columns is set at 9. Cells A1, B1, and C1 contain the column headings Last Name, First Name, and Middle Initial. What is displayed in A1, B1, and C1?

SELF-TEST (by section)

7–1. The term spreadsheet was coined at the beginning of the personal computer boom. (T/F)

7–2. (a) Data in an electronic spreadsheet are referenced by their cell _____.

   (b) The pointer highlights the (a) relative cell, (b) status cell, or (c) current cell.

7–3. The cursor control keys can be used to position the pointer at the cell to be edited. (T/F)

7–4. D20..Z40 and Z20..D40 define the same range. (T/F)

7–5. (a) A label is considered a (a) text entry, (b) numeric entry, or (c) formula entry.

   (b) The arithmetic operators used in spreadsheet formulas are *and* and *or*. (T/F)

7–6. When the formula +H4*$Z$18 is copied from A1 to A3, the formula in A3 is _____.

7–7. (a) TA single formula can contain logic operations or string operations, but not both. (T/F)

   (b) In the formula +A4*(P6-S10/14), which arithmetic operation is performed first?

   (c) The formula @MIN(A1..A20) results in the selection of the minimum value in the range A20..A1. (T/F)

   (d) The concatenation operator is the _____ .

7–8. A cell that contains the value ".1234" and is formatted as percent would be displayed as "12.34%". (T/F)

7–9. After you delete rows 1 and 2 in a spreadsheet, what had previously been rows become 3 and 4 become rows 1 and 2. (T/F)

7–10. (a) A model of a spreadsheet that is designed for a particular application is sometimes called a template. (T/F)

(b) If you change the value of a cell in an electronic spreadsheet, all other affected cells are revised accordingly. (T/F)

(c) The spreadsheet feature that enables the recall and execution of a sequence of keystrokes and/or commands is called a _____.

Self-Test Answers. **7–1**, F; **7–2 (a)**, addresses; **(b)**, c; **7–3**, T; **7–4**, T; **7–5 (a)**, a; **(b)**, F; **7–6**, +H6∗$Z$18; **7–7 (a)**, F; **(b)**, S10/14; **(c)**, T; **(d)**, & (ampersand); **7–8**, T; **7–9**, T; **7–10 (a)**, T; **(b)**, T; **(c)**, macro.

HANDS-ON EXERCISES

1. Complete Hands-On Tutorials 12 through 23 in Chapter 8, "Electronic Spreadsheet Tutorials: Spreadsheet Capabilities."

2. **(a)** The following data represent the unit sales data for the past year for Diolab, Inc., a manufacturer of a diagnostic laboratory instrument that is sold primarily to hospitals and clinics.

Diolab Inc. Sales (units)

Region	Qtr1	Qtr2	Qtr3	Qtr4
NE Region	214	300	320	170
SE Region	120	150	165	201
SW Region	64	80	60	52
NW Region	116	141	147	180

Enter the title, headings, and data in an electronic spreadsheet. Place the title in the range B1, the column headings in the range A2..E2, the row headings in the range A3..A6, and the sales data in the range B3..E6.

In the remaining portion of Hands-On Exercise 2, each part builds on the results of the previous part. If the this exercise is to be handed in, print out the initial spreadsheets and then print them out again for each revision.

(b) Add another column heading called SALES/YR in F2 of the Diolab spreadsheet. Enter a formula in F3 that sums the sales for each quarter for the northeast region. Copy the formula to the range F4..F6. SALES/YR should be 1004 for the NE Region and 636 for the SE Region.

(c) Add average sales per quarter, AVG/QTR, in column G. AVG/QTR should be 251 for the NE Region and 159 for the SE Region.

(d) Add two more columns that reflect sales per salesperson. In column H, add number of salespersons per region, PERSONS: 5, 3, 2, and 4, respectively. In column I, add formulas that compute sales per person, SALES/PER (from the data in SALES/YR and PERSONS columns).

SALES/PER should be 200.8 for the NE Region and 212 for the SE Region.

(e) In the range B8..F8, use functions to total sales for each quarter and for the year. The total sales for all regions should be 2480.

(f) Copy the range A2..A6 to A12..A16 and B2..E2 to B12..E12. Diolab, Inc., sales are estimated to be 120 percent of last year's sales. Complete the newly created spreadsheet by multiplying last year's quarterly sales data by 1.2 and placing the result in the spreadsheet. Title this set of data ESTIMATED DIOLAB INC. SALES - NEXT YEAR. The NE Region first-quarter sales should be 257 (rounded) and the SE Region second-quarter sales should be 180.

(g) Each of the lab analysis units sells for $2,000. Add formulas in column F to compute estimated GROSS sales ($2,000 times the total of the estimated quarterly sales) for each region. Also format the GROSS sales values as currency with no decimal places so that the NE Region amount appears as $2,409,600 and the SE Region as $1,526,400. You may need to expand the width of column F to 11 positions.

3. Create a spreadsheet that summarizes an individual's monthly budget in two general categories: expenditures and income. Use formulas to compute the totals for the two categories, the percent of the total, and the ratio of total expenditures to total income. Format your spreadsheet like the following:

	A	B	C
1	EXPENDITURES		
2	Category	Amount	Percent of total
3	Housing	495.00	33.01%
4	Utilities	125.45	8.37%
5	Food	369.29	24.63%
6	Clothing	85.00	5.67%
7	Transportation	265.17	17.68%
8	Entertainment	100.00	6.67%
9	Other	59.50	3.97%
10		-----------	
11	TOTAL	$1,499.41	
12	=================================		
13	INCOME		
14	Category	Amount	Percent of Total
13	Wages	2,400.00	96.00%
14	Tips	0.00	0.00%
15	Gifts	100.00	4.00%

16	Other	0.00	0.00%
17		-----------	
18	TOTAL	$2,500.00	
19	===========================		
20	Ratio of expenditures to income:	.60	

    (b) Print the spreadsheet.

    (c) Enter new amounts for various categories of expenditures and income, and print out the spreadsheet.

4. **(a)** Create a spreadsheet that will allow you to compare this year's monthly electric utility bills with last year's bills. Use the sample data shown here or use your own data. Format your spreadsheet like the following:

	A	B	C	D
1	Month	This Year	Last Year	Difference
2				
3	January	140.23	154.24	−14.01
4	February	160.54	168.30	−7.76
5	March	90.77	87.22	3.55
6	April	65.12	56.61	8.51
7	May	30.98	50.15	−19.17
8	June	50.00	48.08	1.92
9	July	69.33	74.04	−4.71
10	August	45.20	48.59	−3.39
11	September	35.61	22.62	12.99
12	October	70.02	69.11	0.91
13	November	98.87	106.04	7.17
14	December	128.09	140.01	−11.92
15		-------------------------------		
16	TOTAL	$984.76	$1,025.01	

    (b) Print the spreadsheet.

KEYSTROKE TUTORIALS IN THE *LAB MANUAL*

The *Lab Manual* that accompanies this text contains keystroke tutorials for

- Lotus 1-2-3 (© Lotus Development Corporation)
- The TWiN (© Mosaic Software, Inc.; emulates Lotus 1-2-3)
- SuperCalc4 (©) Computer Associates)

These keystroke tutorials illustrate the use of a particular electronic spreadsheet software package in a domestic and a business application. The more advanced features of the packages are introduced in the business application tutorials.

CHAPTER 8

Electronic Spreadsheet Tutorials: Spreadsheet Capabilities

STUDENT LEARNING OBJECTIVES

- To become familiar with the use and application of spreadsheet capabilities of one or more of the following integrated packages:
  - Lotus 1-2-3
  - The TWiN
  - SuperCalc4
- To acquire the ability to apply the electronic spreadsheet skills demonstrated in the hands-on tutorials.

HANDS-ON TUTORIALS for *Lotus 1-2-3*, *The TWiN*, and *SuperCalc4*

12. Using The Software (Spreadsheet Capabilities)
13. Formatting the Column Width
14. Entering Text Data
15. Entering Numeric Data
16. Entering Formulas
17. Using Predefined Functions
18. Using Logical Operations
19. Formatting the Cell Entries
20. Saving and Retrieving a Spreadsheet
21. Printing a Document and Terminating a Session
22. "What if . . ."
23. Inserting a Column

ADVANCED AND SPECIAL FEATURES TUTORIALS: *Lotus 1-2-3*, *The TWiN*, and *SuperCalc4*

Adding a Template to an Existing Spreadsheet
Retrieving from a Files List
Copying a Block
Using Windows

ELECTRONIC SPREADSHEET TUTORIAL: LOTUS 1-2-3 AND THE TWIN

QUICK REFERENCE GUIDE
Lotus 1-2-3
(Release 2.01)
A>123 ↵

SLASH (/) COMMAND MENU

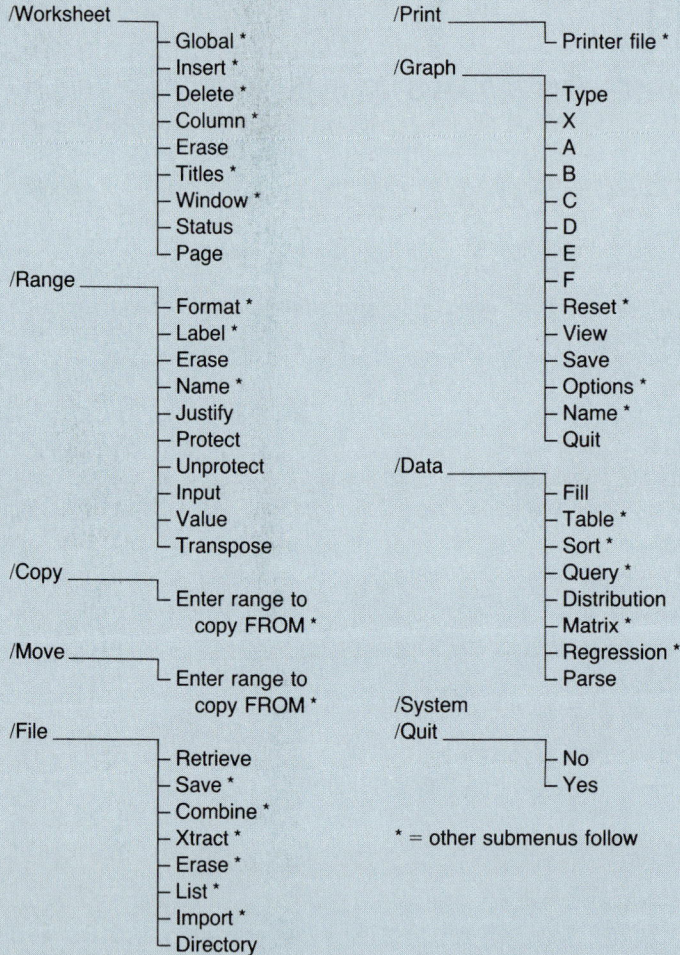

/Worksheet
- Global *
- Insert *
- Delete *
- Column *
- Erase
- Titles *
- Window *
- Status
- Page

/Range
- Format *
- Label *
- Erase
- Name *
- Justify
- Protect
- Unprotect
- Input
- Value
- Transpose

/Copy
- Enter range to copy FROM *

/Move
- Enter range to copy FROM *

/File
- Retrieve
- Save *
- Combine *
- Xtract *
- Erase *
- List *
- Import *
- Directory

/Print
- Printer file *

/Graph
- Type
- X
- A
- B
- C
- D
- E
- F
- Reset *
- View
- Save
- Options *
- Name *
- Quit

/Data
- Fill
- Table *
- Sort *
- Query *
- Distribution
- Matrix *
- Regression *
- Parse

/System

/Quit
- No
- Yes

* = other submenus follow

FUNCTION KEYS

Help	F1	F2	Edit
Name	F3	F4	Absolute
Goto	F5	F6	Window
Query	F7	F8	Table
Calculate	F9	F10	Graph

CELL CURSOR MOVEMENT

To spreadsheet beg./end   HOME   END HOME

HANDS-ON TUTORIAL 12: Using Lotus 1-2-3 and The TWiN (Spreadsheet Capabilities)

Lotus 1-2-3, a product of Lotus Development Corporation, is a high-performance, integrated software package that provides electronic spreadsheet, graphics, and data management capabilities. The focus of this Lotus 1-2-3 tutorial is on its spreadsheet capabilities. This tutorial is based on Lotus 1-2-3 Version 2.01.

This tutorial can also be used with The TWiN (both the full-function and Educational Version 1.4), a Lotus 1-2-3 clone. The TWiN, a product of Mosaic Software, Inc., is distributed as a supplement to the main text. To run The TWiN, enter "twin" at the A prompt (A>twin).

■ Boot the system (see Hands-On Tutorial 1).

■ Load Lotus 1-2-3 to memory. Insert the Lotus 1-2-3 system disk in drive A.

　　A>**123** ↵

■ Insert your data disk in drive B.

■ The display includes a spreadsheet with rows and columns and a user interface. The user interface (control panel) consists of the three lines at the top of the screen. The first line contains status information for the current (highlighted) cell cursor (location, format, column width, location and contents) and the mode indicator (ready, point, menu, edit, wait,

and so on). In the second line, you issue commands and edit data. The third line displays a submenu or a brief description of a highlighted command.

■ Use your cursor control keys to move the cell pointer around the screen and then return it to A1.

　　→ ↓ ← ↑

■ Display the main menu in the user interface by pressing /.

　　/

To select a menu item, press the first letter of the desired menu item or use the left/right cursor control keys to highlight the desired item and press ENTER.

■ ESC erases the current menu.

　　ESC

Three function key commands may prove helpful as you work through the following tutorials.

F1 Context-sensitive Help key.

F2 Permits editing of the contents of the current cell.

F5 Move pointer to or "GoTo" a user-specified cell.

You are now ready to begin your spreadsheet session.

HANDS-ON TUTORIAL 13: Formatting the Column Width

The planned spreadsheet template (see Figure 7–1) has four columns. To make the most effective use of the display screen, revise the column width from the default of 9 positions to 30, 14, 14, and 14 positions for columns A, B, C, and D.

■ Change column A to width 30. HOME positions the pointer at A1.

　　HOME
　　/**W**orksheet **C**olumn **S**et-Width
　　Enter column width (1..240): **30** ↵

■ Change columns B, C, and D to width 14.

Use the cursor control keys to move the pointer to B1 or use the F5 function key to go to (move pointer to) B1 (the latter method is illustrated in the tutorial).

　　F5
　　Enter address to go to: **B1** ↵
　　/**W**orksheet **G**lobal **C**olumn-Width **14** ↵

Columns widths that have been previously set by the user remain unchanged when the "Global" command is issued. In this case, column A will remain at a width of 30.

HANDS-ON TUTORIAL 14: Entering Text Data

In this tutorial we make all of the text entries needed for the spreadsheet of Figure 7–1.

■ First, enter all repeating text (such as the

lines created by = and -) to provide some form to the spreadsheet template.

　　HOME
　　\= → \= → \= → \= ↵

- Follow the foregoing procedure to add the repeated text as illustrated in Figure 7–1 to rows 3, 9, 13, 16, 19, 21, 24, 28, 30, 33, 35, and 39. Notice that on certain rows the repeated text entries begin at column B. For example, the keystroke sequence for row 9 is

  [F5]
  Enter address to go to: **B9** ↵
  \- → \- → \- ↵

- Now make the text entries for column A and row 2, beginning with the entry in A2. If you make an entry error, press F2 to switch to edit mode. Edit the entry as you would text in a word processing document.

  [F5]
  Enter address to go to: **A2** ↵
  ZIMCO INCOME STATEMENT ($1000) ↵

- Enter the column headings in row 2.

  [F5]
  Enter address to go to: **B2** ↵
  "Next Year → "This Year → "Last Year ↵

In Lotus 1-2-3, prefacing a text entry with

a double quote (") causes it to be right justified.

- Make the other text entries (all in column A) for the spreadsheet as illustrated in Figure 7–1. Notice that some entries, such as those in A6 and A10, have either two or four leading spaces. To enter data after row 20, use either the down cursor control key to move one row at a time or the PGDN (page down) key to display rows 21 through 40.

  Notice how the long entries in A34, A37, and A38 "spill over" into empty cells.

  At this point your spreadsheet should look just like Figure 7–1, without the numeric data.

Save option: If at anytime you cannot continue with the tutorials, save your work so that you can pick up where you left off. To do this, see "Hands-On Tutorial 20: Saving and Retrieving a Spreadsheet." When you return, retrieve your spreadsheet and continue the tutorials.

HANDS-ON TUTORIAL 15: Entering Numeric Data

Continue the development of the spreadsheet template of Figure 7–1 by entering the numeric data.

- Enter the numeric values in rows 4, 6, 7, 8, 12, 15, and 18 of columns C and D of the actual income statement (rows 1 through 20). The other values in columns C and D and all values in column B, "Next Year", of the income statement are the results of formulas. Also, enter the values in the ranges B25.D26 and C36.C38. In C36, C37, and C38, enter the values as .2, .01, and 0. We can format these to a percent format later. The actual content of the spreadsheet cells is shown in Figure 7–6. Formulas are entered in the next tutorial. For C4, C6, C7, and C8, enter

  [F5]
  Enter address to go to: **C4** ↵
  153000 ↓ ↓ 115260 ↓ 4125 ↓ 19875 ↓

Notice that the values you entered are not formatted with a dollar sign ($) and a comma (,) as shown in Figure 7–1. We can format or edit these entries later.

- Enter the other nonformula numeric values (identified above) as shown in Figure 7–1.

Lotus 1-2-3 display (rows 1-40) after the completion of Hands-On Tutorial 15.

HANDS-ON TUTORIAL 16: Entering Formulas

Include the calculation capability to the spreadsheet template of Figure 7–1 by entering the formulas.

■ Enter the formulas as illustrated in Figure 7–6 (the actual content of the spreadsheet of Figure 7–1). For B4, enter

> F5
> Enter address to go to: **B4** ↵
> **+C4∗(1+$C$36)** ↓ ↓

Notice that the result, and not the formula, is displayed in cell B4. Validate your entry by comparing the result to the value displayed in B4 in Figure 7–1.

■ Enter the formulas in B6, B7, B8, and B10.

> **+C6∗(1+$C$37)** ↓ **+C7** ↓ **+C8∗(1+$C$38)**
> ↓ ↓ **+B4−B6−B7+B8** ↓

Notice that both the column and row in the absolute cell addresses in formulas of B4, B6, and B8 are prefaced by a dollar sign.

■ Instead of entering the formulas for cells C10 and D10, we can copy the formula from cell B10. B10 is the "copy from" range and C10.D10 is the "copy to" range.

> F5
> Enter address to go to: **B10** ↵
> **/Copy**
> Enter range to copy FROM: B10..B10 ↵
> Enter range to copy TO: **C10.D10** ↵

You can separate the endpoints of the range with one period (C10.D10) or two (C10..D10).

■ Move the pointer to C10 and D10 and notice that the formulas copied to columns C and D apply to columns C and D, not column B.

■ Refer to Figure 7–6 in the text and enter all of the other formulas. Use the copy command as needed to enter like formulas in adjacent columns, just as you did for B10, C10, and D10.

Lotus 1-2-3 display (rows 1-40) after the completion of Hands-On Tutorial 16.

HANDS-ON TUTORIAL 17: Using Predefined Functions

In this tutorial, we will edit B10.D10 to demonstrate the use of predefined functions.

■ Edit the "operating profit" cells to use the SUM function.

> F5
> Enter address to go to: **B10** ↵
> F2 (edit cell)
> B4−B6−B7−B8 BKSP (8 times)
> B4−@**SUM(B6.B8)** ↵

■ Copy B10 to the range C10.D10. You can enter the range C10.D10 directly as illustrated in Hands-On Tutorial 16, or you can use the cursor control keys in combination with the anchor (period or colon). To do this, position the cell pointer at one of the endpoints of the range (C10) and press the anchor. Then, move the pointer to the other endpoint (D10) and press ENTER.

> **/Copy**
> Enter range to copy FROM: B10..B10 ↵
> Enter range to copy TO: → C10. → D10 ↵

The results of these cells are, of course, unchanged.

HANDS-ON TUTORIAL 18: Using Logical Operations

The IF and OR functions along with logical operators are used to integrate data entry validation into the spreadsheet.

■ Display the message "ABOVE 25% LIMIT" in C40 if any of the values entered in C36, C37, or C38 exceeds 25 percent.

> F5
>
> Enter address to go to: **C40** ↵
> **@IF(C36>.25#OR#C37>.25#OR#C38>.25,
> "ABOVE 25% LIMIT"," ")** ↵

For TWiN, use the following formula in C40:

**@IF(C36>.25#OR#C37>.25#OR#C38>.25,
9999999,0)** ↵

A zero appears in C40 if values are 25 percent or below; 9999999 appears if values are greater than 25 percent.

■ Check your formula by entering a value greater than .25 in C36, C37, or C38. The warning message should be displayed in C40 (see Figure 7–10). Replace the test values with the values for the example: .2, .01, and 0, respectively.

HANDS-ON TUTORIAL 19: Formatting the Cell Entries

Complete the spreadsheet template of Figure 7–1 by formatting the cell entries to improve appearance and readability.

■ Edit the entries in B4..D25 to include commas and have no decimal places.

> HOME
>
> /*Range* **F**ormat **,**
> Enter number of decimal places (0..15): **0** ↵
> Enter range to format: **B1.D25** ↵

■ Add dollar signs to the amounts in row 4.

> /*Range* **F**ormat **C**urrency
> Enter number of decimal places (0..15): **0** ↵
> Enter range to format: **B4.D4** ↵

Repeat this command sequence for the amounts in rows 10, 14 and 20. Do the same for the amounts in rows 26 and 27 (the range B26.D27), but for these amounts, accept the default 2 when prompted for decimal places.

■ Format row 29 to be displayed with 2 decimal places.

> F5
>
> Enter address to go to: **B29** ↵
> /*Range* **F**ormat **F**ixed
> Enter number of decimal places (0..15): **2** ↵
> Enter range to format: **B29.D29** ↵

■ Format the amounts in rows 36, 37, and 38 as percent with 2 decimal places.

> F5
>
> Enter address to go to: **C36** ↵
> /*Range* **F**ormat **P**ercent
> Enter number of decimal places (0..15): **2** ↵
> Enter range to format: **C36.C38** ↵

The spreadsheet should look just like Figure 7–1.

Lotus 1-2-3 display (rows 1-40) after the completion of Hands-On Tutorial 19.

HANDS-ON TUTORIAL 20: Saving and Retrieving a Spreadsheet

■ Save the current spreadsheet on disk B with the name of "income".

> /File Save
> Enter save file name: **b:income** ↵

At the prompt, you may need to backspace (BKSP) over the default directory identifier (A:\) and enter "b:".

> If you had already saved "income" to disk storage, you would have been presented with another menu that, in essence, warns you that you will destroy the previous version of the file.
>
> In Lotus 1-2-3, the menu options are

"Cancel" (the Save operation) and "Replace" (the existing file with a file containing the current spreadsheet).

> /File Save
> Enter save file name: **b:income** ↵
> **R**eplace

■ To retrieve a spreadsheet from disk storage, use the following commands to "zap" or clear the current spreadsheet, if necessary, and load the desired file (b:income).

> /File Retrieve
> Name of file to retrieve: **b:income** ↵

HANDS-ON TUTORIAL 21: Printing a Document and Terminating a Session

■ Define the range to be printed and print the current spreadsheet.

> /Print Printer Range **A1.D39** ↵

Turn on your printer, adjust the paper, and reset the printer to the top of the page (Align). Go prints the spreadsheet.

> **A**lign **G**o
> **Q**uit (*to return to the spreadsheet*)

■ Do not exit the spreadsheet package at this time if you intend to continue with Hands-On Tutorial 22. To exit Lotus 1-2-3

> /Quit Yes

HANDS-ON TUTORIAL 22: "What if . . ."

In this tutorial, we answer the question "What if the forecast variables are changed?"

■ Revise the values assigned the forecast variables in C36, C37, and C38 from .2, .01, and 0 to .03, .02, and .04, respectively.

> F5
> Enter address to go to: **C36** ↵
> **.03** ↓ **.02** ↓ **.04** ↓ HOME

Compare your results with those of Figure 7–13.

■ Enter other values for the forecast variables and observe how net profit, earnings per share, and the price-earnings ratio are affected.

HANDS-ON TUTORIAL 23: Inserting a Column

Modify the income statement portion (rows 1-20) of the spreadsheet of Figure 7–1 to include an "After Next" year column (see Figure 7–14). Be sure that the entries for C36, C37, and C38 are .2, .01, and 0, respectively.

■ Insert a new column at column B.

> HOME
> F5
> Enter address to go to: **B1** ↵
> /Worksheet Insert Column
> Enter column insert range: B1..B1 ↵

■ Adjust the width of columns B, C, D, and E to a width of 10 positions so that all columns are displayed on the screen.

> /Worksheet Global Column-Width
> Enter global column width (1..240): **10** ↵

■ Copy the range C1.C20 to B1.B20.

> F5
> Enter address to go to: **C1** ↵
> /Copy
> Enter range to copy FROM: **C1.C20** ↵
> Enter range to copy TO: **B1.B20** ↵

Notice how the projected "Net Sales" in the new column is increased by the value of the forecast variable (projected change in sales) over the amount in the "Next Year" column.

■ Edit the column heading in column B.

[F5]

Enter address to go to: **B2** ↵
[F2] [BKSP] (*9 times*) **After Next** ↵

Switch the pointer between B4 and C4. Notice that the relative addresses were revised during the copy operation, and the absolute addresses remained the same.

■ Print only rows 1 through 20 of the current spreadsheet (see "Hands-On Tutorial 21: Printing a Document and Terminating a Session"). Be sure to identify the range as A1.E20 so that all the columns that appear on the screen are printed.

■ Exit Lotus 1-2-3 without saving the most recent changes, the inserted column.

   /Quit Yes

Lotus 1-2-3 display after the completion of Hands-On Tutorial 23.

ADVANCED AND SPECIAL FEATURES TUTORIAL: Lotus 1-2-3 and The TWiN Spreadsheet Capabilities

In this advanced Lotus tutorial the following skills are introduced: adding a template to an existing spreadsheet, retrieving from a files list, copying a block, deleting lines, and using windows. You should have completed Hands-On Tutorials 12 through 23 before continuing with this advanced tutorial.

Monroe Green, the vice-president of Finance and Accounting, wants to create a three-year summary template (Figure 7–8) of the data presented in Zimco's income statement template (Figure 7–1).

GETTING STARTED

To complete this tutorial, you will need the Lotus system disk and a work disk that contains the Lotus "income" template based on Figure 7–1.

■ Load Lotus 1-2-3 to memory (see Hands-On Tutorial 12). Insert the Lotus 1-2-3 system disk in drive A.

   A>**123** ↵

■ Insert your data disk in drive B.

ADDING A TEMPLATE TO AN EXISTING TEMPLATE

Retrieve the "income" file that you created in Hands-On Tutorials 12 through 23 and create the "Three-Year Summary Data" template in the range A41..D60 (instead of A121..D140 as described in the text).

■ Retrieve the spreadsheet "INCOME.WK1" and position the pointer at "home".

/File **R**etrieve
Name of file to retrieve: [ESC] (*if default is A:*) **b:** ↵
(*highlight "INCOME.WK1"*)
↵
[HOME]

■ Copy A1..D20 to A41..D60.

   /Copy
   Enter range to copy FROM: **A1.D20** ↵
   Enter range to copy TO: **A41** ↵

Note that the goto range was defined by naming only the cell in the upper left corner.

MODIFYING THE "income" TEMPLATE TO CREATE ANOTHER TEMPLATE

Create the template in Figure 7–8.

■ Move the pointer to the template copy.

   [F5]
   Enter address to go to: **A41** ↵

■ Key in the appropriate template title and column headings.

   [F5]
   Enter address to go to: **A42** ↵
   THREE-YEAR SUMMARY DATA → **"Average** → **"Minimum** → **"Maximum** ↵

Entering a new label replaces the existing label. The quote right justifies the heading.

■ Use functions to determine the average, minimum, and maximum values in each category.

F5
Enter address to go to: **B44** ↵
@AVG(B4.D4) → **@MIN(B4.D4)** →
@MAX(B4.D4) ↵

■ Copy the functions to the other ranges.

/Copy
Enter range to copy FROM: **B44.D44** ↵
Enter range to copy TO: **B50** ↵

Use the same procedure to copy range
B44..D44 to B54 and and B60.

■ Delete any unneeded rows in the template copy. Delete rows 55 through 59.

F5
Enter address to go to: **A55** ↵
/Worksheet **D**elete **R**ow ↓ (*4 times*) ↵

Repeat this procedure to delete rows 51 through 53 and then rows 45 through 49. Each time rows are deleted, the remaining rows are moved up to fill the space.

USING WINDOWS

Use the window feature to view the newly created summary template in the lower window and the original template in the upper window.

■ Split the screen into horizontal windows.

(*move template to the bottom of screen*)
F5
Enter address to go to: **A30** ↵
(*position pointer at window division*)
F5
Enter address to go to: **A41** ↵
/Worksheet **W**indow **H**orizontal

■ Move the pointer to A1 in the top window to view the original template. Move the pointer up and down to scroll through the income statements.

HOME

The window feature enables you to scan simultaneously the actual entries in the income statements while viewing summary data. Move the pointer about in the upper window to view different portions of the spreadsheet without affecting the lower window. Press F6 to move the pointer from window to window. Only one window is active at a time.

■ After you have practiced manipulating the windows, clear the bottom window.

/Worksheet **W**indow **C**lear

■ Save the revised spreadsheet.

/File **S**ave ↵ **R**eplace

■ Exit Lotus 1-2-3.

/Quit Yes

Lotus 1-2-3 display after creating the windows in the Advanced and Special Features Tutorial.

QUICK REFERENCE GUIDE
SuperCalc4
(Version 1.0)
A>sc4 ↵

SLASH (/) COMMAND MENU

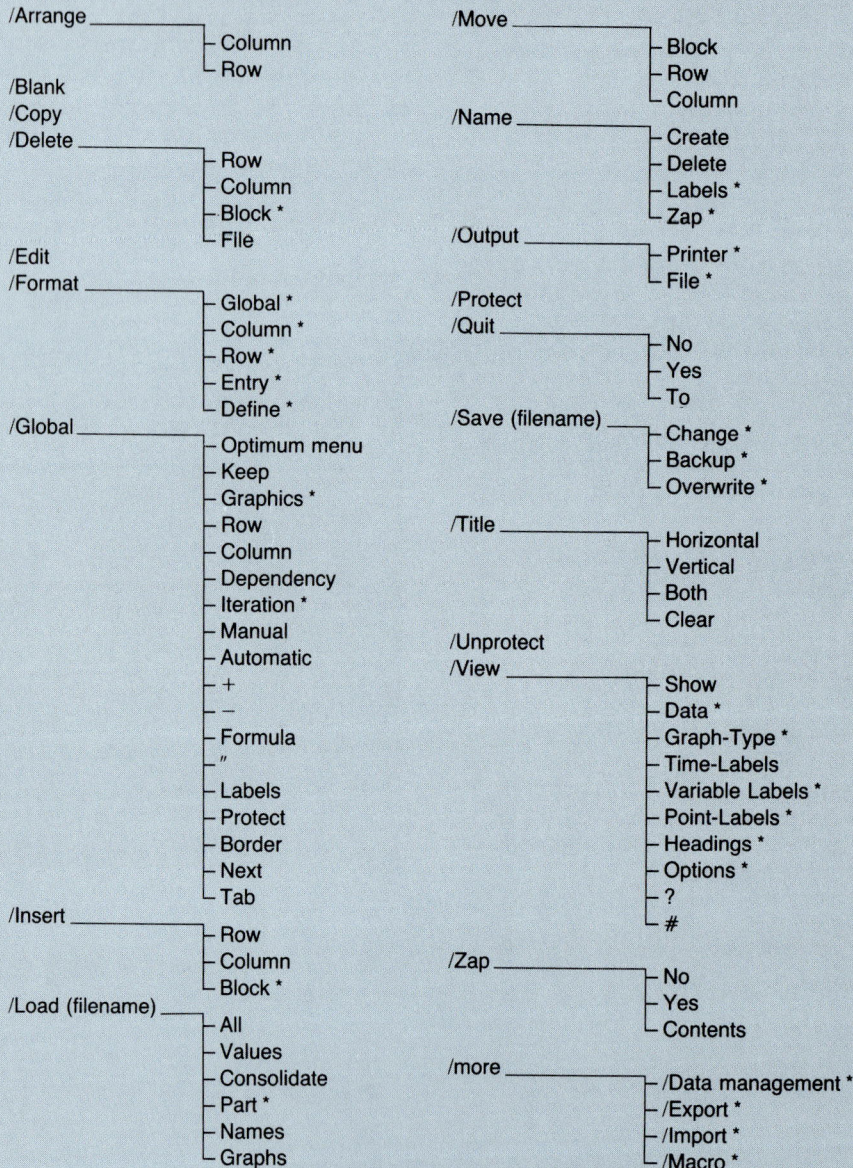

/Arrange
- Column
- Row

/Blank
/Copy
/Delete
- Row
- Column
- Block *
- File

/Edit
/Format
- Global *
- Column *
- Row *
- Entry *
- Define *

/Global
- Optimum menu
- Keep
- Graphics *
- Row
- Column
- Dependency
- Iteration *
- Manual
- Automatic
- +
- −
- Formula
- "
- Labels
- Protect
- Border
- Next
- Tab

/Insert
- Row
- Column
- Block *

/Load (filename)
- All
- Values
- Consolidate
- Part *
- Names
- Graphs

/Move
- Block
- Row
- Column

/Name
- Create
- Delete
- Labels *
- Zap *

/Output
- Printer *
- File *

/Protect
/Quit
- No
- Yes
- To

/Save (filename)
- Change *
- Backup *
- Overwrite *

/Title
- Horizontal
- Vertical
- Both
- Clear

/Unprotect
/View
- Show
- Data *
- Graph-Type *
- Time-Labels
- Variable Labels *
- Point-Labels *
- Headings *
- Options *
- ?
- #

/Zap
- No
- Yes
- Contents

/more
- /Data management *
- /Export *
- /Import *
- /Macro *

* = other submenus follow

FUNCTION KEYS

Help	F1	F2	Edit	
Name	F3	F4	Absolute	
Goto	F5	F6	Window	
Calculator	F7	F8	Resume	
Plot	F9	F10	View	

CELL CURSOR MOVEMENT

To spreadsheet beg./end	HOME	END HOME
To screen beg./end	CTRL-HOME	CTRL-END

HANDS-ON TUTORIAL 12: Using SuperCalc4 (Spreadsheet Capabilities)

SuperCalc4, a product of Computer Associates, is a high-performance integrated software package that provides electronic spreadsheet, graphics, and data management capabilities. The focus of this SuperCalc4 tutorial is on its spreadsheet capabilities. This tutorial is based on SuperCalc4 Educational Version 1.0.

■ Boot the system (see Hands-On Tutorial 1).

■ Load SuperCalc4 to memory. Insert the SuperCalc4 program disk 1 in drive A.

> A>**sc4** ↵
> SPACE

During a SuperCalc4 session, you may need to replace the active program disk with the other program disk. On-screen prompts will tell you when to switch program disks.

■ Insert your data disk in drive B.

■ The display includes a spreadsheet with rows and columns and a user interface. The user interface is the four lines at the bottom of the screen. The first line contains status information for the current (highlighted) cell cursor (location and contents). The second line indicates the width in characters of the current column, available memory (in K or 1024 bytes), and the last column and row in the spreadsheet. In the third line you issue commands, enter data, and edit data. The fourth line lists appropriate help information.

■ Use your cursor control keys to move the cell pointer around the screen, then return it to A1.

> → ↓ ← ↑

■ Display the main menu in the user interface by pressing /.

> /

To select a menu item, press the first letter of the desired menu item or use the left and right cursor control keys to highlight the desired item and press ENTER.

■ ESC erases the current menu.

> ESC

Three function key commands may prove helpful as you work through the following tutorials.

F1 Context-sensitive Help key.

F2 Permits editing of the contents of the current cell.

F5 Move pointer to or "GoTo" a user-specified cell.

You are now ready to begin your spreadsheet session.

HANDS-ON TUTORIAL 13: Formatting the Column Width

The planned spreadsheet template (see Figure 7–1) has four columns. To make the most effective use of the display screen, revise the column width from the default of 9 positions to 30, 15, 15, and 15 positions for columns A, B, C, and D, respectively.

■ Change column A to width 30. HOME positions the pointer at A1. Notice that in SuperCalc4 you enter a comma (,) to accept a default entry displayed in the command line (for example, the comma after A).

> HOME
> /Format,Column,A,**Width**,**30** ↵

■ Change columns B, C, and D to width 15. Use the cursor control keys to move the pointer to B1 or use the F5 function key to go to (move pointer to) B1 (the latter is illustrated in the tutorial).

> F5 =>**B1** ↵
> /Format,Column,B.**D**,Width,**15** ↵

Notice that the period you entered after the letter B is displayed as a colon when you define the range of columns that apply to the format command. Actually, you can enter either a period or a colon. The period or colon serves as the anchor for defining a range. As an alternative, you could enter the period and define the range by moving the pointer to column D.

HANDS-ON TUTORIAL 14: Entering Text Data

In this tutorial we will make all of the text entries needed for the spreadsheet of Figure 7–1.

■ First, enter all repeating text (such as the lines created by = and -) to provide some form to the spreadsheet template. Preface the text string to be repeated text with a single quote.

> HOME
> '= ↵

The text is repeated past the four columns that we need for the spreadsheet. To end the repetitions, fill E1 with blanks.

> F5 =>E1 ↵
> ' ↵

■ Follow the foregoing procedure to add the repeated text as illustrated in Figure 7–1 to rows 3, 9, 13, 16, 19, 21, 24, 28, 30, 33, 35, and 39. Notice that on certain rows the repeated text entries begin at column B. For example, the keystroke sequence for row 9 is

> F5 =>B9 ↵
> '- ↵
> F5 =>E9 ↵
> ' ↵

■ Now make the text entries for column A and row 2, beginning with the entry in A2. If you make an entry error, press F2 to switch to edit mode. Edit the entry as you would text in a word processing document.

> F5 =>A2 ↵
> ZIMCO INCOME STATEMENT ($1000) ↵

In SuperCalc4, text mode entry is the default. Text entries are automatically left justified and a double quote (") is added automatically at the beginning of the entry in the status line. However, you must preface text entries with the double quote when the text entry is preceded by blanks (as in A6) if you wish a numeric or formula entry to be recognized as a text entry.

■ Enter the column headings in row 2.

> F5 =>B2 ↵
> Next Year → This Year → Last Year ↵

These headings for SuperCalc4 are left justified, but we want right justification. To do this, format the range B2.D2 to be right justified.

> F5 =>B2 ↵
> /Format,Entry,B2.D2,TextRight,Accept

Notice that SuperCalc4 often does some of the work for you. When this occurs, enter only those characters needed to complete the command.

■ Make the other text entries (all in column A) to the spreadsheet as illustrated in Figure 7–1. Notice that some entries, such as those in A6 and A10, have either two or four leading spaces. To enter data after row 20, use either the down cursor control key to move one row at a time or the PGDN (page down) key to display rows 21 through 40.

Notice how the long entries in A34, A37, and A38 "spill over" into empty cells.

At this point your spreadsheet should look just like Figure 7–1, without the numeric data.

Save option: If at anytime you cannot continue with the tutorials, save your work so that you can pick up where you left off. To do this, see "Hands-On Tutorial 20: Saving and Retrieving a Spreadsheet." When you return, retrieve your spreadsheet and continue the tutorials.

HANDS-ON TUTORIAL 15: Entering Numeric Data

Continue the development of the spreadsheet template of Figure 7–1 by entering the numeric data.

■ Enter the numeric values in rows 4, 6, 7, 8, 12, 15, and 18 of columns C and D of the actual income statement (rows 1 through 20). The other values in columns C and D and all values in column B, "Next Year", of the income statement are the results of formulas. Also, enter the values in the ranges B25.D26 and C36.C38. In C36, C37, and C38, enter the values as .2, .01, and 0. We can format these to a percent format later. The actual content of the spreadsheet cells is shown in Figure 7–6. Formulas are entered in the next tutorial. For C4, C6, C7, and C8, enter

$\boxed{\text{F5}}$ =>**C4** ↵
153000 ↓ ↓ **115260** ↓ **4125** ↓ **19875** ↓

Notice that the values you entered are not formatted with a dollar sign ($) and

a comma (,) as shown in Figure 7–1. We can format or edit these entries later.

■ Enter the other nonformula numeric values (identified above) as shown in Figure 7–1.

SuperCalc4 display (rows 1-40) after the completion of Hands-On Tutorial 15.

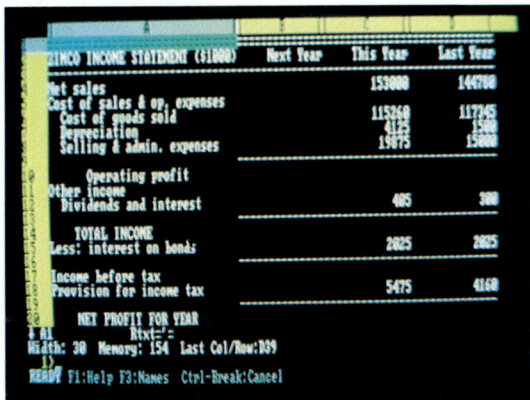

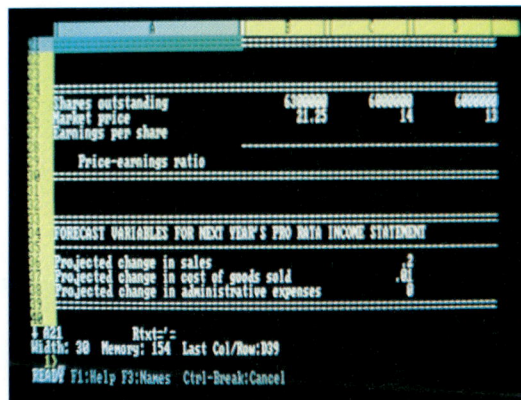

HANDS-ON TUTORIAL 16: Entering Formulas

Include the calculation capability to the spreadsheet template of Figure 7–1 by entering the formulas.

■ Enter the formulas as illustrated in Figure 7–6 (the actual contents of the spreadsheet of Figure 7–1). For B4, enter

$\boxed{\text{F5}}$ =>**B4** ↵
C4*(1+$C$36) ↓ ↓

Notice that the result, and not the formula, is displayed in cell B4. Validate your entry by comparing the result to the value displayed in B4 in Figure 7–1.

The plus (+) sign at the beginning of the formulas in Figure 7–6 is optional in SuperCalc4.

■ Enter the formulas in B6, B7, B8, and B10.

C6*(1+$C$37) ↓ **C7** ↓ **C8*(1+$C$38)** ↓ ↓
B4−B6−B7−B8 ↓

Notice that both the column and row in the absolute cell addresses in formulas of B4, B6, and B8 are prefaced by a dollar sign.

■ Instead of entering the formulas for cells C10 and D10, we can copy the formula from cell B10. B10 is the "copy from" range and C10.D10 is the "copy to" range.

$\boxed{\text{F5}}$ =>**B10** ↵
/Copy,B10,C10.D10 ↵

Move the pointer to C10 and D10 and notice that the formulas copied to columns C and D apply to columns C and D, not column B.

■ Refer to Figure 7–6 in the text and enter all of the other formulas. Use the copy command as needed to enter like formulas in adjacent columns, just as you did for B10, C10, and D10.

SuperCalc4 display (rows 1-40) after the completion of Hands-On Tutorial 16.

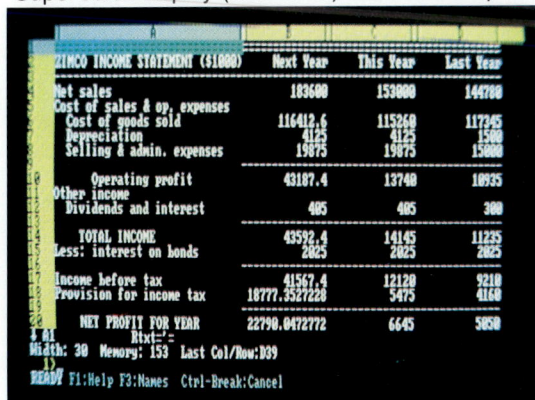

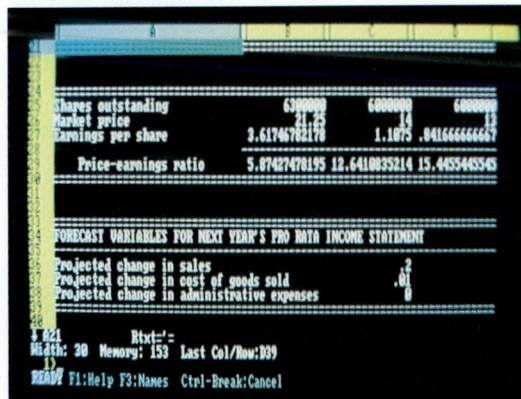

HANDS-ON TUTORIAL 17: Using Predefined Functions

In this tutorial, we will edit B10.D10 to demonstrate the use of predefined functions.

- Edit the "operating profit" cells to use the SUM function.

  [F5] =>**B10** ↵
  [F2] (edit cell)
  B4−B6−B7−B8 [BKSP] (8 times)
  B4−**SUM(B6.B8)** ↵

- Copy B10 to the range C10.D10. You can enter the range C10.D10 directly as illustrated in Hands-On Tutorial 16, or you can use the cursor control keys in combination with the anchor (period or colon). To do this, position the cell pointer at one of the endpoints of the range (C10) and press the anchor. Then, move the pointer to the other endpoint (D10) and press ENTER.

  /**C**opy,B10, → C10. → D10 ↵

The results of these cells are, of course, unchanged.

HANDS-ON TUTORIAL 18: Using Logical Operations

The IF and OR functions along with logical operators are used to integrate data entry validation into the spreadsheet.

- Display the message "ABOVE 25%" in C40 if any of the values entered in C36, C37, or C38 exceeds 25 percent.

  [F5] =>**C40** ↵
  **IF(OR(C36>.25,OR(C37>.25,C38>.25)),
      "ABOVE 25%"," ")** ↵

The SuperCalc4 formula varies slightly from the formula illustrated in the textual material because SuperCalc4 compares only two elements at a time with an OR. To achieve the same result with SuperCalc4, an OR expression is nested within another OR expression. Also, SuperCalc4 limits the message to 9 characters, that is "ABOVE 25%".

- Check your formula by entering a value greater than .25 in C36, C37, or C38. The warning message should be displayed in C40 (see Figure 7–10). Replace the test values with the values for the example: .2, .01, and 0, respectively.

HANDS-ON TUTORIAL 19: Formatting the Cell Entries

Complete the spreadsheet template of Figure 7–1 by formatting the cell entries to improve appearance and readability.

- SuperCalc4 allows the user to define up to 8 different types of number formats. In this tutorial we will define the 5 formats needed in this spreadsheet by making revisions to the default specifications in the first 5 columns of the "User-defined formats".

  [F5] =>**B4** ↵
  /**F**ormat,**D**efine,

Now, use the cursor control keys to alter the default specification in the "User-defined formats." Start with column 1, which represents format 1 options, and revise the default specs to define a format that will apply to row 4 and other like entries (zero "Decimal Places").

  ↓ (5 times) **0**

Revise the column 2 default values in the format table to define a format that will apply to row 6 in the spreadsheet and to other like entries (no "Floating $" and zero "Decimal Places").

We will use the default values in format 3 to apply to rows 26 and 27.

Revise the column 4 default values to define a format that will apply to row 29 (no "Floating $" and no "Embedded Commas").

Revise the column 5 default values to define a format that will apply to the range C36.C38 (no "Floating $", no "Embedded Commas", and yes for "%").

■ Store these user-defined formats and return to the spreadsheet.

    CTRL - BREAK

■ Now, we need to designate which of the 5 user-defined formats applies to which numeric entries. This is done one range at a time. To apply format 1 to row 4, do the following.

    F5 =>**B4** ↵

/**F**ormat,**E**ntry,B4.**D4**,**U**ser-defined**1**,**A**ccept

■ In the same manner, use the above sequence of steps to apply the user-defined formats to the spreadsheet data: format 1 to the ranges B10.D10, B14.D14, and B20.D20; format 2 to the ranges B6.D8, B12.D12, B15.D15, B17.D18, and B25.D25; format 3 to the range B26.D27; format 4 to the range B29.D29; and format 5 to the range C36.C38. After formatting is completed, the spreadsheet should look just like Figure 7–1.

SuperCalc4 display (rows 1-40) after the completion of Hands-On Tutorial 19.

HANDS-ON TUTORIAL 20: Saving and Retrieving a Spreadsheet

■ Save the current spreadsheet on disk B with the name of "income".

    /**S**ave,**b:income**,**A**ll,

At the prompt, you may need to backspace over the default directory identifier (A:\) and enter "b:".

If you had already saved "income" to disk storage, you would have been presented with another menu that, in essence, warns you that you will destroy the previous version of the file.

In SuperCalc4, the menu gives you the option of changing the name of the

spreadsheet file, creating a backup, or overwriting the existing file. To overwrite the file

    /**S**ave,b:income ↵ **O**verwrite,**A**ll,

■ To retrieve a spreadsheet from disk storage, use the following commands to "zap" or clear the current spreadsheet, if necessary, and load the desired file (b:income).

    /**Z**ap-ENTIRE-Spreadsheet? **Y**es
    /**L**oad,**b:income**,**A**ll

SuperCalc4 appends the extension .CAL to user file names (income.CAL).

HANDS-ON TUTORIAL 21: Printing a Document and Terminating a Session

■ Define the range to be printed and print the current spreadsheet. To eliminate the printing of the borders (column letters and row numbers) in SuperCalc4, select "No" for the "Borders" option in the "Output Options Menu".

> ```
> HOME
> ```
> /Output,Printer,Range,A1.**D39** ↵
> /Output,Printer,**O**ptions,Borders,**N**o,**Q**uit
> /Output,Printer,Options,**Q**uit

Turn on your printer, adjust the paper, and reset the printer to the top of the page (Align). "Go" prints the spreadsheet.

> /**O**utput,Printer,**A**lign,**G**o, ↵
> /**O**utput,Printer,**Q**uit

■ Do not exit the spreadsheet package at this time if you intend to continue with Hands-On Tutorial 22. To exit SuperCalc4

> /**Q**uit,**Y**es

HANDS-ON TUTORIAL 22: "What if . . ."

In this tutorial, we answer the question "What if the forecast variables are changed?"

■ Revise the values assigned the forecast variables in C36, C37, and C38 from .2, .01, and 0 to .03, .02, and .04, respectively.

> ```
> F5
> ```
> =>**C36** ↵
> .03 ↓ .02 ↓ .04 ↓ ```HOME```

Compare your results with those of Figure 7–13.

■ Enter other values for the forecast variables and observe how net profit, earnings per share, and the price-earnings ratio are affected.

HANDS-ON TUTORIAL 23: Inserting a Column

Modify the income statement portion (rows 1-20) of the spreadsheet of Figure 7–1 to include an "After Next" year column (see Figure 7–14). Be sure that the entries for C36, C37, and C38 are .2, .01, and 0, respectively.

■ Insert a new column at column B.

> ```
> HOME
> ```
> ```F5``` =>**B1** ↵
> /**I**nsert,**C**olumn,B ↵

■ Adjust the width of columns B, C, D, and E to a width of 11 positions so that all columns are displayed on the screen.

> /**F**ormat,**C**olumn,B.**E**,Width,**11** ↵

■ Copy the range C1.C20 to B1.B20.

> ```F5``` =>**C1** ↵
> /**C**opy,C1.**C20**,**B1.B20** ↵

Notice how the projected "Net Sales" in the new column is increased by the value of the forecast variable (projected

change in sales) over the amount in the "Next Year" column.

■ Edit the column heading in column B.

> ```F5``` =>**B2** ↵
> ```F2``` ```BKSP``` (9 times) **After Next** ↵

Switch the pointer between B4 and C4. Notice that the relative addresses were revised during the copy operation, and the absolute addresses remained the same.

■ Print only rows 1 through 20 of the current spreadsheet (see "Hands-On Tutorial 21: Printing a Document and Terminating a Session"). Be sure to identify the range as A1.E20 so that all the columns that appear on the screen are printed.

■ Exit SuperCalc4 without saving the most recent changes, the inserted column.

> /**Q**uit,**Y**es

SuperCalc4 display after the completion of Hands-On Tutorial 23.

ADVANCED AND SPECIAL FEATURES TUTORIAL: SuperCalc4 Spreadsheet Capabilities

In this advanced SuperCalc4 tutorial the following skills are introduced: adding a template to an existing spreadsheet, retrieving from a files list, copying a block, and using windows. You should have completed Hands-On Tutorials 12 through 23 before continuing with this advanced tutorial.

Monroe Green, the vice-president of Finance and Accounting, wants to create a three-year summary template (Figure 7–8) of the data presented in Zimco's income statement template (Figure 7–1). This tutorial deviates somewhat from the Figure 7–8 discussion in the text because the Educational Version of SuperCalc4 has a 40 row restriction.

GETTING STARTED

To complete this tutorial, you will need the two SuperCalc4 diskettes and a work disk that contains the SuperCalc4 "income" template based on Figure 7–1.

- Load SuperCalc4 to memory (see Hands-On Tutorial 12.) Insert the SuperCalc4 program disk 1 in drive A.

    A>**sc4** ↵
    SPACE

During a SuperCalc4 session, you may need to replace the active program disk with the other program disk. On-screen prompts will tell you when to switch program disks.

- Insert your data disk in drive B.

ADDING A TEMPLATE TO AN EXISTING TEMPLATE

Retrieve the "income" file that you created in Hands-On Tutorials 12 through 23 and create the Three-Year Summary Data template in the range L1..O20 (instead of A121.D140 as described in the text). Use a vertical window to view the copying process.

- Retrieve the spreadsheet "INCOME.cal" and position the pointer at "home".

    /**Load**, F3 *(call up files list)*
    b: *(designate directory)* ↵
    (highlight "INCOME.cal")
    ↵
    /Load,B:\INCOME.cal,**A**ll
    HOME

- Open a vertical window.

    (move cursor to cell B1)
    →
    /**W**indow,**V**ertical

■ Set the column widths of L through O to match the width of columns A through D.

> F5 =>**L1** ↵
> /Format,Column,**L**,Width,**30** ↵
> /Format,Column,**M.O**,Width,**15** ↵

■ Copy the appropriate headings to the summary template.

> F6 (*move pointer to the other window*)
> F5 =>**A4** ↵
> /Copy,A4,**L4** ↵

Copy the content of A10, A14, and A20 to L5, L6, and L7, respectively.

■ Close the window.

> /Window,Clear

■ Position the pointer to the summary template area.

> F5 =>**L1** ↵

■ Add the separator lines in rows 1 and 3. Preface the text string to be repeated text with a single quote.

> '= ↓ ↓
> '- →

To end the repetitions of the text, fill P1 and P3 with blanks.

> F5 =>**P1** ↵
> ' ↵
> F5 =>**P3** ↵
> ' ↵

■ Key in the title and column headings for the summary template.

> F5 =>**L2** ↵
> **THREE-YEAR   SUMMARY** → **Average** → **Minimum** → **Maximum** ←

■ Right justify the column headings.

> /Format,Entry,**M2.O2**,TextRight,*Accept*

■ Use functions to determine the average, minimum, and maximum values in each category.

> F5 =>**M4** ↵
> **AVG(B4.D4)** → **MIN(B4.D4)** → **MAX(B4.D4)** ←

Use the AVG, MIN, and MAX functions above to determine the values in rows 5 through 7. Use the ranges B10.D10, B14.D14, and B20.D20, respectively (for example, M5 should contain the function "AVG(B10.D10)").

■ Format the numbers to improve appearance and readability.

> F5 =>**M4** ↵
> /Format,Entry,M4.**O7**,**U**ser-defined**1**,**A**ccept

Format 1 (currency, embedded commas, and no decimal places) was defined during the preparation of the income statement spreadsheet.

SuperCalc4 display after creating the "THREE-YEAR SUMMARY DATA" screen in the Advanced and Special Features Tutorial.

USING WINDOWS

■ Split the screen into horizontal windows to view two separate parts of the spreadsheet simultaneously.

> HOME
> F5 =>**A13** ↵
> **/W**indow,**H**orizontal
> (display the summary template)
> F5 =>**L1** ↵

■ Move the pointer to A1 in the top window to view the original template. Move the pointer up and down to scroll through the income statements.

> F6   HOME

The window feature enables you to scan simultaneously the actual entries in the income statements while viewing summary data. Move the pointer about in the upper window to view different portions of the spreadsheet without affecting the lower window. Press F6 to move the pointer from window to window. Only one window is active at a time.

■ After you have practiced manipulating the windows, clear the bottom window.

> **/W**indow,**C**lear

■ Save the revised spreadsheet.

> **/S**ave,b:income.CAL**O**verwrite,**A**ll,

■ Exit SuperCalc4.

> **/Q**uit,**Y**es

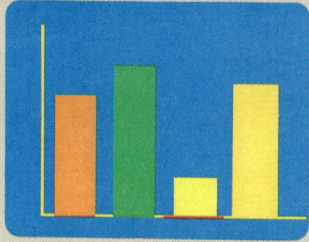

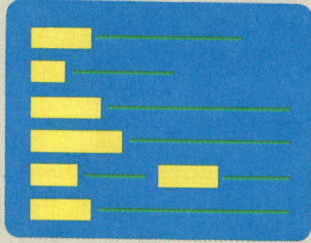

Electronic Spreadsheet Concepts and Tutorials: Database and Graphics Capabilities

CHAPTER 9

STUDENT LEARNING OBJECTIVES

- To explain how a database can be created within the context of a spreadsheet format.
- To describe the database features of electronic spreadsheet software
- To explain how bar graphs, pie graphs, and line graphs are created from spreadsheet data.
- To discuss graphics features of electronic spreadsheet software
- To identify database and graphics applications for integrated spreadsheet software packages.
- To become familiar with the use and application database and graphics capabilities for one or more of the following integrated packages:
    - Lotus 1-2-3
    - The TWiN
    - SuperCalc4
- To acquire the ability to apply the electronic spreadsheet skills demonstrated in the hands-on tutorials.

HANDS-ON TUTORIALS for *Lotus 1-2-3*, *The TWiN*, and *SuperCalc4*

24. Creating a Spreadsheet Data Base
25. Making Inquiries to a Spreadsheet Data Base
26. Sorting a Spreadsheet Data Base
27. Using Spreadsheet Graphics Capabilities
28. Entering Spreadsheet Data
29. Producing a Bar Graph
30. Saving and Printing/Plotting a Graph
31. Producing Stacked-bar and Clustered-bar Graphs
32. Producing a Pie Graph
33. Producing a Line Graph

ADVANCED AND SPECIAL FEATURES TUTORIALS: *Lotus 1-2-3* and *SuperCalc4* (Graphics Capabilities)

Adding labels and subheadings
Changing fonts

9–1 INTEGRATED SPREADSHEET SOFTWARE

The more popular spreadsheet programs, such as Lotus 1-2-3 and SuperCalc4, are actually integrated packages that include database (data management) and graphics capabilities. Chapters 7 and 8 emphasize *spreadsheet* capabilities; that is, those aspects of spreadsheet software that are computer-based extensions of applications for lined paper (spreadsheets). Before reading this chapter, you should have acquired at least a fundamental understanding of the concepts presented in Chapter 7.

This chapter focuses on the *database* (data management) and *graphics* capabilities of integrated spreadsheet software packages. The next section discusses and illustrates how spreadsheet rows and columns can be conceptualized as a data base and applied to data base applications. The remainder of the chapter is devoted to discussing approaches to presenting spreadsheet data in the form of graphs.

9–2 THE DATABASE SIDE OF SPREADSHEETS

A Row is a Record—A Column is a Field

The tabular format of the spreadsheet work area provides a natural setting for the creation, maintenance, and manipulation of a data base. The hierarchy of data organization (bits, characters, *fields*, *records*, *files*, and *data bases*) is discussed in Chapter 2 and illustrated in Figure 2–7.

■ Each row in a spreadsheet data base represents one *record* (related data about a particular event or thing).

■ Each column in a spreadsheet database represents one *field* (the smallest logical unit of data).

The COURSE data base in Figure 9–1 is used to illustrate the database side of spreadsheet software. The concepts embodied in the database example of Figure 9–1 are introduced first in Chapter 7 (Section 7–10, Figure 7–15) and again in Chapter 10, "Database Software Concepts." The common example will help you to contrast the spreadsheet software approach to data management with the database software approach.

Edwina Cool, Zimco's education coordinator, uses spreadsheet software to help her with her record-keeping tasks. Her COURSE data base (see Figure 9–1) contains a record for each course that Zimco offers to their employees and for several courses at the State University. The first row in a spreadsheet data base *always* contains the *labels* for the fields in the records (for example, ID, TITLE, and so on). The second and subsequent rows contain one *course record* each. Each row record in the COURSE data base contains the following fields:

■ *ID*. Identification number (supplied by Zimco for in-house courses, by vendors, and by State University).

A computer-based system that supports the decision-making process is sometimes referred to as a decision support system or DSS. This advertising executive combined the capabilities of an integrated software package that includes spreadsheet, database, and graphics capabilities with that of a powerful portable computer to give him a decision support system. The DSS permits him to get information when he wants it and in the form he wants it. (Photo courtesy of Hewlett-Packard Company)

```
A1:    'ID

        A           B            C        D          E         F
 1   ID     TITLE              TYPE     SOURCE     DURATION
 2   100    MIS Orientation    in-house Staff         24
 3   201    Micro Overview     in-house Staff          8
 4   2535   Intro to Info. Proc. media   Takdel Inc    40
 5   310    Programming Stds.  in-house Staff          6
 6   3223   BASIC Programming  media    Takdel Inc    40
 7   7771   Data Base Systems  media    Takdel Inc    30
 8   CIS11  Business COBOL     college  St Univ       45
 9   EX15   Local Area Networks vendor  HAL Inc       30
10   MGT10  Mgt. Info. Systems college  St. Univ      45
11   VC10   Elec. Spreadsheet  media    VidCourse     20
12   VC44   4th Generation Lang. media  VidCourse     30
13   VC88   Word Processing    media    VidCourse     18
```

FIGURE 9–1
Electronic Spreadsheet:
Database Format
This spreadsheet is organized as a data base. The data base contains a record for each of the 12 courses that Zimco offers to its employees. The labels for the fields are listed in the first row. Each subsequent row containsone record. This data base was first introduced in Figure 7–15.

■ *TITLE.* Title of course.

■ *TYPE.* Type of course (in-house seminar, multimedia, college course, or vendor seminar).

■ *SOURCE.* Source of course (Zimco staff or supplier of course).

■ *DURATION.* Duration (number of hours required to complete course).

Enter Data to a Data Base

You create a spreadsheet data base as you would any other spreadsheet—simply enter data to the individual cells. There are, however, a few basic rules that you must follow.

1. The first row must contain the labels for the fields.
2. The second and each subsequent row (to the end of the data base) must contain a record; that is, blank rows and divider lines are not permitted.
3. A particular field can contain label or numeric entries, but not both.

See "Hands-On Tutorial 24: Creating a Spreadsheet Data Base" at the end of this chapter.

Spreadsheet Database Capabilities

The fundamental capabilities of integrated spreadsheet software and database software are similar.

1. Create and maintain (add, delete, and revise records) a data base.
2. Extract and list or find and highlight those records that meet certain conditions.

As this radiologist interprets x-rays, a nurse enters his verbal comments into a spreadsheet data base.
(Courtesy of Compaq Computer Corporation)

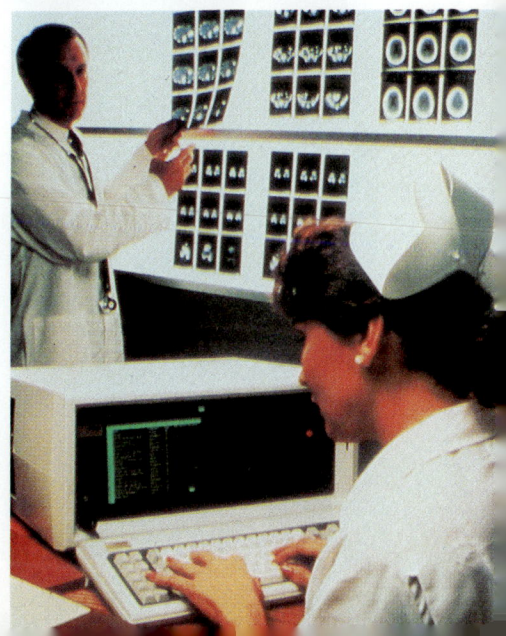

3. Sort records in ascending or descending sequence by primary and secondary fields.

Software that is designed specifically for data management provides considerably more capabilities than spreadsheet software does (see Chapter 11, "Database Software Concepts"). For example, database software permits sorting on three (not just two) fields and has a report generation feature. However, all of the spreadsheet capabilities can be applied to the data in a spreadsheet data base (computing the average value for a particular field, for example).

Making Data Base Inquiries

With spreadsheet software you can retrieve, view, and print records based on preset conditions. You set conditions for the selection of records by associating the desired condition with the appropriate field or fields in the *criterion range*. The user-defined criterion range (A19..E20 in Figure 9-2) would normally contain a copy of the first

FIGURE 9-2
Electronic Spreadsheet: Extracting Information from a Data Base
Records can be extracted from a data base based on preset criteria. In the figure, records that meet the criteria, TYPE="in-house" and DURATION<=10, are extracted and displayed in the user-defined output range (A15..E18).

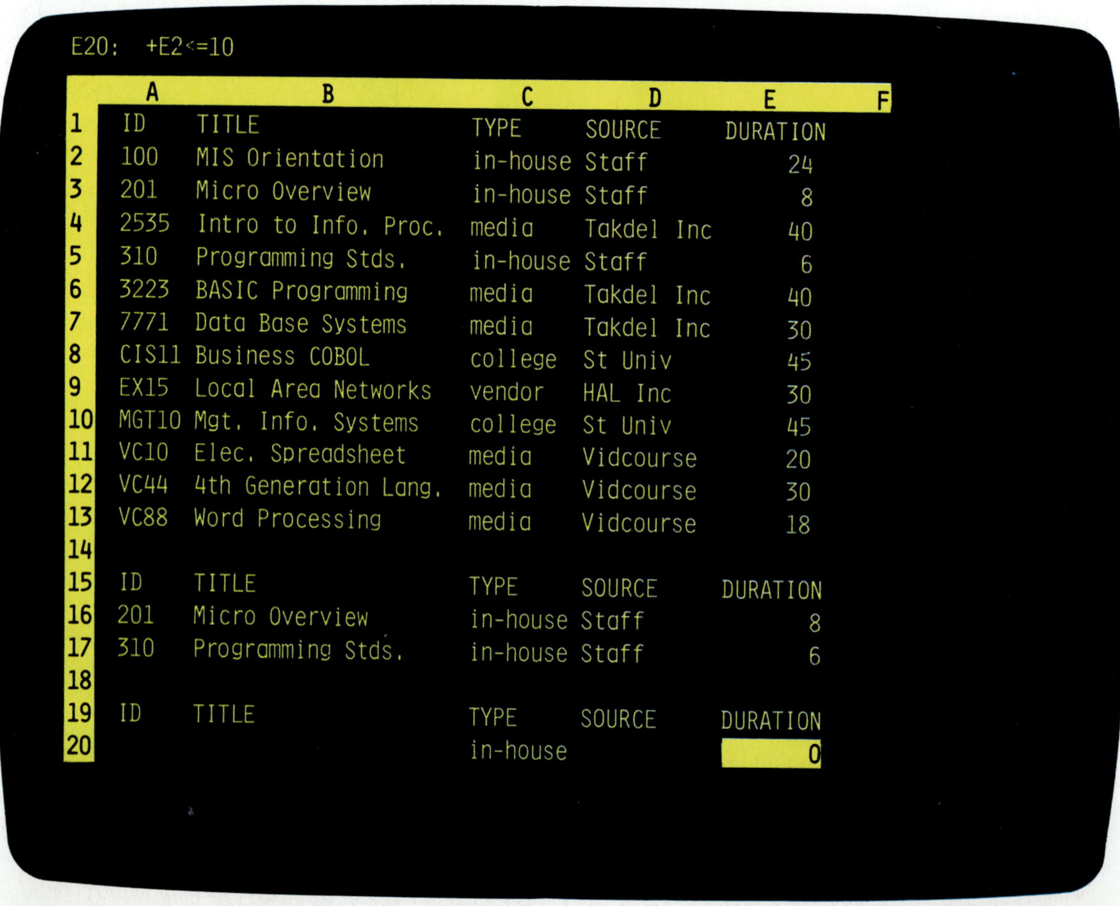

```
E20:   +E2<=10
```

	A	B	C	D	E	F
1	ID	TITLE	TYPE	SOURCE	DURATION	
2	100	MIS Orientation	in-house	Staff	24	
3	201	Micro Overview	in-house	Staff	8	
4	2535	Intro to Info. Proc.	media	Takdel Inc	40	
5	310	Programming Stds.	in-house	Staff	6	
6	3223	BASIC Programming	media	Takdel Inc	40	
7	7771	Data Base Systems	media	Takdel Inc	30	
8	CIS11	Business COBOL	college	St Univ	45	
9	EX15	Local Area Networks	vendor	HAL Inc	30	
10	MGT10	Mgt. Info. Systems	college	St Univ	45	
11	VC10	Elec. Spreadsheet	media	Vidcourse	20	
12	VC44	4th Generation Lang.	media	Vidcourse	30	
13	VC88	Word Processing	media	Vidcourse	18	
14						
15	ID	TITLE	TYPE	SOURCE	DURATION	
16	201	Micro Overview	in-house	Staff	8	
17	310	Programming Stds.	in-house	Staff	6	
18						
19	ID	TITLE	TYPE	SOURCE	DURATION	
20			in-house		0	

row (the field label row) and the conditions (under the appropriate field label). For example, Figure 9–2 illustrates the procedure for *extracting* and displaying the course records that meet both of the following conditions:

TYPE is "in-house"
DURATION is less than or equal to (<=) 10 hours

Those records that meet both criteria are extracted and displayed in the user-defined output range (A15..E18).

Another way to locate and display the records that meet certain conditions is to *find* them. When you issue the find command, the first record that meets the criteria is highlighted in reverse video (see Figure 9–3). To see other records that meet the criteria, simply press the up or down cursor control keys.

You can use the cursor control keys to scan or "page" through the data base. See "Hands-On Tutorial 25: Making Inquiries to a Spreadsheet Data Base."

FIGURE 9–3
Electronic Spreadsheet: Finding Information in a Data Base
Records can be located and highlighted in a data base based on preset criteria. In the figure, the first record that meets the criteria, TYPE="in-house" and DURATION<=10, is highlighted.

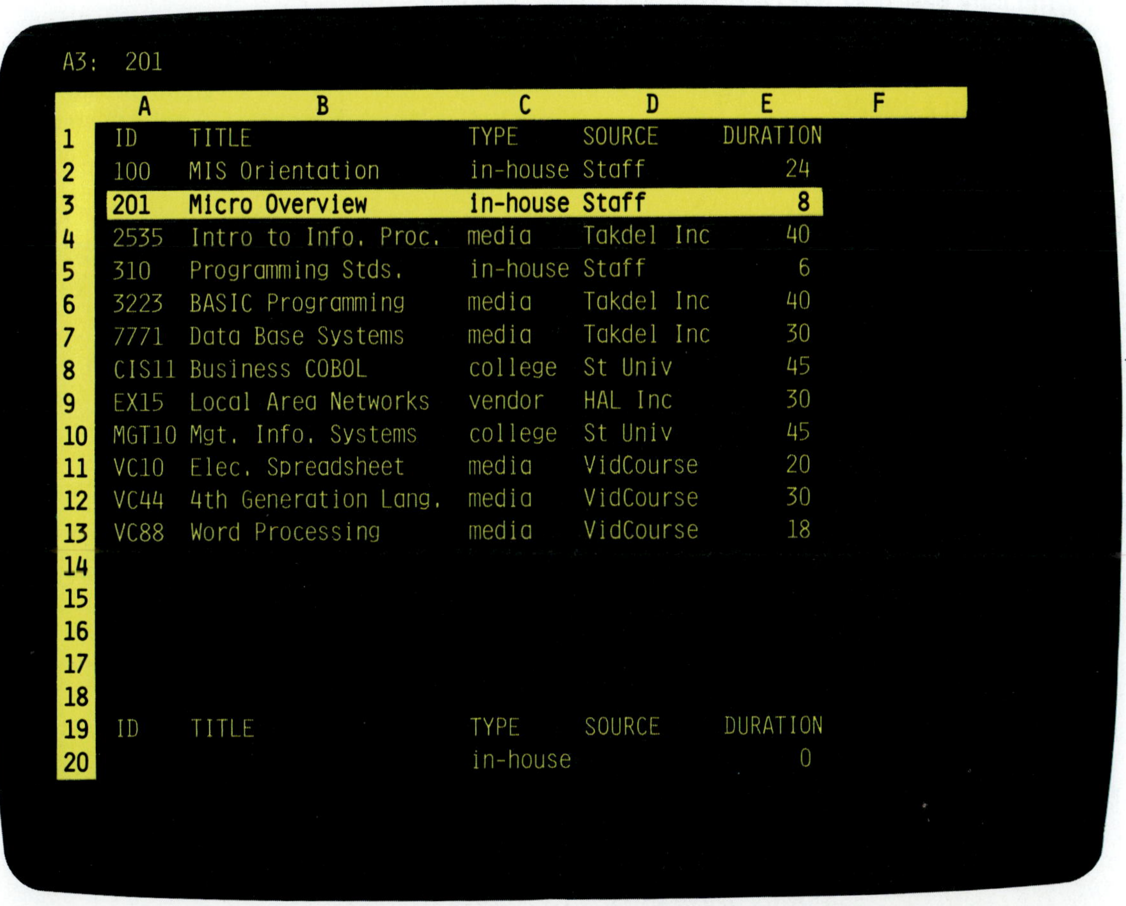

	A	B	C	D	E	F
	ID	TITLE	TYPE	SOURCE	DURATION	
1						
2	100	MIS Orientation	in-house	Staff	24	
3	201	Micro Overview	in-house	Staff	8	
4	2535	Intro to Info. Proc.	media	Takdel Inc	40	
5	310	Programming Stds.	in-house	Staff	6	
6	3223	BASIC Programming	media	Takdel Inc	40	
7	7771	Data Base Systems	media	Takdel Inc	30	
8	CIS11	Business COBOL	college	St Univ	45	
9	EX15	Local Area Networks	vendor	HAL Inc	30	
10	MGT10	Mgt. Info. Systems	college	St Univ	45	
11	VC10	Elec. Spreadsheet	media	VidCourse	20	
12	VC44	4th Generation Lang.	media	VidCourse	30	
13	VC88	Word Processing	media	VidCourse	18	
14						
15						
16						
17						
18						
19	ID	TITLE	TYPE	SOURCE	DURATION	
20			in-house		0	

A3: 201

Sorting Records

The records in a spreadsheet data base can be sorted for display in a variety of formats. The COURSE data base in Figure 9–1 is sorted by ID. Edwina Cool wanted a presentation of the COURSE data base that was sorted by ID within SOURCE (see Figure 9–4). This involves the selection of a *primary key field* and a *secondary key field*. Edwina selected SOURCE as the primary key field, but she wanted the courses offered by each source to be listed in ascending order by ID.

To achieve this record sequence, she selected ID as the secondary key field. You would normally define a secondary key when you expect duplicates in the primary key fields. For example, in Figure 9–1, the SOURCE or primary key field has three entries for Takdel Inc. Once the key fields are identified, the sort command can be issued to rearrange and display records in the desired sequence. Notice in Figure 9–4 that the SOURCE field entries (column D) are in alphabetical order and the three "Staff" records (rows 5, 6, and 7) are in sequence by ID (100, 201, 310). See "Hands-On Tutorial 26: Sorting a Spreadsheet Data Base."

9–3   THE GRAPHICS SIDE OF SPREADSHEETS

Presentation Graphics

With the graphics component of an integrated software package, you can create a variety of **presentation graphics** from data in an electronic spreadsheet or a data base. The use of graphics software has become synonymous with polished presentation. Among the most popular presentation graphics are **bar graphs**, **pie graphs**, and **line**

FIGURE 9–4
Electronic Spreadsheet:
COURSE Data Base
Sorted by ID within SOURCE
This display is the result of a sort operation on the COURSE data base with the SOURCE field as the primary key field and the ID field as the secondary key field.

```
A1:   'ID

      A            B              C        D          E           F
1    ID    TITLE               TYPE     SOURCE     DURATION
2    EX15  Local Area Networks vendor   HAL Inc       30
3    CIS11 Business COBOL      college  St Univ       45
4    100   MIS Orientation     in-house Staff         24
5    201   Micro Overview      in-house Staff          8
6    310   Programming Stds.   in-house Staff          6
7    MGT10 Mgt. Info. Systems  college  St. Univ      45
8    2535  Intro to Info. Proc. media   Takdel Inc    40
9    3223  BASIC Programming   media    Takdel Inc    40
10   7771  Data Base Systems   media    Takdel Inc    30
11   VC10  Elec. Spreadsheet   media    VidCourse     20
12   VC44  4th Generation Lang. media   VidCourse     30
13   VC88  Word Processing     media    VidCourse     18
```

graphs (seen in Figures 9–6, 9–9, and 9–10, respectively). Other types of graphs are possible. Each of these graphs can be annotated with graph *titles*, *labels* for axes, and *legends*. See "Hands-On Tutorial 27: Using Lotus 1-2-3, The TWiN, or SuperCalc4 (Graphics Capabilities)" and "Hands-On Tutorial 28: Entering Spreadsheet Data."

Graphic representations of data have proven to be an effective means of communication. It is easier to recognize problem areas and trends in a graph than it is in a tabular summary of the same data. Compare the data in the spreadsheet of Figure 9–5 to the graphic representation of that data in Figures 9–7 and 9–8.

A number of studies confirm the power of presentation graphics. These studies uniformly support the following conclusions:

- People who use presentation graphics to get their message across are perceived as better prepared and more professional than those who do not.

- Presentation graphics can help to persuade attendees or readers to adopt a particular point of view.

- Judicious use of presentation graphics tends to make meetings shorter. Perhaps it's true that a picture is worth a thousand words!

For many years, the presentation of tabular data was the preferred approach to communicating tabular information. However, this approach was preferred by default: it was simply too expensive and time consuming to produce presentation graphics manually. Today, you can use graphics software to produce perfectly proportioned, accurate, and visually appealing graphs in a matter of seconds. Prior to the introduction of graphics software, the turnaround time for producing a graph was at least a day, and often a week.

One of the real advantages of an integrated package is that any changes made to data in a spreadsheet are reflected in the graphs as well.

With graphics software you can prepare professional-looking graphs for reports and presentations.
(AST Research Inc.)

Preparing a Graph

The data needed to produce a graph already exist in a spreadsheet or data base. You create a graph by responding to a series of prompts. The first prompt asks you to select the type of graph to be produced: bar graph, pie graph, line graph, and so on. You identify the ranges of spreadsheet data that are to be printed or plotted. You can also choose spreadsheet ranges that will be printed as labels on the graph. Once you have identified the source of the data and labels, and perhaps added a title, you can display, print, or plot the graph.

The keystroke tutorials at the end of this chapter demonstrate the step-by-step procedures for preparing a variety of graphs based on the data in the spreadsheet of Figure 9–5.

9–4   GRAPHICS IN PRACTICE

Sally Marcio, the vice-president of Sales and Marketing at Zimco, is an avid user of spreadsheet and graphics software. The spreadsheet of Figure 9–5 is an annual summary of the sales for each of Zimco's four products by sales region. The data from this spreadsheet provide the basis for demonstrating the compilation of bar, pie, and line graphs.

FIGURE 9–5
Electronic Spreadsheet: Sales Data for Graphs
The bar, pie, and line graphs of Figures 9–6 through 9–10 are derived from these sales figures.

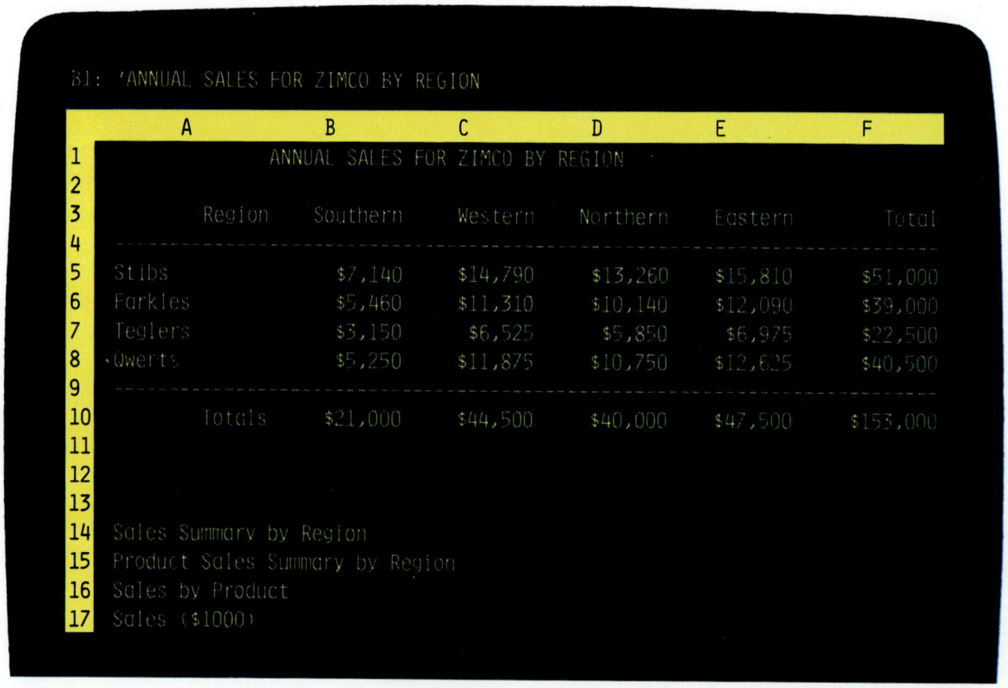

```
B1:  'ANNUAL SALES FOR ZIMCO BY REGION

           A          B          C          D          E          F
 1              ANNUAL SALES FOR ZIMCO BY REGION
 2
 3        Region    Southern   Western    Northern   Eastern      Total
 4        ---------------------------------------------------------------
 5  Stibs            $7,140    $14,790    $13,260    $15,810     $51,000
 6  Farkles          $5,460    $11,310    $10,140    $12,090     $39,000
 7  Teglers          $3,150     $6,525     $5,850     $6,975     $22,500
 8  Qwerts           $5,250    $11,875    $10,750    $12,625     $40,500
 9        ---------------------------------------------------------------
10        Totals    $21,000    $44,500    $40,000    $47,500    $153,000
11
12
13
14  Sales Summary by Region
15  Product Sales Summary by Region
16  Sales by Product
17  Sales ($1000)
```

Bar Graphs

A bar graph contains vertical bars of varying heights. The height of the bars is proportional to a range of numeric values in an electronic spreadsheet. To prepare the bar graph of Figure 9–6, Sally first had to specify appropriate ranges; that is, the values in the "Totals" row (range B10..E10 of Figure 9–5) are to be plotted and the region names (range B3..E3 of Figure 9–5) are to be inserted as labels along the horizontal or x axis. Sally also added a title for the graph, "Sales Summary by Region", titles for the x axis, "Region" and the vertical or y axis, "Sales ($1000)".

The *origin*, or the point at which the x and y axes meet, is automatically set at zero. Sally accepted this default; however, you may want to set the origin at other than zero when you want to highlight the differences between the bars. If Sally had set the origin at $20,000 the bar in Figure 9–6 illustrating the sales for the Eastern Region ($47,500) would be over 27 times the height of the bar illustrating the sales for the Southern Region sales ($21,000); that is, a net of $27,500 would be compared to a net of $1,000. Setting the origin at $20,000 would make the differences between the regional sales figures more apparent—perhaps too apparent for the sales manager for the Southern Region.

The bars (and also the pieces of a pie chart) can be shaded in any one of three ways.

■ Unless otherwise specified, the bars are filled with close parallel lines that slant to the right or left or two sets of parallel lines that intersect, resulting in a *crosshatching* pattern. See the pie chart illustration in Hands-On Exercise 4 for examples.

■ One of the options is to *solid fill* the bars (see Figure 9–6).

■ The remaining option is to add *color* to the lines, crosshatching, or the solid-fill presentations so that each bar or segment of a bar is represented by a different color (see Figure 9–7).

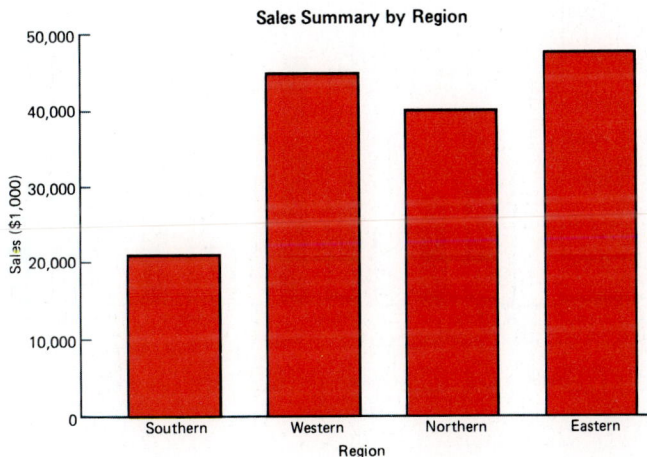

FIGURE 9–6
Electronic Spreadsheet: Bar Graph
The "Total" sales for each region in Figure 9–5 are graphically represented in this bar graph.

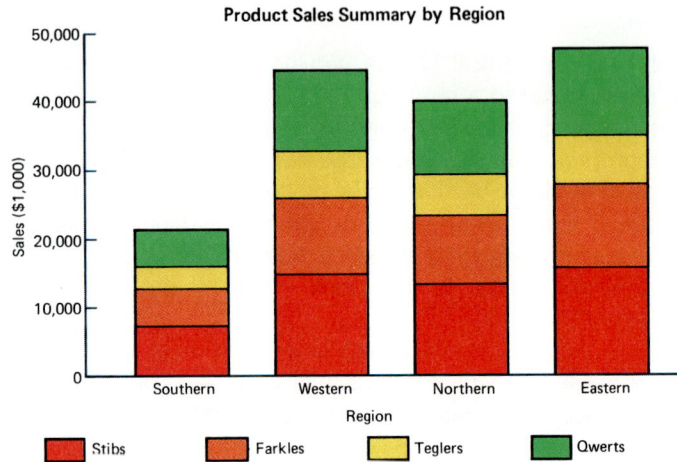

FIGURE 9–7
Electronic Spreadsheet:
Stacked-Bar Graph
Regional sales for each of the
four products in Figure 9–5 are
graphically represented in this
stacked-bar graph.

See "Hands-On Tutorial 29: Producing a Bar Chart" and "Hands-On Tutorial 30: Saving and Printing/Plotting a Graph."

The sales figures for each region in Figure 9–5 (range B5..E8) can be plotted in a **stacked-bar graph**. Each bar is made up of the sales figures for each of the four products. Because of this, a legend is needed to distinguish which parts of the stacked bar for a particular region apply to which product. Sally specified that the range A5..A8 be the range for the legend labels (the names of the products). The resultant graph, shown in Figure 9–7, helps Sally to better understand the distribution of product sales within the four regions. The **clustered-bar graph** in Figure 9–8 is an alternative presentation to the stacked-bar graph. These graphs visually highlight the relative contribution that each product made to the total sales for each region. See "Hands-On Tutorial 31: Producing Stacked-bar and Clustered-bar Charts."

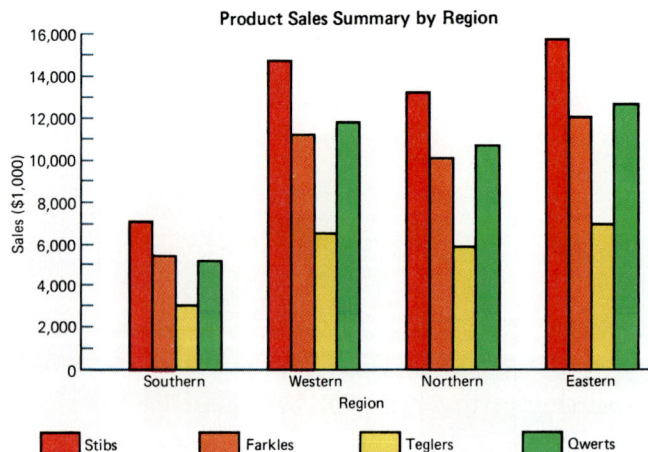

FIGURE 9–8
Electronic Spreadsheet:
Clustered-Bar Graph
Regional sales for each of the
four products in Figure 9–5 are
graphically represented in this
clustered-bar graph.

Pie Graphs

Pie graphs are the most basic of presentation graphics. A pie graph graphically illustrates each "piece" of data in its proper relationship to the whole "pie." To illustrate how a pie graph is constructed and used, refer again to the "Annual Sales" spreadsheet in Figure 9–5.

Sally Marcio produced the sales-by-product pie graph in Figure 9–9 by specifying that the values in the "Total" column (range F5..F8 of Figure 9–5) be the pieces of the pie. She specified further that the product names (range A5..A8) be inserted as labels. She also added a title. The numbers in parentheses represent what percent each piece (total sales for a particular product) is of the whole (total sales, or the value in F10, $153,000). To emphasize the product with the greatest contribution to total sales, Sally decided to *explode* (or separate) the Stibs piece of the pie. See "Hands-On Tutorial 32: Producing a Pie Chart."

Line Graphs

A line graph connects similar points on a graph with one or more lines. Sally Marcio used the stacked-bar graph of Figure 9–7 to visually highlight relative product sales by region. She used the same data in the spreadsheet of Figure 9–5 to generate the line graph of Figure 9–10. The line graph makes it easy for Sally to compare sales between regions for a particular product.

In the line graph of Figure 9–10, four ranges of data from the spreadsheet of Figure 9–5 (B5..E5, B6..E6, B7..E7, and B8..E8) are plotted and each range connected by a line, one line for each product. The graph clearly indicates that the proportion of product sales is similar for each region. See "Hands-On Tutorial 33: Producing a Line Chart."

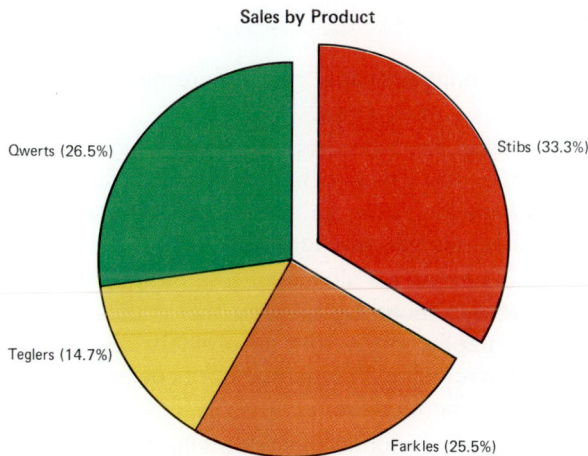

Sales by Product

Qwerts (26.5%)
Stibs (33.3%)
Teglers (14.7%)
Farkles (25.5%)

FIGURE 9–9
Electronic Spreadsheet: Pie Graph
Total sales by product (the "Totals" row, B10..E10) in Figure 9–5 are graphically represented in this pie graph. The "Stibs" piece of the pie is exploded for emphasis.

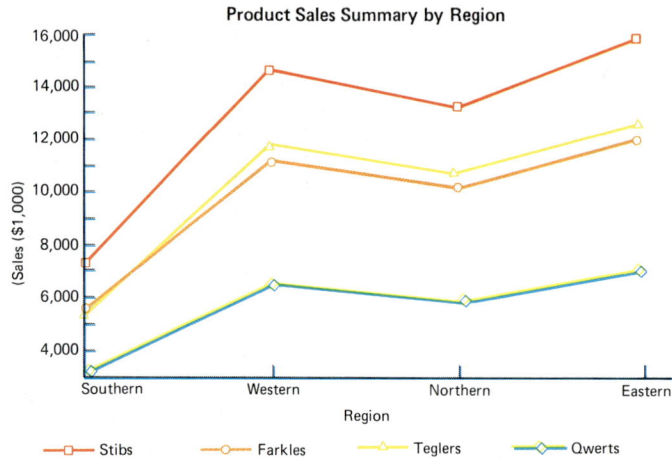

FIGURE 9–10
Electronic Spreadsheet: Line Graph
This line graph shows a plot of the data of Figure 9–5. A line connects the sales for each product by region.

Color ink-jet printers, such as this one, can draw graphic images on paper or directly on a blank acetate. The acetates can be used with an overhead projector to project the graph on a large screen.
(Courtesy of International Business Machines Corporation)

9–5   PRESENTING A GRAPH

The actual physical presentation of a graph is dependent on the available hardware (matrix printer, laser printer, plotter, and so on). Computer-generated graphic images can be recreated on paper, transparency acetates, 35 mm slides, or they can be displayed on a monitor or projected onto a large screen. The use of sophisticated and colorful graphics adds an aura of professionalism to any report or presentation. Some of the more common approaches to presenting a graph are discussed below.

■ Dot-matrix and ink-jet printers, both black on white and color, can be used to reproduce the graphic image on either paper or transparency acetates.

■ Multi-pen plotters can be used to produce professional-quality presentation graphics (in color) on either paper or transparency acetates.

■ Laser printers enable very-high resolution (close to typeset quality) black on white graphs.

■ Desktop film recorders reproduce a high-resolution graphic image on 35 mm film in either black and white or color. Some models provide the facility for users to process and mount their own slides. Others require outside processing.

■ A less expensive alternative to a desktop film recorder is the hood, lens, and mounting brackets that enable the users to photograph the graphic image with an ordinary 35 mm camera. The quality of the resulting 35 mm slide is, of course, dependent on the resolution of the monitor.

■ Screen-image projectors project the graphic image to a large screen, similar to the way television programs are projected to a large TV screen. Another device transfers the graphic image that is displayed

Spice up a presentation with colorful graphics by using a microcomputer. Graphics software permits you to prepare a screen that can be produced instantly on a print for previewing or as a 35mm slide for use in a presentation.
(Digital Research Inc.)

on the monitor to a large screen with the use of an ordinary over-head projector.

9–6   DEDICATED GRAPHICS PACKAGES

The graphics component of integrated software packages is usually limited to producing bar, pie, and line graphs from the data in the spreadsheet. However, dedicated or stand-alone graphics packages offer an extensive array of features. For example, dedicated graphics packages provide the ability to prepare *text charts* (such as lists of key points) and *organization charts* (such as block charts showing the hierarchical structure of an organization), and they provide users with the flexibility to customize graphs. The functionality of graphs prepared by integrated packages and a dedicated graphics packages is about the same, but graphs produced by dedicated graphics packages are usually more visually appealing (for example, pie and bar graphs are three-dimensional).

Besides offering the ability to prepare graphs from spreadsheet data, stand-alone graphics packages let you create and store original draw-ings. To do this, however, your personal computer must be equipped with a mouse, digitizing board, or some type of device that permits the input of curved and angular lines. To make drawing easier to do, such software even offers a data base filled with a variety of frequently used symbols, such as rectangles, circles, cats (yes, even cats), and so on. Some companies draw and store the image of their company logo so it can be inserted on memos, reports, and graphs.

User-friendly software packages that are dedicated to graphics applications let users "paint" pictures on the screen. The "painter" picks the appropriate icon (for example, pencil, paint brush, palette), color (middle left), display pattern (right), and so on to create an image (for example, the lake view in the photo).

SUMMARY OUTLINE AND IMPORTANT TERMS____

9–1 INTEGRATED SPREADSHEET SOFTWARE. Integrated spreadsheet packages often include database and graphics capabilities. Spreadsheet rows and columns can be conceptualized as a data base and applied to data base applications. Spreadsheet data can be presented in the form of graphs.

9–2 THE DATABASE SIDE OF SPREADSHEETS. The tabular format of the spreadsheet work area provides a natural setting for the creation, maintenance, and manipulation of a data base. Each row in a spreadsheet data base represents one record. Each column in a spreadsheet data base represents one field. The first row in a spreadsheet data base always contains the labels for the fields in the records. The second and subsequent rows contain one record each.

Integrated spreadsheet software provides database capabilities to create and maintain a data base, extract or find records that meet certain conditions, and sort records.

With spreadsheet software, records can be retrieved, viewed, and printed based on preset conditions. Set the conditions for the selection of records by associating the desired condition with the appropriate field or fields in the criteria range.

The records in a spreadsheet data base can be sorted for display in a variety of formats. This involves the selection of a primary key field and, if needed, a secondary key field.

9–3 THE GRAPHICS SIDE OF SPREADSHEETS. With the

graphics component of an integrated software package, you can create a variety of **presentation graphics** from data in an electronic spreadsheet or a data base. Among the most popular presentation graphics are **bar graphs**, **pie graphs**, and **line graphs**. Graphic representations of data have proven to be an effective means of communication.

Users create graphs from spreadsheet data by responding to a series of prompts: type of graph, range of data to graphed, labels, and so on.

9–4   GRAPHICS IN PRACTICE.   Bar, pie, and line graphs can be created from the same spreadsheet data. The origin is the point at which the x and y axes of a bar or line graph meet. The bars, and also the pieces of a pie chart, can be distinguished by crosshatching, solid fill, and by adding color.

A bar graph contains vertical bars of varying heights. The height of the bars is proportional to a range of numeric values in an electronic spreadsheet. The **stacked-bar graph** and **clustered-bar graph** can present more information than a simple bar graph.

Pie graphs are the most basic of presentation graphics. A pie graph graphically illustrates each "piece" of data in its proper relationship to the whole "pie."

A line graph connects similar points on a graph with one or several lines.

9–5   PRESENTING A GRAPH.   Computer-generated graphic images can be recreated on paper, transparency acetates, 35 mm slides, or they can be displayed on a monitor or projected to a large screen.

9–6   DEDICATED GRAPHICS PACKAGES.   The variety of graphs that can be produced by an integrated software packages is limited. However, dedicated or stand-alone graphics packages offer the user the capability to create a more extensive array of graphs, such as text charts, organization charts, customized graphs, and even original drawings.

REVIEW EXERCISES

1. Describe the relationship between a spreadsheet row, a spreadsheet column, a record, and a field.
2. What are the three fundamental capabilities of a spreadsheet program when it is organized as a data base?
3. What is the purpose of a criteria range?
4. What would be the sequence of records in a COURSE data base (see Figure 9–1) that was sorted by TITLE within DURATION? Show the sequence by listing only the ID of each record.
5. What condition(s) would be entered to the criteria range to select only media courses? Only CIS11?

6. Name three types of graphs commonly used for presentation graphics.

7. Name and graphically illustrate (by hand) two variations on the bar graph.

8. Under what circumstances is a graphic representation of data more effective than a tabular presentation of the same data?

9. What is meant when a portion of a pie graph is exploded?

10. Is it possible to present the same information in a stacked-bar and a line graph? How about stacked-bar and pie graphs?

11. What advantages does a dedicated graphics package have over the graphics software that is part of an integrated package?

12. Describe three approaches to the physical presentation of a computer-generated graph.

SELF-TEST (by section)

9–1. The more popular integrated software packages include spreadsheet, graphics, and _____ capabilities.

9–2. (a) When used for data base applications, the row of a spreadsheet becomes a field in record. (T/F)

(b) The first row in an electronic spreadsheet that is set up for data base applications is made up of (a) record indices, (b) field labels, or (c) single letter entries.

(c) What record would be selected from the COURSE data base of Figure 9–1 for the criteria SOURCE="VidCourse" and DURATION>25?

(d) If the COURSE data base of Figure 9–1 is to be sorted by TITLE within TYPE, the primary key would be assigned to TYPE. (T/F)

9–3. Among the most popular presentation graphics are bar graphs, pie graphs, and _____ graphs.

9–4. (a) The point at which the x and y axes meet is called the crosshatch. (T/F)

(b) An alternative presentation to the clustered-bar graph is the _____ graph.

(c) The line graph connects similar points on a graph. (T/F)

9–5. Laser printers enable the preparation of very-high resolution color graphs. (T/F)

9–6. Charts that contains a list of key points are called (a) text charts, (b) organization charts, or (c) sequence charts.

Self-Test Answers. **9–1,** database; **9–2 (a),** F; **(b),** b; **(c),** VC44; **(d),** T; **9–3,** line; **9–4 (a),** F; **(b),** stacked-bar; **(c),** T; **9–5,** F; **9–6,** a.

HANDS-ON EXERCISES

1.   Complete Hands-On Tutorials 24 through 26 (data base applications) in the tutorials section of this chapter.

2.   (a)   Set up a spreadsheet data base to accept the following sales data for Diolab, Inc., a manufacturer of a diagnostic laboratory instrument that is sold primarily to hospitals and clinics.

	Diolab Inc. Sales (units)			
Region	Qtr1	Qtr2	Qtr3	Qtr4
NE Region	241	300	320	170
SE Region	120	150	165	201
SW Region	64	80	60	52

Each of the remaining parts of this hands-on exercise is a follow-on to the previous part.

(b)   Enter the Diolab data above into the data base.

(c)   Revise the NE Region first-quarter sales to be 214.

(d)   Add the following NW Region record to the data base.

Region	Qtr1	Qtr2	Qtr3	Qtr4
NW Region	116	141	147	180

(e)   Obtain a printout of the data base and store the data on a disk file named DIOLAB.

(f)   Select and list all Diolab regions (records) that sold more than 150 units in the fourth quarter (all but the SW Region).

(g)   Select and list all Diolab regions (records) that sold more than 150 units in the fourth quarter *and* all regions for which fourth-quarter sales are greater than third-quarter sales (SE and NW Regions).

(h)   Sort the Diolab data base in ascending order by QTR1 sales.

(i)   Sort the Diolab data base in descending order by QTR4 sales.

3.   Complete Hands-On Tutorials 27 through 33 (graphics applications) and the Advanced and Special Features Tutorial (if appropriate) in the tutorials section of this chapter.

4.   (a)   Use the following Diolab, Inc., sales data (from Hands-On Exercise 2 in Chapter 7, "Electronic Spreadsheet Concepts: Spreadsheet Capabilities" and Hands-On Exercise 2 in this chapter). Produce the accompanying bar graph showing the total unit sales by region for Diolab, Inc. Label the *y* and *x* axes as shown.

	Diolab Inc. Sales (units)			
Region	*Qtr1*	*Qtr2*	*Qtr3*	*Qtr4*
NE Region	214	300	320	170
SE Region	120	150	165	201
SW Region	64	80	60	52
NW Region	116	141	147	180

TOTAL SALES BY REGION
DIOLAB, INC.

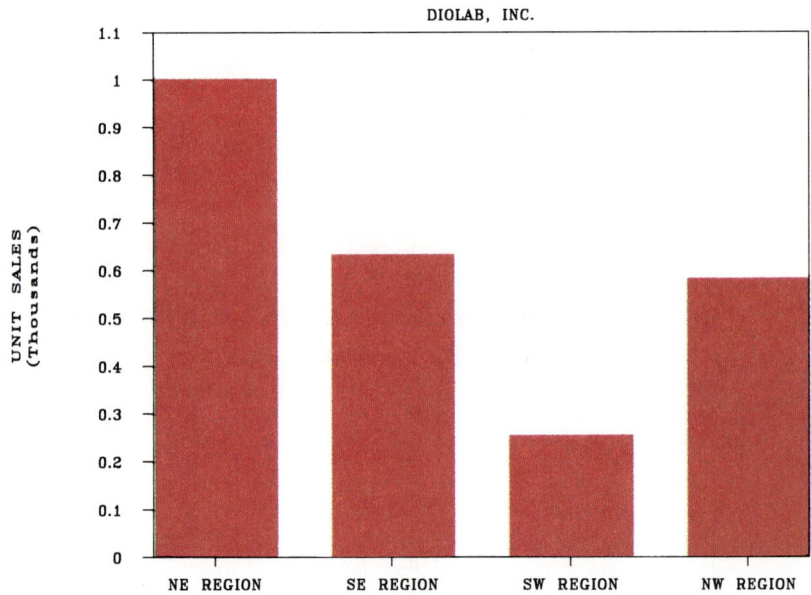

Each of the remaining parts of this hands-on exercise deal with the Diolab, Inc., data or graphs produced from these data.

(b) Produce the accompanying pie graph showing the total unit sales by region for Diolab, Inc. Title the graph and label each piece as shown.

TOTAL SALES BY REGION
DIOLAB, INC.

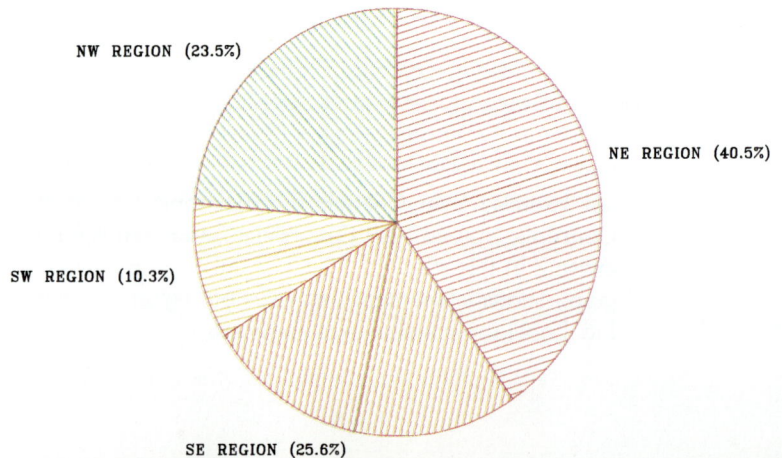

(c) Compare the information portrayed in the bar and pie graphs above.

(d) Produce the accompanying clustered-bar graph showing quarterly unit sales by region for Diolab, Inc. Title the graph, label the axes, and include a legend as shown.

QUARTERLY SALES BY REGION
DIOLAB, INC.

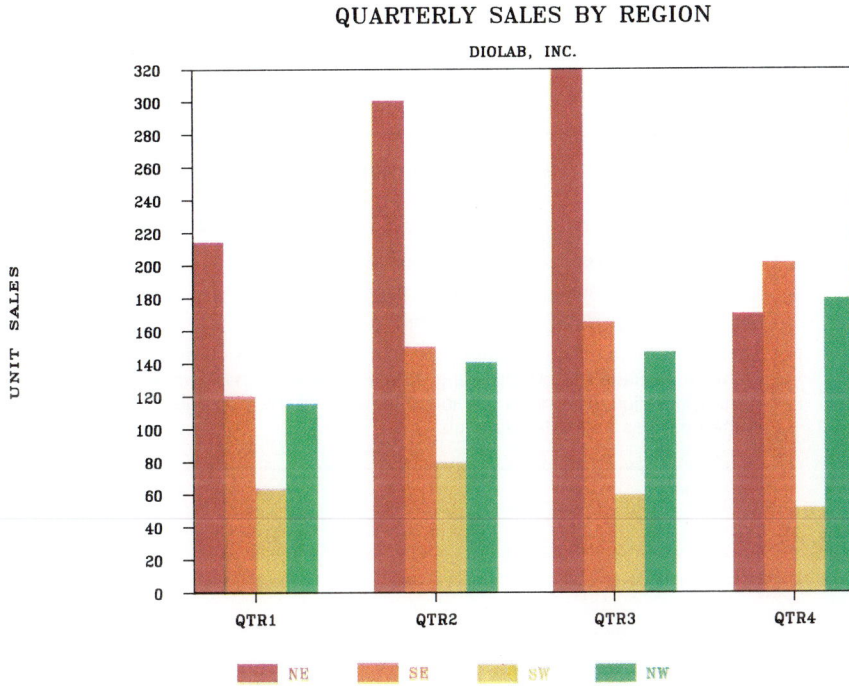

(e) Produce the accompanying line graph showing quarterly unit sales by region for Diolab, Inc. Title the graph, label the axes, and include a legend as shown.

QUARTERLY SALES BY REGION
DIOLAB, INC.

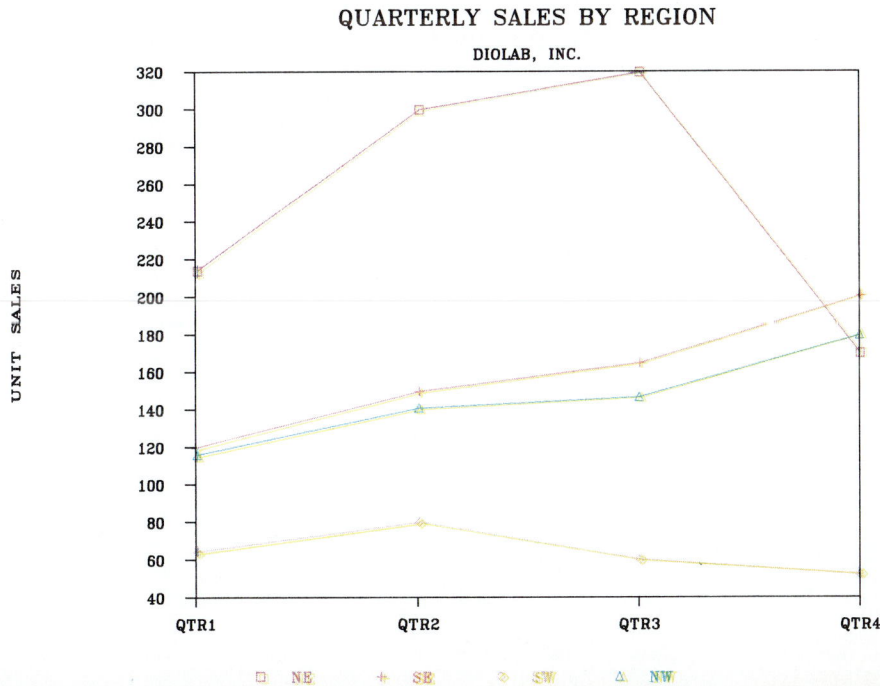

(f) Compare the information shown in the clustered-bar and line graphs above.

5. Use an integrated software package to produce a line graph for the spreadsheet data in Hands-On Exercise 4 in Chapter 7, "Electronic Spreadsheet Concepts: Spreadsheet Capabilities." Label the y axis "Payment" and the x axis "Month." Set the origin at $20 and plot the data for "This Year" and "Last Year." Display the graph and then print it.

KEYSTROKE TUTORIALS IN THE *LAB MANUAL*

The *Lab Manual* that accompanies this text contains keystroke tutorials for:

- Lotus 1-2-3 (Database and Graphics Capabilities)
- The TWiN (Database and Graphics Capabilities)
- SuperCalc4 (Database and Graphics Capabilities)

These keystroke tutorials illustrate the use of a particular electronic spreadsheet software package's database and graphics capabilities in a domestic and a business application. The more advanced features of the packages are introduced in the business application tutorials.

ELECTRONIC SPREADSHEET TUTORIAL (DATABASE CAPABILITIES): LOTUS 1-2-3

HANDS-ON TUTORIAL 24: Creating a Spreadsheet Data Base Using Lotus 1-2-3 (Database Capabilities)

Lotus 1-2-3, a product of Lotus Development Corporation, is a high-performance integrated software package that provides electronic spreadsheet, graphics, and data management capabilities. The focus of this Lotus 1-2-3 tutorial is on its database capabilities. This tutorial is based on Lotus 1-2-3 Version 2.01.

This tutorial can also be used with The TWiN (both the full-function and Educational Version 1.4), a Lotus 1-2-3 clone. The TWiN, a product of Mosaic Software, Inc., is distributed as a supplement to the main text. To run The TWiN, enter "twin" at the A prompt (A>twin).

If you have not completed Hands-On Tutorials 12 through 23 (spreadsheet capabilities), do so before beginning this series of tutorials.

■ Boot the system (see Hands-On Tutorial 1).

■ Load Lotus 1-2-3 to memory. Insert the Lotus 1-2-3 system disk in drive A.

   A>**123** ↵

■ Insert your data disk in drive B.

■ The planned spreadsheet data base template (see Figure 9–1) has five columns. Revise the column width for columns A, B, D, and E from the default of 9 positions to 6, 22, 11, and 8 positions, respectively. Do not change column C. See "Hands-On Tutorial 13, Formatting the Column Width." HOME positions the pointer at A1.

   HOME
   /Worksheet *Column* **Set-Width**
   Enter column width (1..240): **6** ↵

Change columns B, D, and E to 22, 11, and 8 positions, respectively. Use the cursor control keys to move the pointer to B1 or use the F5 function key to "go to" (move pointer to) B1.

■ Enter the labels for the fields in row 1.

   HOME
   ID → **TITLE** → **TYPE** → **SOURCE** → **DU-RATION** ↵

■ Enter the first of the 12 records shown in Figure 9–1 in row 2. Enter all IDs and TI-TLEs (columns A and B) as text entries; that is, begin any numeric ID (100) or TI-TLE (4th. . .) with an apostrophe (').

   F5
   Enter address to go to: **A2** ↵
   '100 → **MIS Orientation** → **in-house** → **Staff** → **24** ↵

Enter the remainder of the records in rows 3 through 13. At this point your spreadsheet should look just like Figure 9–1.

Save option: If at anytime you cannot continue with the tutorials, save your work so that you can pick up where you left off. To do this, see "Hands-On Tutorial 20, Saving and Retrieving a Spreadsheet." When you return, retrieve your document and continue the tutorials.

Lotus 1-2-3 display after the completion of Hands-On Tutorial 24.

HANDS-ON TUTORIAL 25: Making Inquiries to a Spreadsheet Data Base _____

Inquiries to the spreadsheet data base are made in several ways. One method is to extract and display the course records (see Figure 9–2). Another method uses the find command (see Figure 9–3).

■ To use the Data/Query/Extract method, first copy the field labels into rows 15 and 19 (see Hands-On Tutorial 17 for an explanation of the copy command). These rows provide labels for the the output range (A15..E18) and the criterion range (A19..A20).

> HOME
> /Copy
> Enter range to copy FROM: **A1.E1** ↵
> Enter range to copy TO: **A15** ↵

Repeat this procedure to copy the labels to row 19. It is not necessary to define the entire "copy to" range, only the upper-left corner of the range.

■ Identify the conditions (the criteria) in row 20 (the TYPE is "in-house" and the DURATION is less than or equal to 10 hours). See Figure 9–2.

> F5
> Enter address to go to: **C20** ↵
> **in-house** ↵
> F5
> Enter address to go to: **E20** ↵
> **+E2<=10** ↵

The formula result shown in E20 is zero; however, the formula is displayed in the user interface.

■ Identify the following ranges: input, criterion, and output.

> /Data Query Input
> Enter Input range: **A1.E13** ↵
> Criterion
> Enter Criterion range: **A19.E20** ↵
> Output
> Enter Output range: **A15.E18** ↵

■ Extract all the records that meet the criteria specified in row 20 to the output range (A15..E18).

> Extract ↵
> Quit

Records 201 and 310 should have been extracted.

Lotus 1-2-3 display after the completion of the "Extract" operation in Hands-On Tutorial 25.

■ Use the find command to highlight each record that matches the criteria in row 20. First, however, erase the output range so that your results will look like that of Figure 9–3.

> F5
> Enter address to go to: **A15** ↵
> /Range Erase
> Enter range to erase: **A15.E18** ↵
> /Data Query Find

Notice that record 201 is highlighted. Use your down cursor key to find additional records that meet the criteria.

> ↓

You can use the up cursor key to search in reverse. Return to the worksheet when you have finished viewing the records.

> ESC Quit

■ Erase A19..E20 before proceeding to the next tutorial.

> F5
> Enter address to go to: **A19** ↵
> /Range Erase
> Enter range to erase: **A19.E20** ↵

HANDS-ON TUTORIAL 26: Sorting a Spreadsheet Data Base _____

The records in a spreadsheet data base can be sorted in a variety of ways. The COURSE data base from Figure 9–1 is sorted in Figure 9–4 by ID within SOURCE. Specify the primary and secondary key fields to accomplish this sort.

■ Identify the records to be sorted. Do not include the labels (row 1).

/Data Sort Data-Range
Enter Data-Range: **A2.E13** ↵

■ Identify the primary key field as SOURCE and the order as "ascending".

(*in the sort menu*)
Primary-Key
Primary sort key: **D1** ↵
Sort order (A or D): **A** ↵

■ Identify the secondary key field as ID and the order as "ascending".

(*in the sort menu*)
Secondary-Key
Secondary sort key: **A1** ↵
Sort order (A or D): **A** ↵

■ Perform the sort and return to the worksheet.

(*in the sort menu*)
Go

■ Save the current spreadsheet on disk B with the name of "coursedb".

/File Save
Enter save file name: **b:coursedb** ↵
(*if saved earlier*) **R**eplace

■ Print the course data base and exit Lotus 1-2-3 (see "Hands-On Tutorial 21: Printing a Document and Terminating a Session").

/Print Printer Range A1.E13 ↵
Align **G**o
Quit (*to return to the spreadsheet*)
/Quit Yes

ELECTRONIC SPREADSHEET TUTORIAL (DATABASE CAPABILITIES): SUPERCALC4

HANDS-ON TUTORIAL 24: Creating a Spreadsheet Data Base Using SuperCalc4

SuperCalc4, a product of Computer Associates, is a high-performance integrated software package that provides electronic spreadsheet, graphics, and data management capabilities. The focus of this SuperCalc4 tutorial is on its database capabilities. This tutorial is based on SuperCalc4 Educational Version 1.0.

You will need to complete Hands-On Tutorials 12 through 23 before completing the following tutorials on the database capabilities of electronic spreadsheet software.

■ Boot the system (see Hands-On Tutorial 1).

■ Load SuperCalc4 to memory. Insert the SuperCalc4 program disk 1 in drive A.

> A>**sc4** ↵
> SPACE

■ Insert your data disk in drive B.

■ The planned spreadsheet data base template (see Figure 9–1) has five columns. Revise the column width for A, B, D, and E from the default of 9 positions to 6, 22, 11, and 8 positions, respectively. Do not change column C, for it needs to be 9 positions (the default setting). HOME positions the pointer at A1.

> HOME
> /**F**ormat,Column,A,Width,6 ↵

Change columns B, D, and E to 22, 11, and 8 positions, respectively. Use the cursor control keys to move the pointer to B1 or use the F5 function key to "go to" (move pointer to) B1.

■ Enter the labels for the fields in row 1.

> HOME
> ID → TITLE → TYPE → SOURCE → DURATION ↵

■ Enter the first of the 12 records shown in

Figure 9–1 in row 2. Enter all IDs (column A) as text entries; that is, begin any numeric-only ID (for example, 100) with a double quote (").

> F5 =>**A2** ↵
> "100 → **MIS Orientation** → **in-house** → **Staff** → 24 ↵

Enter the remainder of the records in rows 3 through 13. SuperCalc4 interprets "EX15" (the ID of record 9) as a formula entry (EX(P) is exponentiation); therefore you will need to preface this entry with a double quote to indicate that it is a text entry. At this point your spreadsheet should look just like Figure 9–1.

Save option: If at anytime you cannot continue with the tutorials, save your work so that you can pick up where you left off. To do this, see "Hands-On Tutorial 20, Saving and Retrieving a Spreadsheet." When you return, retrieve your document and continue the tutorials.

SuperCalc4 display after the completion of Hands-On Tutorial 24.

HANDS-ON TUTORIAL 25: Making Inquiries to a Spreadsheet Data Base _____

Inquiries to the spreadsheet data base are made in several ways. One method is to extract and display the course records (see Figure 9–2). Another method uses the find command (see Figure 9–3).

- To use the "extract" method, first copy the field labels into rows 15 and 19 (see Hands-On Tutorial 17 for an explanation of the copy command). These rows provide labels for the the output range (A15..E18) and the criterion range (A19..A20).

  HOME
  /Copy,A1.**E1,A15** ↵

Repeat this procedure to copy the labels to row 19. It is not necessary to define the entire "copy to" range, only the upper-left corner of the range.

- Identify the conditions (the criteria) in row 20 (the TYPE is "in-house" and the DURATION is less than or equal to 10 hours). See Figure 9–2.

  F5 =>**C20** ↵
  in-house ↵
  F5 =>**E20** ↵
  +**E2<=10** ↵

The formula result shown in E20 is zero; however, the formula is displayed in the user interface.

- Identify the following ranges: input, criterion, and output.

  HOME
  //Data,Input,A1.**E13** ↵
  //Data,Criterion,**A19.E20** ↵
  //Data,Output,**A15.E18** ↵

- Extract all the records that meet the criteria specified in row 20 to the output range (A15..E18).

  //Data,**Extract** ↵
  //Data,**Quit**

Records 201 and 310 should have been extracted.

SuperCalc4 display after the completion of the "Extract" operation in Hands-On Tutorial 25.

- Use the find command to highlight each record that matches the criteria in row 20. First, however, erase the output range so that your results will look like that of Figure 9–3.

  F5 =>**A15** ↵
  /Blank,A15.**E18** ↵
  //**D**ata,Find

Notice that record 201 is highlighted. Use your down cursor key to find additional records that meet the criteria.

  ↓

You can use the up cursor key to search in reverse. Return to the worksheet when you have finished viewing the records.

  ↵
  //Data,**Q**uit

- Erase A19..E20 before proceeding to the next tutorial.

  F5 =>**A19** ↵
  /Blank,A19.**E20** ↵

HANDS-ON TUTORIAL 26: Sorting a Spreadsheet Data Base _____

The records in a spreadsheet data base can be sorted in a variety of ways. The COURSE data base from Figure 9–1 is sorted in Figure 9–4 by ID within SOURCE. Specify the primary and secondary key fields to accomplish this sort.

■ Identify the primary (column D) and secondary (column A) keys and the records to be sorted (A2.E13). Both keys are sorted in ascending sequence. The "No-Adjust" option tells the program not to alter cell formulas or recalculate values.

> F5 =>**D2** ↵
>
> **/A**rrange,Column,D,**A2.E13,A**scending,
> **N**o-Adjust,Options,**A,A**scending

■ Save the current spreadsheet on disk B with the name of coursedb.

> /Save,**b:coursedb,A**ll,

■ Print the course data base and exit SuperCalc4 (see "Hands-On Tutorial 21: Printing a Document and Terminating a Session").

> HOME
>
> **/O**utput,Printer,**R**ange,A1.**E13** ↵
> /Output,Printer,**A**lign,Go, ↵
> /Output,Printer,**Q**uit
> **/Q**uit,**Y**es

Notice that borders (row and column labels) are included on this printout. To remove the borders, select the "no" option for borders on the Output Options Menu.

ELECTRONIC SPREADSHEET TUTORIAL (GRAPHICS CAPABILITIES): LOTUS 1-2-3

HANDS-ON TUTORIAL 27: Using Lotus 1-2-3 (Graphics Capabilities)

Lotus 1-2-3, a product of Lotus Development Corporation, is a high-performance integrated software package that provides electronic spreadsheet, graphics, and data management capabilities. The focus of this Lotus 1-2-3 tutorial is on its graphics capabilities.

If you have not completed Hands-On Tutorials 12 through 23 (spreadsheet capabilities), do so before beginning this series of graphics tutorials.

■ Boot the system (see Hands-On Tutorial 1).

■ Load Lotus 1-2-3 to memory.

    A>**123** ↵

■ Insert your data disk in drive B.

HANDS-ON TUTORIAL 28: Enter Spreadsheet Data

Use the Lotus 1-2-3 procedures and techniques that you learned in Hands-On Tutorials 12 through 23 to create the sales summary spreadsheet of Figure 9–5.

■ Set the width of column A to 15 positions and the width of columns B through F to 11 positions (see "Hands-On Tutorial 13: Formatting the Column Width").

■ Enter all text (except rows 14 through 17), including repeating text (rows 4 and 9) and numeric data as shown in Figure 9–5 (see Hands-On Tutorials 14, "Entering Text Data," and 15, "Entering Numeric Data"). Notice that the text entries in A3..F3 and A10 are right justified. The numeric data in column F and in row 10 are the results of formulas.

■ Enter the formulas to sum sales by product (rows), by region (columns), and overall. Enter the formula @SUM(B5..E5) in F5 and copy it to F6..F8. Enter the formula @SUM(B5..B8) in B10 and copy it to C10..F10. See Hands-On Tutorials 16, "Entering Formulas," and 17, "Using Predefined Functions."

■ Format all numeric and formula entries (B5..F10) as shown (see "Hands-On Tutorial 19: Formatting the Cell Entries"). Format the entries as currency with 0 decimal places.

■ Save the spreadsheet template as "sales" on disk B (see "Hands-On Tutorial 20: Saving and Retrieving a Spreadsheet").

HANDS-ON TUTORIAL 29: Producing a Bar Graph

Produce the bar graph illustrated in Figure 9–6.

■ Identify the data to be graphed.

    F5

    Enter address to go to: **B10** ↵
    /Graph **A** (define first data range) **B10.E10** ↵

■ Select the type of graph to be "Bar."

    (in Graph menu) Type **B**ar

■ Add the main heading and labels for the x-axis and y-axis.

    (in Graph menu) **O**ptions Titles **F**irst
    Enter graph title, top line: **Sales Summary by Region** ↵

    (in Graph/Options menu) Titles **X**-Axis
    Enter X axis title: **Region** ↵
    (in Graph/Options menu) Titles **Y**-Axis
    Enter Y axis title: **Sales ($1000)** ↵
    Quit (to return to Graph menu)

■ Label the bars for each region.

    (in Graph menu) **X**
    Enter X axis range: **B3.E3** ↵

As you become familiar with graphics capabilities, you will find that there are many things you can do to improve the appearance of a graph.

■ Display the bar graph (the functional equivalent of Figure 9–6).

(*in Graph menu*) **V**iew

A graph that is displayed on a monitor may or may not appear as it would when printed or plotted. On occasion, the program must make certain compromises to fit as much of the graph as possible on the display (for example, writing labels vertically rather than horizontally). Press SPACE or any key to return to the spreadsheet.

$\boxed{\text{SPACE}}$

■ Lotus 1-2-3 saves the settings for the current graph when the spreadsheet is saved. However, if you wish to create and then recall more than one graph from the spreadsheet data, you will need to name each graph.

> (*in Graph menu*) **N**ame **C**reate
> Enter graph name: **bargraph** ↵
> **Q**uit

To recall the settings for a particular graph (make it the current graph), select

"Graph" (from the main menu), "Name," and "Use," and then highlight and select the name of the desired graph.

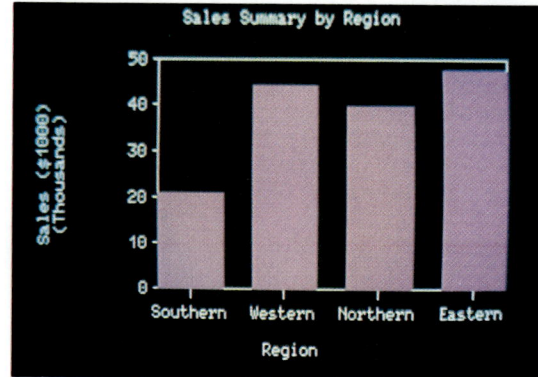

Lotus 1-2-3 display of the bar graph produced in Hands-On Tutorial 29.

HANDS-ON TUTORIAL 30: Saving and Printing/Plotting a Graph

■ In Lotus 1-2-3, the current graph settings are saved when the spreadsheet is saved.

> **/F**ile **S**ave
> Enter save file name: **b:sales** ↵
> (*if "sales" is an existing file*) **R**eplace

If you plan to print/plot a particular graph, you will need to create a separate PrintGraph file. The bar graph is the current graph.

> **/G**raph **S**ave
> Enter graph file name: **b:bar** ↵
> **Q**uit

The commands above create a file, called BAR.PIC (Lotus 1-2-3 adds the PIC extension), from which the bar graph can be printed.

■ Print the bar chart (a bar graph like Figure 9–6). Use Lotus 1-2-3's PrintGraph program, which is on a separate disk, to print the bar graph. First, however, you must exit Lotus 1-2-3.

> **/Q**uit **Y**es

Replace the Lotus 1-2-3 system disk in drive A with the PrintGraph disk.

> A>**pgraph** ↵

Change the default PrintGraph settings so that the program searches disk B for BAR.PIC and identify the device on which the graph will be printed/plotted.

> **S**ettings **H**ardware **G**raphs-Directory
> Enter directory containing picture files
> $\boxed{\text{ESC}}$ (*to clear line*) **B:** ↵
> **P**rinter (*highlight the output device*) $\boxed{\text{SPACE}}$ ↵
>
> **Q**uit **Q**uit
> **I**mage-Select (*highlight BAR*) $\boxed{\text{SPACE}}$ ↵
> **A**lign **G**o

Printing/plotting a graph may take a few minutes. Exit PrintGraph.

> **E**xit
> End PrintGraph session? **Y**es
> A>

Return to Lotus 1-2-3 and retrieve the "sales" spreadsheet (see Hands-On Tutorials 12 and 20).

HANDS-ON TUTORIAL 31: Producing Stacked-Bar and Clustered-Bar Graphs _____

Produce the stacked-bar graph illustrated in Figure 9–7.

■ Identify the range of the data to be graphed.

> /Graph **A** (*define first data range*) **B5.E5** ↵
> (*in Graph menu*) **B** (*define second data range*) **B6.E6** ↵
> (*in Graph menu*) **C** (*define third data range*) **B7.E7** ↵
> (*in Graph menu*) **D** (*define fourth data range*) **B8.E8** ↵

■ Select type of graph to be "Stacked-Bar."

> (*in Graph menu*) **T**ype **S**tacked-Bar

■ Add the main heading and labels for the x-axis and y-axis. The heading and labels for the bar graph are still current in Lotus 1-2-3, and so the labels for the x-axis and y-axis are unchanged. Enter a new title.

> (*in Graph menu*) **O**ptions **T**itles **F**irst
> Enter graph title, top line: **Product Sales Summary by Region** ↵
> **Q**uit (*to return to Graph menu*)

■ Label the variables (the four products).

> (*in Graph menu*) **O**ptions **L**egend **A**
> Enter legend for A range: **Stibs** ↵
> (*in Graph/Options menu*) **L**egend **B**
> Enter legend for A range: **Farkles** ↵
> (*in Graph/Options menu*) **L**egend **C**
> Enter legend for A range: **Teglers** ↵
> (*in Graph/Options menu*) **L**egend **D**
> Enter legend for A range: **Qwerts** ↵
> **Q**uit (*to return to Graph menu*)

■ Display the stacked-bar graph on the screen.

> (*in Graph menu*) **V**iew
> SPACE (*to return to the spreadsheet*)

■ Produce and display the clustered-bar chart illustrated in Figure 9–8. All of the specifications are the same for the stacked-bar and the clustered-bar charts except for the selection of type of graph.

> (*in Graph menu*) **T**ype **B**ar **V**iew
> SPACE (*to return to the spreadsheet*) **Q**uit

Because the data range (B5..E8) has both rows and columns, the request for a "Bar" chart is interpreted as a request for a clustered-bar chart.

■ Save the graph settings as "multibar".

> (*in Graph menu*) **N**ame **C**reate
> Enter graph name: **multibar** ↵
> **Q**uit

Lotus 1-2-3 display of the clustered-bar graph produced in Hands-On Tutorial 31.

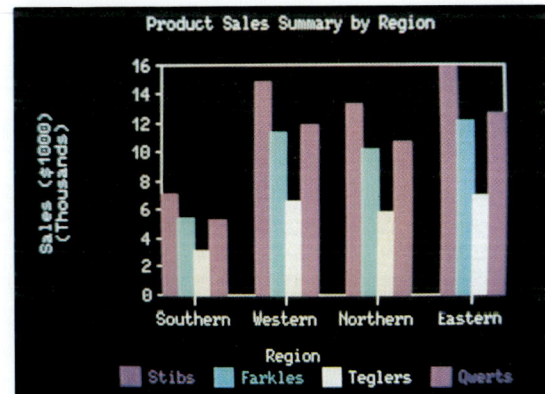

HANDS-ON TUTORIAL 32: Producing a Pie Graph _____

Produce the pie graph illustrated in Figure 9–9.

■ Identify the range of the data to be graphed.

> /Graph **A**
> Enter first data range: **F5.F8** ↵

■ Select type of graph.

> (*in Graph menu*) **T**ype **P**ie

■ Add the main heading and labels.

> (*in Graph menu*) **O**ptions **T**itles **F**irst
> Enter graph title, top line: **Sales by Product** ↵
> **Q**uit
> (*in Graph menu*) **X**
> Enter X axis range: **A5.A8** ↵
> **Q**uit

■ Explode the Stibs piece of the pie (segment 1). In Lotus 1-2-3, add 100 to the shading code (0, 1, 2, 3, . . . 7) for the piece that you wish to explode. These codes must be in adjacent cells of a row or column.

F5
Enter address to go to: **A18** ↵
101 → 2 → 3 → 4 →
/Graph **B**
Enter second data range: **A18.D18** ↵

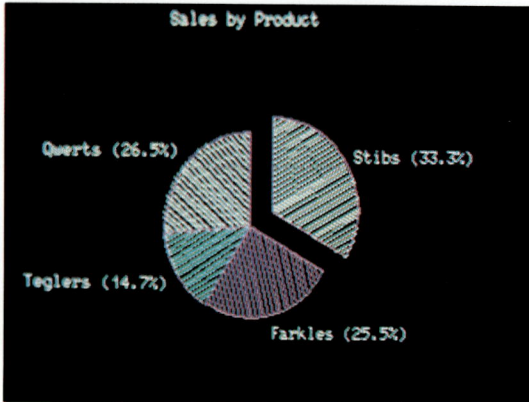

■ Display the pie graph.

(*in Graph menu*) **View**
SPACE (*to return to the spreadsheet*)

■ Save the graph settings as "piegraph".

(*in Graph menu*) **N**ame **C**reate
Enter graph name: **piegraph** ↵
Quit

Lotus 1-2-3 display of the pie graph produced in Hands-On Tutorial 32.

HANDS-ON TUTORIAL 33: Producing a Line Graph

■ Produce and display the line graph illustrated in Figure 9–10. The specifications for this line graph are the same as those for the stacked-bar and clustered-bar graphs of Hands-On Tutorial 31, except for the selection of type of graph.

/Graph **N**ame **U**se (*highlight "MULTIBAR"*) ↵
SPACE (*to return to the spreadsheet*)
(*in Graph menu*) **T**ype **L**ine **V**iew
SPACE (*to return to the spreadsheet*) **Q**uit

■ Save your work and exit:

/File **S**ave
Enter save file name: **b:sales** ↵
(*if "sales" is an existing file*) **R**eplace
/Quit **Y**es

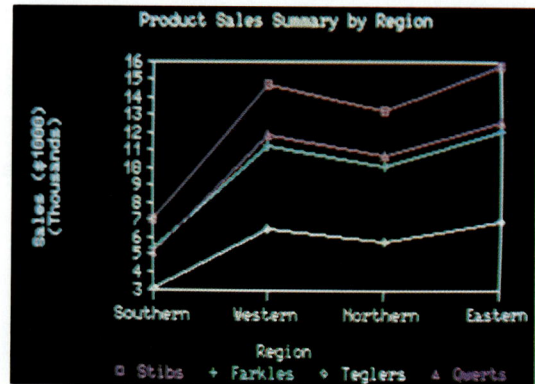

Lotus 1-2-3 display of the line graph produced in Hands-On Tutorial 33.

ADVANCED AND SPECIAL FEATURES TUTORIAL: Lotus 1-2-3 Graphics Capabilities

In this advanced Lotus 1-2-3 tutorial the following skills are introduced: enhancing a clustered-bar graph to include data-labels, subheadings, and different font styles. You should have completed Hands-On Tutorials 12 through 23 and 34 through 40 before continuing with this advanced tutorial.

After Sally Marcio created the clustered-bar graph (see Figure 9–8), she realized that it did not contain enough information to be immediately useful to Zimco's president, Preston Smith. She instructed her staff to add data-labels, a subheading, and choose different font styles to make the graph more visually appealing. The following tutorial describes the steps taken by Sally's staff to enhance the graph.

GETTING STARTED

To complete this tutorial, you will need the Lotus system disk, the PrintGraph disk, and a work disk that contains the Lotus "sales" file for the graph based on Figure 9–8.

- Boot the system (see Hands-On Tutorial 1).
- Load Lotus 1-2-3 to memory (see Hands-On Tutorial 12).

  A>**123** ↵

- Insert your data disk in drive B.

RETRIEVING AND ENHANCING A CLUSTERED-BAR GRAPH

Retrieve the "sales" file created in Hands-On Tutorials 34 through 40 and add data-labels and a subheading.

- Load "sales" from your work disk to memory.

  /File Retrieve ESC (if default is A) **b:sales** ↵

- Recall the settings for the multibar graphs.

  /Graph Name Use
  (highlight "MULTIBAR")
  ↵
  (return to spreadsheet)
  SPACE

- Add a subheading to the graph's title.

  (in Graph menu) Options Titles Second
  Enter graph title, second line: **Zimco Enterprises** ↵

- Add data-labels to state the dollar value of each segment.

  (in Graph menu) Data-Labels
  A (labels for A range data)
  Enter label range for A range data: **B5.E5** ↵
  Center
  B (labels for B range data)
  Enter label range for B range data: **B6.E6** ↵
  Center
  C (Labels for C range data)
  Enter label range for C range data: **B7.E7** ↵
  Center

D (Labels for D range data)
Enter label range for D range data: **B8.E8** ↵
Center
Quit **Q**uit (return to the Graph menu)

- Select and view the clustered-bar graph then return to the Graph menu.

  Type **B**ar **V**iew
  SPACE

In the display of the graph, several of the data-labels are superimposed on one another; however, they are easily readable when the graph is printed or plotted.

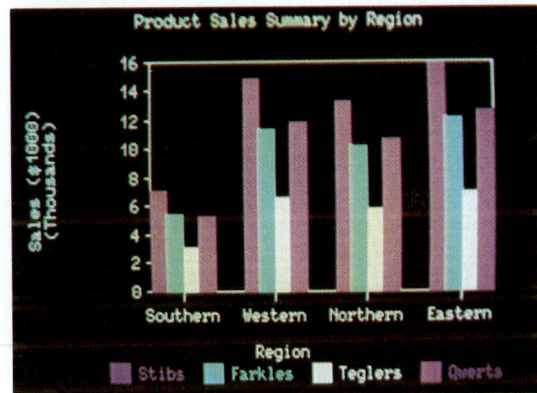

Lotus 1-2-3 display of the clustered-bar graph produced in the Advanced and Special Features Tutorial.

- Save the graph settings under a new name so that the original settings can be retained.

  Name **C**reate **multibar1** ↵

- Create a PrintGraph file of the new graph.

  Save
  Enter graph file name: **b:cluster** ↵
  Quit

- Save the spreadsheet and the new graph settings to disk.

  /File Save B:\SALES.WK1 ↵ **R**eplace

SELECTING FONTS AND PRINTING THE GRAPH

Switch to the PrintGraph program, select fonts for the labels, print the graph, and exit Lotus 1-2-3.

- Exit Lotus 1-2-3 before entering the PrintGraph program.

  /Quit **Y**es

- Remove the system disk from drive A and insert the PrintGraph disk.

A>**pgraph** ↵

■ **Select the primary and secondary font settings.**

> *Settings* **I***mage* **F***ont* **1**
> (*highlight BOLD*)
> SPACE (*to mark*) ↵
> **F***ont* **2**
> (*highlight ROMAN1*)
> SPACE ↵
> **Q***uit*
> (in Settings menu) **H***ardware* **G***raphs-Directory*
> Enter directory containing picture files
> **B:** ↵
> **P***rinter*
> (*highlight the output device*) SPACE ↵
> **Q***uit*

■ **Save the settings to the "cluster" graph file.**

> **S***ave*

■ **Select a graph file and print the graph.**

> **I***mage-Select*
> (*highlight CLUSTER*)
> SPACE ↵
> **A***lign* **G***o*

If the program pauses before printing, press SPACE to continue.

■ **Exit the Lotus PrintGraph program.**

> **E***xit* **Y***es*

GRAPHICS TUTORIAL: THE TWiN

HANDS-ON TUTORIAL 27: Using The TWiN (Graphics Capabilities)

The TWiN, a product of Mosaic Software, Inc., is a clone of Lotus 1-2-3. It uses the standard commands and format, with minor variations, of Lotus 1-2-3 with the exception of the format of its graphics capabilities. This tutorial is based on TWiN's Educational Version 1.4.

If you have not completed Hands-On Tutorials 12 through 23 (spreadsheet capabili-

ties), do so before beginning this series of graphics tutorials.

■ Boot the system (see Hands-On Tutorial 1).
■ Load The TWiN to memory.

   A>**twin** ↵

■ Insert your data disk in drive B.

HANDS-ON TUTORIAL 28: Enter Spreadsheet Data

Use the The TWiN procedures and techniques that you learned in Hands-On Tutorials 12 through 23 to create the sales summary spreadsheet of Figure 9–5.

■ Set the width of column A to 15 positions and the width of columns B through F to 11 positions (see "Hands-On Tutorial 13: Formatting the Column Width").
■ Enter all text (except rows 14 through 17), including repeating text (rows 4 and 9) and numeric data as shown in Figure 9–5 (see Hands-On Tutorials 14, "Entering Text Data," and 15, "Entering Numeric Data"). Notice that the text entries in A3..F3 and A10 are right justified. The numeric data in column F and in row 10 are the results of formulas.

■ Enter the formulas to sum sales by product (rows), by region (columns), and overall. Enter the formula @SUM(B5..E5) in F5 and copy it to F6..F8. Enter the formula @SUM(B5..B8) in B10 and copy it to C10..F10. See Hands-On Tutorials 16, "Entering Formulas," and 17, "Using Predefined Functions."
■ Format all numeric and formula entries (B5..F10) as shown (see "Hands-On Tutorial 19: Formatting the Cell Entries"). Format the entries as currency with 0 decimal places.
■ Save the spreadsheet template as "sales" on disk B (see "Hands-On Tutorial 20: Saving and Retrieving a Spreadsheet").

HANDS-ON TUTORIAL 29: Producing a Bar Graph

Produce the bar graph illustrated in Figure 9–6.

■ Identify the data to be graphed.

   F5
   Enter cell to go to: **B10** ↵
   /Graph 1 (*define first data range*)
   Data range for 1: **B10.E10** ↵

■ Select the type of graph to be "Bar."

   (*in Graph menu*) **Type D**)*VBar*

■ Add the main heading and labels for the x-axis and y-axis.

   (*in Graph menu*) **O**ptions
   (*cursor is in Titles block*)
   Sales Summary by Region ↵ (*6 times to x-axis*)

   X -Axis Label **Region** ↵
   Y1-Axis Label **Sales ($1000)** ↵ ESC

■ Label the bars for each region.

   (*in Graph menu*) *Label* **X**
   Data label range for X: **B3.E3** ↵

As you become familiar with graphics capabilities, you will find that there are many things you can do to improve the appearance of a graph.

■ Display the bar graph (the functional equivalent of Figure 9–6).

   (*in Graph menu*) **V**iew

A graph that is displayed on a monitor may or may not appear as it would when printed or plotted. On occasion, the program must make certain compromises to fit as much of the graph as possible on the display (for example, writing labels vertically rather than horizontally). Press SPACE or any key to return to the spreadsheet.

| SPACE |

■ The TWiN saves the settings for the current graph when the spreadsheet is saved. However, if you wish to create and then recall more than one graph from the spreadsheet data, you will need to name each graph.

> (*in Graph menu*) **N**ame **C**reate
> Graph to create: **bargraph** ↵
> **Q**uit

To recall the settings for a particular graph (make it the current graph), select "Graph" (from the main menu), "Name," "Use," and then ENTER, which highlights and selects the name of the desired graph.

The TWiN display of the bar graph produced in Hands-On Tutorial 29.

HANDS-ON TUTORIAL 30: Saving and Printing/Plotting a Graph

■ In The TWiN, the current graph settings are saved when the spreadsheet is saved.

> **/F**ile **S**ave
> Enter save file name: **b:sales** ↵
> (*if "sales" is an existing file*) **R**eplace

■ Print the current graph on the printer.

> **/G**raph **G**print **P**rinter

Is the printer on-line, and the paper properly positioned? Y/(N) **Y**

Printing/plotting a graph may take a few minutes.

■ Exit the Graph menu and return to the spreadsheet.

> **Q**uit

HANDS-ON TUTORIAL 31: Producing Stacked-Bar and Clustered-Bar Graphs

Produce the stacked-bar graph illustrated in Figure 9–7.

■ Identify the range of the data to be graphed.

> **/G**raph **1** Data range for 1: **B5.E5** ↵
> (*in Graph menu*)
> **2** Data range for 2: **B6.E6** ↵
> **3** Data range for 3: **B7.E7** ↵
> **4** Data range for 4: **B8.E8** ↵

■ Select type of graph to be "Stacked-Bar."

> (*in Graph menu*) **T**ype **D**)VBar

■ Add the main heading and labels for the x-axis and y-axis. The labels for the bar graph are still current in The TWiN and so the labels for the x-axis and y-axis are unchanged. Enter a new title, label the variables (the four products) to create a legend, then return to the Graph menu.

> (*in Graph menu*) **O**ptions
> **Product Sales Summary by Region** ↵
> | PGDN | (*2 times to Legend*)
> 1 **Stibs** ↵
> 2 **Farkles** ↵
> 3 **Teglers** ↵
> 4 **Qwerts** ↵
> (*use* → *and* ↑ *keys and move cursor to "Bars..")*
> Bars (C)luster or (S)tack **S**
> | ESC | (*to return to Graph menu*)

■ Display the stacked-bar graph on the screen and return to the spreadsheet.

> (*in Graph menu*) **V**iew
> | SPACE |

■ Produce and display the clustered-bar chart illustrated in Figure 9–8. All of the specifications are the same for the stacked-bar and the clustered-bar charts except for the selection of type of graph.

(in Graph menu) Type **E**3D-Bar **V**iew
SPACE (to return to the spreadsheet) **Q**uit

The only option for vertical bar in 3D is cluster, so it overrides the S in stacked bar in the options.

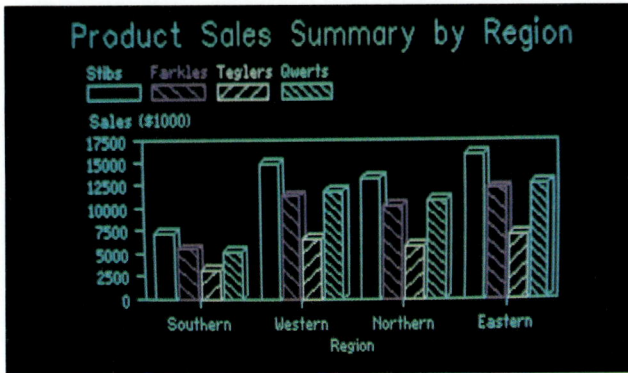

■ Save the graph settings as "multibar".

(in Graph menu) **N**ame **C**reate
Graph to create: **multibar** ↵
Quit

The TWiN display of the clustered-bar graph produced in Hands-On Tutorial 31.

HANDS-ON TUTORIAL 32: Producing a Pie Graph

Produce the pie graph illustrated in Figure 9–9.

■ Identify the range of the data to be graphed.

/**G**raph **1**
Enter first data range: **F5.F8** ↵

■ Select type of graph.

(in Graph menu) **T**ype **G**)3D-Pie

■ Add the main heading and labels.

(in Graph menu) **O**ptions
Sales by Product ↵
PGDN (2 times) TAB (5 times)
Pie data range number or **1**
ESC
(in Graph menu) **X**
Enter X axis range: **A5.A8** ↵

■ Display the pie chart.

(in Graph menu)
View
SPACE

■ Save the graph settings as "piegraph".

(in Graph menu) **N**ame **C**reate
Graph to create: **piegraph** ↵
Quit

The TWiN display of the pie graph produced in Hands-On Tutorial 32.

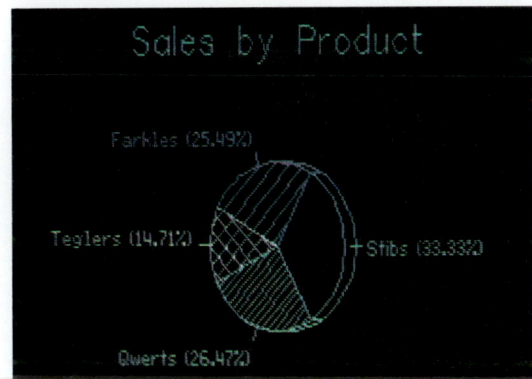

HANDS-ON TUTORIAL 33: Producing a Line Graph

■ Produce and display the line graph illustrated in Figure 9–10. The specifications for this line graph are the same as those for the stacked-bar and clustered-bar graphs of Hands-On Tutorial 38, except for the selection of type of graph.

/Graph **N**ame **U**se
Graph to use: → *(press until see "multibar")*
multibar ↵
SPACE
(in Graph menu) Type **A**)*Line* **V**iew
SPACE **Q**uit

■ **Save your work and exit**:

/File **S**ave
Enter save file name: **b:sales** ↵
(if "sales" is an existing file) **R**eplace
*/Q*uit **Y**es

The TWiN display of the line graph produced in Hands-On Tutorial 33.

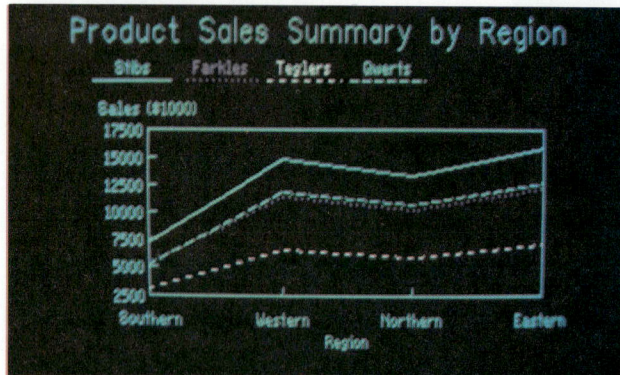

ELECTRONIC SPREADSHEET TUTORIAL (GRAPHICS CAPABILITIES): SUPERCALC4

HANDS-ON TUTORIAL 27: Using SuperCalc4 (Graphics Capabilities)

SuperCalc4, a product of Computer Associates, is a high-performance integrated software package that provides electronic spreadsheet, graphics, and data management capabilities. The focus of this SuperCalc4 tutorial is on its graphics capabilities.

If you have not completed Hands-On Tutorials 12 through 23 (spreadsheet capabilities), do so before beginning this series of graphics tutorials.

■ Boot the system (see Hands-On Tutorial 1).

■ Load SuperCalc4 to memory.

  A>**sc4** ↵
  SPACE

■ Insert your data disk in drive B.

HANDS-ON TUTORIAL 28: Enter Spreadsheet Data

Use the SuperCalc4 procedures and techniques that you learned in Hands-On Tutorials 12 through 23 to create the sales summary spreadsheet of Figure 9–5.

■ Set the width of column A to 15 positions and the width of columns B through F to 12 positions (see "Hands-On Tutorial 13: Formatting the the Column Width").

■ Enter all text, including repeating text (rows 4 and 9) and the chart titles and labels (rows 14-17), and numeric data as shown in Figure 9–5 (see Hands-On Tutorials 14, "Entering Text Data," and 15, "Entering Numeric Data"). Notice that the text entries in A3:F3 and A10 are right justified. The numeric data in column F and in row 10 are the results of formulas.

■ Enter the formulas to sum sales by product (rows), by region (columns), and overall. Enter the formula SUM(B5:E5) in F5 and copy it to F6:F8. Enter the formula SUM(B5:B8) in B10 and copy it to C10:F10. See Hands-On Tutorials 16, "Entering Formulas," and 17, "Using Predefined Functions."

■ Format all numeric and formula entries (B5:F10) as shown (see "Hands-On Tutorial 19: Formatting the Cell Entries"). All column 1 default specifications apply except one: change "Decimal Places" from "2" to "0".

■ Save the spreadsheet template as "sales" on disk B (see "Hands-On Tutorial 20: Saving and Retrieving a Spreadsheet").

HANDS-ON TUTORIAL 29: Producing a Bar Graph

Produce the bar graph illustrated in Figure 9–6.

■ Identify the data to be graphed.

  F5 =>**B10** ↵
  /View,Data,B10.**E10** ↵

■ Select the type of graph to be "Bar." In SuperCalc4, a "1" is added automatically, indicating that this is graph number 1. SuperCalc4 permits you to store up to 9 graphs per spreadsheet.

  /View,1,Graph,**B**ar

■ Add the main heading and labels for the x-axis and y-axis. SuperCalc4 permits

you to associate the contents of a cell with a heading.

  /View,1,Headings,**M**ain,(*move pointer to A14*)
  A14 ↵
  /View,1,Headings,**X**-axis,(*move pointer to A3*)
  A3 ↵
  /View,1,Headings,**Y**-axis,(*move pointer to A17*)
  A17 ↵
  /View,1,Headings,**Q**uit

Notice that your prompts will continue to be "/View,1," while you are describing the chart.

■ Label the bars for each region. SuperCalc4 refers to the labels for the x-axis (and the segments of a pie chart) as time-labels.

/View,1,Time-Labels,**B3.E3** ↵

As you become familiar with graphics capabilities, you will find that there are many things you can do to improve the appearance of a graph.

■ Display the bar graph (the functional equivalent of Figure 9–6).

/View,1,Show,

A graph that is displayed on a monitor may or may not appear as it would when printed or plotted. On occasion, the program must make certain compromises to fit as much of the graph as possible on the display (for example, labels writing vertically rather than horizontally). Press SPACE or any key to return to the spreadsheet.

| SPACE |

Follow the directions on the screen as you swap between the two SuperCalc4 program disks.

SuperCalc4 display of the bar graph produced in Hands-On Tutorial 29.

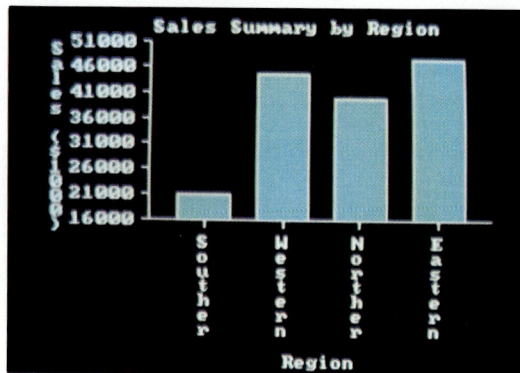

HANDS-ON TUTORIAL 30: Saving and Printing/Plotting a Graph

■ In SuperCalc4 the specifications relating to the graphs associated with a particular spreadsheet template are saved to disk when you issue the SAVE command.

/Save,**b:sales,A**ll,

Or, if you had already saved "sales" to disk storage,

/Save,b:sales ↵ **O**verwrite,**A**ll,

■ Print the bar chart (a bar graph like Figure 9–6) by pressing function key 9 to print the current graph.

| F9 |

HANDS-ON TUTORIAL 31: Producing Stacked-Bar and Clustered-Bar Graphs

Produce the stacked-bar graph illustrated in Figure 9–7.

■ Identify the range of the data to be graphed. Identify this new graph as #2. SuperCalc4 automatically designates each row in a block range as a variable (products).

/View,#2,Data,**B5.E8** ↵

■ Select type of graph to be "Stacked-Bar."

/View,#2,Graph,Stacked-Bar

■ Add the main heading and labels for the x-axis and y-axis.

/View,#2,Headings,**M**ain,(move pointer to A15)
A15 ↵
/View,#2,Headings,**X**-axis,(move pointer to A3)
A3 ↵

/View,#2,Headings,**Y**-axis,(move pointer to A17)
A17 ↵
/View,#2,Headings,**Q**uit

■ Label the bars for each region.

/View,#2,Time-Labels,**B3.E3** ↵

■ Label the variables (the four products).

/View,#2,**V**ariable-Labels,**A5.A8** ↵

■ Display the stacked-bar graph on the screen.

/View,#2,Show,

■ Produce and display the clustered-bar graph illustrated in Figure 9–8. All of the specifications are the same for the stacked-bar and the clustered-bar charts except for the selection of type of graph.

/View,#**2**,Graph,**B**ar
/View,#2,**S**how,
[SPACE] (*to return to the spreadsheet*)

Because the data range (B5:E8) has both

rows and columns, the request for a "Bar" chart is interpreted as a request for a clustered-bar chart.

SuperCalc4 display of the clustered-bar graph produced in Hands-On Tutorial 31.

HANDS-ON TUTORIAL 32: Producing a Pie Graph

Produce the pie graph illustrated in Figure 9–9.

■ **Identify the range of the data to be graphed. identify this new graph as #3.**

/View,#**3**,**D**ata,**F5.F8** ↵

■ **Select type of graph.**

/View,#3,**G**raph,**P**ie

■ **Add the main heading and labels.**

/View,#3,**H**eadings,**M**ain,(*move pointer to A16*) A16 ↵
/View,#3,**H**eadings,**Q**uit
/View,#3,**T**ime-Labels,**A5.A8** ↵

In SuperCalc4, Time-Labels are interpreted as labels for the pieces of the pie.

■ **Explode the Stibs piece of the pie (segment 1).**

/View,#3,**O**ptions,**E**xplosion,**S**egment,**1**,**Q**uit
/View,#3,**O**ptions,**Q**uit

■ **Display the pie graph.**

/View,#3,**S**how,
[SPACE] (*to return to the spreadsheet*)

SuperCalc4 display of the pie graph produced in Hands-On Tutorial 32.

HANDS-ON TUTORIAL 33: Producing a Line Graph

■ **Produce and display the line graph illustrated in Figure 9–10. The specifications for this line graph are the same as those for the stacked-bar and clustered-bar graphs of Hands-On Tutorial 31, except for the selection of type of graph.**

/View,#**2**,Graph,**L**ine
/View,#2,**S**how,

■ **Save your work and exit.**

/**S**ave,b:sales ↵ **O**verwrite,**A**ll,
/**Q**uit,**Y**es

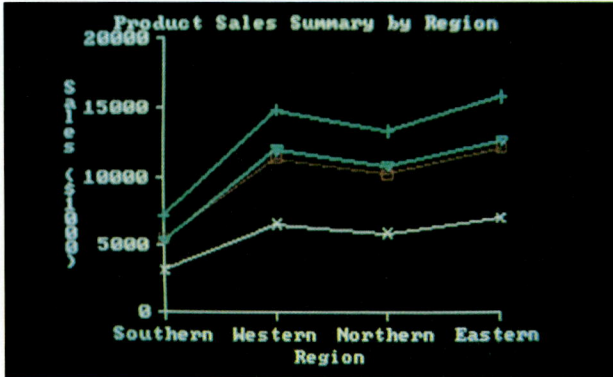

SuperCalc4 display of the line graph produced in Hands-On Tutorial 33.

ADVANCED AND SPECIAL FEATURES TUTORIAL: SuperCalc4 Graphics Capabilities

In this advance SuperCalc4 tutorial the following skills are introduced: enhancing a pie graph to include point labels and subheadings. You should have completed Hands-On Tutorials 12 through 23 and 34 through 40 before continuing with this advanced tutorial.

After Sally Marcio created the pie graph (see Figure 9–9), she realized that it did not contain enough information to be immediately useful to Zimco's president, Preston Smith. She instructed her staff to add point labels and a subheading to make the graph more visually appealing. The following tutorial describes the steps taken by Sally's staff to enhance the graph.

GETTING STARTED

To complete this tutorial, you will need the two SuperCalc4 diskettes and a work disk that contains the SuperCalc4 "sales" graph based on Figure 9–9.

- Boot the system (see Hands-On Tutorial 1).
- Load SuperCalc4 to memory (see Hands-On Tutorial 12).

    A>**sc4** ↵
    ⌷SPACE⌷

During a SuperCalc4 session, you may need to replace the active program disk with the other program disk. On-screen prompts will tell you when to switch program disks.

- Insert your data disk in drive B.

RETRIEVING AND ENHANCING A PIE GRAPH

Retrieve the "sales" file created in Hands-On Tutorials 34 through 40 and make a copy of the graphics settings for the pie chart.

- Load "sales" from your work disk to memory.

    /Load,b:sales ↵

If you need to see the files list on your data disk, press F3 and highlight the appropriate file.

- Make a copy the pie chart settings created in Hands-On Tutorial 39 in view area #5 so that the original settings can be retained.

    /Copy,∗3,5 ↵

- Confirm that the graph file was copied correctly by displaying the graph on the monitor.

    /View,**#5**,Show,

Return to the spreadsheet.

    ⌷SPACE⌷

- Add the text that will be used as headings.

    ⌷F5⌷=>**A18** ↵
    Zimco Enterprises ↓
    Stibs Explosion Version ↓

ADDING A SUBHEADING AND A HEADING BELOW THE GRAPH

■ Add a subheading to the graph's title and a heading below the graph.

> /View,5,Headings,Sub,A18 ↵
> /View,5,Headings,X-axis,A19 ↵
> /View,5,Headings,Quit

■ Display the graph.

> /View,5,Show,

Press SPACE or any key to return to the spreadsheet.

> SPACE

■ Examine the graph definition screen. This is not required but you should know that the option is available.

> /View,?
> (return to the spreadsheet)
> ESC
> (clear the command line)
> ESC   ESC

■ Save the graph settings before printing the graph.

/Save,B:SALES.cal ↵ Overwrite,All,

PRINTING/PLOTTING THE GRAPH

■ Print/plot the graph.

> F9

■ Exit SuperCalc4.

> /Quit,Yes

SuperCalc4 display of the pie graph produced in the Advanced and Special Features Tutorial.

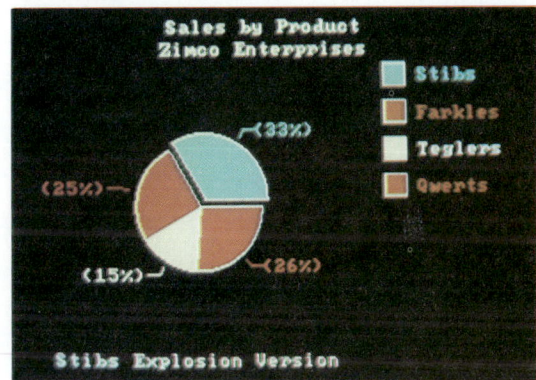

CHAPTER 10

Database Software Concepts

STUDENT LEARNING OBJECTIVES

- To describe the function and purpose of database software.
- To relate the hierarchy of data organization to database software.
- To define the structure of a data base.
- To discuss concepts associated with data base inquiries, sorting, and report generation.
- To discuss the rationale for file indexing.
- To discuss the terminology and concepts associated with database programming.
- To describe the steps to program development.
- To describe various high-level database tools.
- To identify applications for database software.

10–1 THE FUNCTION OF DATABASE SOFTWARE

With database software, you can create and maintain a data base and extract information from the data base. To use database or data management software, you first identify the format of the data, and then design a display format that will permit interactive entry and revision of the data base. Once the data base is created, its *records* (related data about a particular event or thing) can be deleted or revised and other records can be added to the data base. Database, as one word, is an alternative terminology for data management software. Data base, as two words, refers to the highest level of the hierarchy of data organization. The hierarchy of data organization (bits, characters, fields, records, files, and data bases) is discussed in Chapter 2 and illustrated in Figure 2–7.

All database software packages have the following fundamental capabilities:

1. Create and maintain (add, delete, and revise records) a data base.
2. Extract and list all records or only those records that meet certain conditions.
3. Permit inquiries to the data base (for example, the average age of all employees).
4. Sort records in ascending or descending sequence by primary, secondary, and tertiary key fields.
5. Generate formatted reports with subtotals and totals.

The more sophisticated database packages include a variety of other

These marketing managers are using database software to create a microcomputer-based order-entry system. The customer data base will contain pertinent customer information, such as name, address, credit limits, order history, and so on. (Photo courtesy of Hewlett-Packard Company)

features, such as *spreadsheet-type computations*, *graphics*, *programming*, and *applications generators*.

There are many applications for database software. Some of the more popular applications of database software include mailing lists, inventory management, customer accounting, sales reporting, general office filing, business accounting, and personnel record keeping.

10–2   THE DESIGN OF DATABASE SOFTWARE ──

Each Database Software Package Has Its Own Design.   Many similarities exist between commercially available word processing packages and between commercially available electronic spreadsheet packages. With word processing, the user sees and manipulates lines of text. With electronic spreadsheets, the user sees and manipulates data in numbered rows and lettered columns. This is not the case with database packages.

All commercial database software packages permit the creation and manipulation of data bases, but what the user sees on the screen may be vastly different for the various packages. However, the concepts embodied in these database packages are very similar. The conceptual coverage that follows is generic and can be applied to all database packages; however, the examples are oriented to dBASE III PLUS, but for the most part, they are applicable to earlier versions (dBASE II and dBASE III). All are products of Ashton-Tate.

Menu-Driven versus Command-Driven Database Software.   You have the option of using dBASE III PLUS as a *menu-driven* or a *command-driven* software package. Or, you can elect to alternate between the two approaches, depending on which best suits your immediate operational needs. In the dBASE III PLUS tutorial that parallels this explanation (see Chapter 11, "Database Software Tutorials") and in this conceptual description of database software features, we use the command-driven approach. The dBASE III PLUS advanced features tutorial in Chapter 11 introduces "The Assistant," dBASE III PLUS's menu-driven option. If you learn one way, you can easily switch to the alternative.

The difference between the two approaches is implied in their names. When you opt for the menu-driven approach, you select options from a hierarchy of menus. With the command-driven approach, you key in a command that may be comprised of one or several parts. When working with the package as a command-driven system, you must be aware of the *command syntax*, or the way the commands are put together. See "Hands-On Tutorial 34: Using dBASE III PLUS" in Chapter 11, "Database Software Tutorials". All tutorials referenced in this chapter can be found in Chapter 11.

dBASE III PLUS can be a command-driven system or a menu-driven system. The photo illustrates the menu-driven user interface. The main menu is presented as a bar menu at the top of the screen. In the photo, the "Set Up" option of the main menu is highlighted causing a subordinate pull-down menu to be displayed.

10–3   DATA BASE ORGANIZATION

The organization of the data in a microcomputer data base is similar to the traditional hierarchy of data organization. Related **fields**, such as course identification number, course title, and course type, are grouped to form **records** (the course record in the COURSE data base in Figure 10–1). A collection of related records make up a data **file** or a **data base**. In database software terminology, file and data base are often used interchangeably.

The best way to illustrate and demonstrate the concepts of database software is by example. Edwina Cool, Zimco's education coordinator, uses a micro-based database software package to help her with her record-keeping tasks. To do this, Edwina creates two data bases. The

FIGURE 10–1
Database: COURSE Data Base and TRAINING Data Base
The COURSE data base contains a record for each course that Zimco offers to its employees. The TRAINING data base contains a record for each Zimco employee who is enrolled in or has taken a course.

Record#	ID	TITLE	TYPE	SOURCE	DURATION
1	100	MIS Orientation	in-house	Staff	24
2	201	Micro Overview	in-house	Staff	8
3	2535	Intro to Info. Proc.	media	Takdel Inc	40
4	310	Programming Stds.	in-house	Staff	6
5	3223	BASIC Programming	media	Takdel Inc	40
6	7771	Data Base Systems	media	Takdel Inc	30
7	CIS11	Business COBOL	college	St. Univ.	45
8	EX15	Local Area Networks	vendor	HAL Inc	30
9	MGT10	Mgt. Info. Systems	college	St. Univ.	45
10	VC10	Elec. Spreadsheet	media	VidCourse	20
11	VC44	4th Generation Lang.	media	VidCourse	30
12	VC88	Word Processing	media	VidCourse	18

COURSE data base

Record#	ID	EMPLOYEE	DEPARTMENT	START	STATUS
1	VC10	Bell, Jim	Marketing	01/12/87	I
2	VC10	Austin, Jill	Finance	01/12/87	I
3	VC10	Targa, Phil	Finance	01/12/87	C
4	VC88	Day, Elizabeth	Accounting	03/18/87	C
5	VC88	Fitz, Paula	Finance	04/04/87	I
6	MGT10	Mendez, Carlos	Accounting	01/15/87	I
7	EX15	Adler, Phyllis	Marketing	02/10/87	W
8	100	Targa, Phil	Finance	01/04/87	C
9	100	Johnson, Charles	Marketing	01/10/87	C
10	100	Klein, Ellen	Accounting	01/10/87	C

TRAINING data base

COURSE data base (see Figure 10–1) contains a record for each course that Zimco offers to their employees and for several courses at State University. Zimco provides tuition reimbursement for selected courses at the State University. Each record in the COURSE data base contains the following fields:

- Identification number (supplied by Zimco for in-house courses, by vendors, and by State University; provides cross-reference to the TRAINING data base)
- Title of course
- Type of course (in-house seminar, multimedia, college or vendor seminar)
- Source of course (Zimco staff or supplier of course)
- Duration (number of hours required to complete course)

Spreadsheet versions of Edwina's COURSE data base are presented in Chapter 7 (Figure 7–15) and Chapter 9 (Figure 9–1). Compare these presentations to the presentation in this chapter to contrast the spreadsheet and database approaches to data management.

The TRAINING data base (see Figure 10–1) contains a record for each Zimco employee who is enrolled in or has taken a course. Each record contains the following fields:

- Identification number (provides cross-reference to COURSE data base)
- Employee (name of Zimco employee)
- Department (department affiliation of employee)
- Start (date course was begun)
- Status (employee's status code: I=incomplete, W=withdrawn from course, C=completed course)

10–4   CREATING A DATA BASE

To create a data base, the first thing you do is to set up a *screen format* that will enable you to enter the data for a record. The data entry screen format is analogous to a hard-copy form that contains labels and blank lines, like a medical questionnaire or employment application. Data are entered and edited (deleted or revised) with database software one record at a time, just as they are on hard copy forms.

The Structure of the Data Base

To set up a data entry screen format you must first specify the *structure* of the data base by identifying the characteristics of each field in the data base. This is done interactively, with the system prompting you to enter the field name, field type, and other appropriate information (see Figure 10–2). For example, the ID field in Figure 10–2 is a five-character field. The *field name* is ID; the *field length* is five charac-

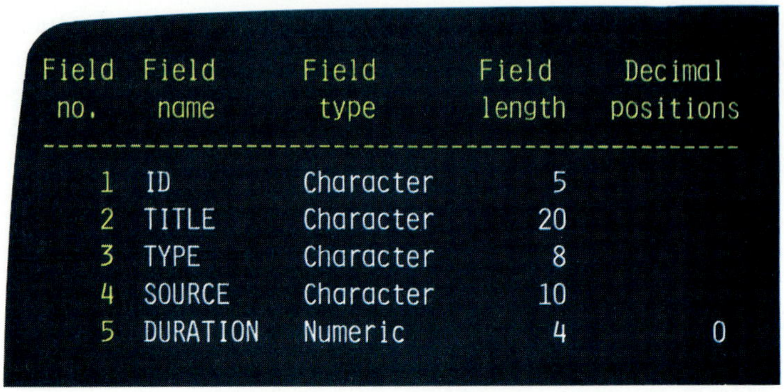

Field no.	Field name	Field type	Field length	Decimal positions
1	ID	Character	5	
2	TITLE	Character	20	
3	TYPE	Character	8	
4	SOURCE	Character	10	
5	DURATION	Numeric	4	0

FIGURE 10–2
Database: Structure of the COURSE Data Base

ters; and the *field type* is "character." The field names for the COURSE and TRAINING data bases are listed at the top of the displays in Figure 10–1 (ID, TITLE, TYPE, and so on). A *character* field type can be a single word or any alphanumeric (numbers, letters, and special characters) phrase up to several hundred characters in length. For *numeric* field types, you must specify the maximum number of digits (field length) and the number of decimal positions that you wish to have displayed. Since the course durations are all defined in whole hours, the number of decimal positions for the DURATION field is set at zero (see Figure 10–2). See "Hands-On Tutorial 35: Creating a Data Base."

Entering and Editing a Data Base

The screen format for entering, editing, and adding records to the COURSE data base is shown in Figure 10–3. This screen is generated automatically from the specifications outlined in the structure of the COURSE data base (see Figure 10–2). To create the COURSE data base, Edwina Cool issues a command that calls up the data entry screen of Figure 10–3. Then she enters the data for the first record, then the second record, and so on. On most database systems, the records are automatically assigned a number as they are entered. The

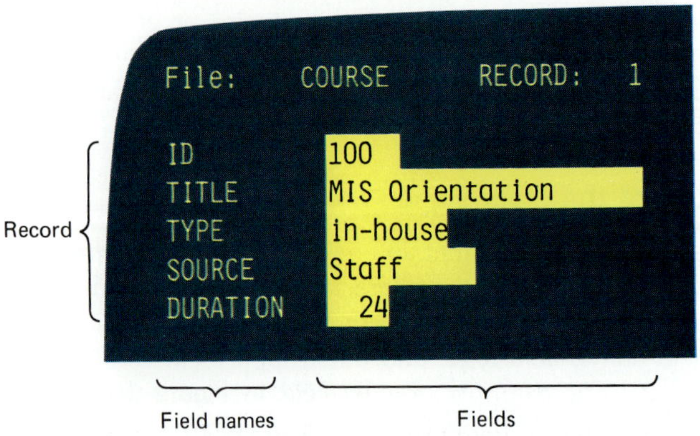

FIGURE 10–3
Database: Data Entry Screen Format
Illustrated is the screen format for entering, editing, and adding records to the COURSE data base. This screen is automatically generated from the specifications outlined in structure of the COURSE data base (see Figure 10–2).

reverse video portion of the screen in Figure 10–3 comprises the data for the five fields in record 1.

To add a record to an existing COURSE data base, Edwina issues a command like *append*. This command displays the format screen of Figure 10–3 (without data) so that she can enter the data for the new record(s). Each additional record is assigned a record number that is one higher than the current total. To edit a record, Edwina issues a command like *edit* in conjunction with the desired record number (for example, record 1) or a qualifier (ID='100'). The desired record would then appear superimposed over the format screen, as in Figure 10–3. Changes are made to fields in the format screen in much the same way that you would change text in a word processing document. See "Hands-On Tutorial 36: Adding Data Base Records," "Hands-On Tutorial 37: Modifying Records in a Data Base," and "Hands-On Tutorial 38: Create and Add Records to the TRAINING Data Base."

10–5 WORKING WITH A DATA BASE

Setting Conditions for Record Selection

Database software also permits you to retrieve, view, and print records based on preset conditions. You set conditions for the selection of records by composing a *relational expression* that reflects the desired conditions. The relational expression normally compares one or more field names to numbers or character strings using *relational operators* (see Figure 10–4). Several expressions can be combined in a single condition with *logical operators* (see Figure 10–4). Relational and logical operators are discussed in Chapter 7, "Electronic Spreadsheet Concepts."

Edwina Cool wants a listing of all in-house seminars; so she issues commands to *locate (search* for) and then *list* the records of all courses

Relational Operators	
COMPARISON	OPERATOR
Equal to	=
Less than	<
Greater than	>
Less than or equal to	< =
Greater than or equal to	> =
Not equal to	<>

Logical Operators AND and OR	
OPERATION	OPERATOR
For the condition to be true: Both sub-conditions must be true	AND
At least one subcondition must be true	OR

FIGURE 10–4
Relational and Logical Operators

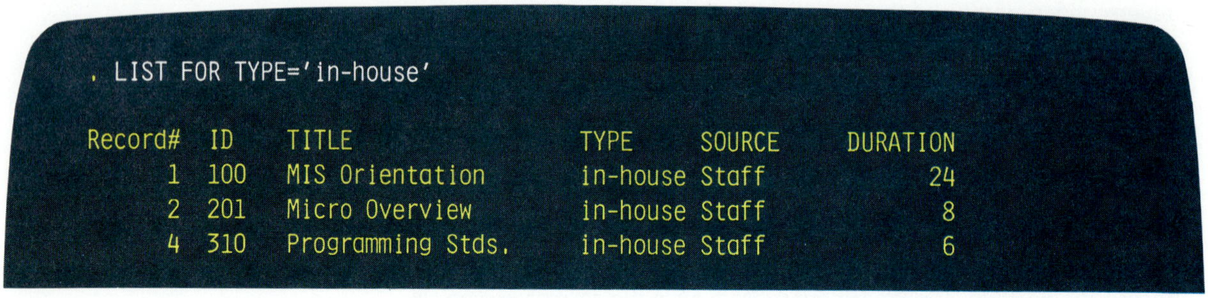

```
. LIST FOR TYPE='in-house'

Record#  ID    TITLE                  TYPE      SOURCE    DURATION
      1  100   MIS Orientation        in-house  Staff          24
      2  201   Micro Overview         in-house  Staff           8
      4  310   Programming Stds.      in-house  Staff           6
```

FIGURE 10–5
Database: Conditional Search and List
For the command, LIST FOR TYPE='in-house', only the records from the
COURSE data base (Figure 10–1) are displayed for which TYPE='in-
house'.

that are of TYPE in-house in the COURSE data base (see Figure
10–1). TYPE is the name of the field that holds type of course data.
To retrieve these records, she sets the condition to

TYPE='in-house'

Depending on the database package, the *search string* will be enclosed
in single or double quotes; here we use single quotes. To produce
the output of Figure 10–5, Edwina keys the command

LIST FOR TYPE='in-house'

Of course, you can route the output to either a display screen or a
printer. If Edwina wanted only the ID and TITLE for those records
that meet the condition TYPE='in-house', she would enter a command
like

LIST ID, TITLE FOR TYPE='in-house'

Figure 10–6 shows the output.

Data Base Inquiries

Filtering.   You can page through the data base by moving from record
to record. You can select and view a particular record by entering
the record number that is supplied by the software or by entering
certain selection conditions (for example, ID='EX15'). Database soft-

FIGURE 10–6
**Database: Conditional Search
and List, Specified Fields
Only**
For the command, LIST ID,
TITLE FOR TYPE='in-house',
only the ID and TITLE fields are
displayed for the records from
the COURSE data base (Figure
10–1) for which TYPE='in-
house'.

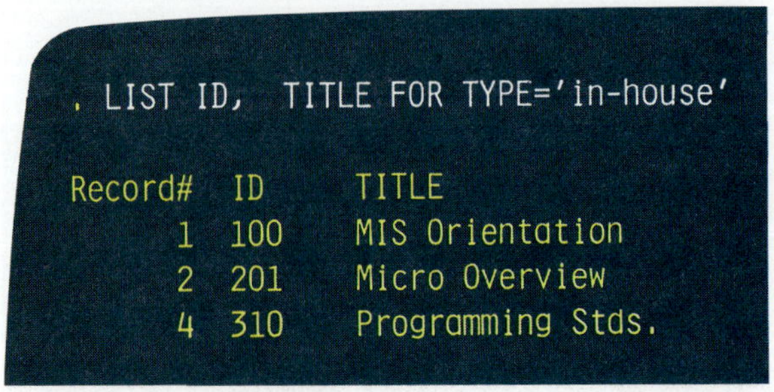

```
. LIST ID, TITLE FOR TYPE='in-house'

Record#  ID    TITLE
      1  100   MIS Orientation
      2  201   Micro Overview
      4  310   Programming Stds.
```

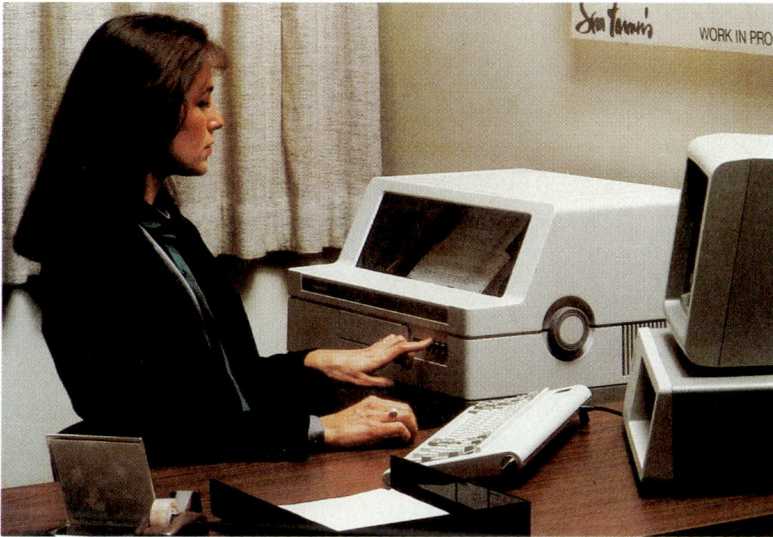

The results of a data base inquiry can be displayed on the screen or they can be printed.
(Dataproducts Corporation)

ware also permits inquiries that involve parts or all of one or more records. To extract and list selected records from a data base, you must first establish the condition or conditions. The process of selecting records by setting conditions is sometimes called **filtering**; that is, those records or fields that you do not want are filtered out of the display.

The following relational expressions establish conditions that will select or extract records (noted to the right of the expression) from the COURSE data base of Figure 10–1.

Expression	Records
TYPE='in-house' .AND. DURATION<=10	records 2 and 4 (see Figure 10–7)
SOURCE='VidCourse' .OR. SOURCE='Takdel Inc'	records 3, 5, 6, 10, 11, 12
DURATION>15 .AND. DURATION<25	records 1, 10, 12
ID='CIS11'	record 7

In the first example, the records selected from the COURSE data base must be of TYPE "in-house" *and* their DURATION must be less than or equal to (<=) 10 hours (see Figure 10–7). Only records 2 and 4 meet *both* conditions. In the second example, the entry in the SOURCE field must be *either* "VidCourse" *or* "Takdel Inc". Six records would be selected: records 3, 5, and 6 meet the "Takdel Inc" condition and records 10, 11, and 12 meet the "VidCourse" condition.

FIGURE 10–7
Database: Conditional Expression with AND Operator
For the command, TYPE='in-house' .AND. DURATION<=10, only the records from the COURSE data base (Figure 10–1) are displayed for which TYPE='in-house' *and* DURATION <= (less than or equal to) 10.

```
. LIST FOR TYPE='in-house' .AND. DURATION<=10
Record# ID    TITLE              TYPE      SOURCE      DURATION
    2 201    Micro Overview     in-house Staff              8
    4 310    Programming Stds.  in-house Staff              6
```

Inquiries Involving Calculations.   Besides filtering, you can also make inquiries to the data base that result in a display of calculated information. For example, Edwina Cool wants to know the total number of available seminar hours that are conducted by the her staff. To do this, she issues the following command for the COURSE data base:

SUM DURATION FOR SOURCE='Staff'

The result, 38 (24+8+6), is displayed on the screen. To obtain the average duration of all courses, Edwina issues this command:

AVERAGE DURATION

This command causes the average of all course durations (28) to be displayed on the screen. Similarly, Edwina issues the command to COUNT the number of "VidCourse" courses in the COURSE data base.

COUNT FOR SOURCE='VidCourse'

The result of 3 is displayed on the monitor. See "Hands-On Tutorial 39: Making Data Base Inquiries."

Sorting Records

The records in a data base can also be sorted for display in a variety of formats. For example, the COURSE data base in Figure 10–1 has been sorted and is displayed in ascending order by course identification number (ID). To obtain this sequencing of the data base records, Edwina Cool selects ID as the *key field* and requests an ascending sort of the COURSE data base. In some software packages, the *collating sequence* is set up so that numbers are considered to be less than alphabetic characters. Other software packages use a collating sequence that treats numbers as greater than alphabetic characters. In Figure 10–1, the numeric IDs are listed before those that begin with a letter.

Edwina also wants a presentation of the COURSE data base that is sorted by ID within SOURCE. This involves the selection of a *primary* and a *secondary key field*. Secondary key fields are helpful when duplicates exist in the primary key field (for example, there are three records for SOURCE='Staff'). Edwina selects SOURCE as the primary key field, but she wants the courses offered by each source to be listed in ascending order by ID. To achieve this record sequence, she selects ID as the secondary key field. A version of the COURSE data base that has been sorted by ID within SOURCE is shown Figure 10–8. Notice in Figure 10–8 that the SOURCE field entries are in alphabetical order and the three "Staff" records (records 4, 5, and 6) are in sequence by ID (100, 201, 310). If the need arises, Edwina can perform sorts that require the identification of primary, secondary, and tertiary key fields.

In most database packages, the issuing of a sort command results in the compilation of a another data base. The sorted version of the data base is stored on disk under another name. After the sort operation, the sorted version of the data base contains the records in the order

```
Record#  ID     TITLE                TYPE       SOURCE      DURATION
      1  EX15   Local Area Networks  vendor     HAL Inc         30
      2  CIS11  Business COBOL       college    St. Univ.       45
      3  MGT11  Mgt. Info. Systems   college    St. Univ.       45
      4  100    MIS Orientation      in-house   Staff           24
      5  201    Micro Overview       in-house   Staff            8
      6  310    Programming Stds.    in-house   Staff            6
      7  2535   Intro to Info. Proc. media      Takdel Inc      40
      8  3223   BASIC Programming    media      Takdel Inc      40
      9  7771   Data Base Systems    media      Takdel Inc      30
     10  VC10   Elec. Spreadsheet    media      VidCourse       20
     11  VC44   4th Generation Lang. media      VidCourse       30
     12  VC88   Word Processing      media      VidCourse       18
```

described in the sort command (see Figure 10–8). Edwina uses the sorted version of the COURSE data base of Figure 10–8 to produce the listing of Figure 10–9. To do this she issues the following command:

LIST SOURCE, ID FOR TYPE='vendor' .OR. TYPE='media'

Because the entries in the SOURCE field are alphabetized in Figure 10–8, the selected SOURCE entries in Figure 10–9 are also alphabetized. See "Hands-On Tutorial 40: Sorting a Data Base."

Quick and Dirty Reports

A data base is a source of information and database software provides the facility to get at this information. A *report* is the presentation of information that is derived from one or more data bases. The simple listings of selected records and fields in Figures 10–5 through 10–9 are "quick and dirty" reports. Such reports are the bread and butter of data base capabilities. These listings may not be fancy, but in most instances the user is more interested in the information than the format in which it is displayed. The generation of formatted reports is discussed in a later section.

FIGURE 10–8
Database: COURSE Data Base Sorted by ID within SOURCE
This display is the result of a sort operation on the COURSE data base with the SOURCE field as the primary key field and the ID field as the secondary key field.

```
. LIST SOURCE, ID FOR TYPE='vendor' .OR. TYPE='media'
Record#  SOURCE       ID
      1  HAL Inc      EX15
      7  Takdel Inc   2535
      8  Takdel Inc   3223
      9  Takdel Inc   7771
     10  VidCourse    VC10
     11  VidCourse    VC44
     12  VidCourse    VC88
```

FIGURE 10–9
Database: Conditional Expression with OR Operator
For the command, LIST SOURCE, ID FOR TYPE='vendor' .OR. TYPE='media', only the records from the COURSE data base (as sorted in Figure 10–8) are displayed for which TYPE='vendor' *or* TYPE='media'.

Micros can be linked together in networks such that they can share a data base. The micros at this management consulting firm are part of such a network. Computer networks are discussed in Chapter 13, "Communications Software Concepts and Tutorials." (Courtesy of Xerox Corporation)

10–6   COMBINING TWO DATA BASES

Edwina Cool wanted to produce a "quick and dirty" status report that contained an alphabetical listing of those employees who had completed courses (STATUS='C' on TRAINING data base of Figure 10–1) along with the IDs and TITLEs of the courses they had taken. She wanted a similar status report for those employees whose STATUS was incomplete (STATUS='I'). Producing these reports is a little more challenging because the data required are on *two different data bases*: the course ID, EMPLOYEE name, and STATUS fields are on the TRAINING data base, and the course ID and TITLE fields are on the COURSE data base. Since the two data bases have a common field (ID), Edwina can *join* the two data bases to get the report she wants.

The following command joins the TRAINING data base with the COURSE data base and generates the temporary data base (TEMP1) of Figure 10–10.

```
JOIN [TRAINING] WITH COURSE TO TEMP1 FOR COURSE->ID=ID
    FIELDS EMPLOYEE, ID, TITLE, STATUS
```

Since Edwina wants the employee names to be listed alphabetically, she had to sort the resultant data base (TEMP1) on the EMPLOYEE field and create another temporary data base called TEMP2 (see Figure 10–10). She then issued the following commands to get the reports she wanted:

```
LIST FOR STATUS='C'
LIST FOR STATUS='I'
```

The resultant reports are shown in Figure 10–11. See "Hands-On Tutorial 41: Combining Data Bases."

10–7   INDEXING FILES

Records in a data base are displayed in the sequence in which they are stored in the data base. There are two approaches that enable the display of records in alternative sequences.

■ Use the sort command and create a sorted version of the data base (see Section 5 in this chapter).

■ Create an **index file**. **Indexing** eliminates the need to create a sorted version of the original data base.

The procedures and mechanics of the way a particular record is accessed are, for the most part, transparent to users. However, it is a good idea to have a basic understanding of the way records are accessed so that you can appreciate one of the major the advantages of indexing—speed of processing. When you activate the TRAINING data base and enter the command,

```
LIST FOR EMPLOYEE='Targa, Phil'
```

the database program begins at the first record and compares the

TRAINING data base

Record#	ID	EMPLOYEE	DEPARTMENT	START	STATUS
1	VC10	Bell, Jim	Marketing	01/12/87	I
2	VC10	Austin, Jill	Finance	01/12/87	I
3	VC10	Targa, Phil	Finance	01/12/87	C
4	VC88	Day, Elizabeth	Accounting	03/18/87	C
5	VC88	Fitz, Paula	Finance	04/04/87	I
6	MGT10	Mendez, Carlos	Accounting	01/15/87	I
7	EX15	Adler, Phyllis	Marketing	02/10/87	W
8	100	Targa, Phil	Finance	01/04/87	C
9	100	Johnson, Charles	Marketing	01/10/87	C
10	100	Klein, Ellen	Accounting	01/10/87	C

+

COURSE data base

Record#	ID	TITLE	TYPE	SOURCE	DURATION
1	100	MIS Orientation	in-house	Staff	24
2	201	Micro Overview	in-house	Staff	8
3	2535	Intro to Info. Proc.	media	Takdel Inc	40
4	310	Programming Stds.	in-house	Staff	6
5	3223	BASIC Programming	media	Takdel Inc	40
6	7771	Data Base Systems	media	Takdel Inc	30
7	CIS11	Business COBOL	college	St. Univ.	45
8	EX15	Local Area Networks	vendor	HAL Inc	30
9	MGT10	Mgt. Info. Systems	college	St. Univ.	45
10	VC10	Elec. Spreadsheet	media	VidCourse	20
11	VC44	4th Generation Lang.	media	VidCourse	30
12	VC88	Word Processing	media	VidCourse	18

TEMP1 data base

Record#	EMPLOYEE	ID	TITLE	STATUS
1	Bell, Jim	VC10	Elec. Spreadsheet	I
2	Austin, Jill	VC10	Elec. Spreadsheet	I
3	Targa, Phil	VC10	Elec. Spreadsheet	C
4	Day, Elizabeth	VC88	Word Processing	C
5	Fitz, Paula	VC88	Word Processing	I
6	Mendez, Carlos	MGT10	Mgt. Info. Systems	I
7	Adler, Phyllis	EX15	Local Area Networks	W
8	Targa, Phil	100	MIS Orientation	C
9	Johnson, Charles	100	MIS Orientation	C
10	Klein, Ellen	100	MIS Orientation	C

TEMP2 data base

Record#	EMPLOYEE	ID	TITLE	STATUS
1	Adler, Phyllis	EX15	Local Area Networks	W
2	Austin, Jill	VC10	Elec. Spreadsheet	I
3	Bell, Jim	VC10	Elec. Spreadsheet	I
4	Day, Elizabeth	VC88	Word Processing	C
5	Fitz, Paula	VC88	Word Processing	I
6	Johnson, Charles	100	MIS Orientation	C
7	Klein, Ellen	100	MIS Orientation	C
8	Mendez, Carlos	MGT10	Mgt. Info. Systems	I
9	Targa, Phil	VC10	Elec. Spreadsheet	C
10	Targa, Phil	100	MIS Orientation	C

FIGURE 10–10
Database: Combining Two Data Bases
A common ID field enables the joining of the TRAINING data base with
the COURSE data base to produce the TEMP1 data base. TEMP1 is
sorted on the EMPLOYEE field to create TEMP2.

```
. LIST FOR STATUS='C'
Record#  EMPLOYEE              ID     TITLE              STATUS
      4  Day, Elizabeth        VC88   Word Processing    C
      6  Johnson, Charles      100    MIS Orientation    C
      7  Klein, Ellen          100    MIS Orientation    C
      9  Targa, Phil           VC10   Elec. Spreadsheet  C
     10  Targa, Phil           100    MIS Orientation    C

. LIST FOR STATUS='I'
Record#  EMPLOYEE              ID     TITLE              STATUS
      2  Austin, Jill          VC10   Elec. Spreadsheet  I
      3  Bell, Jim             VC10   Elec. Spreadsheet  I
      5  Fitz, Paula           VC88   Word Processing    I
      8  Mendez, Carlos        MGT10  Mgt. Info. Systems I
```

FIGURE 10–11
Database: Reports Made Possible by Combining Two Data Bases
For the command, LIST FOR STATUS='C', only the records from the TEMP2 data base (Figure 10–10) for which STATUS='C' (completed course) are displayed in the first list. For the command, LIST FOR STATUS='I', only those records for which STATUS='I' (incomplete) are displayed in the second list.

contents of the EMPLOYEE field to the character string, "Targa, Phil". If there is no match, the program checks the next record, and so on, until a match is found. The match is noted and the search continues to the end of the file. At the end of the search both "Targa, Phil" records (record numbers 3 and 8 in Figure 10–1) are displayed. For a large file this record-by-record comparison can be time consuming, even at computer speeds.

One way to speed up the search process is to create an index file and use two files.

1. *Data file.* The data file (or data base) contains the records (for example, for each employee, for each course, for each inventory item)

2. *Index file.* The smaller index file contains only the key and record number for each record on the data file. The record number is the record's numerical position within the the data file. The first record is record number 1.

A request for a particular record is first directed to the index file, which points, via the record number, *directly* to the memory location of the desired record. This data and index file approach to accessing a record is much faster than searching the entire data file.

One of the advantages to creating an index file is that you can *find* the record or records that contain a particular character string. For example, if Edwina wanted to display all TRAINING records for EMPLOYEE Phil Targa, she would activate both the data and index files (with EMPLOYEE being the designated key) and issue the following commands.

FIND Targa
LIST NEXT 10

The LIST NEXT would cause up to 10 "Targa, Phil" records to be displayed. Indexing is illustrated in the keystroke tutorials. See "Hands-On Tutorial 42: Indexing."

10–8   REPORT GENERATION

Database software provides the ability to create customized or formatted reports. This capability allows you to design the *layout* of the report. This means that you have some flexibility in spacing and can include titles, subtitles, column headings, separation lines, and other elements that make a report more readable. The user describes the layout of the *customized* report interactively, and then stores it for later recall. The result of the description, called a *report form*, is recalled from disk storage and merged with a data base to create the customized report. Managers often use this capability to generate periodic reports (for example, Weekly Training Status Report).

Once a month Edwina Cool generates four reports that summarize the courses being offered for each type of course; that is, one report summarizes Zimco's course offerings for TYPE='in-house', another, TYPE='media' (multimedia), and so on. One of these formatted reports is shown in Figure 10–12. This summary report of MULTIMEDIA COURSES was compiled by merging a predefined report format with the COURSE data base (as sorted in Figure 10–8). The layout of

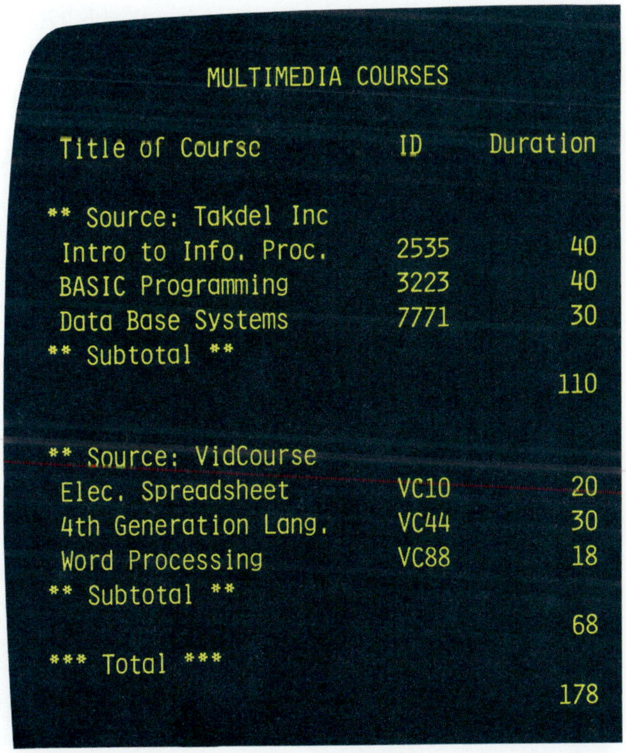

FIGURE 10–12
Database: Formatted Reports
This formatted report was compiled by merging a predefined report format with the COURSE data base as sorted in Figure 10–8.

the report form called for a title, column headings, subheadings (for each SOURCE of TYPE = 'media'), plus subtotals and a total for DURATION. The formatted report of Figure 10–12 is one of dozens that Edwina Cool generates on a weekly and monthly basis by using database software. See "Hands-On Tutorial 43: Retrieving and Saving a Database" and "Hands-On Tutorial 44: Printing a Report and Terminating a Session."

10–9 PROGRAMMING

Our discussions up to this point on database software have assumed that the user enters one instruction or selects one menu option at a time. Database software provides the capability to combine these instructions in the form of a *program*. A database software program, like any other computer program, is made up of a sequence of instructions that are executed one after another. These instructions are executed in sequence unless the order of execution is altered by a test-on-condition instruction or a branch instruction.

An Example Database Program

Typically, a program will accept *input* (from the keyboard or a file), access disk *storage*, accomplish some *processing* activity, and provide some kind of *output* (to a disk file, a printer, or the monitor). To illustrate database programming, we use an example program that

1. Allows the user to make an inquiry to the TRAINING database (*storage*) in Figure 10–1.
2. Allows the user to enter (*input*) the name of an employee (for example, "Targa, Phil").
3. Searches the file and identifies all records that involve the employee in question (*processing*).
4. Displays a "Training History Report" (*output*) that contains all records that apply to the employee in question.

A dBASE III PLUS program that accomplishes these tasks is shown in Figure 10–13. The comment instructions [those that begin with an asterisk (*)] embedded in the program of Figure 10–13 describe the purpose and function of the instructions that follow. An interactive session resulting from the execution of the program in Figure 10–13 is shown in Figure 10–14.

You could, of course, extract and display the information shown in Figure 10–14 by issuing a series of individual database software instructions. However, without a program, you would have to reenter the instructions each time you made a similar inquiry.

Problem Solving and Programming Logic

A single program addresses a particular problem: to compute and report sales commissions or to permit an update of a data base or to analyze

```
******   HISTORY.PRG  ******
*        This program allows the user to make an inquiry to the
*        TRAINING data base. The user enters an employee name to
*        generate an "EMPLOYEE TRAINING HISTORY" report for that
*        employee.
****** ****** ****** ******
*        Activate the TRAINING data base.
USE TRAINING
*        Clear the screen.
CLEAR
*        Position cursor at row 4, column 20 and display title.
@ 4, 20 SAY "EMPLOYEE TRAINING HISTORY"
*        Insert 2 blank lines.
?
?
*        Display an input prompt (inside quotes) with leading and
*        trailing spaces. "Accept" employee name into the variable NAME.
ACCEPT "          Enter employee's name (Last, First):  " TO NAME
CLEAR
*        Position cursor at row 4, column 8 and display heading.
@ 4, 8 SAY "Training History Report for:   " + NAME
*        Display the column headings for the report. A "?" at the
*        beginning of a line causes the output cursor to be
*        positioned at the beginning of the next line. The
*        character string within the quotes is displayed. When
*        nothing follows the "?", a blank line is inserted.
?
? "Department   Course ID   Status"
? "================================"
*        Supress dBASE III PLUS confirmation messages.
SET TALK OFF
*        Set the record pointer to the first record in the file.
GO TOP
*        In the following loop, the EMPLOYEE name for each record
*        in the data base is compared to the name entered to NAME.
*        If a match occurs, then the instructions between the IF
*        and IFEND are executed. DO the loop WHILE the record read
*        is NOT the EOF (end-of-file).
DO WHILE .NOT. EOF ()
 IF EMPLOYEE = NAME
*        The following instructions define the format of the output
*        displayed. A "?" at the beginning of a line causes the
*        output cursor to be positioned at the beginning of the next
*        line. The character string within the quotes and the
*        contents of the field indicated (e.g., EMPLOYEE) are
*        displayed. The "+" indicates that the character string
*        and the value of the field are to be cocatenated (joined
*        together).
   ?
   ? DEPARTMENT + "   " + ID + "         " + STATUS
 ENDIF
*        Advance the record pointer to the next record.
 SKIP
ENDDO
*        Display a legend for the status codes.
@ 18, 1 SAY "Status codes: C=complete; I=incomplete; W=withdrawn"
*        Restore the default display setting.
SET TALK ON
? "End of search"
```

FIGURE 10–13

Database: A dBASE III PLUS Program

When executed, this database program enables a user to make an inquiry
to the TRAINING data base (Figure 10–1).

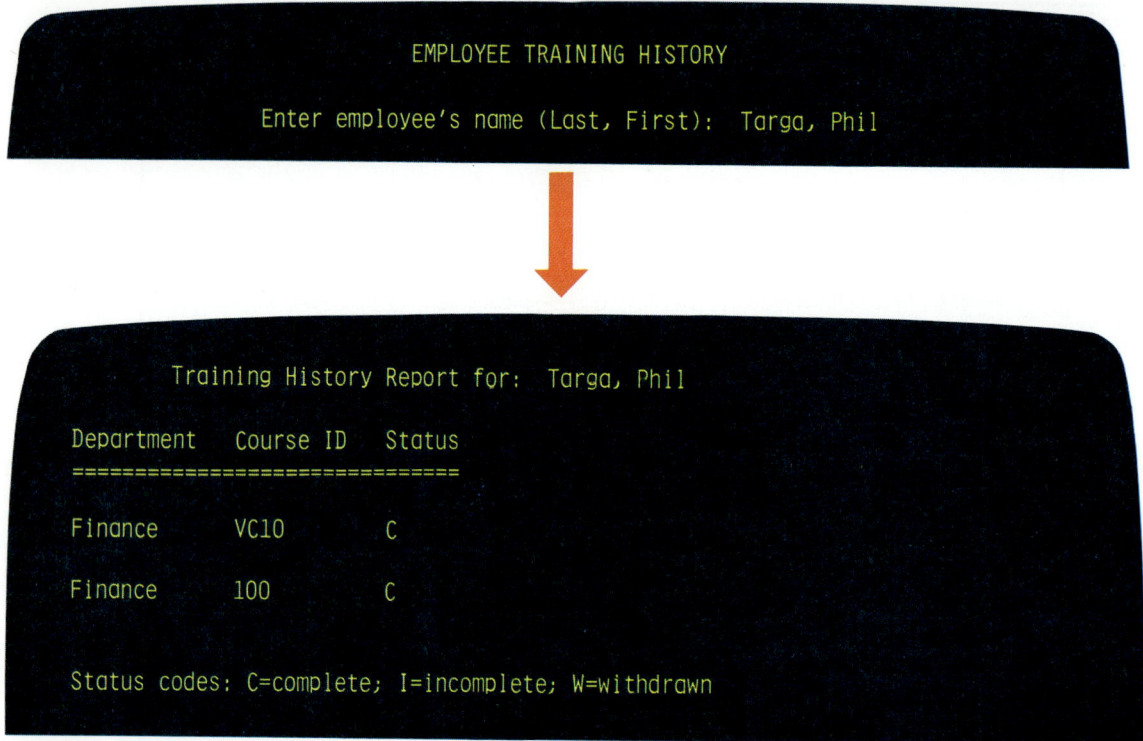

```
          EMPLOYEE TRAINING HISTORY

    Enter employee's name (Last, First):   Targa, Phil
```

```
        Training History Report for:  Targa, Phil

    Department   Course ID   Status
    ===============================

    Finance      VC10        C

    Finance      100         C

    Status codes: C=complete; I=incomplete; W=withdrawn
```

FIGURE 10–14
Database: Program Input/Output
These displays show the interactive session that results from the
execution of the program in Figure 10–13.

These engineers use database
software as a tool for collecting,
maintaining, and analyzing data
from experiments. They wrote a
database program to validate
that the data entered are within
acceptable ranges.
(Photo courtesy of Hewlett-Packard
Company)

marketing data. In effect, when you write a program, you are solving
a *problem*. To solve the problem you must derive a *solution*. And to
do that, you must use your powers of *logic*.

A program is like the materials used to construct a building. Much
of the brainwork involved in the construction of a building goes into
the blueprint. The location, appearance, and function of a building
are determined long before the first brick is laid. And so it is with
programming. The design of a program, or its programming logic (the
blueprint), is completed before the program is written.

Flowcharting.   A number of techniques are available to help programmers analyze a problem and design the program. One of the most
popular techniques is **flowcharting**, in which **flowcharts** are used
to illustrate data, information, and work flow through the interconnection of *specialized symbols* with *flow lines*. The combination of symbols
and flow lines portrays the logic of the program. The flowchart symbols
that are commonly used for database programming are shown in Figure
10–15.

Each symbol indicates the *type of operation to be performed*, and
the flowchart graphically illustrates the *sequence in which the operations*

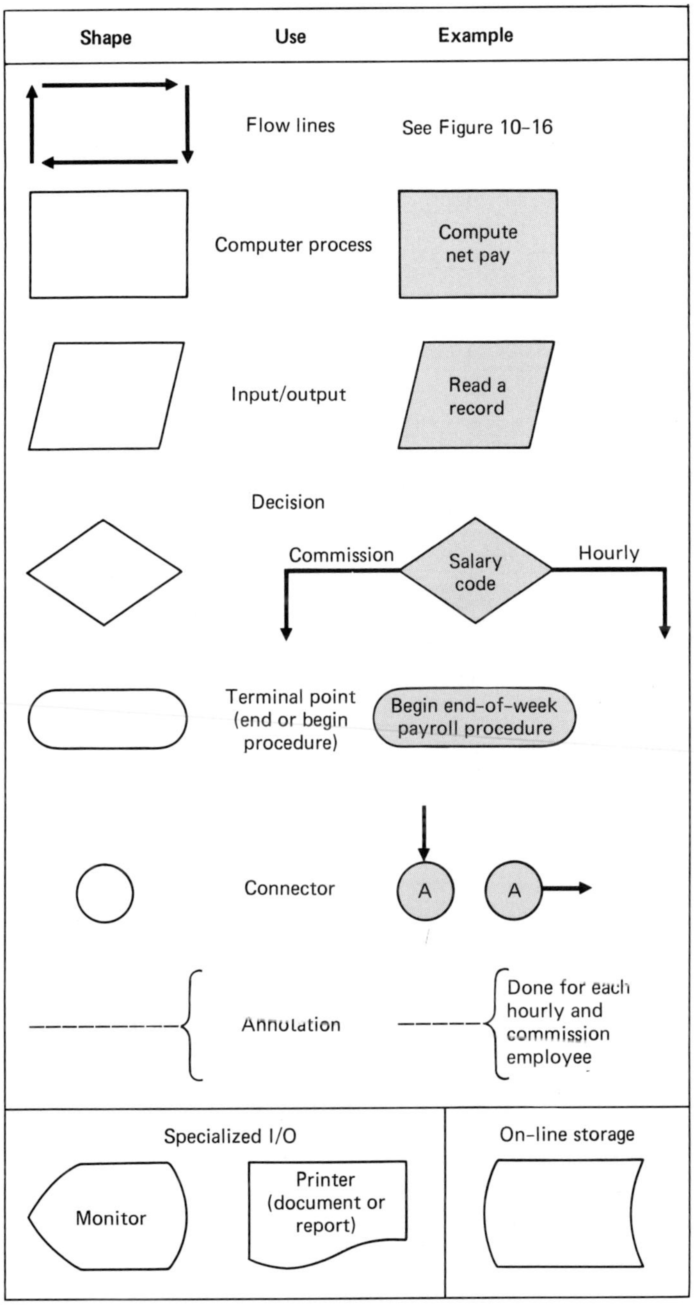

Shape	Use	Example
	Flow lines	See Figure 10–16
	Computer process	Compute net pay
	Input/output	Read a record
	Decision	Commission ← Salary code → Hourly
	Terminal point (end or begin procedure)	Begin end-of-week payroll procedure
	Connector	A A
	Annotation	Done for each hourly and commission employee

Specialized I/O	On-line storage
Monitor Printer (document or report)	

FIGURE 10–15
Flowchart Symbols

are to be performed. Flow lines ——→ depict the sequential flow of the program logic. A rectangle ☐ signifies some type of *computer process*. The parallelogram ▱ is a generalized *input/output* symbol that denotes any type of input to, or output from, the program. The diamond-shaped symbol ◇ marks the point at which a *decision* is to be made. In a program flowchart, a particular set of instructions is executed based on the outcome of a decision. For example, in the program of Figure 10–13, *several* decisions are made during the execution of the program. Each flowchart must begin and end with the oval *terminal point* symbol ⬭. A small circle ○ is a *connector* and is used to break and then link flow lines. The connector symbol is often used to avoid having

281

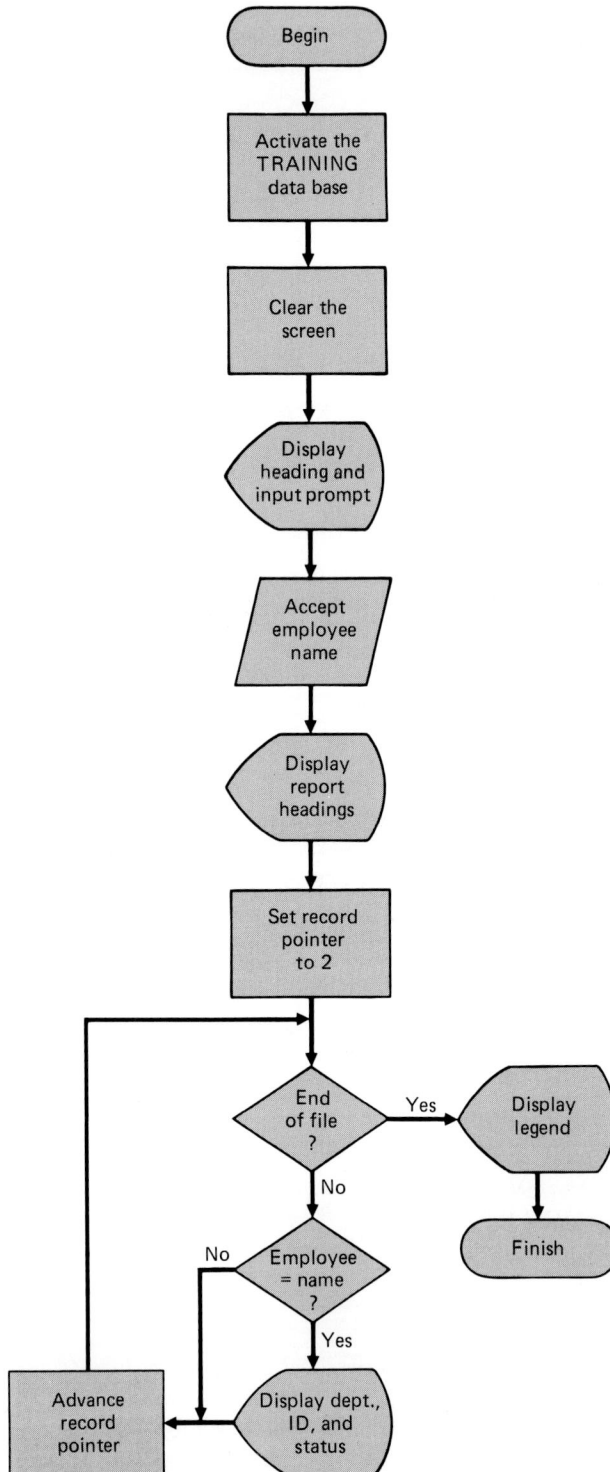

FIGURE 10–16
Program Flowchart
This flowchart graphically illustrates the logic of the dBASE III PLUS
program in Figure 10–13.

to cross lines. The bracket ---{ permits descriptive notations to be added to flowcharts. The *on-line storage* symbol ☐ represents a file or data base. The most common *specialized input/output* symbols are the *monitor* ◯ and the *printer* (hard copy) ▱ symbols.

The program flowchart of Figure 10–16 portrays the logic for the program of Figure 10–13.

Variables and Programming Control Structures. In a program, a location in memory is represented by a **variable name** (NAME, EMPLOYEE, ID). A variable name in a program instruction refers to the *contents* of a particular storage location. In the example program of Figure 10–13, the employee's name was entered in the a memory location referred to by the variable name, NAME. The contents of NAME was compared to the contents of the variable assigned to the employee name field, EMPLOYEE.

Computer scientists have identified three basic *control structures* into which any programs can be segmented. The logic of a program can be conceptualized in these three structures—*sequence*, *selection*, and *loop*. These three control structures are illustrated in Figures 10–17, 10–18, and 10–19, respectively, and their use is demonstrated in the example of Figure 10–16.

FIGURE 10–17
Sequence Control Structure

FIGURE 10–19
Loop Control Structures
The two types of loop structures are DOWHILE and DOUNTIL.

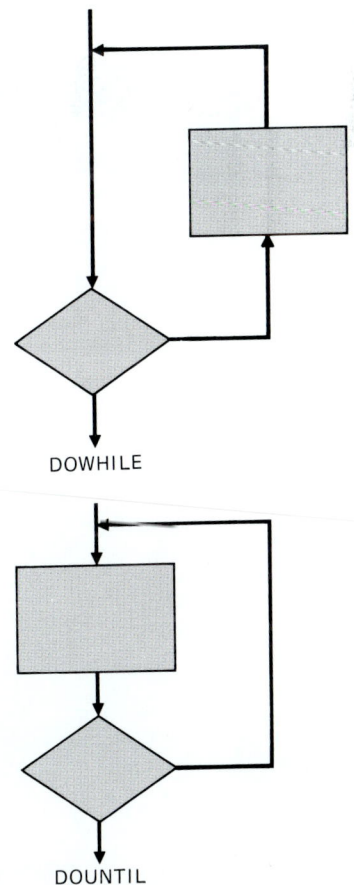

FIGURE 10–18
Selection Control Structures
Any number of options can result from a decision in a selection control structure.

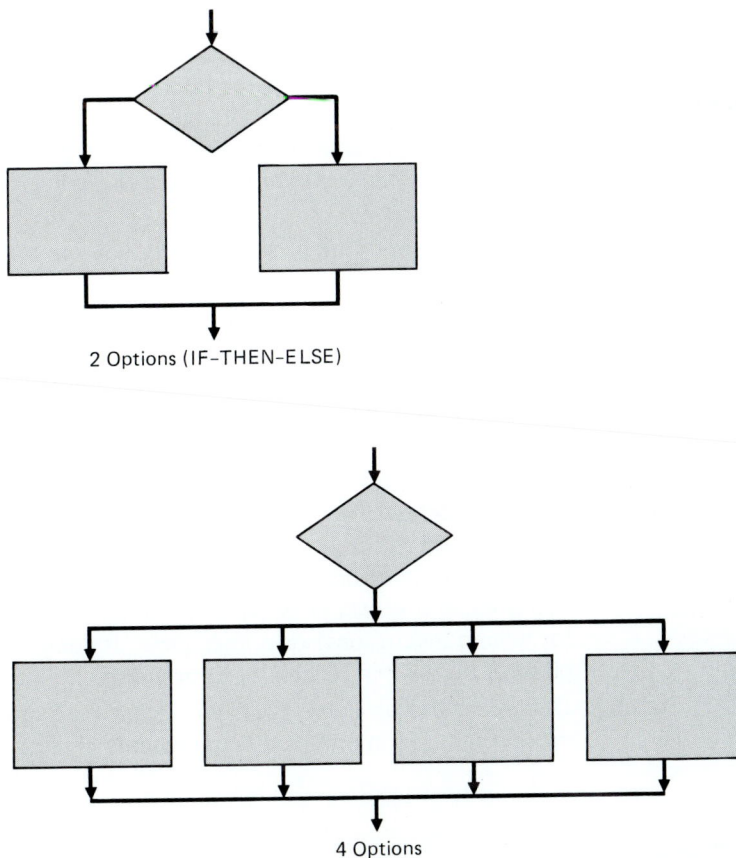

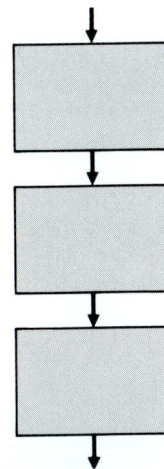

2 Options (IF–THEN–ELSE)

4 Options

DOWHILE

DOUNTIL

In the sequence structure (Figure 10–17), the processing steps are performed in sequence. The selection structure (Figure 10–18) depicts the logic for selecting the appropriate sequence of statements. In Figure 10–16, which depicts the flowchart of our example program, the selection structure is used to illustrate the logic for determining whether or not the information in a particular record is to be displayed. Only those records for which EMPLOYEE equals NAME are selected and displayed in the report.

The loop structure (Figure 10–19) is used to represent the program logic when a portion of the program is to be executed repeatedly until a particular condition is met (such as end of file). When the decision, or *test-on-condition*, is placed at the beginning of the statement sequence, it becomes a *DOWHILE loop*; when placed at the end, it becomes a *DOUNTIL loop*. In the example program of Figure 10–16, the instructions in the loop between the DO WHILE and ENDDO instructions are executed repeatedly while the record that is read is not the end-of-file (EOF) record. See "Hands-On Tutorial 45: Programming Database Software."

Writing Programs

Each program is a project. The following steps are followed for each programming project.

Step 1.   *Describe the problem.* Describing the problem involves identifying exactly what needs to be done.

Step 2.   *Analyze the problem.* Break the problem into its basic components for analysis. Remember: "Divide and conquer." Although different programs have different components, a good place to start with most programs is to analyze the *output, input, processing,* and *file-interaction* components.

Step 3.   *Design the logic of the program.* Next, you have to put the pieces together in the form of a logical program design (for example, a flowchart).

Step 4.   *Code the program.* The design of the program is translated into instructions, or a program. If the logic is sound and the design documentation (narrative description, logic diagram, and so on) is thorough, the coding process is relatively straightforward.

Step 5.   *Test and debug the program.* Once the program has been entered into the system, it is likely that you will encounter at least one of those cantankerous **bugs**. A bug is either a *syntax error* (violation of one of the rules for writing instructions) or a *logic error*. Ridding a program of bugs is the process of **debugging**.

Step 6.   *Document the program.* Over the life of the program, procedures and information requirements change. Updating programs to reflect these changes is much easier with good documentation (narrative description, logic diagram, embedded comments, and so on).

10–10   HIGH-LEVEL DATABASE TOOLS_____

Application Generators

Some database software packages have an **application generator** feature. This feature helps users to develop **information systems—** without having to write programs! An information system is a computer-based system that provides data processing capability and information for making decisions.

Application generators enable users to specify, through an interactive dialogue with the system, what information processing tasks are to be performed. This is essentially a fill-in-the-blank process. After users enter their specifications, the actual instructions are generated automatically. In the creation of an information system, the user describes the data base and then specifies screen layouts for file creation and maintenance, data entry, management reports, and menus. The program modules that perform these task are created, pulled together, and integrated automatically to complete the system.

Application generators are currently in the infant stage of development. Existing application generators do not have the flexibility of database programs; therefore, the code of application generators must occasionally be supplemented with *custom code* to handle unique situations.

The application generator and programming features of database software have made straightforward systems easy to develop. In fact, these tools are often used to develop ad hoc systems that may be used only once or twice. With database software these *throwaway systems* are well within the realm of economic feasibility.

Natural Languages

The next step in the sophistication of database software is the use of **natural language** interfaces. The premise behind a natural language is that the programmer or user needs little or no training. He or she simply writes specifications without regard for instruction format or syntax. To date, there is no such language. Although the creation of such a language is difficult to comprehend, it is probably inevitable.

In the meantime, natural languages with certain syntax restrictions are available with some database software packages. And for limited information processing tasks, such as ad hoc inquiries and report generation for a specific application area, existing natural languages work quite well. With certain limitations, existing natural languages permit users to express *queries* (inquiries to the database) in normal, everyday English. You can phrase a query any way you want. For example, you could say, "Let me see the average salaries by job category in the marketing department." Or you would get the same results if you said, "What is the average salary in the marketing department for each job classification?" If your query is unclear, the natural-language software might ask you questions that will clarify any ambiguities. Other typical natural-language queries might be

- Are there any managers between the ages of 30 and 40 in the northwest region with MBA degrees?
- Show me a pie graph that compares voter registrations for Alabama, Georgia, North Carolina, South Carolina, and Florida.
- What are the top 10 best-selling fiction books in California?

10–11   DATABASE SOFTWARE IN PRACTICE

Data management software earns the productivity tool label by providing users with the capability to organize data into an electronic data base that can be easily maintained and queried. The examples illustrated and discussed in the concepts section merely scratch the surface of the potential of database software. With relative ease, you can generate some rather sophisticated inquiries, reports, data bases, and even information systems.

Database software is designed to provide the user with maximum flexibility. For example, with database software it is easy to change the structure of a data base. If Edwina Cool wanted to add an END field (date course was completed) to the structure of the TRAINING data base in Figure 10–1, she could do so without having to recreate the data base.

Many of the capabilities of electronic spreadsheet software are embodied in database software and vice versa. For example, you can also make "what if" inquiries with database software. Edwina Cool might ask, "What if we discontinued the VidCourse contract, how many courses would we have left to offer?" You might observe that this and some other queries illustrated in this section might best be answered by simply examining a hard copy of the 10- and 12-record data bases. But what if Edwina Cool had 120 different courses in her COURSE data base and 1,500 employees in her TRAINING data base? These numbers are much more realistic for a company the size of Zimco, but procedures for making the inquiries to a data base with 1,500 records are no more difficult than making inquiries to a data base with 10 records.

Students use database software to keep records relating to a wide range of activities: expenses (item, amount, date), friends (name, address, phone), intramural scores (opponent, score, date), courses (title, instructor, credit hours, term, grade), and so on.
(Courtesy of International Business Machines Corporation)

SUMMARY OUTLINE AND IMPORTANT TERMS

10–1   THE FUNCTION OF DATABASE SOFTWARE.   With database software, you can create and maintain a data base and extract information from the data base. All database software packages have the basic fundamental capabilities that allow you to create and maintain a data base, extract and list selected records, make inquiries to the data base, sort records, and generate formatted reports.

The more sophisticated database packages include a variety of other features, such as spreadsheet-type computations, graphics, programming, and applications generators.

10–2   THE DESIGN OF DATABASE SOFTWARE.   All commercial database software packages permit the creation and manipulation of data bases, but what the user sees on the screen may be vastly different for the various packages. However, the concepts embodied in these database packages are very similar. Some database software packages give the user the option of working with it as a menu-driven software package or as a command-driven software package.

10–3   DATA BASE ORGANIZATION.   The organization of the data in a microcomputer data base is similar to the traditional hierarchy of data organization. Related **fields** are grouped to form **records**. A collection of related records make up a data **file** or a **data base**. In database software terminology, file and data base are often used interchangeably.

10–4   CREATING A DATA BASE.   To create a data base, specify the structure of the data base. To do this, enter the field name, field type, field length, and other appropriate information for each field in a record. A character field type can be a single word or an alphanumeric phrase. Defining a numeric field type involves specifying the field length and the number of decimal positions to be displayed.

The data entry screen is generated automatically from the specifications outlined in the structure of the data base. To add a record to a data base, issue an append command. To edit a record, issue an edit command.

10–5   WORKING WITH A DATA BASE.   Database software permits the retrieval, viewing, and printing of records based on preset conditions. Set conditions for the selection of records by composing a relational expression that reflects the desired conditions. The relational expression normally compares one or more field names to numbers or character strings using relational operators. Several expressions can be combined in a single condition with logical operators.

You can page through the data base by moving from record to record. You can select and view a particular record by entering the record number that is supplied by the software or by entering certain selection conditions. The process of selecting records by setting conditions is sometimes called **filtering**. Besides filtering, you can also make inquiries to the data base that result in a display of calculated information.

Records in a data base can be sorted for display in a variety of formats. To sort the records in a data base, select a primary key and, if needed, secondary and tertiary key fields. In most database packages, issuing a sort command results in the compilation of a another data base.

"Quick and dirty" reports are easy-to-produce listings of data base information.

10–6 COMBINING TWO DATA BASES.   Two different data bases can be combined to provide the user with greater flexibility in obtaining information. The data bases are linked through a common key field.

10–7 INDEXING FILES.   One way to speed up the data base search process is to use two files, an **index file** and a data file. The smaller index file contains only the key and record number for each record on the data file. A request for a particular record is first directed to the index file, which points, via the record number, to the memory location of the desired record.

10–8 REPORT GENERATION.   Database software provides the capability to create customized or formatted reports. The user describes the layout of the customized report interactively, then stores it for later recall.

10–9 PROGRAMMING.   Database software provides the capability to combine the database instructions in the form of a program. A database software program is made up of a sequence of instructions that are executed one after another.

Typically, a program will accept input, access disk storage, accomplish some processing activity, and provide some kind of output. In a program, a location in memory is represented by a **variable name**.

A number of techniques are available to help programmers analyze a problem and design the program. One of the most popular techniques is **flowcharting**. In flowcharting, **flowcharts** are used to illustrate data, information, and work flow through the interconnection of specialized symbols with flow lines. The combination of symbols and flow lines portrays the logic of the program.

Computer scientists have identified three basic control structures: sequence, selection, and loop.

These six steps define the programming process: describe the problem; analyze the problem; design the logic of the program; code the program; test and debug the program; and document the program.

10–10 HIGH-LEVEL DATABASE TOOLS.   Some database software packages have an **application generator** feature that helps users to develop **information systems**. The next step in the sophistication of database software is the use of **natural language** interfaces. Natural languages with certain syntax restrictions are available with some database software packages. Within these limitations, existing natural languages permit users to express queries in normal, everyday English.

10–11   DATABASE SOFTWARE IN PRACTICE.   Data management software earns the productivity tool label by providing users with the ability to organize data into an electronic data base that can be easily maintained and queried. With relative ease, a user can generate sophisticated inquiries, reports, data bases, and even information systems.

REVIEW EXERCISES

1. Describe the capabilities of database software.
2. What characteristics describe a field in a data base record?
3. What is the purpose of setting conditions for a data base?
4. In data base terminology, what is meant by filtering?
5. Describe two types of inquiries to a data base that involve calculations.
6. What is the relationship between a field, a record, and the structure of a data base?
7. Give examples and descriptions of at least three other fields that might be added to the record for the COURSE data base of Figure 10–1.
8. Give examples and descriptions of at least three other fields that might be added to the record for the TRAINING data base of Figure 10–1.
9. What would be the employee name for the third record if the TRAINING data base of Figure 10–1 was sorted so that the primary and secondary key fields were DEPARTMENT and EMPLOYEE, respectively?
10. What is contained in each record in an index file?
11. Under what circumstances would the order of execution of the instructions in a database program be altered?
12. What is a natural language interface to a database software program?
13. Draw the flowchart symbols for computer process, terminal point, and decision.
14. What is the purpose of a test-on-condition instruction in a database program?
15. What is involved in Step 2 of the programming process, analyze the problem?
16. What dBASE III PLUS instruction could be applied to the COURSE data base of Figure 10–1 to count the number of in-house courses offered at ZIMCO?
17. What instruction designates the end of a DOWHILE loop in a dBASE III PLUS program?

SELF-TEST (by section)

10–1. Another name for database software is data management software. (T/F)

10–2. Commercial database packages are like commercial electronic spreadsheet packages in that the display of the work area is similar for all packages. (T/F)

10–3. In a data base, related _____ are grouped to form records.

10–4. The definition of the structure of a data base would not include which of the following: (a) field names, (b) selection criteria for fields, (c) field lengths?

10–5. **(a)**   The relational operator for greater than or equal to would be _____.

      (b)   What record(s) would be selected from the COURSE data base of Figure 10–1 for the criteria SOURCE="HAL Inc" and DURATION>40?

      (c)   If the COURSE data base of Figure 10–1 is sorted by TITLE within TYPE, the ID of the third record would be _____.

10–6. To combine two data bases, they must have a common (a) character string, (b) field, or (c) record.

10–7. Generally speaking, the record of an index file will have fewer fields that its accompanying data file. (T/F)

10–8. The layout of a report provides details that describe the structure of a particular data base. (T/F)

10–9. **(a)**   The dBASE III PLUS programming instruction for clearing the screen is _____.

      (b)   The flowcharting symbol that denotes generalized input/output is shaped like (a) a parallelogram, (b) a diamond, or (c) an oval.

10–10. The application generator feature of database software helps users to develop information systems. (T/F)

10–11. Database software has some of the capabilities of electronic spreadsheet software and vice versa. (T/F)

Self-Test Answers.   **10–1,** T; **10–2,** F; **10–3,** fields; **10–4,** b; **10–5 (a),** >=; **(b),** none would be selected; **(c),** 201; **10–6,** b; **10–7,** T; **10–8,** F; **10–9 (a),** CLEAR; **(b),** a; **10–10,** T; **10–11,** T.

HANDS-ON EXERCISES

1. Complete Hands-On Tutorials 34 through 45 in Chapter 11, "Database Software Tutorials."

2. **(a)**   Design a data entry screen to accept the following sales data for Diolab, Inc., a manufacturer of a diagnostic laboratory instrument that is sold primarily to hospitals and clinics.

Diolab Inc. Sales (units)

Region	Qtr1	Qtr2	Qtr3	Qtr4
NE Region	241	300	320	170
SE Region	120	150	165	201
SW Region	64	80	60	52

Each of the remaining parts of this hands-on exercise is a follow-on to the previous part.

(b) Enter the Diolab data above into a data base.

(c) Revise the NE Region first-quarter sales to be 214.

(d) Add the following NW Region record to the data base.

Region	Qtr1	Qtr2	Qtr3	Qtr4
NW Region	116	141	147	180

(e) Obtain a printout of the data base and store the data on a disk file named DIOLAB.

(f) Select and list all Diolab regions (records) that sold more than 150 units in the fourth quarter (all but the SW Region)?

(g) Select and list all Diolab regions (records) that sold more than 150 units in the fourth quarter *and* for which fourth-quarter sales are greater than third-quarter sales (SE and NW Regions)?

(h) Select and list only the REGION and QTR4 fields of those Diolab regions for which the average sales for the first three quarters is less than the sales for the fourth quarter (SE and NW Regions)?

(i) Make an inquiry to the Diolab data base that results in a display of the average unit sales for each quarter (QTR1=128).

(j) Make an inquiry to the Diolab data base that results in a display of the total unit sales for each quarter (QTR1=514).

(k) Sort the Diolab data base in ascending order by QTR1 sales. Print out the sorted data base.

(l) Sort the Diolab data base in descending order by QTR4 sales. Print out the sorted data base.

(m) Generate and print a formatted report from the sorted DIOLAB data base that is entitled DIOLAB INC. SALES (UNITS) and has the following column headings: Sales Region, 1st Qtr, 2nd Qtr, 3rd Qtr, and 4th Qtr. The report should include the total sales for each quarter.

3. (a) Create a database to keep track of an individual's library of recordings: compact discs (CDs), long-playing (LP) records, and audio tapes. The database should have the following fields defined:
    1) FORMAT (CD, LP record, or tape)
    2) ARTIST
    3) TITLE
    4) [Playing] TIME
    5) [Number of] SONGS

(b) Enter the following data into the audio database.

Format	Artist	Title	Time	Songs
CD	Depeche Mode	Some Great Reward	38.59	13
CD	The Cure	The Cure?	32.32	10
RECORD	London Symphony	Mozart: Requiem	61.25	1
TAPE	Pet Shop Boys	Please	32.15	10
CD	Depeche Mode	Black Celebration	41.19	12
RECORD	Depeche Mode	People Are People	32.37	11
TAPE	O.M.D.	The Pacific Age	43.00	12
CD	The Cure	Standing on the Beach	52.18	15
RECORD	The Ramones	End of the Century	36.28	16

(c) Use the audio database and appropriate criteria to generate and print reports that contain
    1) The entire data base sorted alphabetically by title
    2) All LP records and tapes sorted by playing time
    3) All CDs that were recorded by Depeche Mode
    4) All LP records and tapes with playing times in excess of 40 minutes

(d) Make the following inquiries to the audio data base.
    1) The total number of songs on CD
    2) The average playing time for all recordings

(e) Produce and print a formatted report that contains all entries in the data base, is sorted alphabetically by artist, and has subtotals for playing time for each artist. The report should look something like this:

Artist	Title	Playing Time	Total For Artist
Depeche Mode	Some Great Reward	38.59	
Depeche Mode	Black Celebration	41.19	
Depeche Mode	People Are People	32.37	
			112.15
O.M.D.	The Pacific Age	43.00	
			43.00
Pet Shop Boys	Please	32.15	
			32.15

The Cure	The Cure?	32.32	
The Cure	Standing on the Beach	52.18	
			84.50
The Ramones	End of the Century	36.28	
			36.28
London Symphony	Mozart: Requiem	61.25	
			61.25

4. (a) Write an interactive database program that permits a manager to request a quarterly sales summary for any of the four regions of Diolab, Inc. (use the Diolab data base from Hands-On Exercise 2). A sample interactive session is illustrated below.

Enter sales region to be summarized: **NW REGION**

NW REGION SALES SUMMARY

First quarter:	116
Second quarter:	141
Third quarter:	147
Fourth quarter:	180

| Total for year: | 584 |

(b) Activate the DOS printer echo feature and execute the program. Request a sales summary for the SE Region. Deactivate the printer echo.

(c) Document the database program with internal comments. Print out the program.

KEYSTROKE TUTORIALS IN THE *LAB MANUAL*

The *Lab Manual* that accompanies this text contains keystroke tutorials for

■ dBASE III PLUS (© Ashton-Tate, Inc.)
■ Reflex: The Database Manager (© Borland/Analytica)
■ PFS: Professional File (© Software Publishing Corporation)

These keystroke tutorials illustrate the use of a particular data management software package in a domestic and a business application. The more advanced features of the packages are introduced in the business application tutorials.

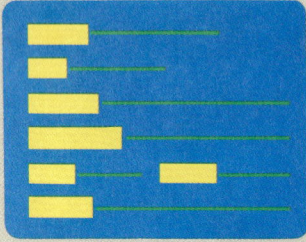

CHAPTER 11

Database Software Tutorials

STUDENT LEARNING OBJECTIVES

- To become familiar with the use and application of database software for one or more of the following packages:
  - dBASE III PLUS
  - Reflex: The Database Manager
  - PFS:Professional File
- To acquire the ability to apply the database software skills demonstrated in the hands-on tutorials.

HANDS-ON TUTORIALS for *dBASE III PLUS, Reflex: The Database Manager, and PFS:Professional File*

DATA MANAGEMENT TUTORIAL: DBASE III PLUS

COMMANDS

Press F1 for on-line help with syntax and description of commands.

Starter Set

?	DELETE FILE	LABEL	REPORT
APPEND	DIR	LIST	SCREEN
AVERAGE	DISPLAY	LOCATE	SEEK
BROWSE	DO	MODIFY	SET
CHANGE	EDIT	PACK	SKIP
CLEAR	ERASE	QUERY	SORT
CONTINUE	EXPORT	QUIT	STORE
COPY	FIND	RECALL	SUM
COUNT	GO/GOTO	RELEASE	TOTAL
CREATE	IMPORT	RENAME	TYPE
DELETE	INDEX	REPLACE	USE

Advanced Set

@			
ACCEPT	IF	ON	RETURN
CANCEL	INPUT	PARAMETERS	RUN/!
CALL	INSERT	PRIVATE	SAVE
CLOSE	JOIN	PROCEDURE	SELECT
COPY FILE	LOAD	PUBLIC	SUSPEND
DISPLAY CMDS	LIST CMDS	READ	TEXT
DO CASE	LOOP	REINDEX	UPDATE
DO WHILE	MACRO/&	RESTORE	VIEW
EJECT	MODIFY CMDS	RESUME	WAIT
EXIT	NOTE/*	RETRY	ZAP

FUNCTION KEYS

Help	F1	F2	Assit
List	F3	F4	Dir
Display structure	F5	F6	Display status
Display memory	F7	F8	Display
Append	F9	F10	Edit

OTHER

ESC — Exit "Assist" mode at dot prompt

↑ ↓ — At dot prompt, permits scrolling between previously issued commands

HANDS-ON TUTORIAL 34: Using dBASE III PLUS

dBASE III PLUS, a product of Ashton-Tate, is a relational database management system that enables users to create, maintain, and manipulate a data base. It also provides users with the flexibility to make inquiries and generate reports. User commands can be combined in files and run like a program to create unique data management applications. Educational version 1.0 is used to create this data management tutorial.

- Boot the system (see Hands-On Tutorial 1).
- Load dBASE III PLUS to memory. Insert the dBASE III PLUS program disk 1 in drive A.

    A>**dbase** ↵

- Wait for the message and then replace the dBASE III PLUS program disk 1 in drive A with program disk 2.
- Insert your data disk in drive B.

    ↵

The default user interface is dBASE III PLUS's Assistant mode, or menu-driven interaction with the system. The initial work screen displays the main menu in a bar menu at the top of the screen and a pull-down menu for the "Set Up" option of the main menu. However, we are going to use the command-driven user interface in this tutorial. To switch from "Assistant" mode to command mode, press ESC. The dBASE III PLUS dot prompt (a period) should appear at the bottom of the screen.

HANDS-ON TUTORIAL 35: Creating a Data Base

To create the COURSE data base of Figure 10–1, you need to define its structure.

- Create the data base structure (see Figure 10–2).

    . **CREATE COURSE** ↵

Study the input and editing keystroke options at the top of the screen, the record definition work area, and the status/user-instruction interface at the bottom of the screen.

- In the field definition work area for field number 1, define the ID field. Enter the Field Name. Use the backspace or delete keys to correct data entry errors.

    ID ↵

The five types of fields are "character" (the default), "numeric," "date," "logical," and "memo." To select a field type, press the first character of the desired field type or press the SPACE bar to toggle through the options.

    C

Define the width of the field, sometimes

|ESC|

At this point you are ready to begin your dBASE III PLUS session. If you wish to return to Assistant mode, enter the command "ASSIST" at the dot prompt. Several function key commands will prove helpful as you work through the following dBASE III PLUS tutorials.

|F1|	dBASE III PLUS's context-sensitive Help key.
|F2|	Changes from command to Assistant mode.
|F3|	Displays contents of active database file.
|F4|	Displays the database files from a specified directory.
|F5|	Displays the structure (data elements) of current database file.
|F9|	Permits the addition of records to the current database file.
|F10|	Permits editing of records in the current database file.

dBASE III PLUS uses the term database file to refer to the actual data base and uses database structure to refer to the definition of the structure of the data base (data elements and their characteristics).

called the field length, in character positions.

    5 ↵

The cursor is automatically positioned for the next field definition because fields of type "character" do not require a "Dec" or decimal positions definition.

- Define the other three character fields in the COURSE data base.

    TITLE ↵ **C 20** ↵
    TYPE ↵ **C 8** ↵
    SOURCE ↵ **C 10** ↵

- The fifth field is of type "numeric." Set "Dec," or the number of spaces to the right of the decimal, to zero.

    DURATION ↵ **N 4** ↵ **0** ↵

- Press ENTER with the cursor at the "Field Name" prompt to signify the end of the record definition for the COURSE database file. Press ENTER again to confirm that the definition is correct.

    ↵ ↵

dBASE III PLUS display after the creation of the data base structure in Hands-On Tutorial 35.

■ Return to the dot prompt with a "No" response.

Input data records now? (Y/N) **N**

A "Yes" response would display the data entry screen for the COURSE data base.

HANDS-ON TUTORIAL 36: Adding Data Base Records

At this point the COURSE data base has no records. Add the records, as shown in Figure 10–1, to the COURSE data base.

■ The APPEND command displays the data entry screen (see Figure 10–3).

. **APPEND** ↵

■ Enter the data for the first record shown in Figure 10–1.

100 ↵
MIS Orientation ↵
in-house

Since "in-house" is exactly as long as the field width definition, the cursor is automatically positioned at the next field. You may hear a warning beep.

Complete the first record with entries for the SOURCE and DURATION fields.

Staff ↵
24 ↵

■ Repeat the record entry procedure described above to enter records 2 through 12 of the COURSE data base (Figure 10–1). After entering the last record, you

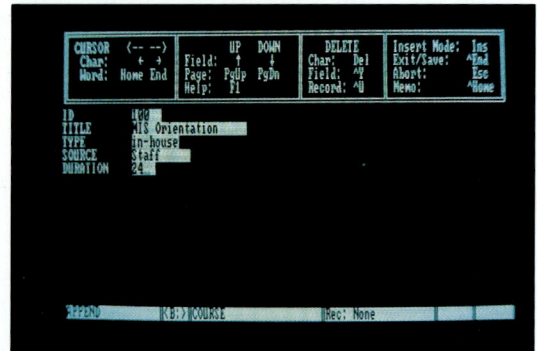

dBASE III PLUS display of the data entry screen for the first record (ID=100) of the COURSE data base in Hands-On Tutorial 36.

should be at the end-of-file (EOF) and record number 12 (see indicators in lower-right corner of screen).

■ Return to the dot prompt.

CTRL - END

HANDS-ON TUTORIAL 37: Modifying Records in a Data Base

■ To modify the contents of any record(s) in a data base, make the desired data base the active data base with the "USE" command.

. **USE COURSE** ↵

■ Select the "BROWSE" command.

. **BROWSE** ↵

dBASE III PLUS "browse" display of the COURSE data base in Hands-On Tutorial 37. The second record (ID=201) is highlighted.

Use the four cursor control keys to browse through the records of the data base. To make corrections or modifications, position the cursor at the proper location and key in the correct data. Use the INS key to toggle between insert and replace data entry modes.

■ Return to the dot prompt.

CTRL - END

One alternative approach to viewing or modifying records of the active data base is to issue the "APPEND" command at the dot prompt and PGUP or PGDN to select the appropriate record. Another alternative, if you know the record number, is to go directly to the desired record with the "EDIT" command (for example, to edit record 4: . EDIT 4).

HANDS-ON TUTORIAL 38: Creating and Adding Records to a Data Base

You now have one of the two permanent data bases illustrated in Figure 10–1. The other is the TRAINING data base.

■ Define the structure of the TRAINING data base.

> **. CREATE TRAINING** ↵

Follow the procedures in Hands-On Tutorial 35 to create the structure for the TRAINING data base.

> **ID** ↵ **C 5** ↵
> **EMPLOYEE** ↵ **C 20** ↵
> **DEPARTMENT** ↵ **C 10** ↵

The START field is of type "date," has a default width of 8 positions, and has a predefined data entry format of MM/DD/YY.

> **START** ↵ **D** 8
> **STATUS** ↵ **C 1** ↵

Exit the data base structure definition screen.

> ↵ ↵

■ Add the records, as shown in Figure 10–1, to the TRAINING data base.

> Input data records now? (Y/N) **Y**

Enter the data for the each of the 10 records in the same manner as described in Hands-On Tutorial 36 and return to the dot prompt.

CTRL - END

Save option: If at anytime you cannot continue with the tutorials, save your work so that you can pick up where you left off. To do this, refer to Hands-On Tutorial 43, "Retrieving and Saving a Database" and to Hands-On Tutorial 44, "Printing a Report and Terminating a Session." When you return, retrieve your file and continue the tutorials.

HANDS-ON TUTORIAL 39: Making Data Base Inquiries

With dBASE III PLUS, it is easy to make inquiries to the data base.

■ It is good practice to clear the display screen.

> **. CLEAR** ↵

■ Display the entire COURSE data base.

> **. USE COURSE** ↵ (to activate COURSE)
> **. LIST** ↵

■ Display records based on a condition.

> **. CLEAR** ↵
> **. LIST FOR TYPE='in-house'** ↵

The display should look like Figure 10–5.

■ Display only the ID and TITLE for the records that meet a condition.

> . CLEAR ↵
> . LIST ID, TITLE FOR TYPE='in-house' ↵

The display should look like Figure 10–6.

As an alternative to keying in the LIST command above, you can edit the first LIST command. Use the up and down cursor control keys to scroll through previous commands. In this instance, you can simply press the up arrow until the desired command is displayed at the dot prompt, and then edit it as needed. Press ENTER to invoke the command. You may need to toggle between replace and insert modes with the INS key (select insert mode and insert "ID, TITLE" in the first LIST command; this creates the second).

■ Display records based on a compound condition.

> . CLEAR ↵
> . LIST FOR TYPE='in-house' .AND.
>   DURATION<=10 ↵

The display should look like Figure 10–7.

■ Display the total number of in-house seminars made available to employees (result should be 38).

> . CLEAR ↵
> . SUM DURATION FOR SOURCE='Staff' ↵

dBASE III PLUS display of the COURSE records that meet the conditions TYPE='in-house' and DURATION<=10 in Hands-On Tutorial 39.

Notice that "Staff" is in upper and lower case, just as it is in the database file.

■ Display the average duration of all courses (result should be 28).

> . CLEAR ↵
> . AVERAGE DURATION ↵

■ Display the total number of VidCourse courses (result should be 3).

> . CLEAR ↵
> . COUNT FOR SOURCE='VidCourse' ↵

HANDS-ON TUTORIAL 40: Sorting a Data Base

Sort the COURSE data base by ID field (secondary key) within the SOURCE field (primary key). Clear your screen if necessary.

■ Create a temporary database file called DBSORT.

> . SORT TO DBSORT ON SOURCE, ID ↵

■ Display the sorted version of the COURSE database file.

> . USE DBSORT ↵
> . LIST ↵

The USE command makes DBSORT the active database file. A display of the results of the sort operation is shown in Figure 10–8.

■ Display the SOURCE and ID of those records for which the TYPE is "vendor" or "media" (Figure 10–9).

> . LIST SOURCE, ID FOR TYPE='vendor' .OR.
>   TYPE='media' ↵

HANDS-ON TUTORIAL 41: Combining Data Bases

dBASE III PLUS permits users to combine or join database files that have common fields (see Figure 10–10). Clear your screen if necessary.

■ Open, or make available for processing, the database files that are to be combined.

> . SELECT 1 ↵
> . USE COURSE ↵
> . SELECT 2 ↵
> . USE TRAINING ↵

The instructions above identify COURSE as the file opened in work area 1 and TRAINING as the file opened in work area

2. dBASE III PLUS has 10 work areas. Because it was named last, TRAINING is the active file, but COURSE is open and can be a part of operations.

■ Create a temporary database file called TEMP1 by combining COURSE and TRAINING. This operation enables the employee's name to be displayed with the full title of the courses he or she has taken.

> .JOIN WITH COURSE TO TEMP1 FOR ID=COURSE->ID FIELDS EMPLOYEE, ID, TITLE, STATUS ↵

The ID field in the active file (TRAINING) is matched with the ID field from the nonactive file (COURSE). "COURSE->ID" is the instruction syntax for "the ID from the COURSE file."

■ Sort TEMP1 on EMPLOYEE to create TEMP2. Make the inquiries as shown in Figure 10–11.

. USE TEMP1 ↵
. SORT TO TEMP2 ON EMPLOYEE ↵
. USE TEMP2 ↵
. LIST FOR STATUS='C' ↵
. LIST FOR STATUS='I' ↵

dBASE III PLUS display after the completion of Hands-On Tutorial 41.

HANDS-ON TUTORIAL 42: Indexing

Indexing permits the display of sorted records without creating a separate sorted version of the data base. Indexing also allows rapid random access of records in a data base.

■ Activate the master TRAINING data base.

. USE TRAINING ↵

■ Create TRINDEX (training index file) from the active TRAINING file. Make EMPLOYEE the key field.

. INDEX ON EMPLOYEE TO TRINDEX ↵

■ TRINDEX, which is now the active data base, is ordered alphabetically by EMPLOYEE. When you issue a LIST command, the result is a display of a similarly ordered TRAINING data base.

. LIST ↵

■ Find all records that contain the character string "Targa" and list them.

. FIND Targa ↵
. LIST NEXT 10 ↵

The LIST NEXT 10 command causes up

to 10 occurrences of "Targa" records to be displayed.

■ Reactivate the master TRAINING data base.

. USE TRAINING ↵

dBASE III PLUS display after the "LIST NEXT" command in Hands-On Tutorial 42.

HANDS-ON TUTORIAL 43: Retrieving and Saving a Data Base

■ To retrieve a particular database file, make it the active file with the USE command. If multiple files are opened with

the SELECT command (see Hands-On Tutorial 41), SELECT the work area that contains the database file that you wish to make the activate file (SELECT 2).

```
. USE TRAINING ↵
. LIST ↵
```

■ The active or open database file is not saved to disk storage until it is closed. Close an active file by issuing a USE command for another database file or the active database file; exiting dBASE III PLUS with a QUIT command (see Hands-On Tu-

torial 44); or by issuing the CLOSE DATA-BASE command. Either of the following commands will close the TRAINING database file and, if it has been altered, save the revised database file to disk storage.

```
. USE TRAINING ↵
```

or

```
. CLOSE DATABASE ↵
```

HANDS-ON TUTORIAL 44: Printing a Report and Terminating a Session

■ Append the qualifier, TO PRINT, to the end of the LIST command to route LIST selections from the active database file to the printer. Print the entire TRAINING database file.

```
. USE TRAINING ↵
```

```
. LIST TO PRINT ↵
```

■ Exit dBASE III PLUS.

```
. QUIT ↵
```

QUIT saves to disk storage those active database files that have been modified.

HANDS-ON TUTORIAL 45: Programming

The programming capability of database software allows you to combine instructions in a logical sequence instead of entering them one at a time. The program in this tutorial allows the user to make an inquiry to the TRAINING data base (see Figures 10–13 and 10–14).

■ If needed, load dBASE III PLUS to memory and progress to the dot prompt (see "Hands-on Tutorial 34: Using dBASE III PLUS").

■ Prepare to create a program called HIS-TORY.

```
. CREATE COMMAND HISTORY ↵
```

Observe the edit window at the top of the screen. Press F1 to toggle the display of the edit window between on and off.

F1 F1

■ Enter the program. The annotated comments (lines beginning with asterisks) in Figure 10–13 explain the purpose of program instructions. The comment lines do not effect the program and can be omitted to save entry time. The format of an interactive session is illustrated in Figure 10–14.

```
USE TRAINING ↵
CLEAR ↵
@ 4, 20 SAY "EMPLOYEE TRAINING HISTORY" ↵
? ↵
? ↵
ACCEPT "        Enter employee's name (Last, First):      "  TO NAME ↵
CLEAR ↵
@ 4, 8 SAY "Training History Report for:     "  +  NAME ↵
? ↵
? "Department Course ID Status" ↵
? "======= ====== ==== " ↵
SET TALK OFF ↵
DO WHILE .NOT. EOF () ↵
  IF EMPLOYEE = NAME ↵
    ? ↵
    ? DEPARTMENT  +  "        "  +  ID  +  "              "  +  STATUS ↵
  ENDIF ↵
  SKIP ↵
ENDDO ↵
@ 18, 1 SAY "Status codes: C=complete; I=incomplete; and W=withdrawn" ↵
SET TALK ON ↵
```

dBASE III PLUS display after the program has been entered in Hands-On Tutorial 45.

Look over the program carefully and correct any keying errors (see the edit box at the top of the screen for instructions).

■ Save your program.

[CTRL]-**W**

The save command returns you to the dot prompt.

■ Run the HISTORY program.

. **DO HISTORY** ↵
. Enter employee's name (Last, First):   **Targa, Phil** ↵

If the program has bugs in it, you may need to modify it. Use the following command to recall the HISTORY program file, and then edit the program.

. **MODIFY COMM HISTORY** ↵
(*make needed corrections*)
[CTRL]-**W** (*save program*)

■ Exit dBASE III PLUS (see Hands-On Tutorial 44).

. **QUIT** ↵

dBASE III PLUS display of the interactive session for the program in Hands-On Tutorial 45.

DATA MANAGEMENT TUTORIAL: REFLEX

QUICK REFERENCE GUIDE
Reflex: The Database Manager
(Version 1.14)
A>reflex ↵

SYSTEM MENUS

Views
- Form *
- List *
- Graph *
- Xtab *
- Close
- Resize
- Expand
- Shrink
- Next view
- Quit

Edit
- Delete
- Insert
- Set column width
- Row select
- Column select
- Window clear

* = other submenus follow

Print/File
- Retrieve file *
- Save file
- Erase file
- Print *
- Global settings *

Records
- Field & sort settings *
- Vary
- Add record
- Delete record
- Perform sort
- Recalc
- Clear database

Search
- Set conditions
- Apply filter
- Remove filter
- Find record
- Keep record

FUNCTION KEYS

Help	F1	F2	Edit
Row	F3	F4	Column
Filter			*Expand*
Find	F5	F6	View
Record			**Record**
First			*Last*
Prior	F7	F8	Next
Sort			
Recalc	F9	F10	Choices
	Shift		
	Normal		

HANDS-ON TUTORIAL 34: Using Reflex

Reflex: The Database Manager is distributed by Borland/Analytica, Inc. Reflex employs five "Views" of the data in a data base (Form View, List View, Graph View, CrossTab View and Report View). Reflex has several "Tools" that facilitate searches, construct subsets of the data base, and perform operations on files. It can use up to three windows simultaneously to display different "views" of the data base. Version 1.14 is used to create this data management tutorial.

■ Boot the system (see Hands-on Tutorial 1).

■ Load Reflex to memory. Insert the Reflex system disk into drive A and key in one of the following commands.

> A>**reflex** ↵ (*systems with IBM graphics card*)
> A>**reflexh** ↵ (*systems with Hercules graphics card*)
> **/** (*to exit title screen*)

When you select an option from the main menu, a pull-down menu appears. Select commands from these menus in one of two ways: press the first letter of the command or use the cursor control and ENTER keys. These tutorials use the first method.

Look at the current pull-down menu. The title of the menu, "Views", is highlighted. The commands are displayed at two intensities. The bold commands are available for selection. Other commands are not available at this time. Use the cursor control keys to scan through the other menus.

> → ← ↑ ↓ (*as desired*)

■ Replace the System Disk in drive A with the Help Disk and insert your data disk in drive B. You are ready to begin a Reflex session. You can complete this tutorial without using the Help Disk, but the F1 Help menu would not be available.

Several function key commands will prove helpful as you work through the following Reflex tutorials.

F1	HELP — the context sensitive Help key.
F2	EDIT—puts Reflex in edit mode so that you can make changes to the selected cell.
F6	NEXT VIEW—makes the next view active when more than one is on the screen.
F7	PREVIOUS RECORD—selects and displays the previous record in the database.
F8	NEXT RECORD—selects and displays the next record in the database.
F10	CHOICES—provides a list of current field names or other valid choices for the current selection.

■ Press ESC now to erase the pull down menu.

> ESC

HANDS-ON TUTORIAL 35: Creating a Data Base

To create the COURSE data base of Figure 10–1, you need to define its structure. Use Form View to set up the structure of the data base.

■ Open the Form View.

> **/V**iews **F**orm

The Form Design screen appears.

■ Key in the field names in the data entry form (see Figure 10–2). Press BKSP to delete mistakes or use the cursor control keys to highlight an entry and reenter the name.

> **ID** ↓
> **TITLE** ↓
> **TYPE** ↓
> **SOURCE** ↓
> **DURATION** ↵

■ Exit Form Design.

> **/F**orm **E**xit **D**esign

Colons have been placed behind each field name and the cursor is positioned to the right of the first field.

■ Define the field type as either text or numeric. In the COURSE data base, all the fields are text except DURATION. Some IDs contain letters as well as numbers, but they are still considered text entries for this specific definition. Use the Field & Sort Settings tool to define the field type. A tool is a group of instructions that help Reflex perform certain commands. These instructions appear in a window that is superimposed over the active view.

> **/R**ecords **F**ield & Sort Settings..

■ Define the field type as "Numeric" or "Text".

> → (*move the cursor to the "Type" column for ID*)
> F10 (*choices key*)
> ↑ (*"Text" is entered for ID*) ↵
> Are you sure? No Yes **Y**es

Enter "Text" for TITLE, TYPE, and SOURCE, and enter "Numeric" for DURATION. After making all other entries, return to Form View.

> ESC (*return to Form View*)

Reflex display after the creation of the data base structure in Hands-On Tutorial 35.

HANDS-ON TUTORIAL 36: Adding Data Base Records

At this point the COURSE data base has no records. Add the records, as shown in Figure 10–1, to the COURSE data base.

■ Enter the data for record 1 in Figure 10–1.

> **100** ↵ (*next field*)
> **MIS Orientation** ↵
> **in-house** ↵
> **Staff** ↵
> **24** F8 (*next record*)

■ Enter the data listed in Figure 10–1 for

records 2 through 12. At the beginning of the second record key in two intentional mistakes to be corrected later.

> **211** (*an intentional data entry error*) ↵
> **Macro Overview** (*an intentional data entry error*) ↵
> **in-house** ↵
> **Staff** ↵
> **8** F8

Key in the remainder of the records (3 through 12).

HANDS-ON TUTORIAL 37: Modifying Records in a Data Base

Use both Form and List Views to correct errors in the data base.

■ Open List View to list the COURSE data base and divide the screen horizontally.

> **/V**iews **L**ist
> Which Way?   Replace   Vertical   Horizontal
> **H**orizontal

"Replace" removes Form View from the screen and replaces it with List View. "Vertical" or "Horizontal" divides the screen in half vertically or horizontally so that both views share the screen. Form View is in the top half and List View is in the bottom half. The word "LIST" is highlighted to show that List View is the active view.

■ Move the cursor Home to the first record in the file.

> HOME

■ Expand the TITLE field.

> → (*move cursor to the TITLE field*)
> **/E**dit **S**et Column Width
> → (*10 times*) ↵

If you use the down cursor key, you can see that this width accommodates the longest TITLE entry (4th Generation Lang.).

■ In List View, correct the entry in the ID field of record 2.

> HOME ↓ F2 (*edit key*)
> BKSP BKSP **01** ↵

■ Corrections can also be made from Form View. In Form View, correct the entry in the TITLE field of record 2.

> F6 (*next View*)
> ↓ F2
> ← (*13 times*) DEL **i** ↵

Save option: If at anytime you cannot continue with the tutorials, save your work so that you can pick up where you left off. To do this, refer to "Hands-On Tutorial 32, Re-

trieving and Saving a Database" and to "Hands-On Tutorial 33, Printing a Report and Terminating a Session." When you return, retrieve your file and continue the tutorials.

Reflex split-screen display of the Form View (top) and the List View (bottom) for the COURSE data base at the completion of Hands-On Tutorial 37.

HANDS-ON TUTORIAL 38: Creating and Adding Records a Data Base _____

Because we will not be using the TRAINING data base from Figure 10–1 in this Reflex tutorial, there is no need to create it.

HANDS-ON TUTORIAL 39: Making Data Base Inquiries _____

In Reflex you can search for a record that meets conditions that you set. You can then filter the data base to create a new or temporary subset of the records that meet those conditions. Use the Search Conditions tool to define a filter and apply the filter to the data base to create a subset of records.

■ Be sure you are in List View (use F6 to switch between Views so that LIST is highlighted) and expand the List View to fill the screen.

    /Views **E**xpand

■ Define a one parameter filter.

    /Search **S**et Conditions..

Move the cursor to the TYPE field and key in the phrase "in-house". Enclose it in double quotes because it is a text entry.

    ↓ (3 times to TYPE) **"in-house"**

Use the quick exit technique to exit from the "Set Conditions" tool.

    CTRL - ↵ (quick exit)

■ Apply the filter to the data base.

    SHIFT - F5 (apply/remove filter)

The List View should display the same information as shown in Figure 10–5. The "FILT" in the lower right corner of the screen indicates that a filter has been applied to the data base.

■ Modify List View to resemble Figure 10–6. Remove unwanted columns so that only the ID and TITLE fields are displayed.

    HOME
    ↑ → → DEL → DEL → DEL

Deleting the columns from List View does not delete the data from the data base.

■ Display the ID and TITLE fields of all the records by removing the filter.

    SHIFT - F5

■ Restore deleted fields by keying the name of the field at the top of the appropriate column.

HOME ↑ → → TYPE → SOURCE →
DURATION ↵

- Add another parameter to the existing filter.

    /Search Set Conditions..
    ↓ (5 times to DURATION) <=10 CTRL -↵

- Apply the filter so that List View resembles Figure 10–7. Return to List View after observing the filtered data.

    SHIFT - F5 (apply the filter)
    SHIFT - F5 (remove the filter)

```
'281
 Views  Edit   Print/File  Records  Search   List
 ID      TITLE            TYPE      SOURCE    DURATION
▶ 281    Micro Overview   in-house  Staff          8
 310     Programming Stds. in-house Staff          6
```

Reflex "filter-on" display of the COURSE records that meet the conditions TYPE="in-house" and DURATION<=10 in Hands-On Tutorial 39.

- Use the CrossTab View to display the number of seminar hours (the sum of DURATION) made available to employees by each of the organizations listed in the SOURCE field. First, however, return to the horizontal split screen.

    /Views Shrink
    /Views Xtab

- Choose the type of summary desired.

    Summary: F10 (choices key)
    ↓ (3 times to highlight @SUM)
    → (select @SUM and move to the next field)

The function, @SUM, totals all rows and columns.

- Select the field whose data will appear in the cells.

    Field: F10 → (select DURATION and move to next field)

- Name the vertical (DURATION) and horizontal (SOURCE) components of the CrossTab table.

    All /Crosstab For Each.. F10 (DURATION is highlighted) CTRL -↵
    ↑ /Crosstab For Each.. F10 ↓ (2 times to highlight SOURCE) CTRL -↵

Each unique entry in the DURATION field occupies its own row and each unique entry in the SOURCE field occupies its own column. Totals appear to the right of each row and at the bottom of each column. For instance, the number of seminar hours taught by the in-house staff is 38 (the total of the third column).

- Replace "@SUM" with "@AVG" in the Summary block.

    ↑ (3 times to position cursor at Summary:)
    F10 ↓ (move cursor to highlight "@AVG") ↵

The average duration of all the courses (28 hours) appears in the the box in the lower-right corner.

- Display the total number of courses offered by each organization.

    F10 HOME (cursor is at @COUNT) ↵

The total number of courses offered by VidCourse is 3 (fifth column).

- Close the CrossTab View.

    /Views Close

HANDS-ON TUTORIAL 40: Sorting a Data Base

Perform a two-level sort on the data base. First sort the SOURCE field then sort the ID field within each SOURCE field grouping.

- Call up the Field & Sort Settings tool and define the sort sequence. Perform the sort.

    /Records Field & Sort Settings..
    → (3 times) 2 (ID is the secondary key)
    ↓ (3 times) 1 (SOURCE is the primary key) ↵

The default is ascending sequence (see the A in the A/D column). Use the quick exit and perform the sort.

    CTRL -↵
    /Records Perform Sort
    HOME

The List View should resemble Figure 10–8.

- Display the SOURCE and ID fields of those records for which the TYPE is vendor or media.

    /Search Set Conditions..
    ↓ (3 times to TYPE) "**vendor**" → "**media**"
    (position cursor to <= 10 for removal)
    ↓ (2 times) ← DEL
    CTRL -↵
    SHIFT - F5 (filter data base)

Modify List View to resemble Figure 10–9 by removing unwanted columns so that

Reflex display of the COURSE data base sorted by ID within SOURCE in Hands-On Tutorial 40.

only the SOURCE and ID fields are displayed.

> HOME
> ↑ → DEL → DEL → → DEL

The List View should resemble Figure 10–9.

■ Restore all records and all fields to List View.

> SHIFT - F5 *(remove filter)*
> /List Show All Fields

The TITLE field is restored to its original width. Reset the column width for the TI-TLE field (see Hands-On Tutorial 37).

HANDS-ON TUTORIAL 41: Combining Data Bases

This tutorial is not applicable to Reflex.

HANDS-ON TUTORIAL 42: Indexing

This tutorial is not applicable to Reflex.

HANDS-ON TUTORIAL 43: Saving and Retrieving a Data Base

Save the COURSE data base to the data disk and then retrieve the "course" file.

■ Save the COURSE data base by using the Save Reflex Database tool.

> /Print/File Save File..

Change the logged drive from A:\ to B:

> ↑ b: ↵

Name the file and quick exit.

> **course** CTRL - ↵

If you had previously saved "course", answer the following:

> Replacing B:\course No Yes **Yes**

The file is saved to your data disk.

■ Retrieve the COURSE file by using the Retrieve Reflex Database tool.

> /Print/File Retrieve File..

Reflex remembers which drive is logged and the name of the current data base. If desired, press F10 for a list of options to choose another data base. Use the quick exit to retrieve the data base currently listed.

> CTRL - ↵
> This will clear your database, Continue?
> No Yes **Yes**

HANDS-ON TUTORIAL 44: Printing a Report and Terminating a Session

Title and print a simple report.

■ Call up the Print Settings tool and title the report.

> /Print/File Print

■ Title the report.

> **ZIMCO ENTERPRISES** ↵
> **COURSE OFFERING** ↵

Check that the printer is on and perform a quick exit to accept all settings and

print the document. The report contains the information found in Figure 10–8.

> CTRL - ↵

Close the Print Settings tool.

> ESC

■ Exit Reflex to DOS.

> /Views Quit
> Are you sure? No Yes **Yes**
> A>

HANDS-ON TUTORIAL 45: Programming

This tutorial is not applicable to Reflex.

DATA MANAGEMENT TUTORIAL: PFS:PROFESSIONAL FILE

QUICK REFERENCE GUIDE
PFS:Professional File
(Version 1.0)
A>pf ↵

MAIN MENU

Design
- Create new design
- Enter/Edit formulas
- Add, move, or delete fields
- Change field names

Add

Search/Update
- Review/Update records
- Review/Edit sorted records
- Replace field data
- Delete records

Copy
- Copy data file
- Copy design
- Copy records
- Copy from ASCII file
- Copy from 1-2-3 worksheet

Report
- Print crosstab
- Print list
- Print records or labels
- Enter/Edit headings

Setup
- Select data file
- Share data file
- Check data file
- Select printer 1
- Select printer 2
- Change data directory
- Change work drive
- Change screen colors
- Change screen update speed

Exit

OTHER

ESC   Cancel action or window and
       return to previous task.

FUNCTION KEYS

Help	F1	F2	Edit
			Quick
Form	F3	F4	entry
Report			
formats	F5	F6	
	F7	F8	
			Previous
			record
	F9	F10	Continue
	Shift		
	Normal		

HANDS-ON TUTORIAL 34: Using PFS:Professional File

PFS:Professional File, a product of Software Publishing Corporation, is a database management system that enables users to create, maintain, and manipulate a data base. It also provides users with the flexibility to make inquiries and generate reports. Version 1.0 is used to create this data management tutorial.

■ Boot the system (see Hands-On Tutorial 1).

■ Load PFS:Professional File to memory. Insert the PFS:Professional File program disk in drive A.

    A>pf ↵

■ Insert your data disk in drive B. At this

point you are ready to begin your PFS:Professional File session. Several function key commands will prove helpful as you work through the following PFS:Professional File tutorials.

[F1]	PFS:Professional File's context-sensitive Help key.
[F2]	Displays the Edit pull-down menu.
[F3]	Displays the Form pull-down menu.
[F4]	Displays the Quick Entry pull-down menu.
[F5]	Displays the Report Formats pull-down menu.
[F10]	Continue to the next record, action, or form.
[SHIFT]-[F10]	Move to the previous record.

HANDS-ON TUTORIAL 35: Creating a Data Base

To create the COURSE data base of Figure 10–1, you need to define its structure.

■ Create the data base structure or a form design in PFS:Professional File (see Figure 10–2).

  1 (select "Design")
  1 (select "Create new design")

■ Enter the name of the database file to be created.

  Filename: B:**course** ↵

Study the display of the design-screen options.

■ Enter the names of the fields from figure 10–2 into the design screen. Place a colon after each field name. Use the backspace or delete keys to correct data entry errors.

  ID: ↵
  TITLE: ↵
  TYPE: ↵
  SOURCE: ↵
  DURATION: [F10]

Pressing F10 signifies the end of the record definition for the COURSE database file and returns you to the Main Menu.

HANDS-ON TUTORIAL 36: Adding Data Base Records

At this point the COURSE data base has no records. Add the records, as shown in Figure 10–1, to the COURSE data base.

■ Select "Add" from the Main Menu.

  2

■ Enter the data for the first record shown in Figure 10–1 and save it to disk storage.

  100 [TAB]
  MIS Orientation [TAB]
  in-house [TAB]
  Staff [TAB]
  24 [F10] (save record)

■ Repeat the record entry procedure described above to enter records 2 through 12 of the COURSE data base (Figure 10–1). After entering the last record, you should be at record number 13 (see indicator at bottom of screen).

■ Return to the Main Menu.

  [ESC]

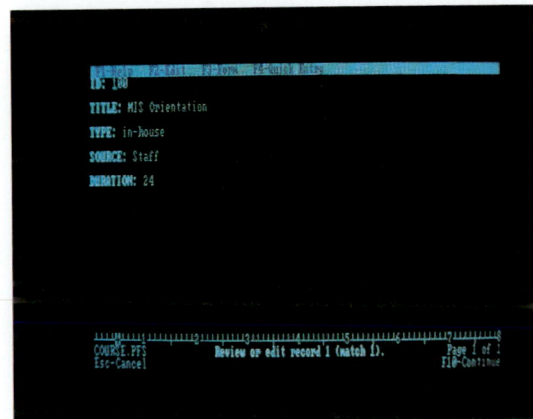

PFS:Professional File display after the creation of the data base structure in Hands-On Tutorial 35.

HANDS-ON TUTORIAL 37: Modifying Records in a Data Base _____

■ To modify the contents of any record(s) in a data base, choose "Search/Update" from the Main Menu.

> 3 (*select "Search/Update"*)
> 1 (*select "Review/Edit records"*)

■ Use the F10 key to browse through the records of the data base. To correct keying errors, use the TAB and cursor control keys to position the cursor at the proper location and make the correction. Use the INS key to toggle between insert and replace data entry modes.

> F10 (*browse through records*)
> ESC ESC (*return to the Main Menu*)

An alternative approach to viewing or modifying records of the active data base, is to enter search criteria on the "Choose records to edit" screen that appears when you choose "Review/Edit records" from the Search/Update Menu. For example, if you entered CIS11 in the ID field (and pressed F10), the record for Business COBOL would be displayed for editing.

Save option: If at anytime you cannot continue with the tutorials, save your work so that you can pick up where you left off. To do this, refer to "Hands-On Tutorial 43: Retrieving and Saving a Database" and to "Hands-On Tutorial 44: Printing a Report and Terminating a Session." When you return, retrieve your file and continue the tutorials.

HANDS-ON TUTORIAL 38: Creating and Adding Records to a Data Base _____

Because we will not be using the TRAINING data base from Figure 10–1 in this PFS:Profes-sional File tutorial, there is no need to create it.

HANDS-ON TUTORIAL 39: Making Data Base Inquiries _____

With PFS:Professional File it is easy to make inquiries to the data base.

■ Select the COURSE data base file and print a list of the records contained in it.

> 6 (*setup*)
> 7 (*change work drive*) b (*if needed, change to drive B*) ↵
> 6 (*setup*)
> 1 (*select data file*)
> Filename: B:**course** ↵

■ Display a list of all the records in the COURSE data base.

> 5 (*report*)
> 2 (*print list*)

Fill in the order in which the fields are to be listed. In this example all fields are displayed. To eliminate a field from the display, do not associate a number with that field.

> ID: **1** TAB
> TITLE: **2** TAB
> TYPE: **3** TAB
> SOURCE: **4** TAB
> DURATION: **5** F10

Include all records in the data base in the list by pressing F10.

> F10

■ Examine the List Options screen. Change the "Print to:" option on the List Options screen to "Screen".

> SHIFT - TAB (*reverse tab*) **2** (*screen*) ↵

Examine the list of records that is produced on the screen. It should resemble the COURSE data base list in Figure 10–1. Return to the Report Menu.

> ESC ESC ESC

■ Display records based on a condition.

> **2** (*print list*)
> ID: **1** TAB
> TITLE: **2** TAB
> TYPE: **3** TAB
> SOURCE: **4** TAB
> DURATION: **5** F10

Include only those records with TYPE "in-house".

> ID: TAB
> TITLE: TAB
> TYPE: **in-house**
> F10

The "Print to:" option on the List Options screen should still be "Screen" since it was changed for the last list.

↵

The display should look like Figure 10–5. Return to the Report Menu.

[ESC] [ESC] [ESC]

■ Display only the ID and TITLE for the records that meet the condition TYPE "in-house".

    2 (*print list*)
    ID: **1** [TAB]
    TITLE: **2** [F10]
    ID: [TAB]
    TITLE: [TAB]
    TYPE: **in-house** [F10]

The "Print to:" option on the List Options screen should still be "Screen" since it was changed for the last list.

↵

The display should look like Figure 10–6. Return to the Report Menu.

[ESC] [ESC] [ESC]

■ Display records based on a compound condition.

    2 (*print list*)
    ID: **1** [TAB]
    TITLE: **2** [TAB]
    TYPE: **3** [TAB]
    SOURCE: **4** [TAB]
    DURATION: **5** [F10]

Include only those records for which TYPE is "in-house" and the DURATION is 10 or fewer hours.

    ID: [TAB]
    TITLE: [TAB]
    TYPE: **in-house** [TAB]
    SOURCE: [TAB]
    DURATION: **<=10** [F10]
    ↵

The display should look like Figure 10–7. Return to the Main Menu.

[ESC] [ESC] [ESC] [ESC]

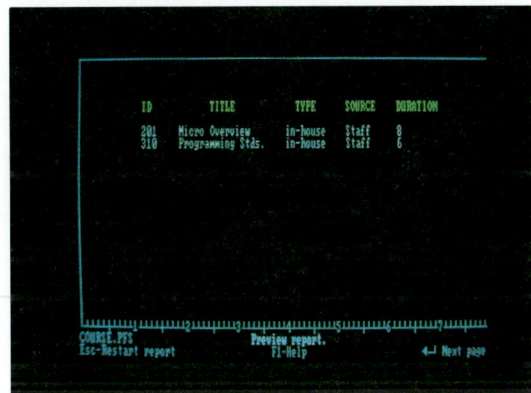

PFS:Professional File display of the COURSE records that meet the conditions TYPE="in-house" and DURATION<=10 in Hands-On Tutorial 39.

HANDS-ON TUTORIAL 40: Sorting a Data Base

Sort the COURSE data base by ID field (secondary key) within the SOURCE field (primary key).

■ Display a list of records sorted by ID within SOURCE. From the Main Menu, select "Report". In PFS:Professional File, the first field in the listing is automatically the primary key. The second field is the secondary key. The records are automatically sorted when a display is requested.

    5 (*report*)
    2 (*print list*)
    ID: **2** (*secondary key*) [TAB]
    TITLE: **3** [TAB]
    TYPE: **4** [TAB]
    SOURCE: **1** (*primary key*) [TAB]
    DURATION: **5** [F10] [F10]

Change the "Print to:" option on the List Options screen to be "Screen" if necessary.

    [SHIFT]-[TAB] **2** ↵

The records should be displayed in the same order as Figure 10–8, but the order in which the fields are displayed will be different (SOURCE will be first, and so on).

Return to the Report Menu.

[ESC] [ESC] [ESC]

■ Display the SOURCE and ID of those records for which the TYPE is "vendor" or "media" (similar to Figure 10–9).

    2 (*print list*)
    ID: **2** [TAB] [TAB] [TAB]
    SOURCE: **1** [F10]

Include only those records for which TYPE is "vendor" or "media".

ID: `TAB` `TAB`
TYPE: **vendor;media** `F10`
↵

The display should look similar to Figure 10–9 except that the SOURCE field is only displayed once for each source.
Return to the Main Menu.

`ESC` `ESC` `ESC` `ESC`

PFS:Professional File display of the COURSE data base sorted by ID within SOURCE in Hands-On Tutorial 40.

HANDS-ON TUTORIAL 41: Combining Data Bases

This tutorial is not applicable to PFS:Professional File.

HANDS-ON TUTORIAL 42: Indexing

This tutorial is not applicable to PFS:Professional File.

HANDS-ON TUTORIAL 43: Retrieving and Saving a Data Base

■ To retrieve a particular database file, make it the active file with the "Setup" selection from the Main Menu.

  6 (setup)
  1 (select data file)
  Filename: B:**course** ↵

Changes that you make to a data base file using PFS:Professional File are saved to disk automatically. There is no need to explicitly save a data base file after making changes.

HANDS-ON TUTORIAL 44: Printing a Report and Terminating a Session

■ Print out the COURSE data base (see Figure 10–1). Add a two-line header. Change the "Print to:" option on the "List Options"

screen to "Printer" to route lists and reports to the printer. Print the entire COURSE database file.

6 (*setup*)
1 (*select data file*)
Filename: B:**course** ↵
5 (*report*)
2 (*print list*)
ID: **1** [TAB]
EMPLOYEE: **2** [TAB]
DEPARTMENT: **3** [TAB]
START: **4** [TAB]
STATUS: **5** [F10]

Include all records in the data base in the list.

[F10]

Add a two-line header (title) for the report.

Header 1: **ZIMCO ENTERPRISES** [TAB]
Header 2: **COURSE OFFERING**

Be sure that the "Print to:" option on the List Options screen is set to "Printer".

[SHIFT]-[TAB] (*2 times*)
1 (*printer*) ↵ ↵ (*accept defaults*)

The printed output should resemble the COURSE data base list in Figure 10–1. Return to the Main Menu.

[ESC] [ESC] [ESC] [ESC]

■ **Exit PFS:Professional File.**

e (*exit*)
A>

HANDS-ON TUTORIAL 45: Programming

This tutorial is not applicable to PFS:Professional File.

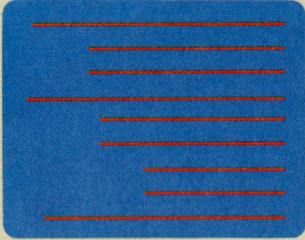

CHAPTER 12

Idea Processor Concepts and Tutorials

STUDENT LEARNING OBJECTIVES

- To describe the function and purpose of idea processors.
- To describe the hierarchical item-orientation of idea processors.
- To discuss idea processing concepts associated with changing the level of an item, inserting or deleting items, block operations, collapsing or expanding an outline, printing an outline, and creating a text file of an outline.
- To identify applications for idea processor software.
- To become familiar with the use and application of idea processor software for one or both of the following packages:
  - The OUTLINER
  - ThinkTank
- To acquire the ability to apply the idea processor skills demonstrated in the hands-on tutorials.

HANDS-ON TUTORIALS for *The OUTLINER and ThinkTank*

46. Using Idea Processor Software
47. Creating an Outline
48. Modifying an Outline
49. Collapsing and Expanding
50. Saving, Retrieving, and Printing an Outline and Terminating a Session
51. The OUTLINER Tutorials (The OUTLINER only)

ADVANCED AND SPECIAL FEATURES TUTORIAL: *The OUTLINER*

Saving an Outline as a Text File
Previewing a Text File
Combining a Text File into a Word Processing Document

12–1 THE FUNCTION OF IDEA PROCESSORS

An **idea processor** is a productivity tool that allows you to organize and document your thoughts and ideas. These versatile software tools have a 1001 uses. Some of these uses are

- Brainstorming
- Outlining project activities
- Preparing speeches and presentations
- Compiling notes for meetings and seminars
- Records keeping
- "To do" lists
- Itineraries

The name idea processors is derived from the fact that the software permits the manipulation of ideas. Actually, these software packages permit the manipulation of descriptions and explanations of *items*. We use the inclusive term *items* to refer to ideas, points, activities, notes, or anything else that can be outlined. When using an idea processor, you work with one item at a time within a hierarchy of other items so that you can easily organize and reorganize your items.

Idea processor software is sometimes referred to as an electronic version of the yellow note pad. The process of outlining inevitably involves both rethinking and the physical reorganization of the items in an outline. When yellow pads are used, thinking and rethinking take a back seat to the physical reorganization of items. When you use idea processor software, you can emphasize thinking and rethinking because it's a breeze to move, add, delete, and revise items. Each action results in a clean presentation of the outline, not the often indecipherable scribbling that results from "yellow pad thinking."

In a nutshell, idea processors have provided us with *a new way of thinking*. Some call it *computer-enhanced thinking*. When you use an idea processor, you can focus your attention on the thought process because the computer and idea processor software help you with documenting and presenting your ideas. See "Hands-On Tutorial 46: Using Idea Processor Software" at the end of this chapter.

Idea processors can be time savers around the office and at home. This woman uses idea processor software to help her with a number of household activities, including preparing the grocery list and maintaining an inventory of household items.
(Courtesy of Apple Computer, Inc.)

12–2 IDEA PROCESSOR CONCEPTS

Like word processing software, idea processor packages permit the manipulation of text, but with a different twist. Idea processors, which are also called *outliners*, can be used to organize these items into an outline format. You create an outline by entering items and using the capabilities of the software to arrange them into a well-organized outline.

Preston Smith, Zimco's president, dictates his letters, memos, and reports from outlines that he prepares with idea processor software. He also prepares notes for his meetings with an idea processor. For example, he prepared the agenda outlined in Figure 12–1 for an execu-

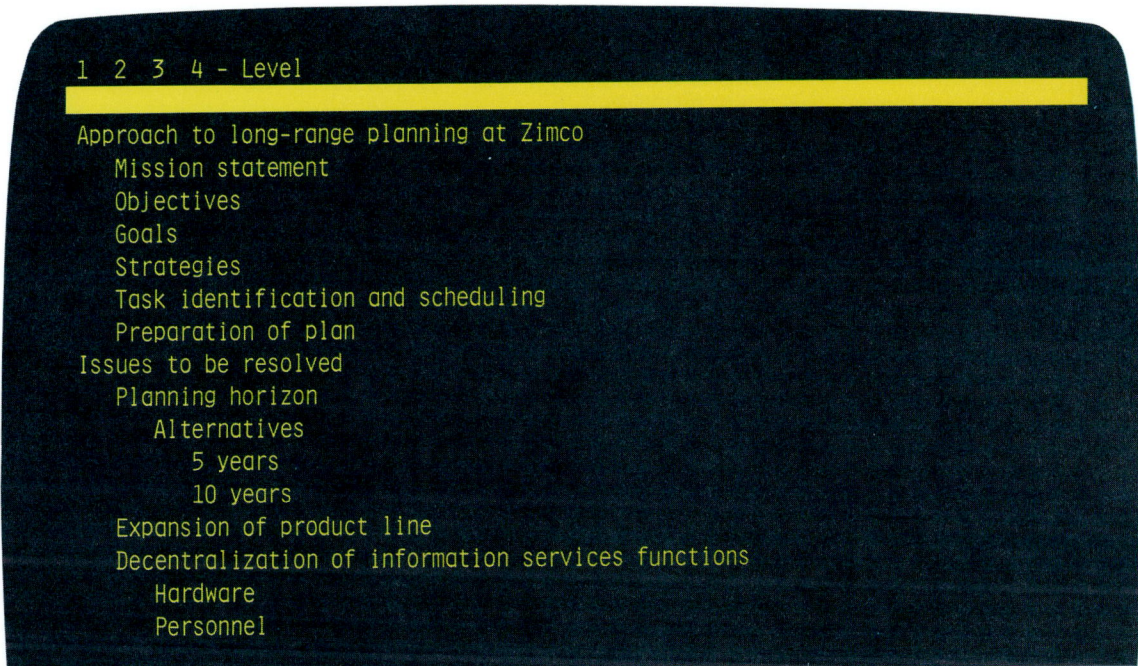

```
1  2  3  4 - Level


Approach to long-range planning at Zimco
    Mission statement
    Objectives
    Goals
    Strategies
    Task identification and scheduling
    Preparation of plan
Issues to be resolved
    Planning horizon
        Alternatives
            5 years
            10 years
    Expansion of product line
    Decentralization of information services functions
        Hardware
        Personnel
```

FIGURE 12–1
Idea Processor: Display of an Outline
The outline shown is an example of an agenda for an executive planning
session. The levels of the items can be equated to the level indicators in
the top left corner of the display.

tive planning session. This example is the basis for demonstrating outliner concepts.

The Item Orientation of Outliners

Idea processors organize items in a hierarchy with several levels of
subordination.

- *First-level items* are flush with the left margin.
- *Second-level items* are indented to show subordination to a first-
  level item.
- *Third-level items* are indented under second-level items.
- *Fourth-level items* are indented under third-level items, and so on.

First through fourth level items are illustrated in Figure 12–1. Notice
the level indicators at the top left corner of the display.

Changing the Level of an Item and Deleting an Item.   One of the
handy features of an outliner is that you can easily change the level
of an item by shifting it to the left or to the right. For example, in
Figure 12–1 the "5 year" and "10 year" items are fourth-level items
under the third-level heading, "Alternatives". Since there is only one

third-level item under "Planning horizon", Preston Smith decided to *delete* the "Alternatives" heading and *shift* the "5 year" and "10 year" items to the third level. The resultant outline is shown in Figure 12–2. Typically, an item in an outline will have at least two subordinate items or it will have none. See "Hands-On Tutorial 47: Creating an Outline."

Inserting Items.   In Preston Smith's draft of the planning agenda outline, the "Objectives" item does not have any subordinate items (*see* Figure 12–1). To better emphasize the two types of objectives, Preston decided to *insert* two third-level headings: "Qualitative results" and "Quantitative results". Under "Hardware", he inserted three fourth-level items: "Personal computers", "Minis", and "Mainframes". Figure 12–3 reflects these additions to the planning agenda outline.

Block Operations.   Like word processing, idea processors provide the facility to *move, copy,* or *delete* a block of items (one or more items). Until moments before the planning session, Preston had "Approach to long-range planning at Zimco" as the first item on the session's agenda (*see* Figure 12–3). Once he decided to make "Issues to be resolved" the first item, he made the revision to the outline by *marking* the lines to be moved, then issuing a *block move* command. The resultant outline is shown in Figure 12–4.

FIGURE 12–2
Idea Processor: Changing the Level of Items in an Outline
This display is the result of modifying the outline in Figure 12–1 so that the "Alternatives" item is deleted and the "5 year" and "10 year" items are changed from the fourth to the third level.

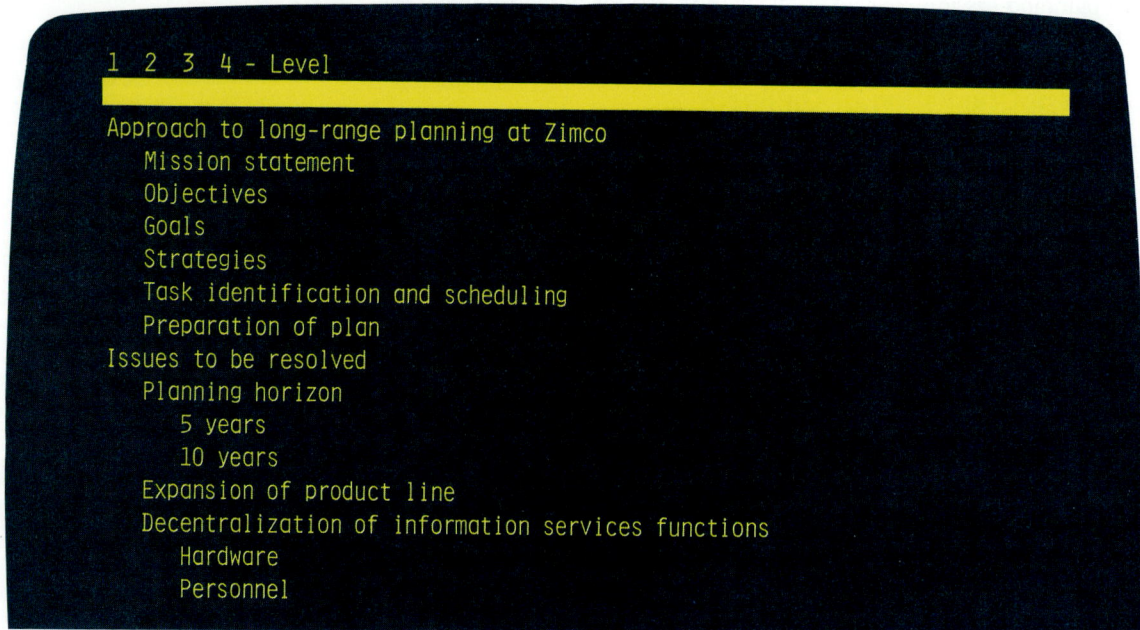
```
1 2  3  4 - Level


Approach to long-range planning at Zimco
    Mission statement
    Objectives
    Goals
    Strategies
    Task identification and scheduling
    Preparation of plan
Issues to be resolved
    Planning horizon
        5 years
        10 years
    Expansion of product line
    Decentralization of information services functions
        Hardware
        Personnel
```

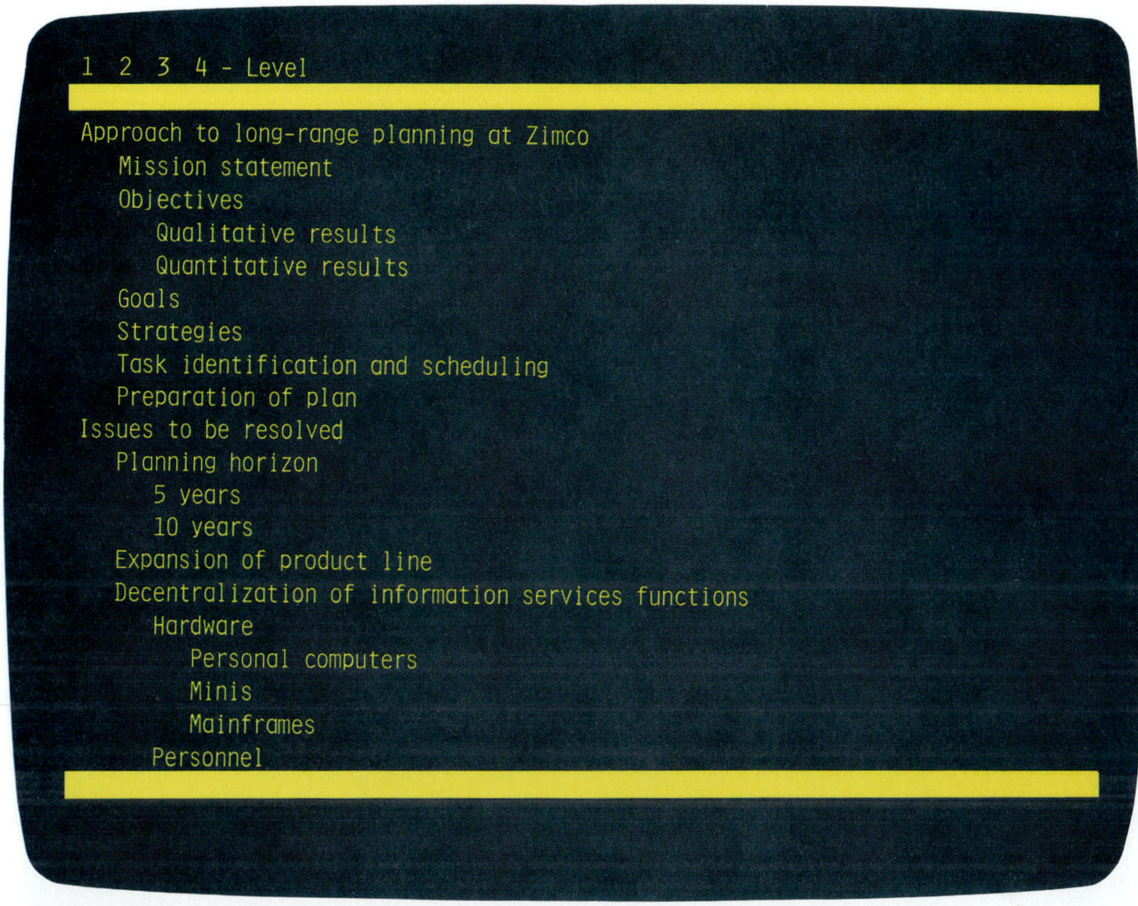

```
1  2  3  4 - Level


Approach to long-range planning at Zimco
    Mission statement
    Objectives
        Qualitative results
        Quantitative results
    Goals
    Strategies
    Task identification and scheduling
    Preparation of plan
Issues to be resolved
    Planning horizon
        5 years
        10 years
    Expansion of product line
    Decentralization of information services functions
        Hardware
            Personal computers
            Minis
            Mainframes
        Personnel
```

FIGURE 12–3
Idea Processor: Inserting Items in an Outline
This display is the result of modifying the outline in Figure 12–2 so that two third-level items are inserted under "Objectives" and three fourth-level items are inserted under "Hardware."

Item Explanations.   Some outliners have a feature that permits users to add an explanation or clarification to an item. The item explanation is usually appended to an item description if the item description does not stand on its own; that is, it needs further explanation or clarification to be understood. The item explanation can be a sentence or even a paragraph. The item explanations can be hidden so that only the item descriptions are displayed. See "Hands-On Tutorial 48: Modifying an Outline."

Collapsing/Expanding an Outline

In outliner terminology, the relationship between an item and its subordinate items is that of a *parent* and *children*. An item, no matter what level, is a parent if it has subordinate items, or children. For example, in Figure 12–4, the second-level heading "Planning horizon" is the

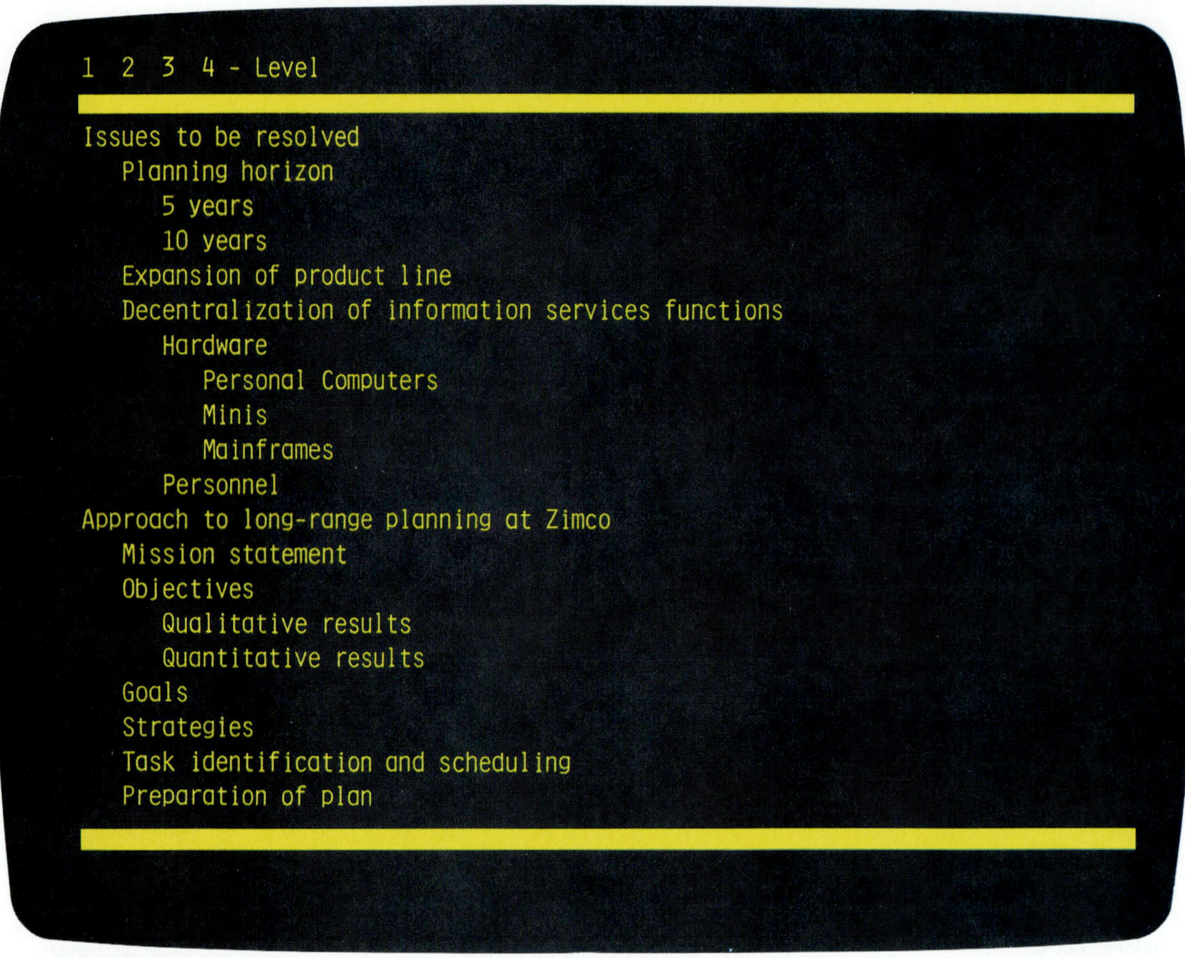

```
 1   2   3   4  -  Level
━━━━━━━━━━━━━━━━━━━━━━━━━━━━━━━━━━━━━━━━
Issues to be resolved
    Planning horizon
        5 years
        10 years
    Expansion of product line
    Decentralization of information services functions
        Hardware
            Personal Computers
            Minis
            Mainframes
        Personnel
Approach to long-range planning at Zimco
    Mission statement
    Objectives
        Qualitative results
        Quantitative results
    Goals
    Strategies
    Task identification and scheduling
    Preparation of plan
━━━━━━━━━━━━━━━━━━━━━━━━━━━━━━━━━━━━━━━━
```

FIGURE 12–4
Idea Processor: Block Operations
This display is the result of modifying the outline in Figure 12–3 so the "Issues to be resolved" item and its children are moved to the beginning of the outline.

parent to its children, "5 years" and "10 years". Notice that the "Planning horizon" item is also a child of "Issues to be resolved": thus, it is both a child and a parent.

The user can selectively *collapse* an outline to hide the children of a particular parent. That is, the children are deleted from the visual display of the outline, but they remain in main memory as part of the complete outline. This feature enables users to hide children from the view for those circumstances where all that is needed is a display of the parent item. For example, Preston Smith collapsed his entire planning agenda outline (see Figure 12–4) to the second-level (see Figure 12–5). In many outliner packages, the parents with hidden children are marked with a "+" (see Figure 12–5). Preston wanted to print out the more detailed outline of Figure 12–4 for himself and the overview outline of Figure 12–5 for the vice-presidents attending the planning session.

An entire outline can be collapsed to a given level or the children

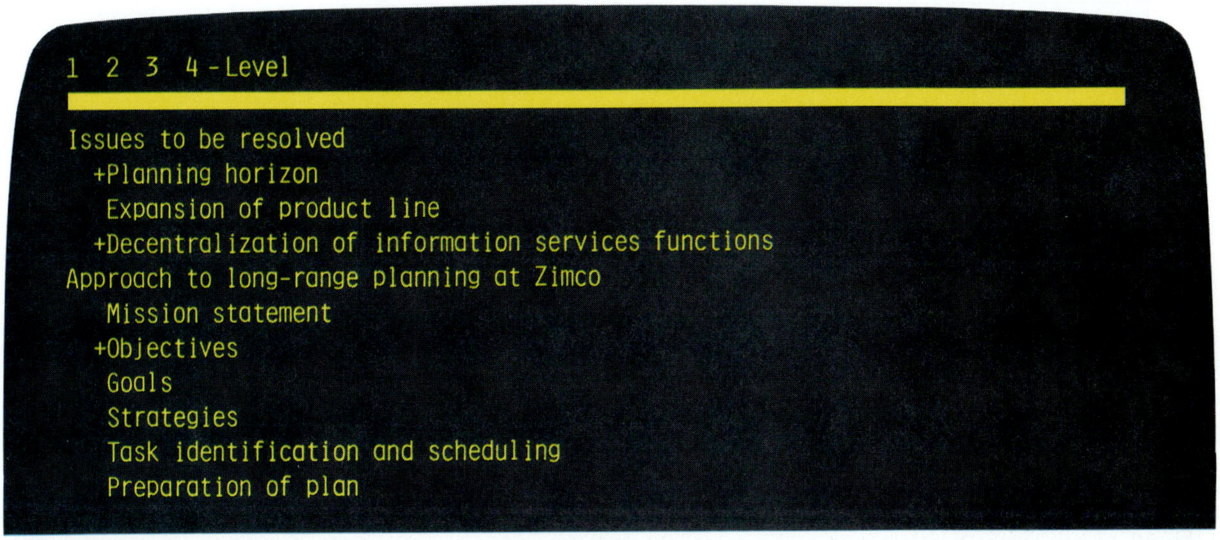

```
1  2  3  4 -Level

Issues to be resolved
   +Planning horizon
    Expansion of product line
   +Decentralization of information services functions
Approach to long-range planning at Zimco
    Mission statement
   +Objectives
    Goals
    Strategies
    Task identification and scheduling
    Preparation of plan
```

FIGURE 12–5
Idea Processor: Display of an Outline with Hidden Children
The outline of Figure 12–4 is displayed after being collapsed to the
second level.

of a single item can be hidden. To redisplay the hidden children, you
issue an *expand* command. Again, the expand can be applied to any
item marked with a plus or it can be applied collectively to an entire
outline. See "Hands-On Tutorial 49: Collapsing and Expanding."

Printing an Outline

While organizing your thoughts, a meeting, the day's activities, and
so on with an idea processor, the relationship between the items is
purely positional (sequence and level of heading). However, on output
(to a printer or a text file), the hierarchical display of items on the
monitor is transformed into a traditional outline format. The hard-copy
output of Figure 12–4 is shown in Figure 12–6. The outline in Figure
12–6 is presented in the traditional outline format. Some outliner packages use the alternative format

1	(vs. I.	)
1.1	(vs. A.	)
1.1.1	(vs.	1.)
1.1.2	(vs.	2.)
1.2	(vs. B.	)
1.3	(vs. C.	)

See "Hands-On Tutorial 50: Saving, Retrieving, and Printing an Outline
and Terminating a Session."

```
                EXECUTIVE PLANNING SESSION

    I.          Issues to be resolved
                A.   Planning horizon
                     1.   5 years
                     2.   10 years
                B.   Expansion of product line
                C.   Decentralization of information services functions
                     1.   Hardware
                          a.   Personal Computers
                          b.   Minis
                          c.   Mainframes
                     2.   Personnel
    II.         Approach to long-range planning at Zimco
                A.   Mission statement
                B.   Objectives
                     1.   Qualitative results
                     2.   Quantitative results
                C.   Goals
                D.   Strategies
                E.   Task identification and scheduling
                F.   Preparation of plan
```

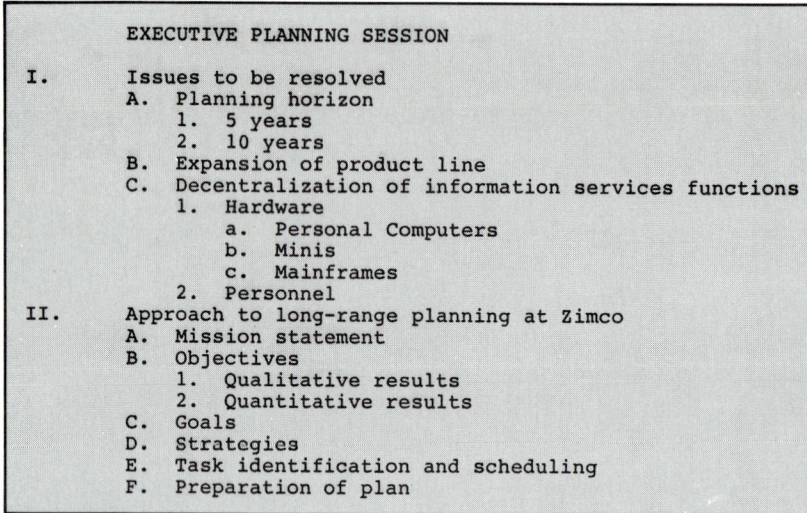

FIGURE 12–6
Idea Processor: Printout of an Outline
On output, the hierarchy of items displayed in Figure 12–4 is transformed to a traditional outline format.

Creating a Text File

You can use word processing software to create an outline that looks just like the one in Figure 12–6. To do so, you would have to perform many functions that are automatic with idea processors. For example, you would have to indent the lines to show appropriate levels and add the numbers and letters. Moreover, using a word processor to work with a document that is formatted as an outline can cause real headaches. For example, if you delete item 4 of 8 items, the last four will have to be manually renumbered.

There are, however, many circumstance where it would be advantageous to merge a completed outline with a word processing document. For example, you might need to insert an outline into a report. To do this, you would use the idea processor to create an *ASCII text file* on disk. Then, use word processing capabilities to merge the outliner text file into the word processing document. Once part of the word

Idea processor software is just one of a growing list of micro productivity software. Each new product increases the demand for micro software education. This demand has created more job opportunities than there are instructors to fill them.
(Courtesy of International Business Machines Corporation)

processing document, the outline can be manipulated like any word processing document.

The procedures for creating a text file of an outline are similar to printing an outline, except that the output is routed to a named file on disk rather than to a printer.

12–3   IDEA PROCESSORS IN PRACTICE

People use idea processors or outliners to organize their thinking, their meetings, their presentations, their dictation, and anything else that can be documented in the hierarchical style of an outline. The number and variety of applications for an idea processor are limitless. The following examples demonstrate a few of the many ways that outliners are used at Zimco.

- Sybil Allen, Zimco's manager of the Systems Analysis Department, has created an outline template for her weekly team meeting. The outline contains a generic list of topics (items) that are common to all meetings, such as progress reports, problem areas, and work schedules for the coming week. Prior to the meeting, she fills in the details (itemizing problems). Sybil works from a detailed outline during team meetings while the team members follow along from a collapsed overview outline.

- Some managers fill out the major heads of the outline and ask their subordinates to fill in the details. For example, before updating the job descriptions in the Personnel Division, Peggy Peoples, Zimco's Vice-President of Personnel, asks all employees in the division to outline what they think should be included in their job descriptions. She provides them with a *template* of an outline that contains the major headings: purpose of position, primary activities, prerequisite experience, prerequisite education, internal interactions, external interactions, and so on.

- Many Zimco managers begin their semi-annual performance review by calling up a template of an evaluation outline. The template includes headings for job knowledge, responsibility, judgement, communication skills, adaptability, and self improvement. From the template, the managers create the draft outlines that they use to prepare their written performance reviews.

- Outliners have become so popular at Zimco that people at all levels use them to prepare weekly itineraries. A typical itinerary template has days of the week as first level headings and hours of the day as second level headings. Activities to be performed are entered as third-level items under the appropriate day and hour. If needed, activity descriptions are included at the fourth level.

- Idea processors can even be used to keep certain types of records. For example, Gram Mertz, Zimco Programming Manager, and his secretary, Sandy Martin, use idea processor software to organize the directories and files on the personal computer that they share.

At the first level are their individual directories (\GRAM and \SANDY). Their subdirectories, which are associated primarily with software packages, are at the second level (\GRAM\LOTUS, \GRAM\DBASE, \SANDY\WP). The files are listed at the third level. For the subdirectory \GRAM\LOTUS, the files at the third level might be COSTSUM.WK1 and SALARY.WK1.

■ Sally Marcio, Vice-President of Sales and Marketing, asked her field salespeople to use idea processors to help them organize their sales calls. Customers respond positively to a salesperson that gives well-organized presentations.

In summary, idea processor software provides the capability for top-down thinking and documentation. That is, you can begin with general ideas or items and break them down into as much detail as desired. Saying that idea processors have 1001 uses might be an understatement. See "Hands-On Tutorial 51: The OUTLINER Tutorials."

SUMMARY OUTLINE AND IMPORTANT TERMS____

12–1   THE FUNCTION OF IDEA PROCESSORS.   An **idea processor** is a productivity tool that allows you to organize and document your thoughts and ideas. These software packages permit the manipulation of descriptions and explanations of items within a hierarchy of other items. The term item refers to ideas, points, activities, notes, or anything else that can be outlined.

12–2   IDEA PROCESSOR CONCEPTS.   Like word processing software, idea processor packages or outliners permit the manipulation of text, but with a different twist. You create an outline by entering items, and then use the capabilities of the software to arrange them into a well-organized outline.

You can use an idea processor to organize items in a hierarchy with several levels of item subordination or shift an item to the left or to the right to change its level. Items can be inserted at any point in an outline. One or more items in an outline can be moved, copied, or deleted. Some outliners have a feature that permits users to add an explanation or clarification to a item.

In outliner terminology, the relationship between an item and its subordinate items is that of a parent and children. The user can selectively collapse an outline to hide the children of a particular parent. An entire outline can be collapsed to a given level or the children of a single item can be hidden. To redisplay the hidden children, issue an expand command. The expand can be applied to any item marked as having hidden items or it can be applied collectively to an entire outline.

On output to a printer or a text file, the hierarchical display of items on the monitor is transformed into a traditional outline format. Create an ASCII text file of an outline if you wish to manipulate the outline with word processing software.

12–3   IDEA PROCESSORS IN PRACTICE.   People use idea processors or outliners to organize their thinking, their meetings, their presentations, their dictation, and anything else that can be documented in the hierarchical style of an outline. Idea processor software provides the capability for top-down thinking and documentation.

REVIEW EXERCISES

1. Describe what advantages an idea processor has over a yellow note pad during brainstorming sessions.

2. What would you do to change a third-level heading in an idea processor-produced outline to a second-level heading? A fourth-level heading?

3. When using an idea processor, what important step must be completed before issuing a command for a block operation?

4. What would be the equivalent label in the traditional outline format for an item at level 2.3.4 in an alternative outline format?

5. How many items would be displayed if the outline in Figure 12–4 were collapsed to level 1?

6. Relate the parent-children concept to collapsing and expanding an outline.

7. Describe a business, a domestic, and a student application for idea processors.

SELF-TEST (by section)

12–1. The software productivity tool that enables computer enhanced thinking is called an _____.

12–2. (a) Second-level items in an idea processor-produced outline are subordinate to third-level items. (T/F)

(b) Idea processor block operations include move, copy, and delete. (T/F)

(c) An item in an outline can be both a parent and a child. (T/F)

(d) It is not possible to merge an idea processor-produced outline with a word processing document. (T/F)

12–3. Idea processors provide the capability for (a) bottom-up thinking, (b) top-down thinking, or (c) substitute thinking.

Self-Test Answers.   **12–1,** idea processor; **12–2 (a),** F; **(b),** T; **(c),** T; **(d),** F; **12–3,** b.

HANDS-ON EXERCISES

1. Complete Hands-On Tutorials 46 through 51 and the Advanced and Special Features Tutorial (if appropriate) in the tutorials section of this chapter.

2. **(a)** Using idea processor software, create an outline that you might use to deliver a 10-minute verbal presentation on word processing, electronic spreadsheet, and database software. Make these three productivity tools the first-level headings and give each of them the following children: function, concepts, and use. Fill in third- and fourth-level headings to complete the outline. Print the outline.

   (b) Use block moves to rearrange the outline that you prepared in the first part of this exercise such that database software is first, followed by electronic spreadsheet and word processing software. Edit the outline if necessary. Print the outline.

   (c) Collapse your outline to the second level and then expand the "function" items. Print the outline.

3. **(a)** Outline your class or lecture notes for the day(s) your instructor covered idea processors. Print the outline.

   (b) Collapse the entire outline to the second level. Print the outline.

KEYSTROKE TUTORIALS IN THE *LAB MANUAL*

The *Lab Manual* that accompanies this text contains keystroke tutorials for

■ The OUTLINER (© Long and Associates)
■ ThinkTank (© Living Videotext, Inc.)

These keystroke tutorials illustrate the use of a particular idea processor software package in a domestic and a business application. The more advanced features of the packages are introduced in the business application tutorials.

IDEA PROCESSOR TUTORIAL: THE OUTLINER

QUICK REFERENCE GUIDE
The OUTLINER
(Version 1.10)
A>outliner ↵

MODES

INS	Switch between Insert and Edit mode.

Insert Mode

ENTER	Enter line, insert a new line

Edit Mode

CTRL-→ or ←	Move cursor a word at a time
HOME/END	Move to beg./end of a line
CTRL-HOME/END	Move to beg./end of outline
ALT-D	Delete a line

Insert and Edit Mode

ALT-1, 2, 3, 4	Change level of line
ESC	Return to Main Menu

FUNCTION KEYS

Mark block	F1	F2	Help
Move block	F3	F4	
Copy block	F5	F6	C/E outline
Collapse heading	F7	F8	Expand heading
		F9	F10	Delete block

HANDS-ON TUTORIAL 46: Using The OUTLINER

The OUTLINER, a product of Long and Associates, is an idea processing tool that helps users to organize their thoughts and ideas. Text files of completed outlines can be merged with files containing word processing documents.

■ Boot the system (see Hands-On Tutorial 1).

■ Load The OUTLINER to memory. Insert The OUTLINER program disk in drive A.

   A>**outliner** ↵

■ Insert your data disk in drive B. The display of the Main Menu indicates that you are ready to begin a session on The OUTLINER.

HANDS-ON TUTORIAL 47: Creating an Outline

■ Create an outline. Select the "create/edit outline" option from the Main Menu.

   1 (*"create/edit outline" option*)

The OUTLINER's work screen is divided into three parts: top, bottom, and the outline (between the thick divider lines). The mode indicator at the top right indicates whether you are in edit, insert, or block mode.

In edit mode, you can move about the outline to change the text and levels of existing items. You can delete the current line (the line with the blinking cursor) by pressing ALT-D. In insert mode, you add lines to the outline above or below the current line, at whatever level you wish, and enter text. Press the INS key to toggle (switch) between insert mode and edit mode. Block mode enables you to perform operations on groups of lines at the same time. You can move, copy, or delete several lines with one operation. Press F1 to enter block mode and mark a block.

The line at the bottom of the work screen indicates which commands and functions are available to you. These change when you switch modes.

The majority of the screen is a window containing the current outline. The four levels of ideas in The OUTLINER are identified by position (indentation) and by the four card suits: spades (level 1), hearts (level 2), diamonds (level 3), and clubs (level 4).

■ Press F2 in either edit or insert mode to call up help screens that summarize The OUTLINER's operations. Read both help screens.

> F2
>
> ↵ *(to view other help screen)*
> ESC *(to return to outline)*

■ Enter all first-, second-, and third-level items of the outline of Figure 12–4 (omit the fourth-level items under "Hardware").

Backspace to correct typos and press ENTER to progress to the next line.

> INS *(if not in insert mode, toggle to insert mode)*
> **Issues to be resolved** ↵

Use the ALT key in combination with 1, 2, 3, or 4 to select the level of the line. The next four lines are at levels 2, 3, 3, and 2, respectively.

> ALT -2 **Planning horizon** ↵
> ALT -3 **5 years** ↵
> **10 years** ↵
> ALT -2 **Expansion of product line** ↵

When in insert mode, press ENTER to insert a line below the current line. To insert a line above the current line, toggle to edit mode (INS) and position the cursor at the home position (the first position in line), then toggle back to insert mode (INS).

■ Enter the remaining text (except the fourth-level items).

HANDS-ON TUTORIAL 48: Modifying an Outline

■ Switch to edit mode and observe available command and function options at the bottom of the screen.

> INS *(toggle to edit mode)*

■ Insert the three fourth-level items under "Hardware" (see Figure 12–4). Use the up and down cursor control keys to position the line cursor at any position on the "Hardware" line except the home position (on the "H"). Toggle to insert mode and enter the fourth-level items.

> ↑ *(to "Hardware")* → *(to "a" in "Hardware")*
> INS *(toggle to insert mode)*
> ALT -4 **Personal computers** ↵
> **Minis** ↵
> **Mainframes** INS *(toggle to edit mode)*

■ Use the cursor control, backspace, and delete keys, to move about the outline

and correct any data entry errors, including blank lines. ALT-D deletes a line.

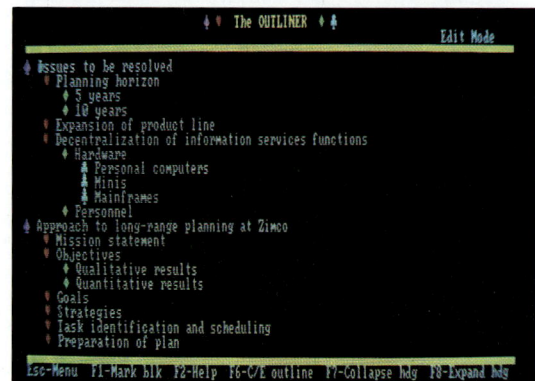

The OUTLINER display after the completion of Hands-On Tutorial 48.

HANDS-ON TUTORIAL 49: Collapsing and Expanding

An entire outline or parent heading can be collapsed to hide children or expanded to redisplay hidden children.

■ Collapse the entire outline to level 2.

> F6 *(collapse/expand outline)* **Collapse 2** *(2nd level)*

Your outline should look like the outline

in Figure 12–5. Headings marked with a "+" have hidden children.

■ Expand the "Planning horizon" heading.
> ↓ *(move cursor to "Planning horizon" line)*
> F8 *(expand heading)*

■ Expand the entire outline to level 4.
> F6 *(collapse/expand outline)* **Expand 4** *(4th level)*

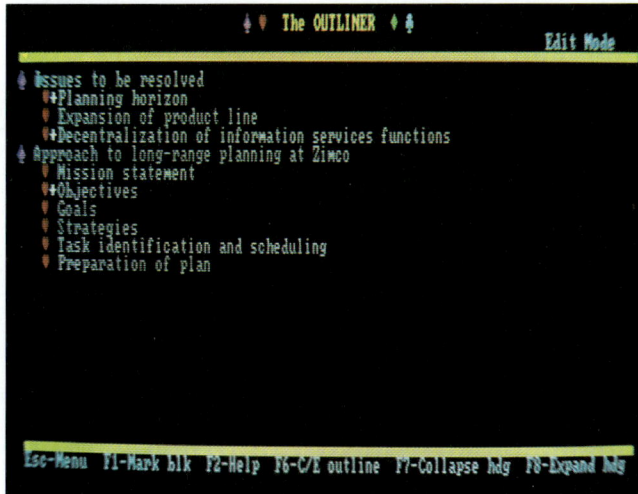

The OUTLINER display after collapsing AGENDA to the second level in Hands-On Tutorial 49.

HANDS-ON TUTORIAL 50: Saving, Retrieving, and Printing an Outline and Terminating a Session

■ Save the outline. Return to the Main Menu and select the file menu option. From the File Menu, select the save option.

> ESC **2** (*file menu option*) **2** (*save option*)

Enter a file identifier (disk and filename) in response to the prompt. The extension, .OUT, is automatically appended to all filenames.

> Save current outline as : **b:agenda** ↵

■ Retrieve a previously saved outline. From the Main Menu, select the file menu option. From the File Menu, select the retrieve option.

> **2** (*file menu option*) **1** (*retrieve option*)

The file identifier of the current outline is displayed after the prompt. If the desired file identifier is not already displayed, enter it in response to the prompt. Respond yes to the confirmation prompt.

> Retrieve OUTLINER file: **b:agenda** ↵
> Current outline will replaced.
>   Continue [Y/N]? **Y**es

■ Print the current outline. Turn on the printer, and then select the print option from the Main Menu.

> ESC
> **3** (*print option*)

Title the outline and accept the remaining defaults on the Print Options screen. Press ENTER to begin printing (see Figure 12–6).

> Outline title (optional) : **EXECUTIVE PLANNING SESSION**
> ↵

■ Exit The OUTLINER. Return to the Main Menu and select the exit option. Respond yes to the confirmation prompt.

> ESC **9** (*exit option*)
> Do you really want to exit The OUTLINER [Y/N]? **Y**es

HANDS-ON TUTORIAL 51: The OUTLINER Tutorials

The OUTLINER program disk contains four interactive tutorials. Tutorial 1 covers introductory concepts plus edit and insert modes. Tutorial 2 covers block mode operations and collapse-expand features. Tutorial 3 covers file operations and print operations. Tutorial 4 covers helpful hints, tricks, and shortcuts.

■ Load The OUTLINER into memory (see "Hands-on Tutorial 46, Using The OUTLINER").

■ Retrieve Tutorial 1 from program disk. Return to the Main Menu and select the file menu option. From the File Menu, select the retrieve option.

ESC **2** (*file menu option*) **1** (*retrieve option*)

At the prompt, enter the filename of Tutorial 1.

Retrieve OUTLINER file: **tutor1** ↵

Read each line of the tutorial outline and follow the instructions. If you get lost or want to start over, simply retrieve the tutorial from disk again.

■ After completing Tutorial 1, work through Tutorials 2, 3 and 4 ("tutor2", "tutor3", and "tutor4").

■ After completing the tutorials, exit The OUTLINER in the manner described in Hands-On Tutorial 50.

ADVANCED AND SPECIAL FEATURES TUTORIAL: THE OUTLINER

In this advanced tutorial of The OUTLINER the following skills are introduced: saving an outline as a text file (also called an ASCII file), previewing a text file, and combining a text file into a word processing document. You should have completed Hands-On Tutorials 41 through 46 before continuing with this advanced tutorial.

Preston Smith, Zimco's President, wanted to be able to merge the agenda outline that he created (see Figure 12–4) for an upcoming executive planning session with a word-processing produced memo that is to be sent to all the vice-presidents. To do this, he will need to change the "agenda" OUTLINER file to a text file and then use word processing software to combine the outline with the memo.

GETTING STARTED

To complete this tutorial, you will need The OUTLINER diskette, a work disk that contains The OUTLINER "agenda" file, and any word processing software. (This tutorial demonstrates the procedure with WordPerfect.)

■ Boot the system (see Hands-on Tutorial 1).
■ Load The OUTLINER to memory. Insert The OUTLINER program disk in drive A.

A>**outliner** ↵

■ Insert your data disk in drive B.
■ Retrieve the "agenda" outline created in Hands-On Tutorials 41 through 45.

2 (*file menu option*) **1** (*retrieve option*)
Retrieve OUTLINER file: **b:agenda** ↵

SAVING AN OUTLINER FILE AS A TEXT FILE

■ To create a text file of the current outline, select the create a text file option from the main menu.

ESC (*return to main menu*)
3 (*create a text file option*)

■ Add the title "EXECUTIVE PLANNING SESSION".

Outline title (optional): **EXECUTIVE PLANNING SESSION**

■ Press TAB to move the cursor to the printer/text file option and change from the default setting of "P" to "T".

TAB (*5 times to printer/text file option*)
Print to printer/text file [P/T] : **T**ext

■ Press ENTER to accept the settings and create the text

↵
Name of text file: **b:agenda.txt** ↵
Do you want page breaks [Y/N]? **N**o

■ Preview the text file.

Do you want to preview the text file [Y/N]? **Y**es

Notice that the spade, heart, diamond and club symbols have been replaced with standard outline symbols (I. A. 1. a.). You are only able to preview this file, not edit it.

```
        ♦ ♥ The OUTLINER ♦ ♣
           Preview Text File

I.    Issues to be resolved
      A. Planning horizon
         1. 5 years
         2. 10 years
      B. Expansion of product line
      C. Decentralization of information services functions
         1. Hardware
            a. Personal computers
            b. Minis
            c. Mainframes
         2. Personnel
II.   Approach to long-range planning at Zimco
      A. Mission statement
      B. Objectives
         1. Qualitative results
         2. Quantitative results
      C. Goals
      D. Strategies
      E. Task identification and scheduling
      F. Preparation of plan

Esc - End preview        PgDn - Next page        PgUp - Last page
```

The OUTLINER preview display of AGENDA in the Advanced and Special Features Tutorial.

- Complete the preview by pressing ESC.

    `ESC` (*end preview*)

- Exit The OUTLINER.

    `ESC` **9** (*exit option*) **Yes**

You will need to replace The OUTLINER disk with the DOS disk after exiting The OUTLINER.

COMPARING THE OUTLINER FILE WITH A TEXT FILE

- Load DOS. At the DOS prompt, use the "type" command to view the text file.

    A>**type b:agenda.txt** ↵

- For comparison, view the "agenda.out" file that was saved as an OUTLINER file.

    A>**type b:agenda.out** ↵

Unlike "agenda.txt", "agenda.out" is not actually an outline. It is a file that is used by The OUTLINER to create an outline.

- Clear the screen to end this session.

    A>**cls** ↵

COMBINING A TEXT FILE WITH A WORD PROCESSING DOCUMENT

- Create the memo from Preston Smith with word processing software (WordPerfect is used in this example).

Use the techniques (and same margin settings) presented in WordPerfect Hands-On Tutorials 4 through 11 to create the following memo.

To: Vice-Presidents, Zimco Enterprises
From: Preston Smith, President
Re: Executive Planning Session

Please plan to meet in the executive conference room after the Annual Meeting next Saturday. The following is a copy of the proposed agenda.

- Save the newly created memo as "planning" on your work disk.

- Merge the text file "agenda" to the "planning" file.

    (*position the cursor two lines below the memo*)
    `CTRL`-`F5` (*text in/out*)
    Selection: **2** (*retrieve file*)
    Document to be Retrieved: **b:agenda.txt** ↵

The "agenda" file is combined with the "planning" memo. Page up and down to view the revised memo.

- Save the "planning" memo, print it, and exit the word processing software (see Hands-On Tutorials 10 and 11).

IDEA PROCESSOR TUTORIAL: THINKTANK

QUICK REFERENCE GUIDE
ThinkTank
(Version 2.30NP)
A>tank ↵

MAIN COMMAND MENU

Press F10 to call the Main Command Menu:

Expand	Keyword
Collapse	— Search
Insert	— Xchange
Move	— Mark
Window	Port
Delete	Files
— Outline	Function
— Document	Extra
— Undo	
Edit	
— Headline	
— Document	

CURSOR MOVEMENT

CTRL-→ or ←	Move cursor a word at a time
HOME/END	Move to beg./end of a line
CTRL-HOME/ END	Move to beg./end of outline

HANDS-ON TUTORIAL 46: Using ThinkTank

ThinkTank, a product of Living Videotext, Inc., is an idea processing tool that helps users to organize their thoughts and ideas. Text files of completed outlines can be merged with files containing word processing documents. In addition, word processing documents may be contained within ThinkTank outlines. This tutorial is based on ThinkTank Version 2.30NP.

■ Boot the system (see Hands-On Tutorial 1).

■ Load ThinkTank to memory. Insert the ThinkTank program disk in drive A.

    A>**tank** ↵

■ Insert your data disk in drive B.

■ The title screen gives you an opportunity to update the date. Assume that the date is correct and answer no to the prompt.

    press "y" for yes, "n" for no **n**

HANDS-ON TUTORIAL 47: Creating an Outline

■ ThinkTank opens the most recently active file (for example, from a previous session). If you had been working on another file, follow the steps below. Create an outline by first closing the current outline.

F10 (*call up command menu*)
files (*select the files option*)
close (*close the file*)

However, if this is the initial session, you will be creating a new file; so use the following technique.

■ Create an outline. Select the new file option from the files command menu and name the file "agenda".

> **new** (*new file*)
> name of new outline file? **b:agenda** ↵

ThinkTank creates a new file with the extension .db and opens a work screen for data entry. In the work screen, the bottom four lines are used to display command options and messages. The upper portion of the screen is reserved for the outline itself. Currently, the outline consists of one line, called the home headline, and a highlight bar. The home headline is reserved for outline titles. No other headline in the outline can be as far to the left as is the home headline.

■ Edit the home headline to make the heading read "EXECUTIVE PLANNING SESSION".

> F10
>
> **edit** (*select edit option*)
> edit headline or document? **h**eadline

Use F10 to call up the command menu, or, if you know the commands that can be activated by pressing the first letter of the menu option, there is no reason to display the command menu. Notice that the highlight bar disappears and a rectangular edit cursor appears to the right of the word, "Home".

> BKSP (*4 times*)

EXECUTIVE PLANNING SESSION ↵

■ Press the insert key to move to the next line.

> INS (*move to the first line of the outline*)

During text entry, all headlines are prefaced by a question mark.

■ Enter all first-, second-, and third- level items of the outline of Figure 12–4 (omit the fourth-level items under "Hardware"). Use the backspace to correct any data entry errors. At this point, you are at level one of the outline.

> **Issues to be resolved** ↵

Indent the next line one level (to level 2) by pressing the right cursor control key.

> → (*move one level*) **Planning horizon** ↵
> → (*change to level 3*) **5 years** ↵
> **10 years** ↵
> ← **Expansion of product line** ↵
> (*enter remaining text. . .*)
> **Preparation of plan** ESC

The "+" sign in front of an item denotes that it has sub-headings (or children) beneath it. A "−" sign indicates that an item has no children.

Instead of pressing ENTER after keying in the last line of Figure 12–4 ("Preparation of plan"), press ESC. This will allow you to modify the outline in the next tutorial.

HANDS-ON TUTORIAL 48: Modifying an Outline _____

Insert the fourth-level items under "Hardware" (see Figure 12–4).

■ Use the left cursor control key to position the line cursor on the "Hardware" line. Press the insert key and enter the three fourth-level items.

> ← (*move cursor to highlight "Hardware"*)
> INS (*create a new headline*)
> → **Personal computers** ↵
> **Minis** ↵
> **Mainframes** ESC

ThinkTank display after the completion of Hands-On Tutorial 48.

HANDS-ON TUTORIAL 49: Collapsing and Expanding

An entire subhead can be collapsed to hide children or expanded to redisplay hidden children.

■ Move the headline cursor through the outline and press the collapse key to collapse the outline to level 2.

> → *(move cursor to "Objectives")*
> − *(grey minus key, the collapse heading key)*
> ← *(move cursor to "Personnel")*
> ↑ ← *(move cursor to "Decentralization. . .")*

Using the up and down cursor keys move the highlight bar at the same level for faster movement.

‾
↑ *(move cursor to "Planning horizon")*
‾

Your outline should look similar to the outline in Figure 12–5. Headings marked with a "+" have hidden children.

■ Expand the "Planning horizon" heading.

> + *(the grey plus key, the expand heading key)*

■ Expand the entire outline to level 4.

> CTRL - HOME *(highlight the home headline)*
> * *(expand all)*

ThinkTank display after collapsing AGENDA to the second level in Hands-On Tutorial 49.

HANDS-ON TUTORIAL 50: Saving, Retrieving, and Printing an Outline and Terminating a Session

■ Save the outline. ThinkTank saves the current file to disk when the close file option is chosen.

> files *(select the files option)*
> close *(close the file)*

ThinkTank returns to the title screen and displays the files command menu.

■ Since the agenda file already exists, press "e" to call up the existing file menu then choose the last option ("agenda" is the last active file).

> exists
> last

If you wish to call another ThinkTank file, choose the enter option to designate the file. The browse option lets you observe the titles of .db files on both drives A and B.

■ Print the current outline. Be sure the cursor is on the home headline.

> CTRL - HOME
> port *(select the port option)*
> select a device   printer
> select an output style   formatted
> look at the format settings? yes

ThinkTank has 17 format options and default values for each. Change the default
selection for option 10, accept the other
defaults, and print the outline.

> → (*9 times*)
> format setting #10 of 17
> table of contents IS printed ↵
> do you want a table of contents? **n**o
> ESC (*exit the format settings*)
> "exit settings" command menu   **n**osave
> press (spacebar) to start printing SPACE

Selecting the nosave option causes the
new setting to be applicable for this
printing only.

■ Return to the outline when the printing
is complete.

> press (spacebar) to continue SPACE

■ Press the escape key to exit ThinkTank.

> ESC
> call it a day? **Y**es

CHAPTER 13

Communications Software Concepts and Tutorials

STUDENT LEARNING OBJECTIVES

- To describe the function and purpose of communications software.
- To describe microcomputer-oriented applications for data communications.
- To demonstrate an understanding of data communications terminology.
- To detail the function and operation of data communications hardware.
- To describe the alternatives and sources for data transmission services.
- To illustrate the various types of computer networks.
- To become familiar with the use and application of communications software for one or both of the following packages:
  - Crosstalk XVI
  - PC-Talk4
- To acquire the ability to apply the communications software skills demonstrated in the hands-on tutorials.

HANDS-ON TUTORIALS for *Crosstalk XVI* and *PC-Talk4*

52. Using Data Communications Software
53. Setting Up the Software for Data Communications
54. Establishing a Data Communications Link
55. Terminating a Data Communications Link

13-1 DATA COMMUNICATIONS: FROM ONE ROOM TO THE WORLD

For many years we have depended on telephone conversations and the postal service to communicate data and information from one location to another. Now, thousands of memos and charts can be sent to locations around the world in a matter of seconds. This is possible because of **data communications** capabilities. Data communications is, very simply, the collection and distribution of electronic data from and to remote locations—in the next room or around the world.

Through the 1960s, a company's computing hardware was located in a single room, called the machine room. Since that time, microcomputers and data communications have made it possible to move hardware and information systems closer to the source and to the people who use them. Before long, micros will be as much a part of our work environment as desks and telephones are now. The integration of computer systems, terminals, and communications links is referred to as a **computer network**.

13-2 COMMUNICATIONS SOFTWARE VERSUS OTHER MICRO PRODUCTIVITY SOFTWARE

People with little or no computer experience can readily identify with memos, sales reports, bar graphs, name and address files, and meeting outlines—applications for word processing, spreadsheet, graphics, database, and outliner software. These applications are part of our everyday business and domestic experiences. Because of this familiarity, we are able to jump right in and begin the conceptual discussions of the various software packages. However, the application addressed by *communications software* is data communications, a technical area that is a mystery to most micro users. This jump-right-in approach is not as easy with data communications software.

To effectively use the capabilities of communications software, it is important that you be familiar with the fundamental concepts associated with data communications. Therefore, much of this chapter is devoted to familiarizing you with the field of data communications.

13-3 THE FUNCTION OF COMMUNICATIONS SOFTWARE

Communications software expands the capability of a microcomputer. With communications software, a micro becomes more than a small stand-alone computer: It becomes capable of interacting with a remote computer, in the next room or in Japan.

In a nutshell, communications software performs two basic functions.

While watching a college football game, this sports writer composed a story for the morning paper on his portable personal computer. After the game he edited the copy, then used communications software to transmit the story electronically over a telephone line to the newspaper's computer system.
(Photo supplied courtesy of Epson America)

1. *Terminal emulation.* Communications software transforms a micro into a video display terminal (VDT) that can be linked to another computer.

2. *File transfer.* Communications software enables the transfer of files between a micro and another computer.

Before accomplishing either of these functions, an electronic link must be established between the micro and the other computer. To establish this link the micro user initiates the **logon procedure**. Typically the logon procedure involves

1. Dialing up a remote computer (another micro or a mainframe). The remote computer answers with a high-pitched tone.

2. Entering a preassigned **password** and **personal identification number** or **PIN**. The use of passwords and PINs helps protect a computer system against unauthorized access and use.

Once the remote computer validates the password, PIN, or both, the link is established. At this time, the remote computer will normally prompt the user to enter a command or it will present the user with a menu of options.

Terminal Emulation

Mainframes, minis, and multiuser micros are designed to provide service to remote terminals. Large mainframes can serve thousands of end users at remote terminals. Multiuser micros can serve up to 10 end users. These **host computers** have direct control over the terminals, processors, storage devices, and input/output devices that are linked to them. When an end user at a terminal logons (establishes a link) to a host computer, the host immediately responds by asking the end user to enter the type of terminal he or she is using. Of course, a micro is not a terminal, but with the aid of communications software, a micro can emulate or act like one of the terminals that can be interfaced with the host. Communications software can transform a micro into any of a variety of popular terminals, including DEC's VT100, IBM's 3101, and AT&T's BCT series.

The two most distinguishing characteristics of terminals are the keyboard layout and the manner in which they send and received data. When a micro is in **terminal emulation mode**, the keyboard, monitor, and data interface are like that of the terminal that is being emulated. From the host computer's perspective, the workstation being serviced is a terminal (for example, DEC VT100), not a micro.

Most terminals are *dumb terminals*, that is they do not have standalone processing or storage capabilities. Communications software transforms a micro into an *intelligent terminal* that can provide capabilities above and beyond that of the terminal being emulated: For example, it can store an interactive session on a disk file.

Communications software makes it possible for this warehouse supervisor to convert his micro to terminal emulation mode so that he can communicate with the company's mainframe computer. (Photo courtesy of Hewlett-Packard Company)

File Transfers

Once the link between the micro and host has been established, data, program, or text files can be transmitted from disk storage on the host computer to disk storage on the micro. This process is called **downloading**. You can also transmit files from the micro to the host in a process called **uploading**.

The file transfer capability afforded by communications software can be invaluable when you need to transfer files between incompatible computers (computers of different manufacturers and/or different operating systems). In today's information society, the need to transfer files between incompatible systems is commonplace.

13–4   MICROCOMPUTER-ORIENTED APPLICATIONS FOR DATA COMMUNICATIONS

The applications for on-line data communications are limited only by the imagination. Some of the more popular micro-oriented applications include the following, most of which have been mentioned or discussed in previous chapters.

- *Electronic mail.* Computer networks enable us to route messages to each other. A message can be a note, letter, report, chart, or even the manuscript of a book. Each person in an organization can be assigned an "electronic mailbox" in which messages are received and stored on secondary storage. To "open" and "read" your **electronic mail**, or **E-mail**, you simply go to the nearest micro or terminal and recall the message from storage.

  The mainframe computers at most companies enable users to send and receive electronic mail within the confines of the company. External electronic mail can be sent and received via public bulletin boards, commercial information services, and public E-mail services.

- *Information services.* Commercial information services make a wide variety of services available through data communications. You can use your home or office micro to do your banking, catch up on the stock prices, check out the menu at a local restaurant, make a hotel reservation, and send or receive a message via electronic mail.

  A few information services are gratis, but most require some kind of fee. The fee can include a one-time initiation fee, a monthly service charge, plus an amount based on usage. A few of the more popular commercial information services are *CompuServe, The Source, Dow Jones News/Retrieval Service, Western Union, Delphi,* and *NewsNet.* The scope of the information services offered by these companies is discussed in more detail in Chapter 1.

- *Bulletin board systems.* Special-interest **bulletin board systems** (**BBS**) offer users a forum for the exchange of ideas and information. The themes for BBSs run the gamut: Apple computer users,

Data communications opens the door to a wide variety of information services, from "up-to-the-minute" news to electronic mail.
(Copyright Viewdata Corporation of America 1984)

Lotus 1-2-3 users, IBM PC users, local politics, introductory computer education, and so on. As the name implies, a BBS is the electronic counterpart of its wall-mounted cousin. Both serve essentially the same function, but a BBS can be accessed from any modem-equipped micro. You can tap into a BBS by using your micro and communications software to establish a link. Once logged on, you can scan or read existing messages, leave messages, or respond to existing messages.

Several thousand bulletin board systems are made available free of charge by individuals, companies, and computer clubs. The person or group sponsoring the BBS is referred to as the *system operator* or **sysop**, for short. Individuals do it as a hobby. Companies do it to provide a service to their customers. Computer clubs do it to facilitate the exchange of information.

■ *On-line information systems*. Data communications makes it possible to tap into a company's host computer and its on-line information systems. You can use your micro to *make an inquiry* to the information system's data base and *receive a response*. For example, the director of personnel might wish to see the training record of an employee, or a salesperson in a department store might inquire about a customer's credit limit.

■ *Data entry*. Data can be entered on-line directly from the source location. For example, field sales representatives can use their portable micros in conjunction with the telephone system and communications software to enter order data from a customer's office.

13–5 DATA COMMUNICATIONS HARDWARE

Special Function Processors

Data communications hardware is used to transmit data in a computer network between terminals and computers, and between computers (micros and mainframes). This hardware includes a variety of *special function processors* that are strategically placed within the network to facilitate the flow of information. For the most part, the function of these special function processors is transparent to the end user; that is, they function automatically without any direction from the end user.

The micro, terminal, or computer sending a **message** is the *source*. The micro, terminal, or computer receiving the message is the *destination*. The contents of a message could be anything from a single character to an electronic memo. A special-function processor, which is connected to the mainframe, establishes and maintains the link between source and destination in a process called **handshaking**. Handshaking is discussed in more detail in Section 13–9.

The Modem

Communications software provides you with the capability to link your microcomputer to a remote computer system anywhere in the world.

At the end of each month, this plant manager downloads cost data from the company's mainframe computer to his microcomputer (see external modem in foreground). He then uses micro-based graphics software to compare expenditures for the Boston plant with those of the Phoenix and Indianapolis plants.
(Reproduced by permission of Hayes Microcomputer Products, Inc. (c) 1987)

However, to do this, you must have ready access to a telephone line and your micro must be equipped with a *modem*. Telephone lines were designed for voice communication, not data communication. The **modem** (*mo*dulator-*dem*odulator) converts computer-to-terminal and computer-to-micro electrical *digital* signals to *analog* signals so that the data can be transmitted over telephone lines (see Figure 13–1). The digital electrical signals are modulated to make sounds similar to those you hear on a touch-tone telephone. Upon reaching their destination, these analog signals are demodulated by another modem to computer-compatible electrical signals for processing. The process is done in reverse for terminal or micro-to-computer communication.

A modem is always required when you dial-up the computer on a telephone line. For transmission media other than telephone lines, the modulation-demodulation process is not needed, and therefore, modems are not required.

Internal and External Modems.   There are two types of modems for micros: *internal* and *external*. On most micros, the modem is internal; that is, it is contained on an optional add-on circuit board that is simply plugged into an empty expansion slot in the processor unit. The external modem is a separate component, as illustrated in Figure 13–1. Both internal and external modems are connected to the common electrical bus to which all micro components are connected, but in different ways. The contacts on the circuit board of the internal modem are plugged directly into the bus. The external modem is connected via an RS-232C serial interface port (see Chapter 3, "Interacting with a Microcomputer"). To make the connection with a telephone line, you simply plug the telephone line into the modem, just as you would when connecting the line to a telephone.

FIGURE 13–1
The Modulation/Demodulation Process
Electrical digital signals are modulated to analog signals for transmission over telephone lines and demodulated for processing at the destination.

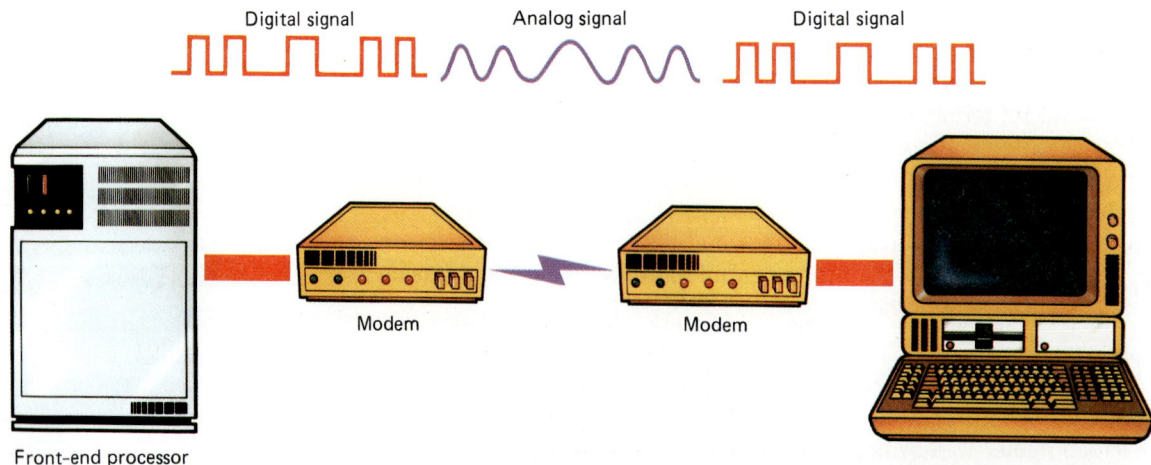

Digital signal   Analog signal   Digital signal

Modem   Modem

Front-end processor

Smart Modems.   Modems have varying degrees of "intelligence" due to embedded microprocessors. For instance, some modems can automatically dial-up the computer (*auto-dial*), establish a link (*logon*), and even answer incoming calls from other computers (*auto-answer*). **Smart modems** have also made it possible to increase the rate at which data can be transmitted and received.

Acoustical Couplers.   If you need a telephone hookup (for a voice conversation) on the same line and do not want to deal with the hassle of disconnecting the phone with each use, you can purchase a modem with an **acoustical coupler**. To make the connection, you mount the telephone handset directly on the acoustical coupler. For travelers who routinely make micro-mainframe connections from public telephones, acoustical couplers are essential items.

13–6   THE DATA COMMUNICATIONS CHANNEL: DATA HIGHWAYS

Channel Capacity

A **communications channel** is the facility by which data are transmitted between locations in a computer network. Data are transmitted as combinations of bits (0s and 1s). A channel's *capacity* is rated by the number of bits that can be transmitted per second. A specially conditioned telephone line can transmit up to 9600 **bits per second** (**bps**), or 9.6K bps (thousands of bits per second). However, common capacities for microcomputer modems are 300 bps, 1200 bps, and 2400 bps. Under normal circumstances, a 1200 bps line would fill a micro's screen in 8 to 16 seconds.

   In practice, the word **baud** and *bits per second* are used interchangeably. In reality they are quite different. Baud is a measure of the maximum number of electronic signals that can be transmitted via a communications channel. It is true that a 300 bps modem operates at 300 baud, but both 1200 bps and 2400 bps modems operate at 600 baud. A technical differentiation between baud and bits per second is beyond the scope of this book. Suffice it to say that when someone says baud, and they are talking about computer-based data communications, they probably mean bits per second. The erroneous use of baud is so common that some communications software packages ask you to specify baud rather than bits per second.

Direction of Data Flow

The direction of *data flow* in a channel, also called a **line**, is either simplex, half-duplex, or full-duplex (see Figure 13–2). Lines that transmit data in only one direction are called **simplex lines**. Those that transmit data in both directions, but not at the same time are called **half-duplex lines**. A line that transmits data in both directions at the same time is called a **full-duplex line**. Since virtually all informa-

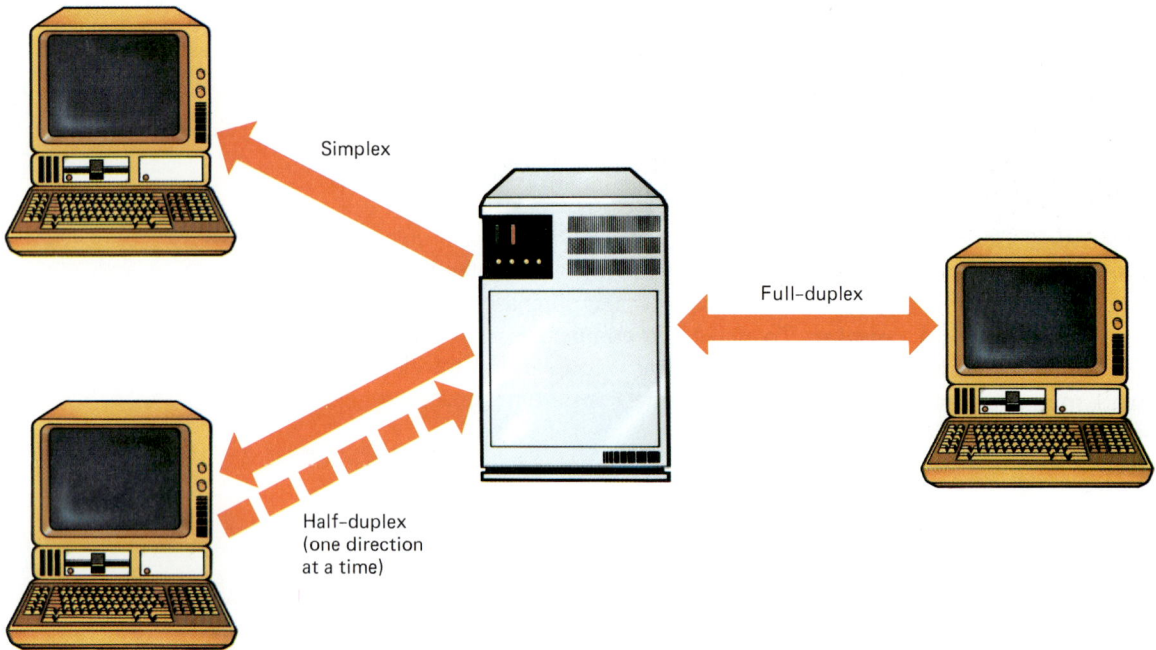

FIGURE 13–2
Direction of Data Flow
Data flow in a channel is either simplex, half-duplex, or full-duplex.

Copper wire in the telephone network is being replaced by the more versatile optical fiber. Laser-generated light pulses are transmitted through these ultrathin glass fibers. A pair of optical fibers can simultaneously carry 1,344 voice conversations and interactive data communications sessions. (AT&T Technologies)

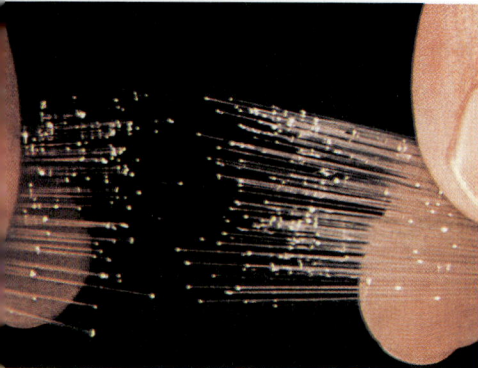

tion systems and services are interactive, bidirectional transmission lines, either half- or full-duplex, are required. "Line" is actually a misnomer, because a full-duplex line is simply two half-duplex lines.

Transmission Media

The channel, which is also called a **data link**, that links a micro and another computer may be comprised of one or a combination of the following transmission media.

- *Telephone lines*. The same transmission facilities that we use for telephone conversations can also be used to transmit data.
- *Optical fiber*. Very thin transparent fibers have been developed that will eventually replace the copper wire that has been used in the telephone system for decades. These hairlike fibers carry data faster and are lighter and less expensive than copper wire.
- *Coaxial cable*. Coaxial cable contains electrical wire and is constructed to permit high-speed data transmission with a minimum of signal distortion. Among other uses, it is used to connect micros, terminals, and computers in a local area (from a few feet to a few miles).
- *Microwave*. Communications channels do not have to be wires or fibers. Data can also be transmitted via microwave radio signals. Transmission of these signals is line-of-sight; that is, the radio signal

This control console monitors data communications traffic between satellites and earth stations.
(RCA)

travels in a direct line from one repeater station to the next until it reaches its destination. Because of the curvature of the earth, microwave repeater stations are placed on the tops of mountains and on towers, usually about 30 miles apart.

Satellites have made it possible to overcome the line-of-sight problem. Satellites are routinely launched into orbit for the sole purpose of relaying data communication signals to and from earth stations. A satellite, which is essentially a repeater station, is launched and set in a geosynchronous orbit 22,300 miles above the earth. A geosynchronous orbit permits the communications satellite to maintain a fixed position relative to the surface of the earth. The big advantage of satellites is that data can be transmitted from one location to any number of other locations anywhere on (or near) our planet.

Data Transmission in Practice

A communications channel from computer A in Seattle, Washington, to computer B in Orlando, Florida (see Figure 13–3), would usually consist of several different transmission media. The connection between computer A and a micro in the same building is probably coaxial cable. The Seattle company might use a communications company, such as AT&T, to transmit the data. The company would then transmit the data through a combination of transmission facilities that might include copper wire, optical fiber, and microwave.

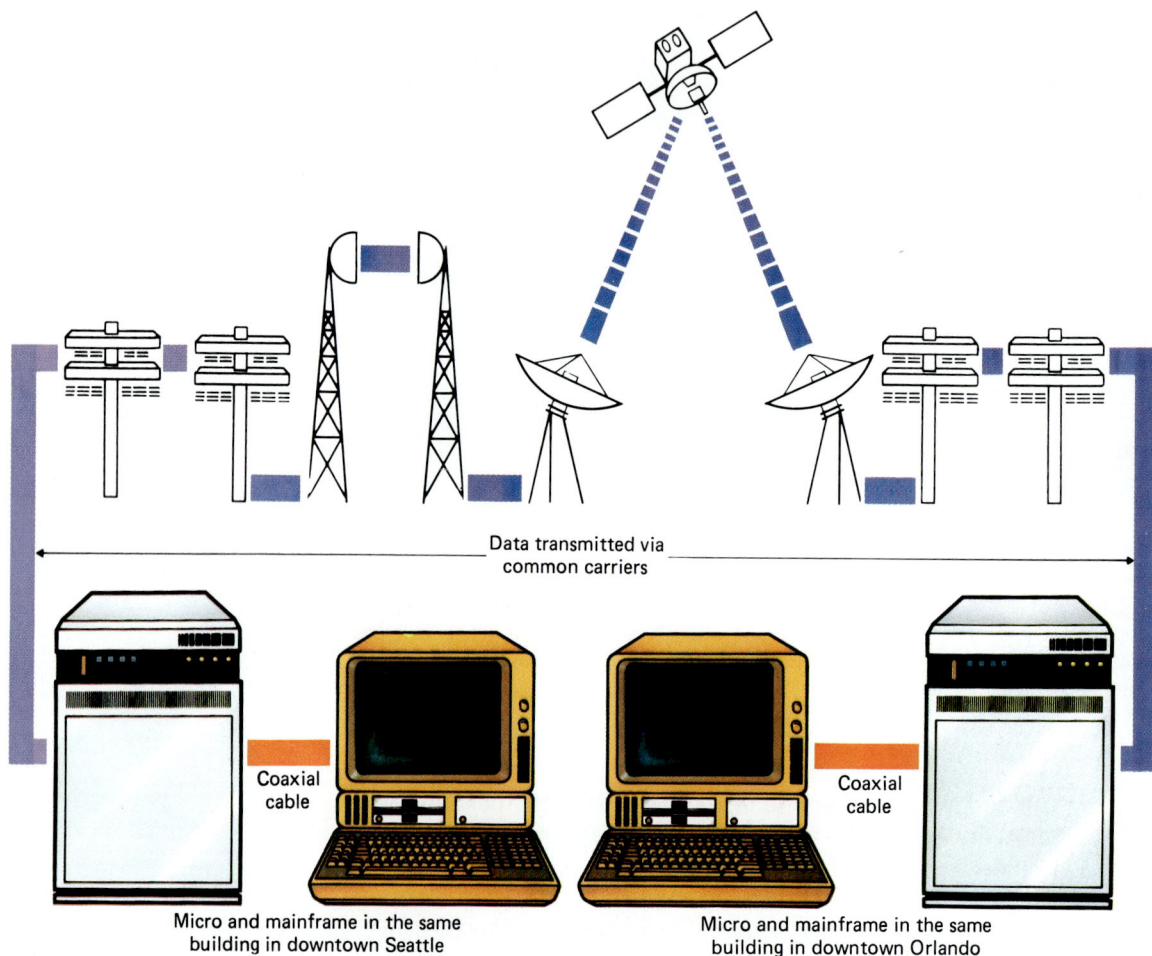

Data transmitted via common carriers

Coaxial cable

Coaxial cable

Micro and mainframe in the same building in downtown Seattle

Micro and mainframe in the same building in downtown Orlando

FIGURE 13–3
Data Transmission Path
It is more the rule than the exception that data are carried over several transmission media between source and destination.

13–7   DATA TRANSMISSION SERVICES

It is impractical for companies to string their own coaxial cables between distant cities and to set their own satellites in orbit. Therefore, companies turn to **common carriers**, such as AT&T and Western Union, to provide channels for data communications. Data communications common carriers, which are regulated by the Federal Communications Commission (FCC), offer two basic types of service: private lines and switched lines.

A **private line** (or **leased line**) provides a dedicated data communications channel between any two points in a computer network. The charge for a private line is based on channel capacity (bps) and distance (air miles).

A **switched line** (or **dial-up line**) is available strictly on a time-and-distance charge, similar to a long-distance telephone line. You make a connection by dialing-up the computer; then a modem sends and receives data.

13–8 NETWORKS: LINKING COMPUTERS AND MICROS

Computer Networks

Network Configurations. Each time you use the telephone, you use the world's largest computer network—the telephone system. A telephone is an endpoint, or a **node**, that is connected to a network of computers that route your voice signals to another telephone, or node. The node in a computer network can be a terminal or another computer. Computer networks are configured to meet the specific requirements of an organization. The basic computer network configurations—star, ring, and bus—are illustrated in Figure 13–4.

The **star configuration** involves a centralized host computer that is connected to a number of smaller computer systems (minis or micros). The smaller computer systems communicate with one another through the host and usually share the host computer's data base.

The **ring configuration** involves computer systems that are approximately the same size, and no one computer system is the focal point of the network. Each intermediate computer system must read a message and pass it along to the destination computer system.

The **bus configuration** permits the connection of terminals, peripheral devices, and microcomputers along a central cable. Devices can be easily added to or removed from the network. Bus configurations are most appropriate when the devices linked are close to one another (see the discussion of local area networks that follows).

A pure form of any of these three configurations is seldom found in practice. Most computer networks are *hybrids* or combinations of these configurations.

The Micro-Mainframe Link. Micros initially designed for use by a single individual have even greater potential when they can be linked with mainframe computers. To give micros this dual-function capability, vendors developed the necessary hardware and software to have **micro-mainframe links**. There are three categories of these links:

1. The microcomputer serves as an intelligent terminal (see discussion in Section 13–3).
2. Data, programs, and text files can be downloaded from and uploaded to the mainframe.
3. Both microcomputer and mainframe work together to process data and produce information.

Micro-mainframe links of the first two types have been made possible by communications software, but achieving the third is no easy task.

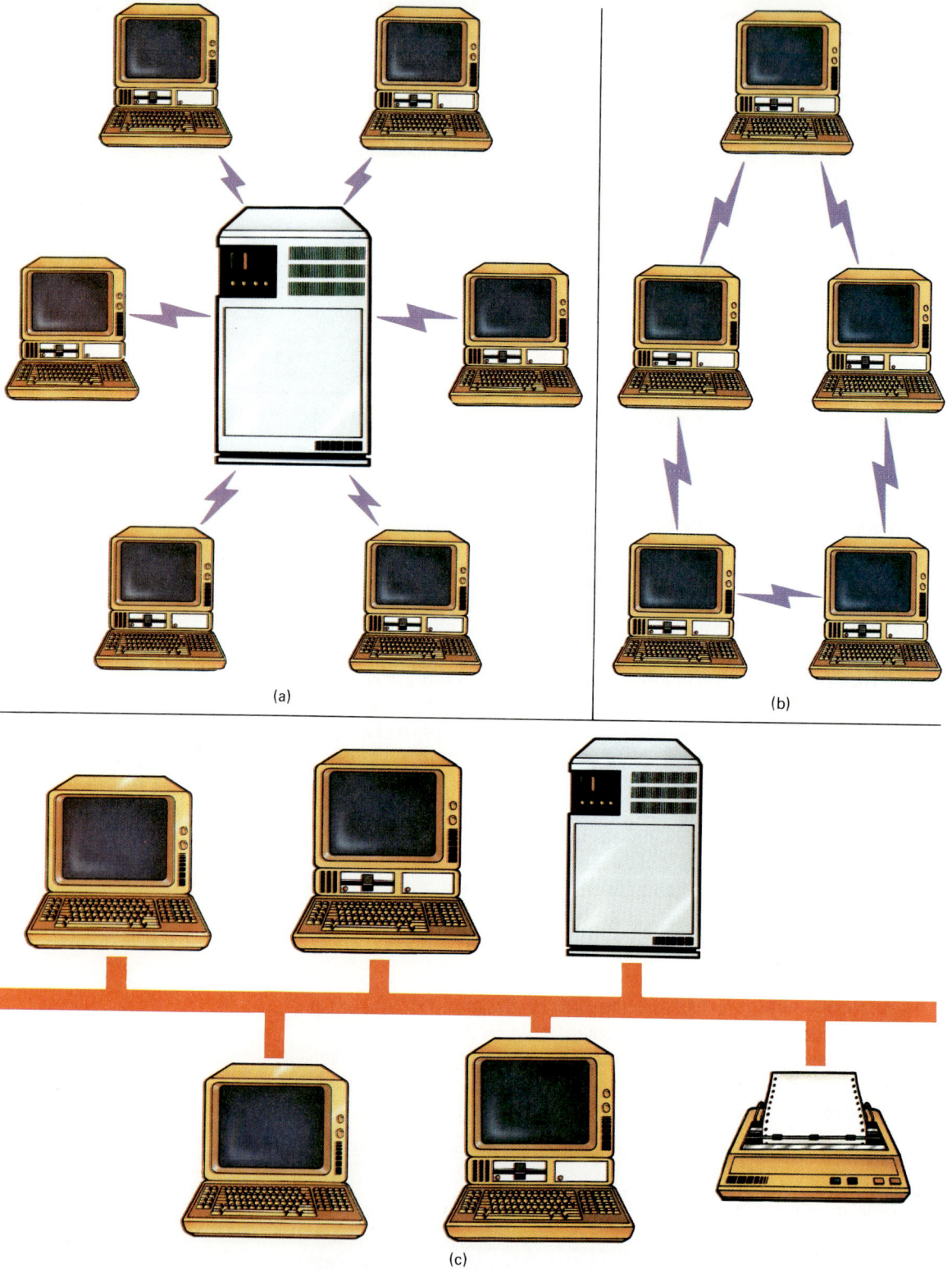

FIGURE 13–4
Network Configurations
(a) Star; (b) Ring; (c) Bus.

There are tremendous differences in the way computers and software are designed. This makes the complete integration of micro-mainframe activities difficult and, for some combinations of micros and mainframes, impossible.

Local Area Networks

A **local area network** (**LAN**), or **local net**, is a system of hardware, software, and communications channels that connect devices locally, as, for example, in a suite of offices. The distance separating devices in the local net may be a few feet to a few miles. A local net permits the movement of data (including text, voice, and graphic images) between mainframe computers, personal computers, terminals, and I/O devices. For example, your micro can be connected to another micro, to mainframes, and to *shared resources*, such as printers and disk storage.

The unique feature of a local net is that a common carrier is not necessary to transmit data between computers, terminals, and shared resources. Because of the proximity of devices in local nets, a company can install its own communications channels (such as coaxial cable or optical fiber). In a LAN, a micro is linked to the network via a channel that is connected directly to one of the micro's RS-232C ports. Since the LAN does not depend on telephone lines and modems for data transmission, data transmission rates of 9600 bps and higher are possible to and from micros.

Like computers, cars, and just about everything else, local nets can be built at various levels of sophistication. At the most basic level they permit the interconnection of PCs in a department so that users can send messages to one another and share files and printers. The more

A local area network links microcomputers in this office so that employees can share hardware, software, and data resources.
(Courtesy of International Business Machines Corporation)

sophisticated local nets permit the interconnection of mainframes, micros, and the gamut of peripheral devices throughout a large, but geographically constrained area, such as a cluster of buildings.

In the near future, you will be able to plug a micro into a communications channel just as you would plug a telephone line into a telephone jack. This type of data communications capability is being installed in the new "smart" office buildings, in college dormitories, and even in some hotel rooms.

Local nets are often integrated with long-haul networks so that people at micros and terminals are not limited to the scope of the local area network.

13–9 COMMUNICATIONS PROTOCOLS _____

Communications protocols are rules established to govern the way that data are transmitted in a computer network. The two general classifications of protocols, **asynchronous** and **synchronous**, are illustrated in Figure 13–5.

FIGURE 13–5
Asynchronous and Synchronous Transmission of Data
Asynchronous data transmission takes place at irregular intervals, where synchronous data transmission requires timed synchronization.

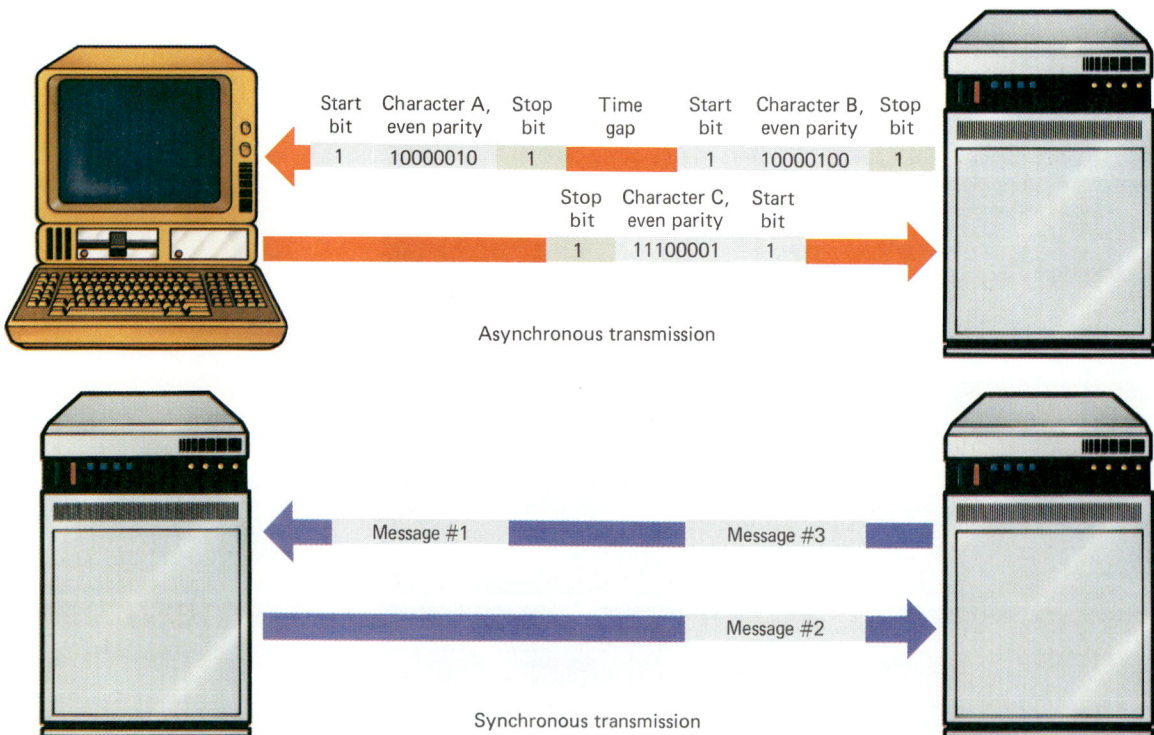

Start bit	Character A, even parity	Stop bit	Time gap	Start bit	Character B, even parity	Stop bit
1	10000010	1		1	10000100	1

Stop bit	Character C, even parity	Start bit
1	11100001	1

Asynchronous transmission

Message #1   Message #3

Message #2

Synchronous transmission

Asynchronous Protocols. Data communication between a micro-computer and any other computer is typically asynchronous. In asynchronous data transmission, data are transferred at irregular intervals on an as-needed basis. *Start/stop bits* are appended to the beginning and end of each message. The start/stop bits signal the receiving terminal or computer at the beginning and end of the message. In microcomputer data communications, the message is a single byte or character (see Figure 13–5).

Both sending and receiving devices maintain and coordinate data communications through *handshaking*. They do this by sending and receiving data in accordance with the rules set forth in a communications protocol. The defacto standard protocol for microcomputer data communications is **XON/XOFF** (pronounced ex-on ex-off). There are other protocols, but the most important thing to remember is that both the sending and receiving devices must adhere to the same handshaking protocol. The data communications protocol used to upload and download files may be different from the handshaking protocol. Again, the sending and receiving devices must follow the same file transfer protocol. The **XMODEM** protocol is the defacto standard for file transfer activities.

Typically, the host computer will **echo** or return the characters that are received from a micro; that is, the characters entered at the micro appear on the micro's monitor in context with those originated by the host computer. In effect, the entire interactive session is displayed when the echo is on. When the host does not echo characters, the user will have to specify "local echo" to display characters entered via the keyboard.

Synchronous Protocols. In synchronous transmission, the source and destination operate in timed synchronization to enable high-speed data transmission (see Figure 13–5). Start/stop bits are not required in synchronous transmission. Data transmission between mainframe computers and between special function processors is normally synchronous.

13–10 PARITY CHECKING

Within a computer network, data in the form of coded characters are continuously transferred at high rates of speed between the computer, the input/output (I/O) and storage devices, and the remote micros and terminals. Each device uses a built-in checking procedure to help ensure that the transmission is complete and accurate. This procedure is called **parity checking**.

Logically, an ASCII character may be represented using seven bits, but physically there are actually *eight* bits transmitted between hardware devices. Confused? Don't be. The extra **parity bit**, which is not part of the character code, is used in the parity-checking procedure to detect whether a bit has been accidentally changed, or "dropped," during transmission. A dropped bit results in a **parity error**.

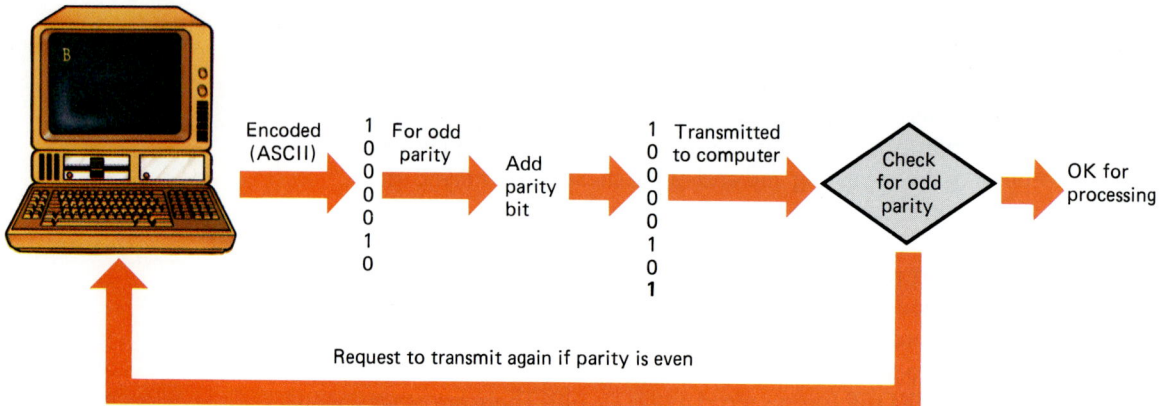

FIGURE 13–6
Parity Checking
The letter B is entered and transmitted to the computer for processing.
Since the ASCII "B" has an even number of bits, an on-bit must be added
to maintain odd parity.

To maintain **odd parity** (see Figure 13–6), the extra parity bit is turned *on* when the seven-bit ASCII byte has an *even* number of on-bits. When the ASCII byte has an *odd* number of on-bits, the parity bit is turned *off*. The receiving device checks for this condition. A parity error occurs when an even number of on-bits is encountered. When the receiving device detects a parity error, the receiving device sends a message to the sending device requesting that the message be transmitted again. Some computer systems are designed to maintain **even parity**, but odd and even parity work in a similar manner.

Parity checking is optional when using communications software. As a rule, if the message length or **data bits** is specified to be 7 bits, parity checking is activated, but if it is specified as 8 bits, parity checking is not activated. If activated, the type of parity checking procedure must be the same (even or odd) for both the sending and receiving devices.

13–11 PREPARING FOR DATA COMMUNICATIONS

When you use a micro, modem, and communications software to establish a link with another computer, you will need to specify the *telephone number* to be called and certain data communications *parameters*. These parameters may include

- *Type of terminal to be emulated* (for example, DEC VT100, IBM 3101)
- *Communications protocol* (for example, XON/XOFF, XMODEM)
- *Data flow* (half- or full-duplex)

- *Data bits* (typically 7 or 8)
- *Parity checking activated* (yes or no)
- *Type of parity checking (if used)* (even or odd)
- *Bits per second (sometimes labeled as baud)* (300, 1200, 2400, 4800, 9600).
- *Stop bits* (usually 1 for micro-based data communications)
- *Echo* (usually echo is provided by the remote computer)

Depending on the protocol and communications package, you may need to specify other parameters as well.

Communications software offers a variety of handy, time-saving features. For example, you can store the settings (the parameters) for a particular bulletin board, information service, or mainframe computer in a *communications profile*. To establish a link with another computer, simply recall and activate the appropriate communications profile. From there, the communications software takes over and automatically dials and logs on to the remote computer. It will even redial if a busy signal is detected. A micro with a modem and communications software can be on the receiving end as well. That is, it can automatically answer "calls" from other computers.

Most communications software packages provide the feature that enables the micro to *capture* all input/output during an interactive session to a disk file. At a later time, the user can use word processing software to recall the session from disk storage and browse through it at a more leisurely rate. Of course, all or part of the information gathered during an interactive session can be integrated into word processing documents, such as memos, letters, and reports.

13–12   COMMUNICATIONS SOFTWARE IN PRACTICE

Information Services, Bulletin Boards, and E-mail.   A variety of *information services* are available to microcomputer owners with communications capabilities. A few of these services include up-to-date real estate information, interactive health information, and movie reviews, to mention a few. You can even shop-at-home in the comfort of your own living room for just about anything from microcomputers to automobiles.

Most cities with a population of 25,000 or more have at least one electronic *bulletin board system*, often sponsored by a local computer club. Members "post" messages, announcements, for-sale notices, and so on, to the computer bulletin board by transmitting them to a central computer, usually another micro. To scan the bulletin board, members again use communications software to link to the central computer.

Communications software also opens the door for sending and receiving *electronic mail* or *E-mail*, either through a local bulletin board, a public electronic mail service, or an information service.

This stockbroker uses his micro and communications software to telecommute at least one day a week; that is, he commutes to work via data communications. Once on-line, he can keep in touch with office activities and retrieve critical information.
(Photo courtesy of Hewlett-Packard Company)

Telecommuting and the Cottage Industry. In the coming years, we will probably see a shift to smaller briefcases. Why? With communications software and an ever-growing number of home computers, people won't need to lug their paperwork between home and office every day. For a great many white-collar workers, at all levels, much of their work is on computers. Working at home is simply a matter of establishing a link between their home and office computers. This is sometimes referred to as **telecommuting**. In the years to come, many white-collar workers will elect to telecommute at least one day a week.

The combination of microcomputers and communications software has fueled the growth of *cottage industries.* The world has been made a little more compact with the computer revolution. Stock brokers, financial planners, writers, programmers, and people from a wide variety of professions may not need to "go to the office." Also, they can live wherever they choose. Micros make it possible for these people to access needed information, communicate with their clients, and even deliver products of their work (programs, stories, or recommendations).

In Summary. Microcomputers have placed the power of computers at our fingertips. Communications software expands that capability by enabling micro users to become a part of any number of computer networks. Once part of the network, a user can take advantage of the awesome power of mainframe computers, the information in their data bases, and the opportunity to communicate electronically with others on the network.

Having mastered the contents of this book and this course, you are now in a position to exploit the benefits of microcomputers in your personal and professional life. This course, however, is only the beginning. The computer learning process is ongoing. The dynamics of a rapidly advancing computer technology demands a constant updating of skills and expertise. Perhaps the excitement of technological innovation and ever-changing opportunities for application is part of the lure of computers.

By their very nature, computers bring about change. However, you and others who use them are the agents of this change.

SUMMARY OUTLINE AND IMPORTANT TERMS ____

13–1 DATA COMMUNICATIONS: FROM ONE ROOM TO THE WORLD. Modern businesses use **data communications** to transmit data and information at high speeds from one location to the another. Data communications makes information more accessible. The integration of computer systems, terminals, and communications links is referred to as a **computer network**.

13–2 COMMUNICATIONS SOFTWARE VERSUS OTHER MICRO PRODUCTIVITY SOFTWARE. People can readily identify with applications for most microcomputer software tools. However, the effective use of communications software requires some familiarity with the fundamental concepts associated with data communications.

13–3 THE FUNCTION OF COMMUNICATIONS SOFTWARE. Communications software expands the capability of a microcomputer by performing two basic functions: terminal emulation and file transfer. The terminal emulation capability transforms a micro into a video display terminal (VDT) that can be linked to another computer. The file transfer capability enables the transfer of files between a micro and another computer.

Perform a **logon procedure** to establish a link between the micro and another computer. The logon procedure involves dialing up a remote computer and entering a preassigned **password** and **personal identification number** or **PIN**.

Host computers, which can serve from one to thousands of remote users, have direct control over the terminals, processors, storage devices, and input/output devices that are linked to them. When a micro is in **terminal emulation mode**, the keyboard, monitor, and data interface are like that of the terminal that is being emulated.

Once the link between the micro and host has been established, data, program, or text files can be **downloaded** or **uploaded**.

13–4 MICROCOMPUTER-ORIENTED APPLICATIONS FOR DATA COMMUNICATIONS.   Some of the more popular micro-oriented applications for data communications include the following: **electronic mail** or **E-mail**, commercial information services, special-interest **bulletin board systems** (**BBS**) (run by the **sysop**), on-line information systems, and data entry.

13–5 DATA COMMUNICATIONS HARDWARE.   Data communications hardware is used to transmit data in a computer network between computers, and between terminals and computers. This hardware includes a variety of special function processors that are strategically placed within the network to facilitate the flow of information.

The micro, terminal, or computer sending a **message** is the source. The micro, terminal, or computer receiving the message is the destination. A special-function processor, which is connected to the mainframe, establishes and maintains the link between source and destination in a process called **handshaking**.

The **modem** converts computer-to-terminal and computer-to-micro electrical signals to a form that can be transmitted over telephone lines and converts telephone signals to digital electrical signals. A modem is always required when you dial-up the computer on a telephone line. **Smart modems** have varying degrees of "intelligence" due to embedded microprocessors.

13–6 THE DATA COMMUNICATIONS CHANNEL: DATA HIGHWAYS. A **communications channel** is the facility by which data are transmitted between locations in a computer network. A channel's capacity is rated by the number of bits that can be transmitted per second or **bits per second (bps)**. In practice, **baud** and bits per second are used interchangeably. In reality they are quite different.

The direction of data flow in a channel, also called a **line**, is through a **simplex line**, a **half-duplex line**, or a **full-duplex line**.

The channel, which is also called a **data link**, may be comprised of telephone lines, optical fiber, coaxial cable, and/or microwave.

13–7 DATA TRANSMISSION SERVICES. **Common carriers** provide communications channels to the public, and lines can be arranged to suit the application. A **private line** (or **leased line**) provides a dedicated communications channel. A **switched line** (or **dial-up line**) is available strictly on a time-and-distance charge.

13–8 NETWORKS: LINKING COMPUTERS AND MICROS. The basic computer network configurations are the **star configuration**, **ring configuration**, and **bus configuration**. A **node** is an endpoint in a computer network.

There are three categories of **micro-mainframe links**: the microcomputer serves as an intelligent terminal; data, programs, and text files can be downloaded from and uploaded to the mainframe; and both microcomputer and mainframe work together to process data and produce information.

A **local area network** (**LAN**), or **local net**, is a system of hardware, software, and communications channels that connects devices locally, as in a suite of offices. The distance separating devices in the local net may be from a few feet to a few miles. The unique feature of a local net is that a common carrier is not necessary to transmit data between computers, terminals, and shared resources. Local nets are often integrated with long-haul networks so that people at micros and terminals are not limited to the scope of the local area network.

13–9 COMMUNICATIONS PROTOCOLS. **Communications protocols** are rules established to govern the way that data are transmitted in a computer network. The two general classifications of protocols are **asynchronous** and **synchronous**. In asynchronous data transmission, data are transferred at irregular intervals on an as-needed basis. Both the sending and receiving devices must adhere to the same handshaking and file transfer protocols.

In synchronous transmission, the source and destination operate in timed synchronization to enable high-speed data transmission.

13–10 PARITY CHECKING.   Hardware devices in a computer network use a **parity checking** procedure to help ensure that the transmission is complete and accurate. The **parity bit** is used in the parity-checking procedure. To maintain **odd parity**, the parity bit is turned *on* when the seven-bit ASCII code has an *even* number of on-bits. Odd and **even parity** work in a similar manner. As a rule, parity checking is activated when the message length or **data bits** is specified to be 7 bits.

13–11 PREPARING FOR DATA COMMUNICATIONS.   Specify the following parameters when using communications software: type of terminal to be emulated, communications protocol, data flow, data bits, parity checking activated, type of parity checking (if used), bits per second (sometimes labeled as baud), stop bits, and echo. Communications software allows you to store the settings for a particular remote computer in a communications profile.

13–12 COMMUNICATIONS SOFTWARE IN PRACTICE.   A variety of information services are available to microcomputer owners with communications capabilities. *Bulletin board systems* are popular throughout the country. Communications software also opens the door to sending and receiving electronic mail.

In the years to come, many white-collar workers will elect to **telecommute** at least one day a week. The combination of microcomputers and communications software has fueled the growth of cottage industries.

Microcomputers have placed the power of computers at our fingertips. Communications software expands that capability by enabling micro users to become a part of any number of computer networks.

REVIEW EXERCISES _____

1. What device converts digital signals to analog signals for transmission over telephone lines? Why is it necessary?
2. Why is it not advisable to spread microwave relay stations 200 miles apart?
3. Describe circumstances for which a leased line would be preferred over a dial-up line.
4. What are the two basic functions performed by communications software?
5. Describe what is involved in a typical logon procedure.
6. How is an external modem connected to a microcomputer?

7. Describe the relationship between a micro-mainframe link and communications software.

8. Contrast local area networks with long-haul networks.

9. Why would you download data? Upload data?

10. Some communications software has automatic dial and redial capabilities. Describe these capabilities.

11. What are the two general classifications of communications protocols? Which is used for microcomputer-based communications applications?

12. Which network configuration permits the connection of terminals, peripheral devices, and micros along a central cable?

13. One popular information service is home banking. Describe an interactive session with at least one transaction to both a checking and savings account. Begin from the time you turn on your microcomputer.

SELF-TEST (by section)

13–1. The collection and distribution of electronic data to and from remote facilities is called _____.

13–2. The application addressed by communications software is data communication. (T/F)

13–3. (a) A PIN is a primary intermediate node. (T/F)

(b) Communications software enables a micro to emulate (a) a mainframe computer, (b) a color monitor, or (c) a terminal.

(c) The process of transmitting files from a host to a micro is called downloading. (T/F)

13–4. By relying on advertising revenue, commercial information services are able to provide their services for free. (T/F)

13–5. The _____ converts digital signals to analog signals for the purpose of transmitting data over telephone lines.

13–6. (a) Bits per second is a measure of (a) storage capacity, (b) channel capacity, or (c) electrical distance.

(b) A full-duplex line is essentially two half-duplex lines. (T/F)

(c) A _____ orbit enables a communications satellite to maintain a fixed position relative to the surface of the earth.

13–7. The two basic types of services offered by common carriers are private line and leased line. (T/F)

13–8. (a) The _____ configuration involves a centralized host that is connected to a number of smaller computer systems.

(b) A LAN is designed for long-haul data communications. (T/F)

13–9. In asynchronous data transmission, start/stop bits are appended to the beginning and end of each message. (T/F)

13–10. Parity checking is mandatory when downloading data but it is optional when uploading data. (T/F)

13–11. A micro with a modem and communications software can make calls to other computers but it cannot receive calls. (T/F)

13–12. Microcomputers and communications software have helped to spur the growth of cottage industries.

Self-Test Answers. **13–1,** data communications; **13–2,** T; **13–3 (a),** F; **(b),** c; **(c),** T; **13–4,** F; **13–5,** modem; **13–6 (a),** b; **(b),** T; **(c),** geosynchronous; **13–7,** F; **13–8 (a),** star; **(b),** F; **13–9,** T; **13–10,** F; **13–11,** F; **13–12,** T.

HANDS-ON EXERCISES

1. Complete Hands-On Tutorials 52 through 55 in the tutorials section of this chapter.

2. **(a)** Use communications software, a microcomputer (with a modem), and a telephone line to establish a communications link with a local electronic bulletin board system.

   (b) Explore the BBS and make a list of the available commands and features.

   (c) Read a few of the recent public messages.

   (d) Respond to an existing message or leave a public message for the other users of the BBS.

   (e) Wait a few days and call the BBS again. Scan the messages to see if anyone replied to your response or your message.

3. **(a)** From a microcomputer, establish link with a BBS that supports file transfers for your type of computer. Examine the files that are available for downloading.

   (b) Download a file from the BBS to your computer.

KEYSTROKE TUTORIALS IN THE *LAB MANUAL*

The *Lab Manual* that accompanies this text contains keystroke tutorials for

■ Crosstalk XVI (© DCA/Crosstalk Communications, Inc.)

■ PC-Talk4 (© The Headlands Press)

These keystroke tutorials illustrate the use of a particular communications software package in a domestic and a business application. The more advanced features of the packages are introduced in the business application tutorials.

COMMUNICATIONS TUTORIAL: CROSSTALK XVI

QUICK REFERENCE GUIDE
CROSSTALK XVI
(Version 3.61)
A>xtalk ↵

COMMAND SUMMARY

ABORT	DO	LWAIT	SAVE
ACCEPT	DPREFIX	MESSAGE	SBREAK
ALARM	DRIVE	MODE	SEND
ANSWERBACK	DSUFFIX	NAME	SKIP
APREFIX	DUPLEX	NO	SNAPSHOT
ASK	EDIT	NUMBER	SPEED
ATTENTION	EMULATE	OUTFILTER	STOP
BKSIZE	EPATH	PARITY	SWITCH
BLANKEX	ERASE	PICTURE	TABEX
BREAK	FILTER	PMODE	TIMER
BYE	FKEYS	PORT	TURNARND
CAPTURE	FLOW	PRINTER	TYPE
CDIR	GO	PWORD	UCONLY
CLEAR	HELP	QUIT	WAIT
COMMAND	IF	RCVE	WHEN
CSTATUS	INFILTER	RDIAL	WRITE
CWAIT	JUMP	REPLY	XDOS
DATA	LABLE	RQUEST	XMIT
DEBUG	LFAUTO	RUN	XXMODEM
DIR	LIST	RWIND	
DNAMES	LOAD	RXMODEM	

HANDS-ON TUTORIAL 52: Using CROSSTALK XVI

CROSSTALK XVI, a product of DCA/Crosstalk Communications, Inc., is a popular communications software package that enables micros to emulate terminals and to transfer files between computers. This tutorial is based on CROSSTALK XVI Version 3.61.

■ Boot the system (see Hands-On Tutorial 1).

■ Load CROSSTALK XVI to memory. Insert the CROSSTALK XVI program diskette in drive A.

    A>**xtalk** ↵

CROSSTALK's status screen appears.

■ Insert your data diskette in drive B. You are now ready to begin your CROSSTALK XVI session.

HANDS-ON TUTORIAL 53: Setting Up CROSSTALK XVI for Data Communication

To use CROSSTALK XVI you must set it up to communicate with a particular computer; that is, the transmission rate, communications protocols, and so on must be consistent between the two computers. You must set the number of *data bits* (bit pattern of each character that is transferred, usually seven or eight), the number of stop bits (usually one), the parity (usually parity is not checked), and local echo (you may need to turn this on if the remote computer does not echo characters that you enter).

This tutorial demonstrates how CROSSTALK XVI can be used to establish a link with CompuServe, a popular commercial information service.

■ Create a CROSSTALK XVI command file for CompuServe. Read through the explanation in the upper part of the screen before entering the data on the command line.

> Enter number for file to use (1   -   #   ):
>   **1** (*NEWUSER*) ↵
> Press ENTER to continue: ↵

The number of the NEWUSER file may differ from that shown here if any other command files have been created.

> Choose a service to set up: **B** (*CompuServe*)
> Enter phone number: **555-9090** (*your CompuServe phone number*) ↵
> 0110, 300, 600, 1200, 2400, 4800, 9600, 19200, etc., baud? **1200** ↵
> Please enter your Compuserve account number: **70000,2611** ↵
> Please enter your CompuServe password: **YOUR-PASSWORD** (*enter own password*) ↵

Your setup for CompuServe is now complete. However, do not call CompuServe now.

> Would you like to call CompuServe now? **no** ↵
> Press ENTER to continue: ↵

■ Exit the NEWUSER command file.

> Please choose a service: **X**

Crosstalk XVI display of the resultant status screen in Hands-On Tutorial 53.

HANDS-ON TUTORIAL 54: Establishing a Data Communications Link

■ Establish a communications link with CompuServe.

> Enter number for the file to use (1 - #):
>   **1** (*CSERV*) ↵

The number of CSERV may differ from that shown here. The message "Dialing - 555-9090 - Waiting for connection . . ." indicates that CROSSTALK XVI is automatically dialing the CompuServe number.

> User ID: 70000,2611
> Password: (*YOUR-PASSWORD*)
>
> CompuServe Information Service
> 11:44 EDT Sunday 26-Apr-88
>
> Last access: 22:15 27-Feb-88
>
> Copyright (C) 1987
> CompuServe Incorporated

> What's New This Week   NEW-1
>
> 1 Online Today
> 2 CompuServe Community News
> 3 Forum Conference Schedules
> 4 Daytime Connect Charges Lower
> 5 Subscriber Directory Revised
> 6 News-A-Tron Updated Daily
> 7 Monogram Software Adds Forum
> 8 Spring Weather Info Online
> 9 Shop "Springtime At The Mall"
> 10 SpaceWAR Tournament Coming
> 11 New Nodes in TX, CA and AK

CompuServe has its own set of commands. Use these commands to work with the plethora of activities and services offered by CompuServe.

HANDS-ON TUTORIAL 55: Terminating a Data Communications Link

■ Terminate the communications link with CompuServe.

> Enter choice **!bye** ↵
> Thank you for using CompuServe!
> Off at 11:47 EDT 26-Apr-88
> Connect time = 0:03

■ Exit CROSSTALK XVI and return to DOS.

> ESC
> Command? **quit** ↵
> Call terminated - returning to DOS
> A>

COMMUNICATIONS TUTORIAL: PC-TALK4

QUICK REFERENCE GUIDE
PC-TALK4
(Version 1.37)
A>pc-talk4 ↵

COMMAND SUMMARY

ALT-A	Display ALT (1-0)		ALT-N	Execute DOS command
ALT-B	Bell toggle		ALT-O	Toggle emulation
ALT-C	Clear screen		ALT-P	Communication parameters
ALT-D	Dialing directory		ALT-Q	Quick redial
ALT-E	Echo toggle		ALT-R	Receive file (PGDN)
ALT-F	Program defaults		ALT-S	Screen dump
ALT-G	Get new subdirectory		ALT-T	Transmit file (PGUP)
ALT-H	Hang up		ALT-U	Store ALT (1-0) files
ALT-I	Retrieve .ALT file		ALT-V	View files
ALT-J	Macro keys		ALT-W	Margin width alarm
ALT-K	Macro keys		ALT-X	Exit PC-TALK4 to DOS
ALT-L	Change logged drive		ALT-Y	Delete a file
ALT-M	Message Toggle		ALT-Z	Display elapsed time

OTHER

HOME	Display Command Summary on screen
ESC	Terminate file transfer

HANDS-ON TUTORIAL 52: Using PC-TALK4

PC-TALK4, a product of The Headlands Press, Inc., is a popular communications software package that enables micros to emulate terminals and to transfer files between computers. This tutorial is based on PC-TALK4 Version 1.37.

■ Boot the system (see Hands-On Tutorial 1).

■ Load PC-TALK4 to memory. Insert the PC-TALK4 program diskette in drive A.

   A>**pc-talk4** ↵

■ Insert your data diskette in drive B. You are now ready to begin your PC-TALK4 session.

HANDS-ON TUTORIAL 53: Setting Up PC-Talk4 for Data Communication

To use PC-TALK4 you must set it up to communicate with a particular computer; that is, the transmission rate, communications protocols, and so on must be consistent between the two computers. You must set the number of *data bits* (bit pattern of each character that is transferred, usually seven or eight), the number of stop bits (usually one), the parity (usually parity is not checked), and local echo (you may need to turn this on if

the remote computer does not echo characters that you enter).

This tutorial demonstrates how PC-TALK4 can be used to establish a link with CompuServe, a popular commercial information service.

When using PC-TALK4 for the first time you need to define a dialing directory entry for the remote computer that you wish to call. Since we are going to call CompuServe, we will use the protocol that is described in the CompuServe guide for new subscribers (8 data bits, no parity, and one stop bit).

- Add an entry for CompuServe to the PC-TALK4 dialing directory.

    ALT-D (*dialing directory*)
    R (*revise or add to directory*)
    Revise/add DD#: **12** (*make CompuServe entry number 12*) ↵
    Name: **CompuServe** (*names directory entry*) ↵
    Phone number: **555-9090** (*enter your own CompuServe phone number*) ↵

Enter the proper communications parameters as required by the remote system.

    Communications parameters ok (Y/N ↵)? **no** ↵
    Baud rate: **1200** ↵
    Parity: **no** ↵
    # data bits: **8** ↵
    # stop bits: **1** ↵

Accept the rest of the default communications parameters.

    Are the remaining parameters ok (Y/N ↵)? **yes** ↵

- Store the CompuServe entry (#12) in the directory.

Is entry #12 ok (Y/N)? **yes** ↵

The Dialing Directory will be redisplayed.

- Return to the terminal screen.

    X (*exit to terminal*)

PC-TALK4 display of the resultant status screen in Hands-On Tutorial 53.

HANDS-ON TUTORIAL 54: Establishing a Data Communications Link _____

- Establish a communications link with CompuServe.

    ALT-D
    12 (*dial entry 12, CompuServe*) ↵

The message "===DIALING CompuServe" will appear and PC-TALK4 will automatically dial the number you assigned (555-9090) and connect with CompuServe.

    ===CONNECT===
    ↵
    User ID: **70000,2611** ↵
    Password: **YOUR-PASSWORD** ↵

    CompuServe Information Service
    11:44 EDT Sunday 26-Apr-88

    Last access: 22:15 27-Feb-88

Copyright (C) 1987
CompuServe Incorporated
All Rights Reserved

What's New This Week   NEW-1

1 Online Today
2 CompuServe Community News
3 Forum Conference Schedules
4 Daytime Connect Charges Lower
5 Subscriber Directory Revised
6 News-A-Tron Updated Daily
7 Monogram Software Adds Forum
8 Spring Weather Info Online
9 Shop "Springtime At The Mall"
10 SpaceWAR Tournament Coming
11 New Nodes in TX, CA and AK

CompuServe has its own set of commands. Use these commands to work with the plethora of activities and services offered by CompuServe.

HANDS-ON TUTORIAL 55: Terminating a Data Communications Link _____

- Terminate the communications link with CompuServe.

    Enter choice !**bye** ↵
    Thank you for using CompuServe!
    Off at 11:47 EDT 26-Apr-88
    Connect time = 0:03

- Exit PC-TALK4 and return to DOS.

    ALT-**X** (*exit*)
    Are you SURE you wish to terminate PC-TALK4 (Y/N ↵=N)? **yes** ↵

GLOSSARY

Absolute cell address A cell address in an electronic spreadsheet that always refers to the same cell.

Access arm The disk drive mechanism used to position the read/write heads over the appropriate track.

Access time The time interval between the instant a computer makes a request for a transfer of data from a secondary storage device and the instant this operation is completed.

Acoustical coupler A device in which a telephone handset is mounted for the purpose of transmitting data over telephone lines. Used with a modem.

Add-on boards Circuit boards that contain the electronic circuitry for a wide variety of computer-related functions. Same as *add-on cards*.

Add-on cards Same as *add-on board*.

Address A name, numeral, or label that designates a particular location in primary or secondary storage.

Alpha A reference to the letters of the alphabet.

Alphanumeric Pertaining to a character set that contains letters, digits, punctuation, and special symbols (related to *alpha* and *numeric*).

Application A problem or task to which the computer can be applied.

Application generators Programming languages in which programmers specify, through an interactive dialog with the system, which processing tasks are to be performed.

Applications software Software that is designed and written to address a specific personal, business, or processing task.

Arithmetic and logic unit That portion of the computer that performs arithmetic and logic operations.

Arithmetic operators Mathematical operators [add (+), subtract (−), multiply (∗), divide (/), and exponentiation (^)] used in electronic spreadsheet and database software for computations.

ASCII [American Standard Code for Information Interchange] An encoding system.

ASCII file A generic text file that is stripped of program-specific control characters.

Asynchronous transmission Data transmission at irregular intervals that are synchronized with start/stop bits (contrast with *synchronous transmission*).

Backup Pertaining to equipment, procedures, or data bases that can be used to restart the system in the event of system failure.

Backup file Duplicate of an existing production file.

Bar graph A graph that contains vertical bars that represent specified numeric values.

Bar menu A menu in which the options are displayed across the screen.

BASIC A multipurpose programming language that is popular on microcomputers.

Batch file A disk file that contains a list of commands and/or programs that are to be executed immediately following the loading of DOS to RAM.

Baud (1) A measure of the maximum number of electronic signals that can be transmitted via a communications channel. (2) Bits per second (common-use definition).

Binary notation Using the binary (base two) numbering system (0, 1) for internal representation of alphanumeric data.

Bit A *binary digit* (0 or 1).

Bits per second [bps] The number of bits that can be transmitted per second over a communications channel.

Block A group of data that is either read from or written to an I/O device in one operation.

Boilerplate Existing text in a word processing file that can in some way be customized so that it is applicable to a variety of word processing applications.

Boot The procedure for loading the operating system to primary storage and readying a computer system for use.

Bug A logic or syntax error in a program, a logic error in the design of a computer system, or a hardware fault.

Bulletin board system [BBS] The electronic counterpart of a wall-mounted bulletin board that enables end users in a computer network to exchange ideas and information via a centralized data base.

Bus An electrical pathway through which the processor sends data and commands to RAM and all peripheral devices.

Bus architecture Same as *open architecture*.

Bus configuration A computer network that permits the connection of terminals, peripheral devices, and microcomputers along a central cable.

Byte A group of adjacent bits configured to represent a character.

C A transportable programming language that can be used to develop both systems and applications software.

CAI [Computer-assisted instruction] Use of the computer as an aid in the educational process.

Carrier Standard-sized pin connectors that permit chips to be attached to a circuit board.

Carrier, common [in data communications] A company that furnishes data communications services to the general public.

CD ROM disk [Compact Disk Read-Only Memory disk] A form of optical laser storage media.

Cell The intersection of a particular row and column in an electronic spreadsheet.

Cell address The location, column and row, of a cell in an electronic spreadsheet.

Central processing unit [CPU] Same as *processor*.

Character A unit of alphanumeric datum.

Clone A hardware device or a software package that emulates a product with an established reputation and market acceptance.

Closed architecture to micros with a fixed, unalterable configuration (contrast with *open architecture*).

Clustered-bar graph A modified bar graph that can be used to represent a two-dimensional set of numeric data (for example, multiple product sales by region).

COBOL [COmmon Business Oriented Language] A programming language used primarily for administrative information systems.

Code The rules used to translate a bit configuration to alphanumeric characters.

Column A vertical block of cells that runs the length of a spreadsheet and is labeled by a letter.

Command driven Pertaining to software packages that respond to user directives that are entered as commands.

Common carrier (in data communications) See *carrier, common*.

Communications See *data communications*.

Communications protocols Rules established to govern the way that data are transmitted in a computer network.

Communications channel The facility by which data are transmitted between locations in a computer network. Same as *line* and *data link*.

Communications software Software that enables a microcomputer to emulate a terminal and to transfer files between a micro and another computer.

Compatibility (1) Pertaining to the ability of one computer to execute programs of, access the data base of, and communicate with, another computer. (2) Pertaining to the ability of a particular hardware device to interface with a particular computer.

Compiler Systems software that performs the compilation process.

Computer Same as *processor*.

Computer network An integration of computer systems, workstations, and communications links.

Computer system A collective reference to all interconnected computing hardware, including processors, storage devices, input/output devices, and communications equipment.

Concatenation The joining together of labels or fields and other character strings into a single character string in electronic spreadsheet or database software.

Configuration The computer and its peripheral devices.

Control unit That portion of the processor that interprets program instructions.

Coprocessor In the context of microcomputers, an extra processor that helps relieve the main processor of certain tasks.

CP/M [Control Program for Microcomputers] A microcomputer operating system.

Cursor A blinking character that indicates the location of the next input on the display screen.

Cyberphobia The irrational fear of, and aversion to, computers.

Daisy-wheel printer A letter-quality serial printer, with its interchangeable character set located on a spoked print wheel.

Data A representation of fact. Raw material for information.

Data base (1) An organization's data resource for all computer-based information processing in which the data are integrated and related so that data redundancy is minimized. (2) Same as a file in the context of microcomputer usage.

Data bits A data communications parameter that refers to the number of bits in a message.

Data communications The collection and/or distribution of data from and/or to a remote facility.

Data communications specialist A person who designs and implements computer networks.

Data element The smallest logical unit of data. Examples are employee number, first name, and price (same as *field*; compare with *data item*).

Data entry The transcription of source data into machine-readable form.

Data item The value of a data element (compare with *data element*)

Data link Same as *communications channel*.

Debug To eliminate bugs in a program or system (related to *bug*).

Decimal The base-10 numbering system.

Decision support system [DSS] A computer-based system that uses available data, computer technology, models, and query languages to support the decision-making process.

Decode The reverse of the encoding process (contrast with *encode*).

Default options Preset software options that are assumed valid unless specified otherwise by the user.

Density The number of bytes per linear length of track of a recording medium. Usually measured in bytes per inch (bpi) and applied to magnetic tapes and disks.

Desktop computer Any computer that can be placed conveniently on the top of a desk (*microcomputer, personal computer*).

Desktop publishing Refers to the hardware and software capability of producing near typeset-quality copy from the confines of a desktop.

Dial-up line Same as *switched line*.

Digitize To translate an image into a form that computers can interpret.

Digitizing tablet and pen A pen and a pressure-sensitive tablet with the same *x-y* coordinates as the screen. The outline of an image drawn on a tablet is reproduced on the display screen.

Direct access Same as *random access*.

Directory A list of the names of the files that are stored on a particular diskette or in a named area on a hard disk.

Disk, magnetic A secondary storage medium for random-access data storage. Available as microdisk, diskette, disk cartridge, or disk pack.

Disk drive, magnetic A magnetic storage device that records data on flat rotating disks (compare with *tape drive*).

Diskette A thin flexible disk for secondary random-access data storage. Same as *floppy disk* and *flexible disk*.

Distributed processing Both a technological and an organizational concept based on the premise that information systems can be made more responsive to users by moving computer hardware and personnel physically closer to the people who use them.

DOS [disk operating system] A generic reference to a disk-based operating system.

Download The transmission of data from a mainframe computer to a workstation.

Downtime The time during which a computer system is not operational.

EGA [Enhanced Graphics Adapter] A circuit board that enables the interfacing of high resolution monitors to microcomputers.

Electronic dictionary A disk-based dictionary that is used in conjunction with a spelling checker program to verify the spelling of words in a word processing document.

Electronic mail A computer application whereby messages are transmitted via data communications to "electronic mailboxes." Also called E-mail.

Electronic spreadsheet Refers to software that permits users to work with rows and columns of data.

Encode To apply the rules of a code (contrast with *decode*).

Encoding system A system that permits alphanumeric characters to be coded in terms of bits.

End user The individual providing input to the computer or using computer output. Same as *user*.

End-of-file [EOF] marker A marker placed at the end of a file.

Expansion slots Slots within the processing component of a microcomputer into which optional add-on circuit boards can be inserted.

Field Same as *data element*.

File (1) A collection of related records. (2) A named area on a secondary storage device that contains a program, data, or textual material.

Filtering The process of selecting and presenting only that information which is appropriate to support a particular decision.

Fixed disk Same as *hard disk*.

Flexible disk Same as *diskette*.

Floppy disk Same as *diskette*.

Flowchart A diagram that illustrates data, information, and work flow via specialized symbols which, when connected by flow lines, portray the logic of a system or program.

Full-duplex line A communications channel that transmits data in both directions at the same time.

Full-screen editing This word processing feature permits the user to move the cursor to any position in the document to insert or replace text.

Function A predefined operation that performs mathematical, logical, statistical, financial, and character-string operations on data in an electronic spreadsheet or a data base.

Function key A special-function key on the keyboard that can be used to instruct the computer to perform a specific operation. Same as *soft key*.

Grammar checker An add-on program to word processing software that highlights grammatical concerns and deviations from conventions in a word processing document.

Grandfather-father-son method A secondary storage backup procedure that results in the master file having two generations of backup.

Hacker A computer enthusiast who uses the computer as a source of enjoyment.

Half-duplex line A communications channel that transmits data in both directions, but not at the same time.

Handshaking The process by which both sending and receiving devices in a computer network maintain and coordinate data communications.

Hard carriage return In word processing, a special character that is inserted in the document when the carriage return is pressed. Typically the character denotes the end of a paragraph or a string of contiguous text.

Hard copy A readable printed copy of computer output.

Hard disk Permanently installed, continuously spinning magnetic storage medium that is made up of one or more rigid disk platters. Same as *fixed disk*. See also *Winchester disk*.

Hardware The physical devices that comprise a computer system (contrast with *software*).

Hard-wired Logic that is designed into chips.

Help command A microcomputer software feature that provides online explanation or instruction on how to proceed.

Host computer The processor in a computer network that has direct control over the terminals, processors, storage devices, and input/output devices in the network.

Icons Pictographs that are used in

place of words or phrases on screen displays.

I/O [Input/Output] Input or output, or both.

Index file Within the context of database software, a file that contains logical pointers to records in a data base.

Information Data that have been collected and processed into a meaningful form.

Information service An on-line commercial network that provides remote users with access to a variety of information services.

Information system A computer-based system that provides both data processing capability and information for managerial decision making (same as *management information system* and *MIS*).

Input Data to be processed by a computer system.

Inquiry An on-line request for information.

Insert mode A data entry mode in which the character entered is inserted at the cursor position.

Instruction A programming language statement that specifies a particular computer operation to be performed.

Integrated software Two or more of the six major microcomputer productivity tools integrated into a single commercial software package.

Interactive Pertaining to on-line and immediate communication between the end user and computer.

Joystick A single vertical stick that moves the cursor on a screen in the direction in which the stick is pushed.

K (1) An abbreviation for kilo, meaning 1,000. (2) A computerese abbreviation for 2 to the 10th power or 1,024.

Key data element The data element in a record that is used as an identifier for accessing, sorting, and collating records.

Keyboard A device used for key data entry.

Keyboard templates Typically a plastic keyboard overlay that indi-

cates which commands are assigned to particular function keys.

Layout A detailed output and/or input specification that graphically illustrates exactly where information should be placed or entered on a VDT display screen or placed on printed output.

Layout line A line on a word processing screen that graphically illustrates appropriate user settings (margins, tabs). Sometimes called format lines.

Leased line A permanent or semipermanent communications channel leased through a common carrier.

Line Same as *communications channel.*

Line graph A graph in which conceptually similar points are plotted and connected so that they are represented by one or several lines.

Load To transfer programs or data from secondary to primary storage.

Local area network [LAN or local net] A system of hardware, software, and communications channels that connects devices on the local premises.

Logical operators Used to logically combine relational expressions in electronic spreadsheet and database software (such as AND, OR).

Logon procedure The procedure by which a user establishes a communications link with a remote computer.

Loop A sequence of program instructions that are executed repeatedly until a particular condition is met.

M [Megabyte] Referring to one million bytes of primary or secondary storage capacity.

Machine language The programming language in which a computer executes all programs, without regard to the language of the original code.

Macro A sequence of frequently used operations or keystrokes that can be recalled and invoked to help speed user interaction with microcomputer productivity software.

Magnetic disk See *disk, magnetic.*

Magnetic disk drive See *disk drive, magnetic.*

Magnetic tape See *tape, magnetic.*

Magnetic tape drive See *tape drive, magnetic.*

Main memory Same as *primary storage.*

Mainframe computer A large computer that can service many users simultaneously.

Management Information system [MIS] Same as *information system.*

Master file The permanent source of data for a particular computer application area.

Memory Same as *primary storage.*

Memory-resident program A program, other than the operating system, that remains operational while another applications program is running.

Menu A workstation display with a list of processing choices from which an end user may select.

Menu driven Pertaining to software packages that respond to user directives that are entered via a hierarchy of menus.

Message A series of bits sent from a workstation to a computer or vice versa.

Micro-mainframe link Linking microcomputers and mainframes for the purpose of data communication.

Microcomputer [or **micro**] A small computer.

Microcomputer specialist A specialist in the use and application of microcomputer hardware and software.

Microdisk A rigid $3\frac{1}{4}$- or $3\frac{1}{2}$-inch disk used for data storage.

Microprocessor A computer on a single chip. The processing component of a microcomputer.

Microsecond One millionth of a second.

Millisecond One thousandth of a second.

Minicomputer [or **mini**] Computers with slightly more power and capacity than a microcomputer.

MIS [Management Information System] Same as *information system.*

Modem [Modulator-Demodulator] A device used to convert computer-compatible signals to signals suitable for data transmission facilities and vice versa.

Monitor A televisionlike display for soft copy output in a computer system.

Motherboard A microcomputer circuit board that contains the microprocessor, electronic circuitry for handling such tasks as input/output signals from peripheral devices, and memory chips.

Mouse A small device that when moved across a desktop a particular distance and direction causes the same movement of the cursor on a screen.

MS-DOS [MicroSoft Disk Operating System] A microcomputer operating system.

Multifunction add-on board An add-on circuit board that performs more than one function.

Multiuser microcomputer A microcomputer that can serve more than one user at any given time.

Nanosecond One billionth of a second.

Natural language A programming language in which the programmer writes specifications without regard to instruction format or syntax. Essentially, using common, human language to program.

Nested loop A programming situation where at least one loop is entirely within another loop.

Network, computer See *computer network*.

Node An endpoint in a computer network.

Numeric A reference to any of the digits 0–9 (compare with *alpha* and *alphanumeric*).

Off-line Pertaining to data that are not accessible by, or hardware devices that are not connected to, a computer system (contrast with *on-line*).

Office automation [OA] Pertaining collectively to those computer-based applications associated with general office work.

On-line Pertaining to data and/or hardware devices that are accessible

to and under the control of a computer system (contrast with *off-line*).

Open architecture Refers to micros that give users the flexibility to configure the system with a variety of peripheral devices (contrast with *closed architecture*). Same as *bus architecture*.

Operating environment (1) A user-friendly DOS interface. (2) The conditions in which a computer system functions.

Operating system The software that monitors and controls all input/output and processing activities within a computer system.

Optical laser disk A read-only secondary storage medium that uses laser technology.

Optical scanners Devices that provide input to computer systems by using a beam of light to interpret printed characters and various types of codes.

Orphan The first line of paragraph that is printed as the last line on a page in a word processing document.

Output Data transferred from primary storage to an output device.

Page break In word processing, an in-line command or special character that causes the text that follows to be printed on a new page.

Page offset The distance between the left edge of the paper and the left margin in a word processing document.

Pagination The word processing feature that provides automatic numbering of the pages of a document.

Parallel port A direct link with the microcomputer's bus that facilitates the parallel transmission of data, usually one byte at a time.

Parity bit A bit appended to a bit configuration (byte) that is used to check the accuracy of data transmission from one hardware device to another (related to *parity checking* and *parity error*).

Parity checking A built-in checking procedure in a computer system to help ensure that the transmission of data is complete and accurate (related to *parity bit* and *parity error*).

Parity error Occurs when a bit is dropped in the transmission of data from one hardware device to another (related to *parity bit* and *parity checking*).

Pascal A multipurpose procedure-oriented programming language.

Password A word or phrase known only to the end user. When entered, it permits the end user to gain access to the system.

Path The logical route that an operating system would follow when searching through a series of directories and subdirectories to locate a specific file on disk storage.

PC-DOS [PC Disk Operating System] A microcomputer operating system.

Peripheral equipment Any hardware device other than the processor.

Personal computer [PC] Same as *microcomputer*.

Personal computing A category of computer usage that includes individual uses of the computer for both domestic and business applications.

Personal identification number [PIN] A unique number that is assigned to and identifies a user of a computer network.

Picosecond One trillionth of a second.

Pie graph A circular graph that illustrates each "piece" of data in its proper relationship to the whole "pie."

Pitch Horizontal spacing (characters per inch) in printed output.

Pixel An addressable point on a display screen to which light can be directed under program control.

Plotter A device that produces hard copy graphic output.

Pointer The highlighted area in an electronic spreadsheet display that indicates the current cell.

Pop-up menu A menu that is superimposed in a window over whatever is currently being displayed on the monitor.

Port An access point in a computer system that permits communication between the computer and a peripheral device.

Primary storage The memory area in which all programs and data must reside before programs can be executed or data manipulated (same as *main memory*, *memory*, and *RAM*; compare with *secondary storage*).

Printer A device used to prepare hard copy output.

Printer spooler A circuit board that enables data to be printed while a microcomputer user continues with other processing activities.

Private line A dedicated communications channel between any two points in a computer network.

Processor The logical component of a computer system that interprets and executes program instructions (same as *computer*, *central processing unit*, *CPU*).

Program (1) Computer instructions structured and ordered in a manner that, when executed, cause a computer to perform a particular function. (2) The act of producing computer software (related to *software*).

Programmer One who writes computer programs.

Programming The act of writing a computer program.

Programming language A language in which programmers communicate instructions to a computer.

Prompt A program-generated message describing what should be entered by the end user of a computer.

Proportional spacing A spacing option for word processing documents for which the spacing between characters remains relatively constant for any given line of output.

Proprietary software Vendor-developed software that is marketed to the public.

Pull-down menu A menu that is "pulled-down" and superimposed in a window over whatever is currently being displayed on a monitor.

Query language A programming language with Englishlike commands used primarily for inquiry and reporting.

RAM [Random Access Memory] Same as *primary storage*.

Random access Direct access to records, regardless of their physical location on the storage medium (contrast with *sequential access*).

Random file A collection of records that can be processed randomly.

Random processing Processing of data and records randomly (same as *direct-access processing*; contrast with *sequential processing*).

Range A cell or a rectangular group of adjacent cells in an electronic spreadsheet.

Read The process by which a record or a portion of a record is accessed from the magnetic storage medium (tape or disk) of a secondary storage device and transferred to primary storage for processing (contrast with *write*).

Read/write head That component of a disk drive or tape drive that reads from and writes to its respective magnetic storage medium.

Record A collection of related data elements.

Relational operators Used in electronic spreadsheet and database formulas to show the equality relationship between two expressions [= (equal to), < (less than), > (greater than), <= (less than or equal to), >= (greater than or equal to), <> (not equal to)]. See also *logical operators*.

Relative cell address Refers to a cell's position in an electronic spreadsheet relative to the cell containing the formula in which the address is used.

Replace mode A data entry mode in which the character entered overstrikes the character at the cursor position.

Reserved word A word that has a special meaning to a software package.

Resolution Referring to the number of addressable points on a monitor's screen. The greater the number of points, the higher the resolution and the greater the clarity.

Reverse video Normal screen display characteristics are reversed. For example, may have black letters on a light background; used for highlighting.

Ring configuration A computer network that involves computer systems that are approximately the same size, and no one computer system is the focal point of the network.

Robotics The integration of computers and industrial robots.

ROM [Read-Only Memory] RAM that can only be read, not written to.

Root directory The directory at the highest level of a hierarchy of directories.

Row A horizontal block of cells that runs the width of a spreadsheet and is labeled by a number.

Run The continuous execution of one or more logically related programs.

Scrolling Using the cursor keys to view parts of a word processing document or an electronic spreadsheet that extends past the bottom or top or sides of the screen.

Secondary storage Permanent data storage on magnetic disk and tape (same as *auxiliary storage*; compare with *primary storage*).

Sector A disk storage concept. A pie-shaped portion of a disk or diskette in which records are stored and subsequently retrieved.

Self booting diskette A diskette that contains both the operating system and an applications software package.

Sequential access Accessing records in the order in which they are stored (contrast with *random access*).

Sequential files Files that contain records that are ordered according to a key data element.

Sequential processing Processing of files that are ordered numerically or alphabetically by a key data element (contrast with *direct access* or *random processing*).

Serial port A direct link with the microcomputer's bus that facilitates the serial transmission of data, one bit at a time.

Simplex line A communications channel that transmits data in only one direction.

Smart modems Modems that have embedded microprocessors.

Soft carriage return In word processing, an invisible special character that is automatically inserted after the last full word within the right margin of entered text.

Soft copy Temporary output that can be interpreted visually as on a workstation monitor (contrast with *hard copy*).

Soft key Same as *function key*.

Software The programs used to direct the functions of a computer system (contrast with *hardware*).

Software package One or more programs that are designed to perform a particular processing task.

Sort The rearrangement of data elements or records in an ordered sequence by a key data element.

Spelling checker An add-on program to word processing that checks the spelling of every word in a word processing document against an electronic dictionary.

Spreadsheet See *electronic spreadsheet*.

Stacked-bar graph A modified bar graph in which the bars are divided to visually highlight the relative contribution of the components that make up the bar.

Star configuration A computer network that involves a centralized host computer that is connected to a number of smaller computer systems.

Style checker An add-on program to word processing software that that identifies deviations from effective writing style in a word processing document (for example, long and complex sentences).

Subdirectory A directory that is subordinate to a higher-level directory.

Subscripts Characters that are positioned slightly below the line of type.

Superscripts Characters that are positioned slightly above the line of type.

Switched line A telephone line used as a regular data communications channel. Also called dial-up line.

Synchronous transmission Transmission of data at timed intervals between terminals and/or computers (contrast with *asynchronous transmission*).

Syntax error An invalid format for a program instruction.

Sysop [system operator] Sponsor of an electronic bulletin board system.

Systems software Software that is independent of any specific applications area.

Tape, magnetic A secondary storage medium for sequential data storage. Available as a reel or a cassette.

Tape cassette Magnetic tape storage in cassette format.

Tape drive, magnetic The hardware device that contains the read/write mechanism for the magnetic tape storage medium.

Telecommuting "Commuting" via a communications link between home and office.

Template A model for a particular microcomputer software application.

Terminal Any device capable of sending and receiving data over a communications channel.

Terminal emulation mode The software transformation of a microcomputer so that its keyboard, monitor, and data interface emulate that of a terminal.

Thesaurus, on-line An add-on program to word processing software that enables users to display synonyms for words in a document.

Throughput A measure of computer system efficiency; the rate at which work can be performed by a computer system.

Toggle The action of pressing a single key on a keyboard to switch between two or more modes of operation such as, insert and replace.

Track, disk That portion of a magnetic disk face surface that can be accessed in any given setting of a single read/write head. Tracks are configured in concentric circles.

Transcribe To convert source data to machine-readable format.

Transmission rate The number of characters per second that can be transmitted beteen primary storage and a peripheral device.

Transparent A reference to a procedure or activity that occurs automatically and does not have to be considered in the use or design of a program or an information system.

Upload The transmission of data from a workstation to a mainframe computer.

User Same as *end user*.

User friendly Used to describe an on-line system that permits a person with relatively little experience to interact successfully with the system.

Utility program An often-used service routine such as a program to sort records.

Variable A primary storage location that can assume different numeric or alphanumeric values.

Variable name An identifier in a program that represents the actual value of a storage location.

VDT [Video Display Terminal] A terminal on which printed and graphic information is displayed on a televisionlike monitor and data are entered on a typewriterlike keyboard.

Version number A number that identifies the release version of a software package.

Video display terminal See *VDT*.

Video disk A secondary storage medium that permits storage and random access to video or pictorial information.

Voice data entry device A device that permits voice input to a computer system. Same as *voice recognition device*.

Voice recognition device Same as *voice data entry device*.

Widow The last line of a paragraph that is printed as the first line on a page in a word processing document.

Wildcard (character) Usually a ? or an * that is used in microcomputer software commands as a generic reference to any character or any combination of characters, respectively.

Winchester disk Permanently installed, continuously spinning magnetic storage medium that is made up of one or more rigid disk platters. Generally, the type of *hard disk* or a *fixed disk* in a microcomputer.

Window A rectangular display that is temporarily superimposed over whatever is currently on the screen.

Window panes Simultaneous display of subareas of a particular window (see *window*).

Word For a given computer, an established number of bits that are handled as a unit.

Word processing Using the computer to enter, store, manipulate, and print text.

Word wrap A word processing feature that automatically moves or wraps text to the next line when text that is added line to exceed the right margin limit.

Workstation The hardware that permits interaction with a computer system, be it a mainframe or a multi-user micro. A VDT and a microcomputer can be a workstation.

Write To record data on the output medium of a particular I/O device (tape, hard copy, workstation display; contrast to *read*).

WYSIWYG [What You See Is What You Get] A word processing package in which what is displayed on the screen is very similar in appearance to what you get when the document is printed.

XMODEM A standard data communications protocol for file transfers.

XON/XOFF A standard data communications protocol.

Zoom An integrated software command that expands a window to fill the entire screen.

INDEX

HANDS-ON TUTORIALS INDEX*

* *Key*: (CT) Crosstalk XVI; (DB) dBASE III PLUS; (LT) Lotus 1-2-3; (MM) MultiMate; (OT) The OUTLINER; (PC) PC-Talk4; (PF) PFS:Professional File; (PW) PFS:Professional Writer; (RF) Reflex; (SC) SuperCalc4; (TT) ThinkTank; (TW) the TWiN; (WB) Webster's NewWorld Writer; (WP) WordPerfect; (WS) WordStar Professional

SUBJECT INDEX**

** *Note*: When several page references are noted for a single entry, boldface denotes the page(s) on which the term is defined or discussed in some depth. Page references refer not only to the text material, but also to the photo captions and figure captions. The index does not include references to terms in the software-specific tutorials.